THE FUTURE OF THE GERMAN-JEWISH PAST

THE FUTURE OF THE GERMAN-JEWISH PAST

Memory and the Question of Antisemitism

Edited by
GIDEON REUVENI AND
DIANA FRANKLIN

PURDUE UNIVERSITY PRESS | WEST LAFAYETTE, INDIANA

Copyright 2021 by Purdue University.
Printed in the United States of America.

Cataloging-in-Publication data is on file at the Library of Congress.
Paperback ISBN: 978-1-55753-711-9

An electronic version of this book is freely available, thanks to the support of libraries working with Knowledge Unlatched. KU is a collaborative initiative designed to
make high-quality books Open Access for the public good. The Open Access ISBN
for this book is 978-1-61249-703-7.

Cover artwork: Painting by Arnold Daghani from *What a Nice World*, vol. 1, 185.
The work is held in the University of Sussex Special Collections at The Keep,
Arnold Daghani Collection, SxMs113/2/90. The authors are grateful to the Centre
for German-Jewish Studies at the University of Sussex for granting us permission to
use the image for the cover.

This book is dedicated to the memory of Professor Edward Timms OBE—scholar, mentor, friend, and founder of the Centre for German-Jewish Studies at the University of Sussex.

CONTENTS

NEW PERSPECTIVES FOR GERMAN-JEWISH STUDIES

ACKNOWLEDGMENTS

T HIS BOOK WAS conceived as part of the anniversary celebrations for the Centre for German-Jewish Studies at the University of Sussex. The center was initially set up in 1994, but officially inaugurated by Lord Richard Attenborough, who was Sussex University's chancellor, in 2000. The purpose of the center is to study the contribution of German-Jewish communities to modern life and to research the experiences and achievements of German-Jewish refugees and their families. Financial support has come from a range of educational trusts, including Steven Spielberg's Righteous Persons Foundation and the Anne Frank-Fonds, as well as individual donors, most of whom were first- or second-generation German-Jewish refugees. The founding director of the center was Professor Edward Timms, a preeminent authority on the Austrian satirist Karl Kraus and a defining scholar of Austrian and German-Jewish studies. For Timms the mission of the center was not only historical, but also contemporary and critical. In his autobiography, *Taking up the Torch* (2010), he noted that racial prejudice constitutes a continuing political danger and that German-Jewish studies may serve as a model for understanding the challenges of multiethnic societies in present-day society. This insight regarding the relevance and contemporary significance of the German-Jewish experience continues to inspire the work of the center and to a large extent comprises the common thread connecting the twenty contributions in this volume. Edward Timms died at the age of eighty-one on November 21, 2018. This book is dedicated to his memory.

Several people helped us to bring this volume to fruition. We would like to thank the Centre for German-Jewish Studies' London-based Advisory Board for their advice and encouragement with this and all our other current projects. Nicola Glucksmann,

Lilian Levy, and Yvonne Crampin have assisted us in preparing the manuscript for publication. The two anonymous reviewers of the volume made some excellent suggestions, which helped us to shape our ideas about the book. At Purdue University Press we found a supportive team that believed in this project from the outset. We would like to extend our sincere gratitude to each author whose work has been included in the ensuing pages. Their insights have enriched the field of German-Jewish studies and we are most grateful to them for helping us to initiate this discussion on the future of the German-Jewish past.

THE FUTURE OF THE GERMAN-JEWISH PAST STARTS HERE

GIDEON REUVENI

PONDERING THE FUTURE of the German-Jewish past is not a new concept. When struggling for their rights, many German Jews reflected on the past with growing dismay, envisioning a bright future for the period after emancipation. Before the First World War it was mainly Zionist thinkers who dominated the debates about the future of the Jews.[1] Swayed by the conviction that there were no prospects for Jews in (mainly Eastern) Europe, they campaigned for a so-called national rebirth of the Jewish people in what was conceived as the place of Jewish origin—the Land of Israel. After the upheavals of the First World War and during the times of uncertainty and rapid change that ensued, the need to discuss the future prospect of German Jewry seemed even more pressing. Between the end of the Great War and the rise of National Socialism in 1933, expectations of German Jews oscillated between, on the one hand, hopes for renewal and on the other hand, gloomy prophecies of disintegration. What is certain is that despite the upheavals and conflicting visions for the future, most German-speaking Jews could not imagine Germany without Jews.[2] This applies all the more to the so-called Jewish "prophets of the past," the German-Jewish historians.[3] Thus, for example, in the first issue of the revived *Zeitschrift für die Geschichte der Juden in Deutschland* in 1929, the historian Raphael Strauss (1887–1947) called for a review of German-Jewish historiography by acknowledging all aspects of Jewish history in Germany.[4] His plan for a more comprehensive German-Jewish historiography was based on the observation that scholarship in this field was divided between two main groups, each driven by different interests and methods of research. According to Strauss, the first group comprised Jewish scholars who were predominantly interested in intellectual study or *Geistesgeschichte*, while the other group comprised mainly non-Jewish scholars dealing with social and economic aspects of Jewish life from the past. Strauss's concept of a comprehensive German-Jewish historiography was thus designed to bring together different groups of scholars—Jews and non-Jews alike— combining their diverse methods and research interests in order to create what Leopold Zunz (1794–1886) had referred to as an all-encompassing science of Judaism.[5] This vision of interdisciplinary or "connecting" Jewish studies in Germany corresponded to the Jewish demand for recognition and the long-standing desire to belong to the majority non-Jewish society.

After the Holocaust, in the first volume of the newly founded *Leo Baeck Institute Year Book* (LBIY), Bernard Dov Weinryb (1905–1982) wrote his own vision of the prospects for German-Jewish history, confirming many of Strauss's contentions.[6] While Weinryb accepted Strauss's initial observation regarding the division of research between two groups of researchers, he attacked the narrow approach of both Jewish and non-Jewish scholars that focused predominantly on the question of the Jews' place within their German host society. For Weinryb, the general tendency of German-Jewish historiography to overstress Jewish/non-Jewish relations had come to a close with the Second World War. "Today," he wrote, "the return to internal Jewish history and thus 'to clear figures' and 'non-illusionistic' pictures seems to be a logical result of the new situation."[7] Based on this observation, Weinryb moved away from Strauss's notion of a comprehensive history and the ideal of "connecting" histories. Instead he proposed that German-Jewish history should deal with Jewish life in Germany within the confines of its own space or what he called "social field." Shifting the center of grav- ity of German-Jewish history back to the Jewish sphere was supposed to undermine the overemphasis on Jewish/non-Jewish relations and to separate research once and for all from the so-called "contribution" approach to German-Jewish relations, and for that matter from the "symbiosis" paradigm as well. Moreover, as opposed to the so-called *Kleinarbeit* (microhistory) approach to Jewish history of the period between the World Wars, Weinryb suggested placing German-Jewish history within "a large-scale synthetic narrative of Jewish history" that would underpin general trends and parallels in the history of the Jews in different places.[8]

More than a half a century after these programmatic outlines were designed, research on German-Jewish history has become a more diverse and sophisticated field of study than it was at the beginning of the twentieth century. The "contribution," as well as the "symbiosis" conceptualization of German-Jewish history are now matters of the past. A more carefully nuanced and refined approach to the interplay between Jews and other Germans dominates scholarship today. No doubt this revision is linked to the emergence of a new, so-called post-émigré generation of Jewish and non-Jewish scholars working in the field.[9] Until very recently, the study of the German-Jewish past was still informed by the assumption that German-Jewish history came to a close with the Holocaust. For most historians of the émigré generation, German-Jewish history was seen as similar to the history of Jews in Spain up to the expulsion in 1492. Recalling Simon Rawidowicz's famous essay entitled: "Israel: The Ever-Dying People," first published in Hebrew at the onset of the greatest catastrophe in Jewish history, Michael Brenner reminds us in his contribution to this volume that there was "hardly a generation in the Diaspora that did not consider itself the final link in Israel's chain."[10] According to Brenner, Jewry has indulged so much in the fear of its end that its constant vision of the end has helped it to overcome every crisis, to emerge from every threatening end as a living unit, though much wounded and reduced.

Following the collapse of the Soviet Union and German reunification, we were suddenly faced with a different reality in which the Jewish community in Germany became the fastest growing in Europe. To what extent the reinstating of Jewish life in Germany can serve as a connecting link between the present and the past of the German-Jewish experience is a question that scholars have begun to ponder in recent years. At the beginning of the new millennium, two special issues of the *Leo Baeck Institute Year Book* were dedicated to this subject and to other questions about the future prospects of German-Jewish studies.[11] Both collections underpin the importance of continuity in German-Jewish history, suggesting a reading of the German-Jewish experience as a constant interplay between destruction and reconstruction of community.[12]

While previous collections focused on historiography, mainly targeting an exclusive audience of professional scholars, this volume is more ambitious in its scope and stimulating in its approach. It gives voice to a diverse group of people from differing backgrounds who have an interest in the past and future of the German-Jewish experience as a field of study. Moreover, since the publication of the last *Leo Baeck Institute Year Book* collection in 2009, social and political realities have shifted dramatically and we seem, yet again, to have arrived at the stage when we are compelled to look back and reexamine the German-Jewish past. I would like to mention a few developments that have prompted this revision.

In the United States under Trump, and in the United Kingdom since the unfortunate vote to leave the European Union, a growing number of Jews are seeking to reclaim their parents' or grandparents' German identities. For some, acquiring German or Austrian citizenship is a symbolic act of reclaiming a bit of the humanity that was stolen from their families by the Nazis, as for example in the case of Nicola Glucksmann in this volume. Despite the longing to redress the past, Glucksmann conveys in her personal reflections the ambivalence that seems to define her experience of the German-Jewish legacy of her family. Yet for most British and American Jews, it is mainly anxiety about the growing xenophobic and antisemitic sentiments in their home countries as well as the opportunities the European Union offers, particularly to younger people, that prompts them to apply for German or Austrian passports. The precarious situation in Israel has encouraged many Israeli Jews to become German or Austrian nationals and, after the expansion of the European Union in Eastern Europe, an increasing number of Israelis have started reclaiming Polish, Hungarian, Romanian, and other passports of the new European Union member states. It is indeed ironic that German and Austrian citizenships provide an "exit" or a "backup plan" for Jews living in countries that originally provided a safe haven when fleeing from Nazi Germany. It seems that the German state is encouraging this proclivity. Pondering the question of Jewish migration in postunification Germany, Hannah C. Tzuberi notes in her contribution that since Germany's readmission into the circle of "civilized states" involved a commitment to overcome the past, the "return of Jews" was thought to provide evidence of just that. Nationalizing descendants of German-Jewish refugees and the lenient, if not welcoming policy toward Jewish migration from the former Soviet Union, Israel, and the United States appears to intertwine with a nation-building project that renders Jews, present and absent, an inherent part of a collective German identity.

Germany's acceptance of its direct responsibility for the Holocaust has strengthened its friendship with Israel and has led to a deep commitment to combat antisemitism and rebuild Jewish life in Germany. This effort has also included substantial investment in Jewish studies, making Germany and Austria important places for (academic) Jewish learning. As we approach the time when there will be no firsthand experience of the horrors of the Holocaust, there is great concern about what will happen when that sense of responsibility turns into history. One possible prospect is that the taboo against open antisemitism will be lifted as collective memory fades. There are alarming signs in the rise of the Far Right, which includes blatantly antisemitic elements already visible in public discourse. The attack on the synagogue in the East German city of Halle on October 9, 2019 marked a significant escalation in right-wing violence against Jews in Germany. The Covid-19 pandemic has been seized by the Far Right, who have been prominent in demonstrations of the so-called Querdenken 711 (lateral thinking) movement, directed against government measures attempting to combat the disease. But it is mainly the radicalization of the otherwise moderate Muslim population that seems to make German and other European societies less tolerant and less inhibited about articulating antisemitic attitudes.[13]

This volume deals with the formidable challenges created by these developments. It is conceptualized to offer a variety of perspectives and views on the topic, and authors were encouraged to develop their own approach to the question about the future of the German-Jewish past. The thread that seems to align this somewhat eclectic miscellany of texts is the recognition of the intrinsic value of the German-Jewish past and the importance of studying it for the future. Revisiting and carrying forward the discussions about the future of the German-Jewish past is not merely a theoretical matter, but also a practical one. It calls for a reevaluation of how the history of Jews in German-speaking

lands should be studied in an age in which interest in this history is radically changing, if not dwindling. Frank Mecklenburg reminds us in his contribution that while
in the past the *Yekkes* (Jews of German-speaking origin) dominated German-Jewish
studies both as scholars and the recipients of its products, very few first-generation
Yekkes now remain to attend lectures and events on German-Jewish topics or to read
the many publications that this field of study still yields.

Today we are faced with the challenge of engaging younger audiences who come
from diverse backgrounds and whose interest in the topic predominantly derives from
the "relevance approach" to the German-Jewish experience. Even in Germany, the
German-Jewish community shows no particular interest in this history, and the study
of the German-Jewish past is dominated by non-Jewish scholars and is part of German
identity politics. The predisposition to engage with Judaism without Jews is best represented in an institution like the Jewish Museum Berlin. For Alan Posener, the Jewish
Museum Berlin epitomizes the high point of German-Jewish reconciliation efforts and
German philosemitism.[14] The museum has portrayed Jews just like ordinary Germans,
providing information about the contributions of individual Jews, but does not say
much about what constitutes Jewish difference in the German context. According to
Posener, this approach has made the Jewish Museum Berlin less Jewish and more of a
Museum of Tolerance. Even after the opening of the museum's new permanent exhi-
bition in August 2020, Posener did not change this view.[15]

Michal Friedlander's chapter provides unique—insider—insights on the challenges
and constraints the Jewish Museum Berlin team of curators encountered while preparing the museum's new permanent exhibition. According to Friedlander, the new exhibition aims to redress the previously imbalanced approach to the German-Jewish past.
We learn that the new exhibition is committed to demonstrating the entangled histories of Jews and other Germans, but that it is supposed to be much more "Jewish" than
the former exhibition. Friedlander valiantly questions what precisely that involves and
how the Jewish Museum Berlin defines what is Jewish. This created a challenge for the
primarily non-Jewish museum team.

While representing the German-Jewish past as a paragon of integration and acculturation is part of an ongoing effort to forge a German identity based on inclusion
and multiculturalism, from a Jewish perspective the image of the alleged assimilationist German Jew has also yielded somewhat peculiar, if not disturbing, consequences. Discussing the question of Jewish conversion in postwar Germany, Sandra
Anusiewicz-Baer, in her chapter, shows how internalizing this image of a non-Jewish
German Jew has created an inferiority complex among Jews living in Germany today.
She claims that the Jewish leadership in Germany seems to take a back seat in all questions about Judaism, delegating decision-making powers over identity issues, such as
conversion, to Orthodox rabbis from outside Germany. In Israel too, Orthodox Judaism

calls the shots in all matters Jewish, including the politically fraught question of who is a Jew according to Israeli law. According to Moshe Zimmermann, the consolidation of Orthodox Judaism as a leading force in Israeli politics and, as a result, the transformation of Israel into what he sees as an illiberal democracy is best encapsulated by the country's official reading of Jewish history. In Israel, Zimmermann explains, the German Jew is seen as the embodiment of the liberal/intellectual/peace-seeking/upper-middle-class Ashkenazi (European) Jew who ended up in the country only as a result of the collapse of the German-Jewish assimilationist model. As a result, in Israel's search for a usable past, there is no place, at least not a constructive one, for German-Jewish history. Looking at German-Jewish writers, the Israeli scholar Galili Shahar reaches a similarly gloomy conclusion in his chapter. According to Shahar, the German-Jewish author is neither "Western" nor "Eastern," but rather an in-betweener who experiences permanent self-estrangement. What future, Shahar asks, can be imagined based on such distorted experiences of the past?

Two other essays deal with what this volume calls the "German-Israeli complex." Hannah C. Tzuberi's chapter, which I briefly alluded to earlier, explores the place Jews have in the construction of German identity, while Dani Kranz discusses the convoluted feelings of attraction and repulsion toward Germany among Israeli Jews living there. She notes that while most Israeli migrants to Germany had an affiliation to Germany and Europe transmitted to them from their families, their reasons for leaving Israel vary. According to Kranz, Israelis in Germany cannot escape the past and, for many of them, coming to Germany is a way of coming to terms with the "memory luggage" they accumulated while growing up in Israel.

The interplay between the personal, the historical, and memory is the main thread that connects the essays in the first section of the book. Both Glucksmann and Posener write as descendants of German-Jewish refugees. Trauma, loss, and ambivalence about any form of belonging is omnipresent in their reflections on the future of the German-Jewish experience. As we learn from Sheer Ganor's chapter, such reactions are not untypical among families of German-speaking Jews. Ganor observes that if parents succeeded in instilling German-Jewishness within their children, it was in the form of a remembered and constructed heritage, not as a lived reality. A striking manifestation of this shift, from living experience (in Central Europe) to remembered history (in exile), is the fact that nowadays the most comprehensive collections and archives dealing with the German-Jewish past are located outside German-speaking countries. One of the places that holds such an archive is the Centre for German-Jewish Studies at the University of Sussex. Since its foundation in the mid-1990s, the center has acquired archival family papers from people who came as refugees from Nazi persecution to the United Kingdom. Although the life trajectory of these families is similar, each of their stories is unique, relating in different ways the dramatic passage of integration, expulsion, and new beginnings in their place of sanctuary. The papers these families kept illustrate and confirm what we know about the past, but sometimes they also question prevailing historical narrative.[16]

Forced to flee Germany after National Socialism assumed power, German-speaking Jews were scattered around the globe, creating a distinct diaspora group that, at least initially, struggled to maintain a distinctive German-Jewish identity. One such story is that of a German Jew named Fritz Pinkuss, as discussed in Björn Siegel's essay. Leaving Germany in 1936, Pinkuss became the chief rabbi of the Congregação Israelita Paulista, São Paulo where he proceeded to implement ideas and traditions in his work from Germany. Pinkuss was also involved in ongoing efforts to promote German-Jewish reconciliation, for which he received the highest honors from the Federal Republic of Germany. Yet, despite his strong ties with Germany, similarly to the majority of German-speaking Jews, Pinkuss remained in Brazil, choosing not to return to the place he formerly considered his homeland.[17]

Taking into account the dispersion of German Jews raises challenging questions about the nature and future of German-Jewishness in the diaspora. From a historiographical perspective, looking at German Jews as a diaspora group implies that beyond the so-called "connecting approach"—which calls for research to put more emphasis on similarity and interconnectedness instead of focusing on difference and separation—and the "contribution approach" that celebrates the involvement of German Jews in the cultural life of their host countries, as well as the more recent "continuity approach" that focuses on postwar Jewish life in Germany and Austria, what we may define as the "relevance approach" of the German-Jewish experience is becoming more predominant. Thus, for example, Mathias Berek discusses in this volume the German-Jewish philosopher Moritz Lazarus's (1824–1903) notion of a "thin blanket of culture" that protects European society from the destructive forces that threaten modern civilization. According to Berek, lessons from the German-Jewish past might add important patches to this fragile covering blanket. A different manifestation of the "relevance approach" can be found in Guy Miron's chapter. The rich German-Jewish historiography, Miron argues, should serve as a source of inspiration for the exploration of other hyphenated Jewish experiences, especially in Muslim countries. According to him, deploying the all too familiar German-Jewish concepts such as "assimilation," "acculturation," and perhaps even "co-constitutionality" in research on Jews living in the Middle East may free this historiography from the simplistic Arab-Jewish dichotomy and help to develop more subtle models to interpret the process of Jewish integration and acculturation in Islamic societies.

Although exclusion and anti-Jewish sentiments feature in many of the contributions to this book, only two essays address antisemitism as their main topic. Lisa Silverman looks at the concept of Jewish difference as a conceptual framework that might explain the persistence of antisemitism. She writes that while the view that Jews played a major role in the creation of culture in modern Central Europe is far from new, research has only recently begun an in-depth probe of the role that the socially constructed category of the "Jew" played beyond prejudices and antisemitism. As a result, Silverman argues, the study of the Jewish past is still biased, to a large degree, in favor of the constructed Jew as a figment of the antisemitic imagination, displacing responsibility for the consequences of focusing solely on antisemitism. It is interesting to juxtapose Silverman's reflections with Klaus Hödl's call to overcome the binary view of the interplay between the "Jewish" and "non-Jewish," so ingrained in Jewish historiography. Without undermining the notion of difference, Hödl proposes that research should put more emphasis on entanglement, rather than simply focus on dissimilarity.

It feels very much as though research on antisemitism is at an impasse and, despite all efforts to understand anti-Jewish sentiment, time and again we seem to be caught off guard in the face of antisemitic attacks, dubbing them "new antisemitism."[18] In his chapter, Anthony D. Kauders offers a fresh impulse to research on antisemitism based on psychological theories that, as he notes, have always informed the study of antisemitism. Kauders suggests that revisiting the psychology of Jew-hatred and the search for alternative (social) psychological models will allow a better understanding of antisemitism as a social phenomenon.

Several other chapters explore new prospects for the study of the German-Jewish past. Liliane Weissberg reflects on the relationship between genre and authorship in the context of the German newspaper feuilleton. She notes that while the paper's news section looked to the past and reported about what had already happened, feuilleton articles aimed to describe the present situation and look forward, thus comprising a fertile source for the study of future expectations of German Jews. In his chapter, Joachim Schlör highlights the significance of material culture in our quest to preserve and explore German-Jewish culture, both in Germany and in the diaspora. Schlör observes that talking and writing about "belongings," owned and then lost, became a means of reassertion for surviving family members and friends, enabling exiles to grapple with questions of belonging. And finally, according to Kerry Wallach, the future of the German-Jewish past is digital. By 2024, she asserts, college courses will serve primarily *post-Millennial students*, a new generation born after the year 2000. Often referred to as "Generation Z," these young people are "digital natives," and the way they communicate and consume information will influence the ways in which scholars, institutions, and cultural producers choose to present their work. Wallach presents some stimulating ideas on how the study of the German-Jewish past will have to change in order to survive in the digital age.

The twenty chapters in this book do not comprise a single narrative, nor offer a roadmap to the future of German-Jewishness. They invite readers to ponder the polysemy of this history and to reflect on the nature of the relationship between the "German" and the "Jewish." It becomes apparent that the construction of the "German-Jewish" juncture is in constant flux and means different things to different people depending upon time and place. On a very basic level, most of us associate German-Jewishness with Jews living in or originating from German-speaking countries. I would suggest that we should expand this somewhat narrow view of the concept of German-Jewishness based on the idea of origin, and develop a more inclusive approach driven by the notion of experience.[19]

National Socialism and the Holocaust rendered Germany a particular place in modern Jewish memory and self-understanding. But this is not a mere abstract matter allied to Jewish identity politics: Germany played a decisive role in the reconstruction of Jewish life after the Holocaust. On September 10, 1952, the State of Israel and the Federal Republic of Germany signed a reparations settlement, also known as the Luxembourg Agreement, according to which West Germany was to pay Israel the costs for "the heavy burden of resettling so great a number of uprooted and destitute Jewish refugees from Germany and from territories formerly under German rule."[20] For the young Israeli state facing major existential challenges, the three billion marks (worth approximately 7.5 billion dollars in 2020) West Germany agreed to pay Israel as "global recompense for the cost of the integration ... of [Jewish] refugees" constituted a Marshall Plan that boosted Israel's struggling economy. Since most of this aid was given in the form of German goods and investments in infrastructure that also utilized German know-how, one palpable outcome of the Luxembourg Agreement was the entanglement of the developing Israeli economy with the growing German industry in ensuing years.[21]

The agreement between Germany and Israel also acknowledged the right of Holocaust survivors to claim personal compensation for deprivation of liberty and losses of livelihood and property resulting from Nazi persecution. The majority of these survivors were not of German origin and compensation claims came from all over the world. In German archives there are around five million such claims that were made from the beginning of the 1950s, and the process is still ongoing. The claims contain testimonies as well as supporting evidence of all kinds, providing ample information on Jewish life before, during and after the Holocaust. Not only European Jews, but also North African Jews who lived under Nazi occupation made claims for personal indemnification, most of which were initially rejected by the German authorities.[22] During the first wave of personal compensation claims made in the 1950s and 1960s applications were submitted in German and German Jews—lawyers, notaries, physicians, and translators—played decisive roles as mediators between non-German-speaking survivors and the German authorities. The German state registered all claimants and those who were successful in getting reparations became part of the German welfare system.[23] Most of them had to remain in regular contact with German officials for the rest of their lives, reporting to the German authorities about changing personal and family circumstances. This collection of documents comprises one of the most comprehensive, still untapped, Holocaust-related archives. While scholars have studied the political, legal, and economic implications of the reparation agreement, primarily depicting it as a successful reconciliation model, research has only recently started to appreciate the full bearing of personal indemnification on survivors and their families.[24] This shift toward the personal experience of reparation also divulges the omnipresence of Germany, German bureaucracy, and the German language in the lives of Holocaust survivors and their families. In other words, the scope and range of the German-Jewish experience is much broader than so far presumed.

The inexhaustible richness of the German-Jewish interrelationship explains its attractiveness for scholars, students, and the public. While this book has done scarcely more than set out some preliminary markers for future thinking, it comprises a centerpiece of the anniversary celebrations of the Centre for German-Jewish Studies at the University of Sussex. When the center was first set up in the mid-1990s, German-Jewish studies hardly featured at British universities, even though Britain, in proportion to its size, had received more refugees from Nazi Germany than any other country. In those early days, Edward Timms, the founding director of the center, recalled: "To insist on the centrality of Exile and Holocaust studies has been regarded as bad form in certain circles."[25] In November 2018 Edward Timms died and we dedicate this book to his memory. Since the center's inception it has benefited from the financial support of a number of German-Jewish refugees who were keen to ensure that the legacy of their parents' and grandparents' achievements in what they regarded as the period of German-Jewish "symbiosis" were not overlooked or forgotten. Thanks to them, the center has grown from strength to strength, actively contributing to scholarship on the unique history of German-speaking Jews and engaging audiences from beyond the ivory towers of academia in its diverse activities. The Centre for German-Jewish Studies is currently going through a period of transformation and growth, and together with fellow scholars and Friends of the Centre, we look forward to addressing changes in contemporary culture, politics, and society while continuing to pose new questions about the German-Jewish past in the years to come.

NOTES

1. Prominent examples include: Max Nordau, *Degeneration* (London: William Heineman, 1895); Arthur Ruppin, *Die Juden der Gegenwart: Eine sozialwissenschaftliche Studie* (Berlin: Calvary, 1904); Alfred Nossig, *Die Zukunft der Juden: Sammelschrift* (Berlin: Komitee der gedenkfeier, 1906); Felix Theilhaber, *Der Untergang der deutschen Juden. Eine volkswirtschaftliche Studie* (Munich: E. Reinhardt, 1911).

2. With Germany, I mean here German-speaking countries. For such future visions of German Jews before 1933 see for example Moshe Zimmermann, "Die aussichtslose Republik—Zukunftsperspektiven der deutschen Juden vor 1933," Menora: Jahrbuch für Deutsch-Jüdische Geschichte (1990): 152–183; idem., "Zukunftserwartungen deutscher Juden im ersten Jahr der Weimarer Republik," Archiv für Sozialgeschichte (1997): 55–72.

3. Michael Brenner, *Prophets of the Past: Interpreters of Jewish History* (Princeton: Princeton University Press, 2010).

4. Raphael Strauss, "Zur Forschungsmethode der jüdischen Geschichte," Zeitschrift für die *Geschichte der* Juden *in Deutschland* 1 (1929): 4–12.

5. For extensive bibliography on Zunz see http://www.jewish-archives.org/nav/class ification/11219.

6. Bernard D. Weinryb, "Prolegomena to an Economic History of the Jews in Germany in Modern Times," Leo Baeck Institute Year Book 1 (1956): 279–306.

7. Ibid., 284.

8. Ibid., 285.

9. On this notion see David Sorkin, "The Immigration Synthesis on the German-Jewish History," Central European History 34, no. 4 (2001): 531–559; as well as his "Beyond the Émigré Synthesis," Leo Baeck Institute Year Book 44 (2000): 209–210; Andreas Daum, Hartmut Lehmann, and James J. Sheehan, eds., *The Second Generation: Émigrés from Nazi Germany as Historians* (New York: Berghahn Books, 2016).

10. Simon Rawidowicz, "Israel: The Ever-Dying People," in *State of Israel, Diaspora, and Jewish Continuity, ed. Benjamin C. I. Ravid* (Hanover: New England University Press, 1998), 53–54.

11. Two special issues of the *Leo Baeck Institute Year Book* were dedicated to the question about the future of German-Jewish studies. One was published in 2000, the other in 2009.

12. On this approach see also Konrad H. Jarausch and Michael Geyer, *Shattered Past: Reconstructing German Histories* (Princeton: Princeton University Press, 2003).

13. Günther Jikeli, *Muslim Antisemitism in Europe: Why Young Urban Males Say They Don't Like Jews* (Bloomington: Indiana University Press, 2015).

14. See also Thomas Lackmann, *Jewrassic Park: Wie baut man (k)ein Jüdisches Museum in Berlin* (Berlin: Philo Verlag, 2000).

15. Alan Posner, "Die Leerstellen im Jüdischen Museum," Die Welt (19.08.2020).

16. For more information on the Sussex German-Jewish archive see http://www.sussex .ac.uk/cgjs/archive.

17. On Jewish remigration to Germany after 1945 see the special section on the topic in vol. 49 of the *Leo Baeck Institute Year Book* (2004).

18. See for example Alvin H. Rosenfed, ed., *Deciphering the New Antisemitism* (Bloomington: Indiana University Press, 2015), as well as *American Historical Review* 123, no. 4 (2018),

xxiv   THE FUTURE OF THE GERMAN-JEWISH PAST STARTS HERE

which features a Roundtable titled "Rethinking Antisemitism" that challenges scholars to reflect on the concepts, epistemologies, narratives, methodologies, and theories that animate our approach to the topic.

19. For an interesting discussion on the tension between Jews in Germany and German Jews see Jeffrey M. Peck, *Being Jewish in the New Germany* (Piscataway, NJ: Rutgers University Press, 2006).

20. The *Luxembourg Agreement* is also available at the online project 100(0) key documents of German history in the twentieth century: https://www.1000dokumente.de /index.html?c=dokument_de&dokument=0016_lux&object=context&st=&l=de.

21. Jacob Tovy, *Destruction and Accounting: The State of Israel and the Reparations from Germany, 1949–1953* [in Hebrew] (Tel Aviv: Tel Aviv University Press, 2016).

22. Hanna Yablonka, *Off the Beaten Track—the Mizrahim and the Shoah* [in Hebrew] (Beer Sheva: Chemed Books, 2008).

23. In order to get compensation some Holocaust survivors from Eastern Europe were even asked to prove their belonging to the German culture. For a detailed discussion of this Kafkaesque procedure see José Brunner and Iris Nachum, "Vor dem Gestz steht ein Türhüter: Wie und warum israelische Antragsteller ihre Zugehörigkeit zum deutschen Sprach- und Kulturkreise beweisen mußten," in *Die Praxis der Wiedergutmachung: Geschichte, Erfahrung und Wirkung in Israel und Deutschland, ed.* Norbert Frei, José Brunner, and Constantin Goschler (Göttingen: Walstein Verlag, 2009), 387–324.

24. For a pioneering account see Susan Slyomovics, *How to Accept German Reparations* (Philadelphia: University of Pennsylvania Press, 2014).

25. Edward Timms, *Taking Up the Torch: English Institutions, German Dialectics and Multicultural Commitments* (Brighton: Sussex Academic Press, 2011).

The Personal, the Historical, and the Making of German-Jewish Memory

"NO MORE MR. NICE GUY"

Questioning the Ideal of Assimilation

ALAN POSENER

A S FAR AS I know, my father never visited a concentration camp. He rarely talked about what we now call the "Holocaust," a word he never used. He had watched and despised the U.S. TV series that introduced the term to the German public. Born in Berlin in 1904 into a rich family of assimilated German Jews, none of whom had to work for a living, Julius Posener had left Germany in 1933 and returned in 1961 to the city of his birth with an English wife and three Christian children.

Julius Posener's autobiography—*Fast so alt wie das Jahrhundert* (Almost as old as the century), first published in 1993—is very discreet about the extermination of the Jews.[1] The fact that his uncle Alfred, his aunt Mathilde, and the widow of his uncle George, Margarete, were deported and murdered is not mentioned in the memoir and was never mentioned in family conversation. The only thing I knew about Alfred, for instance, was that he had been "rather soft in the head" and rode around Lichterfelde on his bike greeting everyone with a polite "Heil Hitler," and that the surviving family members had received compensation for his apparently very valuable stamp collection that had disappeared with him during the war. Indeed, I suspect my cousins in Israel and their children and grandchildren don't even know Alfred, Mathilde, and Margarete ever existed, and I only bothered to ask myself what had happened to them after my father had died. It is almost as if the family were ashamed to admit that this kind of thing had happened to them, too, the way families used to be ashamed of cancer, as if somehow it was their fault.

I'm not sure how typical this voluntary amnesia was for families such as the Poseners, but I have a feeling that it was fairly widespread. Possibly this had to do with the fact that many assimilated German Jews had refused to believe what was really happening in Germany; it was *their* country that had perpetrated these horrors. After all, they were, or had been until 1933, Germans first and foremost and Jews more or less as an afterthought. "*Trotzjuden*," my father called them, Jews by defiance who refused to convert to Christianity or abandon the Jewish community, not out of sympathy for the Jewish religion or—God forbid—Zionism, but because they did not want to bow to the antisemites.

My father often told anecdotes about the *Yekkes*, the German émigrés in Palestine, many of whom had fought in World War I for Kaiser and Fatherland and who could hardly suppress their admiration for Hitler's victory over France. My father, on the other hand, had spent the first years of exile in France, loved the country, and joined the British Army in 1940. He claimed to have been "the first Palestinian to cross the Rhine" into Germany. Yet even he writes to his brother Ludwig in Jerusalem on August 2, 1945: "Strangely enough, I had a Nazi ideal of Germany in my head . . . that made me sure we would find every house in Germany a fortress, every morsel of food poisoned, as Hitler said. This is not the case, and that is disappointing. I have encountered . . . so much servility, denunciation, profiteering, complaining that it sometimes makes me sick."[2] To his sister-in-law, Lotte, he writes a few weeks later: "During the war, I had refused to believe that more than a tenth of the things that were reported were true. And that tenth was bad enough. Now it is proven beyond doubt that everything is true."[3]

Over and above this refusal to believe the worst about one's own country and people, I believe my father and quite a few German Jews like him felt a certain patrician pride in not complaining too much about their own fate. It simply wasn't done. To quote my father's letter to his brother—an ardent Zionist—again: "It is not about forgiving and forgetting, but about pity, which has nothing to do with forgiveness. Whoever tells me I should save my pity for my own is wrong and cannot be more wrong. I made myself guilty of this wrong . . . when a poor devil told me in the first days [of the occupation, A.P.] that he had seen his young wife die in the ruins of their house. I answered that Jews had experienced worse things. But you cannot trump the worst with worse. All that remains is pity."[4]

And then, finally, how did you live among those who had been complicit in the Nazi crimes without some form of forgiving and forgetting? My father returned to Berlin in 1961, when almost everyone he had to deal with had something shameful to hide. In 1949—the year of my birth in London—he was contacted by an old friend from student days in Berlin, Klaus Müller-Rehm, who had become a successful architect. Writing back to Müller-Rehm, my father explains why he had made no effort to contact him before: "We"—meaning we German Jews—"don't enquire about people, unless they were very close or unless . . . we know how they got through those years. Although I often thought about you, Klaus, I wouldn't have enquired about you. I remember a conversation we had in 1932, when you said: 'You of all people, Posener, will sympathise with the solution these people [i.e., the Nazis, A.P.] find when they finally have their say.' I have often wondered when you stopped sympathising with the solution. I did quite early on, but since I didn't know how broad your sympathies were, I kept silent." In a postscript, he comes back to the subject: "You might find my sharp memory and the consequences I drew from a long-ago conversation stupid. And they would be stupid if I were to play the judge and hold a private trial to condemn every German who ever had anything to do with that movement or some of its ideas concerning Jews. On the contrary, I still think that under the circumstances prevailing in Germany in 1931–1932 it was quite possible, indeed it was hard not to be influenced by those ideas and that movement. People like me had it easier, as we simply couldn't—indeed, were not allowed to. All I wanted to say was that after everything that happened, people like me don't spontaneously seek contact with people who were in that situation. And I meant this primarily as an explanation for my not trying to contact you. All the better that you found the way. Once again, many thanks."[5]

Twelve years later Müller-Rehm, who held a professorship in Berlin, pulled some strings and got my father, who had neither a PhD nor any other requisite academic qualification, a professorship in architectural history at his university. As far as I know, they never talked about the past. In his privately published memoirs,[6] Müller-Rehm doesn't even mention my father, let alone his own sympathies for the Nazis and their solutions, glosses over his years as an architect for the Wehrmacht in Crimea and elsewhere in occupied Eastern Europe, and claims in an endnote entitled "Das Judenproblem": "When the ghosts had departed, I received letters of thanks from émigrés, although I don't know how or whether I deserved them. Two things remain totally incomprehensible to me. Firstly, the celebrations with which an overwhelming percentage of the German people enthroned Hitler in 1933, and secondly how all the celebrators disappeared from one day to the next when the war was lost and Hitler dead."[7]

The Jewish émigrés who returned, thankful or not—and being, like my father, indebted to people like Müller-Rehm and his ilk for one's job and position in society was surely not a comfortable position to be in—were thorns in the side of a Germany eager to declare that the adulation for Hitler was as "incomprehensible" as the sudden "servility" my father had complained about as a British soldier in 1945.

A bad conscience was the last thing Germany seemed to be suffering from in the 1960s. Attacking the Social Democrat candidate Willy Brandt, who had spent the Nazi years in exile, the Bavarian conservative Franz-Josef Strauß thundered during the election campaign of 1961: "We surely must be allowed to ask Herr Brandt one thing: What were you doing in those twelve years outside the country? We know what we were doing inside."[8] So, for many returning Jewish émigrés, keeping a low profile and not asking too many questions about the past was not only a matter of pride and pity but also made professional and private sense.

Heinz Galinski, for instance, who survived Auschwitz and Bergen-Belsen and went on to be a very vocal leader of the Jewish community in Berlin and later of the Central Council of Jews in Germany, was universally despised and constantly vilified and threatened with death. In 1975 he survived a parcel bomb attack and since his death in 1992 his grave has been repeatedly desecrated. Being visibly and uncompromisingly Jewish, demanding that Germany face up to its past, supporting Jewish claims against the German state and Israel's right to self-defense, was not a position that helped you make friends and influence people in Adenauer's Germany or, indeed, later. For my father, Galinski was an embarrassment—the kind of "pushy" Jew he never wanted to be or to be associated with, although he realized that this *gène* was in essence antisemitic. (Galinski's daughter, Evelyn Hecht, left the Jewish community and has made a name for herself as a vociferous, radical left-wing critic of Israel, tacking her father's name onto her husband's in order to claim his mantle for her anti-Zionist stance. The extreme Right, which was behind most, though by no means all, of the attacks on Galinski, has discovered its love for Israel, which it sees as a Western bulwark against Islam. Such are the reversals of history.)

There's that word: history. What does Jewish history—specifically: the Jewish past in Germany—teach us? Because what we think it means will define how we remember it. My father couldn't face the past in all its brutality, because that would have meant not being able to face the present. Zionism was not an option—he'd tried it and realized that it wasn't for him and certainly not for the family he had created. Living in England would have been his first choice, but jobs were hard to come by. Returning to Germany, he chose a kind of *doublethink*: knowing and yet not knowing.

To give an example: I was twelve when the family moved to Berlin, but my father never talked to me about what I might expect as a schoolboy with a "Jewish" name and a Jewish father. No matter that I thought of myself as British and Anglican, not Jewish, and certainly not German-Jewish: did my father really think my teachers and the parents of my fellow students wouldn't draw their own conclusions? I remember one history lesson when we were discussing theories about the decline and fall of the Roman Empire. Our teacher, an admirer of the reactionary German novelist Erwin Guido Kolbenheyer, quoted the assertion of the nineteenth-century historian Theodor Mommsen that the Jews had been "the ferment of decomposition" in antiquity and remarked: "You, Alan, as a leader of the antiauthoritarian movement at this school, with your long hair and love of American Negro music, are a prime example of the truth of this statement"—adding that he did not mean this as criticism On the contrary, I was the best student in his class and, in his opinion, the order represented by our boarding school definitely needed some "decomposing."

Today, Jewish schoolchildren in Germany would be happy to have to deal with this kind of more or less academic antisemitism. Many routinely experience bullying, verbal and physical abuse from fellow students, most of them of Arab or Turkish extraction. I never experienced anything of that sort at school or later. The situation in Europe and in Germany is getting more uncomfortable for Jews, trapped between Muslim antisemitism on the one hand and the rise of right-wing populism on the other. In Western Europe, the populists have learned to deny their traditional antisemitism, knowing that it is still a powerful taboo that can ruin their chances of achieving political influence; in Eastern Europe, however, there are fewer inhibitions—and fewer Muslim migrants on whom the populists might vent their nationalist rage. How, then, should Jews read their past—and explain it to non-Jews—in order to cope with the present and the future?

The Jewish Museum in Berlin represents one answer to this question. It symbolizes the high point of German-Jewish reconciliation—or, to be more precise, German philosemitism—that was reached in the mid-nineties. The generation of the victims and perpetrators was fading from history. The big trials of Nazi war criminals were over. An end to compensation payments—*"Wiedergutmachung"*—was in sight. The generation that had come of age in the legendary years around "'68"—my generation—prided itself on having broken with Germany's past and being open to "multiculturalism." And the Jewish Museum with its postmodern architecture and liberal American director seemed the ideal flagship for the message that Germany was no longer the country my father and other émigrés had returned to in the 1950s and 1960s.

The permanent exhibition at the Jewish Museum celebrated "2,000 years of German-Jewish history" and the essential message that the Jewish Museum's director, W. Michael Blumenthal, conveyed was reassuring: the Jews aren't threatening anybody. The permanent exhibition reinforced this message: apart from a few dietary quirks and strange rituals, for instance for male babies, Jews are just like ordinary Germans and always have been. The exhibition said a lot about the contributions of individual Jews to German society—as businesspeople, scientists, politicians, intellectuals, and artists—and almost nothing about Judaism as a religion, or anti-Judaism as a driving force in Western civilization since the earliest days of Christianity. It also said next to nothing about Zionism or about Israel, where German-Jewish life continued after 1933 and German Jews played a key role in the formation of the Jewish state.[9]

The museum as conceived by Blumenthal was less a Jewish Museum than a Museum of Tolerance. In the spirit of this concept, Blumenthal established an "Academy" of the museum devoted to "Jewish-Muslim dialogue." Under a Muslim director, the "Academy" hosted discussions in which critics of Israel and its policies were often prominent, while Muslim antisemitism—a main concern of Jews living in Germany—was referred to only to be dismissed as a construction of Islamophobic and right-wing elements.

Blumenthal's successor, a non-Jewish German academic called Peter Schäfer, went out of his way to accommodate the Muslim narrative—for instance in an exhibition on Jerusalem that failed to mention Arab pogroms and the cooperation of the Grand Mufti with Nazi Germany in World War II. When Schäfer hosted the cultural attaché of the Iranian Embassy and seemed to endorse criticism of a Bundestag resolution condemning the antisemitic BDS movement, even the usually tame Central Council of Jews in Germany was enraged and called the museum—correctly—an "Un-Jewish Museum." Schäfer resigned.[10]

It remains to be seen how the new director, Hetty Berg, will deal with the difficult legacy of the museum. The new permanent exhibition, which opened recently, was conceived by the same team that had developed the exhibition that opened in 2001. While it does devote more space to explaining Judaism, it otherwise avoids divisive issues like Zionism, Israel, and the diverse forms of contemporary antisemitism: precisely the issues that for many Jews define their life in Germany.[11]

As Muslim immigration has grown, the German image of "the Jew" has split: Israel has assumed most of the perceived negative aspects of Jewishness, whereas German Jews have begun to be seen not as "the other" vis-à-vis German society, not as an obstacle in Germany's path to postwar normalcy, or money-grubbing profiteers of the Holocaust,[12] but as a better sort of "other" as portrayed by the Jewish Museum: ready to integrate and assimilate, unlike the Turks and Arabs; intelligent, diligent, successful, almost more German than the Germans.

The banker and politician Thilo Sarrazin, who almost singlehandedly started the right-wing populist movement in 2010 with his book *Deutschland schafft sich ab* (Germany gets rid of itself), explicitly contrasted Jews and Muslims in an interview with *Lettre International*.[13] Berlin had never recovered from the "bloodletting" under the Nazis, Sarrazin said, as "the banks and the retail trade had been by and large in Jewish hands." Thirty percent of the doctors and lawyers in Berlin and 80 percent of the theater directors had been Jewish, whereas today "a great number" of Berlin's Arabs and Turks had "no productive function whatsoever, except for the vegetable market" and their "little girls with headscarves," who lowered the general IQ in Berlin's schools.[14]

Thus facts, or half-facts, that had been used against the Jews under the Nazis—their presumed dominance in the banking and retail sector, in law and cultural activities, as opposed to the Aryan concentration on producing goods in industry and agriculture— were now being used against Turks and Arabs. Quite apart from the slim factual basis (to put it mildly) of Sarrazin's social Darwinism, the pitting of "*Musterjuden*"[15] (ideal Jews) against new immigrants was calculated to promote even more anti-Jewish feeling among the Muslims. Unfortunately, some Jews have adopted this narrative, too. Possibly they feel that being praised by the goyim, even the racist goyim, is such a change from their usual lot that they might as well play along. Possibly they do feel superior to the new immigrants. Almost certainly they feel threatened by Muslim antisemitism and feel that it might be useful to have German Islamophobes on their side. As John F. Kennedy reportedly said when he appointed Lyndon B. Johnson as his vice-presidential running mate: "Better to have him inside the tent pissing out than outside the tent pissing in."[16]

It seems to me, however, that, as Sarrazin's example shows, German philosemitism is often just reversed antisemitism. As my colleague Henryk M. Broder has repeatedly shown, the new German love of all things Jewish seldom extends to Israel.[17] It's fine shedding a tear about the terrible "bloodletting" during the Nazi era and deploring the loss of the Jewish elite; most Germans are less comfortable when Israel does the blood-letting and proves time and again that its defense, intelligence, and scientific elite is able to ensure the existence of the Jewish state in a hostile environment. Germans have developed a taste for klezmer in recent years, but not much sympathy for Zionism.

Furthermore, while Jews may enjoy being portrayed as paragons of integration and assimilation, the fact remains that they would not exist today had they not resisted integration and assimilation for almost 2,000 years. It was not only Christian discrimination that kept the Jews in Western Europe's ghettos or the Russian Pale of Settlement: it was their own determination not to be absorbed by the Gentiles, not to give up their religious heritage, their self-determination, for instance through rabbinical courts, and their own language, be it Yiddish or Ladino. The "parallel societies" decried by critics of Muslim immigration were for centuries what kept the Jews and Judaism alive.

Many modern Jews—not to mention non-Jews—shudder at the sight of Mea Shearim or parts of Brooklyn, let alone at the pictures of Roman Vishniac's "Vanished World" of the Eastern European shtetl. My father's family certainly actively disliked the "*Ostjuden,*" and I remember my father's disdain not only for the musical *Fiddler on the Roof,* which was a huge success in 1960s Germany, and which he considered kitsch of the worst kind, but also for Gershom Scholem, Martin Buber, and other representatives of the Jewish renaissance in the 1920s and 1930s. Writing from Jerusalem to his confidante Ursula Phillip in London shortly after his arrival in Palestine in 1935, my father describes the "devout people of the Wailing Wall" and goes on to say: "We learn (from those of us who view the Holy East with awe because their fathers spat on it) that swaying before us in the stench and mess of the Old City is a race of heroes, ecstatics and scholars. I can believe it.... But my first reaction is disgust."[18]

Neither disgust nor idealization, it seems to me, are adequate answers to the question about the past that today's and tomorrow's Jews in Germany need to reclaim. Instead of papering over cultural differences, a Jewish view of Jewish history needs to stress them; needs to celebrate the strangeness of being Jewish, of being the archetypical Other not only in Christian, but also in Enlightenment thought, as David Nirenberg has shown.[19] Jewish assimilation was a noble enterprise, but it was doomed and, in certain moments, even my father knew that. Writing to his mother from France in February 1935, he says he intends to go to Palestine, because he "can't always be the little man who apologises for his existence" and that he "cannot imagine passing this fate along to a child—again to love, where he is hated, and to live where he is only tolerated."

A Jew who does not feel sympathy and solidarity with today's immigrants who feel caught in the same bind forgets his or her own past. The German footballer Mesut Özil, a member of the national team, wrote bitterly that he was a German when they won, but became a Turk again when they went down to defeat. Indeed, what lessons should Jews in Germany be teaching the newer Germans from the Middle East and Africa? "Integrate, assimilate the way our fathers and grandfathers did!" Look how far it got them.

Young Jews, mostly from Eastern Europe or Israel, recently staged a "Disintegration Congress" in Berlin. One of the organizers, the poet Max Czollek, criticized the role of Jews "as extras in the German Theatre of Memory." In return for "material and social recognition" they "perform the role of 'Jews for Germans'"—all too often "kippa-wearing figures with a Shoah past."[20] Yet young Ukrainian Jews whose grandparents fought with the Red Army do not accept the narrative of victimhood. Nor do young Israelis. Czollek again: "De-integration also means: No, things won't be all right again. No, I won't light those candles with you. No, our mothers and fathers did not go to Auschwitz together. No, my biography is not available to you. No, when I write poetry it is not so that you understand everything. No, my opinion about Israel has nothing to do with you, damn it. No, you're not going to get off that lightly! . . . This is Jud Sauer. These are the Inglorious Poets. We won the war!"[21]

NOTES

1. Julius Posener, *Fast so alt wie das Jahrhundert* (Munich: Siedler, 1990; revised edition Birkhäuser, 1993).

2. Julius Posener, *Ein Leben in Briefen*, edited by Matthias Schirren and Sylvia Claus (Basel: Birkhäuser, 1999), 154f. In the following all translations from the German are mine (A.P.).

3. Ibid., 157.

4. Ibid., 155.

5. Ibid., 178, 181.

6. Klaus Müller-Rehm, *Lenchen Piepkorn. Erinnerungen aus acht Jahrzehnten* (Berlin: self-published, 1990).

7. Ibid., 208.

8. Quoted in Gregor Schöllgen, *Der Auftritt. Deutschlands Rückkehr auf die Weltbühne* (Berlin: Propyläen 2003), 119.

9. See, for instance, my criticism of the Jewish Museum in "Jüdische Allgemeine," https://www.juedische-allgemeine.de/article/view/id/6517.

10. MENA-Watch on some of Schäfer's escapades: https://www.mena-watch.com /mena-analysen-beitraege/antisemiten-im-juedischen-museum-berlin-deutsche -deutsche-bundesregierung-hat-keine-einwaende.

11. See my criticism of the new permanent exhibition in *Die Welt*: https://www.welt.de/kultur/plus213765208/Berlin-Die-Leerstellen-im-Juedischen-Museum.html.

12. Norman Finkelstein's book *The Holocaust Industry* was translated into German and became a bestseller.

13. Thilo Sarrazin's new book *Feindliche Übernahme: Wie der Islam den Fortschritt behindert und die Gesellschaft bedroht,* which was published in August 2018, became an Amazon bestseller in less than a month.

14. The interview is behind a paywall at *Lettre* (https://www.lettre.de/content/frank-berberich_klasse-statt-masse), but the full text of the interview can be found at http://www.zukunftskinder.org/wp-content/uploads/2016/06/Thilo-Sarrazin-Klasse-statt-Masse.pdf.

15. *Der Musterjude* is the title of a novel by Rafael Seligmann, reviewed in English at https://www.jstor.org/stable/1433080?seq=1#page_scan_tab_contents.

16. Quote in the *New York Times*, October 31, 1971.

17. See, for instance, Henryk M. Broder's recent book, *Vergesst Auschwitz!* https://www.randomhouse.de/Special-zu-Henryk-M-Broder-Vergesst-Auschwitz/Vergesst-Auschwitz/aid35755_7865.rhd.

18. Julius Posener, *In Deutschland 1945 bis 1946*, ed. Alan Posener (Munich: Siedler, 2001), 201.

19. David Nirenberg, *Anti-Judaism: The Western Tradition* (New York: W. W. Norton, 2013).

20. Max Czollek and Sasha Marianna Salzmann, eds., *Desintegration. Exhibition Catalogue* (Berlin: Kerber 2017), 11.

21. Ibid., 101.

GENERATION IN FLUX

Diasporic Reflections on the Future of German-Jewishness

SHEER GANOR

I N HIS 1950 account of traveling through Israel, Manfred George shared the story of a conversation that took place between a boy and a girl on the topic of marriage. The boy claimed to know exactly what matrimony is all about: "First, the couple goes to the rabbi, then they celebrate in a feast, and afterwards, they go into a room." "And then?" the girl pressed him to proceed. "Then," the boy continued, "one locks the door and starts talking in German."[1] George offered this light-hearted anecdote to show his readers how wide the linguistic gap remained between parents and children within Israel's German-speaking community. Even though most members of that community had arrived in the land at least a decade earlier, the realm of adults, as it appeared to the young discussants, remained the realm of German, a room behind locked doors.

The following essay explores the generational gap observed in George's account. It weaves together perceptions of parents and children who populated the diaspora of German-speaking Jews, illuminating how older and younger members came to understand demarcations that surfaced between them as they navigated their places of settlement around the world. Approximately 400,000 German-speaking Jews fled Nazi-dominated Central Europe between 1933 and 1941, among them families with children of all ages.[2] In new locales, young Jewish refugees established their own families and reared children who lived as natives of the new homelands. Parents who migrated with young children, as well as those with children born in the immediate years following displacement, witnessed them growing up in environments distant from the ones they had known.

For the most part, parents encouraged the integration of their offspring. But the acculturation of their children involved adopting norms and customs that were quite literally foreign. Language was a central component, as Manfred George's story indicated, though not the only one. Tastes, manners, and values common in the German-Jewish milieu of Central Europe often seemed out of sync when transplanted into new surroundings. Child refugees and children of refugees may not always have felt themselves fully embedded in the receiving societies,[3] but they were usually better able than their parents to acclimatize.[4] With their cultural identity still linking them to old homelands and denoting their foreignness in new ones, adults perceived a widening gulf between their own generation and the one that followed.

The emergence of a fraught generational gap within immigrant families is a notable characteristic of migratory movements and was certainly not unique to twentieth-century Central European Jews. What sets the case of the German-Jewish diaspora apart from other mass migration waves is the emergence of such a generational divide at the precise moment when German-speaking Jewry faced the threat of extinction. National Socialism violently negated claims to German-Jewishness as a culture and identity: its claimants and bearers faced expulsion and dispersion, or worse, deportation and annihilation. The children of the German-Jewish diaspora, it became increasingly clear, would have no physical "metropole" to observe from a distance. If their parents succeeded in instilling German-Jewishness in them, it was in the form of a remembered and constructed heritage, not as a lived reality. Under these conditions, refugee parents had to come to terms with the fact that the world that had shaped them would remain foreign to their children.

Familial relationships and intergenerational tensions remain little explored in scholarship on the German-Jewish diaspora.[5] This essay places them at the focus of investigation. In the following pages I examine the different ways in which German-speaking Jews understood the nature and consequences of the boundaries between the generation still attached to *drüben*—the geographic and mental terrain of the past—and the younger generation immersed foremost in its immediate environments. Synthesizing perspectives from parents as well as children (often writing as adults), I explore their relationship as a locus of hopes and fears, of comfort and conflict. As these tensions unfolded in various geographies and different societal contexts, a question echoed in the background: in light of the Nazi attacks on Germany's Jews and in the aftermath of displacement and dispersion, could German-Jewishness still have a future in the diaspora?

THE GENERATIONAL GAP
AND THE SUSTAINABILITY OF
GERMAN-JEWISH CULTURE

After Ernst Simon traveled at the behest of the Jerusalem Leo Baeck Institute to German-Jewish communities in Latin America, he authored a detailed report on the experience. Youth in the countries that he visited, Simon wrote in 1958, generally understood the German language, though they seldom read it and could speak it only with difficulty. With some bitterness, Simon noted that children of former refugees were rapidly absorbing the local culture, which was quickly "consuming the fragments of the Jewish culture that their parents still possess, and which they attempt to pass on to their children with inadequate means." In Rio de Janeiro, Simon reported, the community branded itself not as "German-Jewish" but as "liberal," and in doing so, he thought that "it loses a part of its German-Jewish character, but wins over the youth." In Buenos Aires, he lamented the strong influence of "North-American culture" but found that a significant portion of children continued to attend the German-Jewish "Pestalozzi-School."[6]

Filled with contradictions, Simon's analysis made no attempt to formulate a coherent characterization of the conditions of the younger generation. His report is instructive, however, in highlighting the urgency with which German-Jewish community leaders observed their descendants growing up across the diaspora. They sought to identify patterns of integration and opportunities to foster communal cohesion. During his journey, Simon gave several lectures on such topics as "The Cultural Legacy of Germany Jewry," "New Developments in Hebrew Literature," or "How to Educate Our Children as Jews." These events were very well attended and Simon attributed their success to the hope that one might learn how to "remain Jewish" and to safeguard one's children within the community.[7] While the general intention was to secure the continued existence of the Jewish minority writ large, German-speaking Jews prioritized doing so within the framework of their own communities. The popular interest in Simon's lectures indicates that the concern around the growing distance of the next generation from "our circles," as Simon referred to it, extended beyond community leaders, pedagogues, and organizations such as the Leo Baeck Institute (LBI), who were explicitly invested in preserving German-Jewishness.

Around the time that Simon composed his report, similar questions were voiced across the German-Jewish diaspora. In New York members of the American Jewish K.C. Fraternity, one of the successor organizations to the Kartell-Convent (KC) umbrella association of Jewish university fraternities, tried to initiate an exchange program in which children of members from various countries would be hosted by KC families in another country. The purpose, beyond the international experience afforded to young participants, was to expose descendants of former *Burschen* to the KC traditions and the bond shared by its members worldwide.[8]

The initial invitation to participate in the program was unsuccessful. In 1961 another attempt to revive it carried an appeal for members to acknowledge that the KC teetered on its "deathbed" and to consider the youth exchange program as a response to its otherwise certain demise. "Isn't it a wonderful thought," John Elton wrote in the organization's bulletin, "that the next generation and the one after that ... will build friendships on cornerstones laid by ourselves? That we were able to contribute something to the possibility that a group of people from different parts of the world would feel close to each other?" Elton recognized that the ideals that motivated his generation and his parents' generation to join the fraternities could no longer suffice, but he still believed in the ability to sustain the KC "when not in name then in spirit."[9] Elton's plea may very well have resonated with fellow KC members (the organization's bulletins and reunion speeches addressed its uncertain future on other occasions as well), but the exchange program failed once again to come to fruition. The majority of the *KC Brüder*, as they referred to themselves, either came to terms with the foreseeable end of their union, or did not believe in the exchange as a viable option. During the postwar decades KC chapters around the world focused their efforts on chronicling their fraternities' history, debating their ideological motivations, and reminiscing at local and international reunions. With no new recruits, no institutional future in the most literal sense, KC members spent the remainder of their active years engaging with their past.

Ernst Simon's inquiry on behalf of the LBI and the unsuccessful attempts at securing the next generation of *KC Brüder* offer two examples of diasporic collectives investigating the possibilities and limitations of a German-Jewish future. These initiatives reveal a concern with the growing detachment of the youth from the culture that had given birth to both the LBI and the KC. While these two institutions were founded specifically as representative bodies for German Jewry (albeit in different time periods and under very different circumstances), they were not alone in sensing a widening divide between parents and children across the diaspora. As the following examples show, the confrontation with this generational gap was present in everyday family environments and experienced directly by parents as well as their children.

THE GERMAN-JEWISH FAMILY

Like all parents, German-Jewish parents strove to guarantee a secure future for their progeny. To that end, they generally promoted and supported their children's integration. Indeed, many observed the process with pride and happiness, grateful to see their sons and daughters developing into locals in their adoptive countries. But a bittersweet sentiment accompanied that sense of joy and accomplishment, especially as the parents themselves often faced material loss and cultural disorientation.

Grete Mahrer's short story entitled "The Letter" illustrates how the generational gap found its manifestations in intimate, everyday spaces. Mahrer submitted it to a writing competition held by the *Mitteilungsblatt*, the press organ of the Central European Immigrant Association in Palestine/Israel. Awarded third prize in the contest, "The Letter" was printed in December 1949. It told the story of Edith Grüner, who had received a letter from her daughter, Jael. Edith knew the origin of the letter even before reading it closely, since Jael was the only person who ever wrote to her in Hebrew and not in German. Having trouble deciphering the foreign language, Edith wrongfully surmised that Jael would be visiting the following day, when the letter had in fact stated that Jael would be getting married that day. This not inconsequential misunderstanding then led to the unfolding of a comedy of errors.

Mahrer's short story is filled with moments of cultural clashes between the Sabra generation and their parents. Particularly interesting is Mahrer's narration of Edith's struggle with Jael's letter: "She sat facing the bookcase with the works of Thomas Mann and Hermann Hesse, books by André Gide and Sigmund Freud, books about political economy and history, books about art and music and psychology that seemed to watch in refined silence as she tried, with the help of a dictionary, to read what her child had written her."[10] Mahrer intentionally delayed over this image of the cultivated woman struggling to read simple words that her daughter had written without effort. It was only a somewhat exaggerated depiction of German-Jewish *Bildungsbürgertum* postdisplacement, one that the *Mitteilungsblatt* editors could safely assume would resonate among their readers.

If Mahrer's story was meant to occasion amusement with a slightly melancholic touch, Edith Kurzweil's memoir offers a more somber version of the parental loss of status. Narrating her escape from her hometown of Vienna to the United States, Kurzweil paid particular attention to the strains that displacement had placed on her relationship with her parents. Her relationship with her father became especially strenuous. She disdained his constant complaining about New York and his romanticization of life "*bei uns*," back in Europe.[11] In her memoir, Kurzweil applied the gift of hindsight when she noted that "it didn't occur to me that without his business and status he had lost his moorings and his dashing spirit. Or that much of his bravado was covering up his feelings of inferiority: he was a foreigner who now perceived himself as a nobody."[12] The sense of losing his self-worth translated into a dominating attitude at home, leading to frequent clashes with his daughter, for whom "Vienna was dissolving into New York."[13]

For many parents and young adults across the German-Jewish diaspora, the relief of having escaped Nazism did not ease the difficulties of relinquishing their former world. When raising children, they tried to introduce pieces of that world that they cherished and missed. Sonja Mühlberger's parents regularly read German fairytales to her while living as refugees in Shanghai. They tried their best to visualize the landscape in which these stories took place and, when their daughter was incapable of understand-ing the meaning of a forest, they explained that it is one tree, and then another tree, and then even more trees together. On one rare occasion when snow fell in the city, her father climbed a ladder to the roof of their house and filled a bowl with the white matter. Young Sonja was instructed to put her hands inside and feel the snow, "and so the story of Snow White became more tangible."[14] On the other side of the world in Bolivia, Leo Spitzer received from his father the book *Beethoven: El Sacrificio de un Niño* (Beethoven: The Sacrifice of a Child), an illustrated biography of the composer his father so admired. The book provided the young Spitzer (born in 1939 in La Paz) with a tangible link to his father's faraway home.[15] The Spanish-language book was something of a boundary object. It simultaneously educated Spitzer about his fami-ly's past and embedded him in their present space of temporary refuge in Bolivia.

ENCOUNTERS OF A GERMAN-JEWISH KIND

Responses to the generational gap were not united in character. Parents reacted differently upon realizing that their offspring acquired mentalities and sensibilities that they perceived as foreign. Marjorie Perloff, for example, felt that her fondness for American pop culture disappointed her parents. Despite the fact that even as a child she was also immersed in the German literary canon, her interest in what her parents disapprovingly called "kitsch" was met with disdain. When she shared her enthusiasm with her family, she said, "my mother and grandmother gave each other a look, as if to say, 'Poor child, she doesn't yet understand.'"[16] Young Perloff, on the other hand, secretly hoped that her mother would become more like other mothers who already knew who Frank Sinatra was.[17]

Parents could tacitly accept their children's acculturation, even when they were not entirely comfortable with the local culture. Hedy Axelrad came to terms with what she had considered the poor etiquette and absent manners displayed by American children. She even accepted that her own daughter, Evi, fell short in this regard. In a 1940 letter to her parents (who were stranded in Vienna), she laughed at the suggestion that Evi be allowed to play only with well-mannered children: "There's no such thing here. I've never seen children so naughty before. There are absolutely no consequences, they do as they please and the adults find it entirely natural." Evi, she wrote, was not misbehav-ing, but "generally does what she wants," while the children of a family friend, Axelrad confided, "are already completely *amerikanisch*." Concluding the matter, Axelrad reas-sured her parents that there was no need to worry about something they could not control, and that "the older ones here are nice and good, so it will work out."[18]

In the diaspora, perpetuating the cultural ideals and behavioral norms that guided Central European Jews before their displacement seemed untenable, particularly for children and youth. The extent to which parents regretted this futility often depended on their own biographies—their previous lives, the circumstances surrounding their migration, the conditions encountered thereafter, and their individual attitudes toward host societies. Consider the cases of Lazar Herrmann and Hans Elias, both of whom had emigrated to the United States but formulated opposing approaches to American influences on their children. Under the pseudonym Leo Lania, Herrmann published an article on the occasion of his son entering U.S. military service in 1943. When his wife declared that she would like to accompany their son, Fred, to the train station, Herrmann hesitated. He recalled his own service during World War I and the stifling atmosphere of militant masculinity. Assuming that Fred would be embarrassed, he was surprised to hear him respond: "Of course you're coming!" Observing Fred going through an experience so close to his own yet so radically different revealed to Herrmann a gulf between their generations: "So it is for us, European fathers, with our American sons," he wrote. "In day-to-day life we don't notice how fast and how fully they are developing away from us. But on that morning I felt it stronger than ever."

Thinking back on European critiques of American education, Herrmann noted that he had once believed that American children, too coddled by their mothers, grew to become "soft." Seeing Fred and his generation, he realized that "the American lad does not become a 'mother's boy,' rather, even in uniform he remains a mother's son. And that's the best protection against the rise of militarism in America." Herrmann thus cheered ex-European youth for quickly Americanizing themselves. He recalled how his son once admonished him when Herrmann brushed off an argument as "nonsense." Fred proclaimed that presenting different perspectives in a reasonable manner is a cornerstone of democratic society. Remarking that, just two years before, Fred had been surrounded by hatred and terror, Herrmann felt immensely pleased at his son's lucid convictions.[19]

Hans Elias saw things differently. In 1940 Elias published an article titled "Liberalistic Education as the Cause of Fascism." Using historical examples from Europe in the eighteenth and nineteenth centuries, as well as from his own experience in Weimar-era Germany, he described progressive education as dangerous. It failed to provide children with the opposition required to mature into thoughtful, responsible human beings. Sensing "that the American youth may come into the same danger," Elias hoped "to awaken the attention of American educators and parents."[20] In his view, educational norms in the United States were not promoting sensible values, as Herrmann had believed, but instead fostered illiberal tendencies, as was the case in Europe.

When in 1945 Elias and his family moved from Massachusetts to Atlanta, Georgia, he and his wife, Anneliese, were disturbed by the rampant racism they witnessed. They were especially concerned that their two young sons might grow up to internalize the

injustice of racial segregation as normal. To make sure that their sons would not acculturate to their surroundings too much, they went together to a local African American
school and met with the principal—who declined their invitation to visit their house
for fear of getting lynched if seen in their white neighborhood.[21] In that particular
social surrounding, Hans and Anneliese Elias were deliberately trying to prevent their
children from feeling at home.

Herrmann celebrated his son's receptiveness to the democratic ideals of his new
country; Elias feared that his children could absorb prevalent bigotry and violence. One
father extolled American children's education as a contrast to rigid European norms;
the other warned that the two were dangerously alike. Significantly, both looked back
at their previous life in Central Europe for clues to determine what their children could
and should learn from new surroundings while building their own futures.

LOOKING BACK TO THE
GERMAN-JEWISH FUTURE

One intriguing facet in the history of the German-Jewish diaspora is a supposed contradiction in integration. Many immigrants experienced a relatively swift and smooth
socioeconomic assimilation, but meanwhile sought to safeguard particular cultural
codes, sustaining a living connection to a world that seemed out of reach. In their previous homelands, genocide and war were destroying what remained of their communities; in their new ones, the younger generation was attuned to coordinates different
from their own. Under these circumstances, if German Jewry still had a future, could
it resemble its past in any meaningful way?

One member of the German-Jewish diaspora considered that question directly in
July 1939. Under the title "Confessions of a Former Assimilationist," Tristan Leander
proclaimed that, from his home in Palestine, he no longer felt a connection to the
German people. His connection to the German language, however, remained strong.
He recognized that his unborn children could not share this link to the language
and culture of his own youth. "But once in a while, when they are not at home," he
predicted, "I will hide in a corner and secretly read a little Goethe or Karl Kraus." He
pleaded with his new compatriots who were unable to understand this need, "because
they never felt themselves to be truly Polish or Russian," to "leave us be. It's only a
matter of one last generation."[22] The deep sense of betrayal that the author—and many
others in his position—felt toward their former homelands did not weaken his strong
commitment to his native culture. Indeed, it was his fear that it would have no lineage,
no room in the future of his own family and by extension the future of the Jewish
people, that compelled him to cling to the idea of German-Jewishness.

The children of the German-Jewish diaspora may or may not have learned the native language of their parents. Many grew to espouse, with some measure of pride, the identity of second-generation *Yekkes*. But the lives, experiences, and memories discussed here show that both parents and children were acutely aware of the chasm that existed between them. Responses to that realization varied, but acceptance prevailed. After all, the existence of a generational gap between parents and their children was perhaps the only *normal* experience that German-speaking Jewish families negotiated during an era of unprecedented rupture.

NOTES

1. Manfred George, *Das Wunder Israel. Eindrücke von einer Reise durch den jungen jüdischen Staat* (New York: Aufbau, 1950), 21.

2. Exact numbers are difficult to determine, but the percentage of children and youth among the refugees was substantial. Hagit Lavsky's research shows that 29 percent of the arrivals to Palestine between 1933 and 1938 were between ages 1 to 20; 15 percent of arrivals between 1933 and 1939 in England were between ages 1 to 18; and in the United States between 1934 and 1938, 30 percent were between ages 1 to 20, dropping to 18 percent between 1938 and 1941. These numbers include children migrating independently, not with their families. Hagit Lavsky, *The Creation of the German-Jewish Diaspora: Interwar German-Jewish Immigration to Palestine, the USA, and England* (Oldenburg: De Gruyter, 2017), 69, 78, 81.

3. For two particularly illuminating discussions of the prolonged sense of otherness experienced by children of German-Jewish refugees see Carol Ascher, Renate Bridenthal, Atina Grossmann, and Marion Kaplan, "Fragments of a German-Jewish Heritage in Four 'Americans,'" in *The German-Jewish Legacy in America, 1938–1988: From Bildung to the Bill of Rights,* ed. Abraham J. Peck (Detroit: Wayne State University Press, 1989), 365–384; Thomas W. Laqueur, "Diary: Memories in German," *London Review of Books* 25, no. 23 (December 2003): 38–39.

4. For the legal regimes that administered the mass forced migration out of Europe in the 1930s and 1940s, children's relative assimilability made them stronger candidates than adults for receiving legal immigration papers. See Tara Zahra, *The Lost Children: Reconstructing Europe's Families after World War II* (Cambridge, MA: Harvard University Press, 2015), loc. 321 in Kindle.

5. Notable exceptions that have dealt specifically with children and youth who came of age in the diaspora include Christian Bauer and Rebekka Göpfert, *Die Ritchie Boys: Deutsche Emigranten beim US-Geheimdienst* (Hamburg: Hoffmann und Campe, 2005); Andreas W. Daum, Hartmut Lehmann, and James J. Sheehan, eds., *The Second*

Generation: Émigrés from Nazi Germany as Historians (New York: Berghahn Books, 2016); Gerald Holton and Gerald Sonnert, *What Happened to the Children Who Fled Nazi Persecution* (New York: Palgrave Macmillan, 2006); Walter Laqueur, *Generation Exodus: The Fate of Young Jewish Refugees from Nazi Germany* (Hanover, NH: I. B. Tauris, 2001). On rescue programs of child refugees, see Brian Amkraut, *Between Home and Homeland: Youth Aliyah from Nazi Germany* (Tuscaloosa, AL: University of Alabama Press, 2006); Judith Tydor Baumel-Schwarz, *Never Look Back: The Jewish Refugee Children in Great Britain, 1938–1945* (West Lafayette, IN: Purdue University Press, 2012); Iris Guske, *Trauma and Attachment in the Kindertransport Context: German-Jewish Child Refugees' Accounts of Displacement and Acculturation in Britain* (Newcastle: Cambridge Scholars Publishing, 2009). On family dynamics in the diaspora, see Judith Gerson, "Family Matters: German-Jewish Masculinities among Nazi Era Refugees," in *Jewish Masculinities. German Jews, Gender and History,* ed. Benjamin Maria Baader, Sharon Gillerman, and Paul Lerner (Bloomington, IN: Indiana University Press, 2012), 210–232; Andrea Hammel, "Representations of Family in Autobiographical Texts of Child Refugees," *Shofar* 23, no. 1 (Fall 2004): 121–132.

6. Ernst Simon, "Bericht über meine Reise nach Süd-Amerika," October 1958. In CENTRA Collection 1958–1971, LBIJER 1016, folder 3, Leo Baeck Institute (LBI) Jerusalem.

7. Ibid.

8. Unsigned, "Für KC—Eltern und Grosseltern," Kartell-Convent deutscher Studenten Jüdischen Glaubens Collection; AR 966, box 1, folder 17, LBI.

9. John H. Elton, "Gedanken über das 'Weiterleben des KC,'" *American Jewish K.C. Fraternity, Inc. Bulletin* no. 5 (September 1961). Kartell-Convent Collection, box 2, folder 6, LBI.

10. Grete Mahrer, "Der Brief," *Mitteilungsblatt* no. 52 (December 30, 1949): 5. Accessed July 2018 at http://www.infocenters.co.il/massuah/multimedia/Docs/pdf/disk20091224 /51141.pdf#search.

11. Ibid., 101.

12. Ibid., 88.

13. Ibid., 121.

14. Sonja Mühlberger, *Geboren in Shanghai als Kind von Emigranten—Leben und Überleben im Ghetto von Hongkew (1939–1947)* (Berlin: Hentrich und Hentrich Verlag, 2006), 32.

15. Leo Spitzer, *Hotel Bolivia: The Culture of Memory in a Refuge from Nazism* (New York: Hill & Wang, 1998), 76.

16. Marjorie Perloff, *The Vienna Paradox: A Memoir* (New York: New Directions, 2004), 185.

17. Ibid., 187.

18. Hedy Axelrad to Adolf and Cäcilie Traub, September 9, 1940, Axelrad Family Collection, AR 25003, box 3, folder 1, LBI.

19. Leo Lania, "Gedanken eines europäischen Vaters: Mein Sohn Ist in der US Armee," *Aufbau* 9, no. 25 (June 18, 1943): 4.

20. Hans Elias, "Liberalistic Education as the Cause of Fascism," *School and Society* 51, no. 1324 (May 11, 1940): 593–598.

21. Hans Elias, "Abenteuer in Emigration und Wissenschaft. Ein Beitrag von Aufklärung des Krebsproblems von Hans Elias," SPE XMS Elias 81.8, SUNY Albany, chapter 7.

22. Tristan Leander, "Bekenntnisse eines Ex-Assimilanten," *Jüdische Welt Rundschau* (July 28, 1939): 6.

HOME ON THE BALCONY

New Initiatives for the Preservation
of Documents and Material Objects
Relating to German-Jewish History

JOACHIM SCHLÖR

A UTUMN 1990.[1] Germany celebrated its reunification, but I heard the news from afar and looked at my own country with a new feeling of distance. As a fellow of the Institute for German History at Tel Aviv University, I had developed a plan to write about the history of the city of Tel Aviv, seen through the eyes and the experiences of German-speaking Jews who had arrived here after the Nazis' rise to power, between 1933 and 1940. My research brought me to an area of the city that some people called "*Yekkesland*": Ben Yehuda, Gordon, Frishman, Mapu, and Ruppin streets, north of the city center, close to the sea, and—then, not anymore— characterized by the public use of the German language (or Hebrew with a German or Austrian accent) and the existence of some institutions such as Landsberger's bookshop or Café Mersand where those *Yekkes* regularly met and exchanged views about their lives between *Herkunft* and *Zukunft*, between a European past and a Middle Eastern present. Fortunately, I also had the opportunity to visit some wonderful people, Eli and Marianne Rothschild, Viola and Mordechai Virshubsky, Ernst Laske, Eva Sänger, Nadja Taussig, and many others. All of these private apartments contained elements of a partly saved German and European cultural heritage that had found their way to Palestine and now lived together with more recent Israeli material objects: musical instruments and music sheets, paintings and drawings on the walls, bookshelves with German titles, letters, diaries, photo albums.[2] Nadia Taussig told me about the German-speaking circle that had met in her and her husband Ernst's flat on Mapu 3 for fifty years, from 1941 to 1991. She showed me a list of all the lectures and debates held at this place, and on that list we encounter many of the important names of deracinated German-speaking Jewish intellectuals, Shalom Ben Chorin, Max Brod, Sammy Gronemann, Margot

Klausner, Helmar Lerski, Leo Perutz, Arnold Zweig; and the important topics of the time: the land and its future, the Zionist movement and the idea of a binational state, music, film, theater, photography, and literature. I managed to make a copy of the list (and have used it in many ways), but when I asked Mrs. Taussig for a copy of the letters that must have been stored somewhere in these desks and cupboards, she hesitated and asked me to visit her again after her move to an *Elternheim*. She passed away just a week or so after that move; none of her friends had the chance to search for the documents and they were all thrown away. Such losses must have occurred many times, due to a lack of interest among the younger generation or maybe, in more general terms, due to the prevailing Zionist idea that the cultures of the diaspora had little value in the process of the Israeli nation-building process. One could often see German books and papers on the street, awaiting disposal.

One of the most impressive visits took place in Gordon Street. Walter Grab, who had immigrated from Vienna as a nineteen-year-old and made a living selling handbags on the street, later redefined and established himself as a historian and became the founder of the Institute for German History at Tel Aviv University. His study was crammed with books and manuscripts, copies of archival sources about the libertarian movements in German history, from the Peasants' War through 1848 to the German anti-Nazi resistance. When I asked him where he felt at home—what *Heimat* meant for him—he also hesitated. It couldn't be Vienna, he maintained, because of the antisemitism that had driven him out of his hometown and was still not defeated; it couldn't be Jerusalem either, because of the dominance of religion which made him uncomfortable. In the end, he said, it was "this balcony," a place from which he could look out to the sea and to his own international connections—and back into his study. I remember wondering what would happen to all these papers in the future, but I didn't dare to ask.

As it turned out, they have been preserved. At that time in the early 1990s, there were only few places that would—or even could—accept such collections. The Zionist Archives in Jerusalem concentrated on the preservation of papers and documents relevant for the study of the political movement; the Central Archives for the History of the Jewish People, also in Jerusalem, kept the memories of (mostly destroyed) Jewish communities in Europe and elsewhere; and while the Leo Baeck Institute's archives in New York, the London-based Wiener Library, or the archive of the Centre for German-Jewish Studies at Sussex University could have been possible repositories, not many people wanted their papers to leave Israel. In the mid-nineties, the little Museum in Honour of German Jewry, founded in 1970 by Israel Shiloni in Nahariya, was offered a new home in Stef Wertheimer's Open Museum in Tefen, Galilee. Ruthi Ofek commenced her work as curator there, and at long last there was a place where children and grandchildren could donate the estates of their parents and grandparents.³ Alongside this positive development in the institutionalization and professionalization of archival work in Israel, another contribution should be discussed: More and more young researchers from all over the world, but specifically from Germany and Austria, began to write about different aspects of German-Jewish and Austrian-Jewish history and culture, and even if their specific topics concerned events, institutions, or personalities from the period before 1933, they had to use the archives in Israel and to take into account the effect of forced emigration both on the persons they interviewed and on their libraries and private archives. In addition, there has been an enormous growth in the number (and quality) of studies that research and discuss this emigration itself, the many different experiences of the *Yekkes*, and the development of both private and public memory cultures related to it. These young researchers continued to visit witnesses of the time in their private homes and asked to see personal documents they might use for their projects—and this interest in turn helped to create a new awareness among those Jews of German or Austrian origin, and their families, about the importance of the preservation of such documents. Finally, with the growing list of publications, with new research projects developed in newly funded or invigorated research centers for Jewish studies in Germany and Austria (Potsdam, Leipzig, Hamburg, Berlin, Graz, Salzburg), and with the continuity of academic collaboration between German universities and partners elsewhere, in Israel and the United States, but also in the UK (not least the Centre for German-Jewish Studies at the University of Sussex), the need to preserve such documents and to make them accessible for research has led to a stronger involvement of German cultural institutions.

As a result of all these developments, the Franz Rosenzweig Minerva Research Center in Jerusalem and the German Literary Archive in Marbach created a project, funded by the German Foreign Office, entitled "Traces and Treasures of German-Jewish History in Israel." This initiative owns its existence to the scholarly and humane engagement of a new generation of scholars—the last generation to meet the surviving *Yekkes* in person and to visit them in their homes. Caroline Jessen, who wrote an excellent PhD dissertation on the "literary canon" of German Jews in Israel, their libraries, and on the place these collections had in their new lives in Israel, coordinated the project from 2012 to 2015. Her successor is Lina Barouch, who specializes in twentieth-century German-Jewish writing and specifically the overlaps between German and Hebrew. The project description on their website reads as follows:

> Personal archives and collections were rescued from Nazi Germany by emigrants, refugees and Jewish institutions with considerable difficulty during the years 1933–1945 and in the immediate aftermath of the Holocaust. Many of these collections were brought to Mandate Palestine and are now preserved in public archives or private collections in Israel. Despite the efforts of Israeli archives, a significant

part of the rescued materials has not yet been made available for international research. Few Israeli archives can provide personnel with sufficient language skills to make these mostly German-language holdings accessible. The project 'Traces of German-Jewish History' promotes the arrangement and description of archives of scholars, writers, and artists and encourages archive-based research in the fields of Cultural Transfer, the History of Science, the Migration of Knowledge and the History of Ideas. In order to preserve significant collections and to open them up to international research, the project draws on the DLA's development of flexible cataloging and conservation measures, while the Rosenzweig Minerva Research Center offers its scholarly expertise and a forum for discussions between established scholars, junior researchers and archivists. Personal archives, literary estates, and historical collections do not only represent a threatened "cultural heritage", but they also provide an essential foundation for new cultural and scholarly discussions. Traces of German-Jewish History offers junior scholars and students the opportunity to participate in projects combining academic research and archival practice. In addition to this, the project aims at locating relevant German-Jewish collections, which are neither archived nor accessible to the public, in order to facilitate their transfer to a suitable public archive in Israel.[4]

Among the collections, we find files of the Hebrew theater *Habimah* and of the Leo Baeck Institute in Jerusalem, as well as private collections of Ruth Enis, Gideon Kaminka, Samuel (Shmuel) Hugo Bergmann, Shlomo Dov (Fritz) Goitein, C. Z. Kloetzel, Heinrich Loewe, Nadia Stein, Curt Wormann, and Walter Grab. At a conference in Jerusalem in September 2016, "Contested German-Jewish Cultural Property after 1945: The Sacred and the Profane," Yonatan Shiloh-Dayan summarized his research on the Walter Grab collection in a lecture with the beautiful title: "What Does a Displaced Historian Keep?" Not only were the documents saved, ordered, systematized, but the preservation enables us to discuss new questions around Grab's work and to enter his world of thought through the documents he kept. This would have pleased Walter Grab immensely. Similarly, the papers of Heinrich Loewe have been preserved. Loewe was a—maybe, *the*—central figure of the Zionist movement in Berlin from the late 1890s to 1933. His name appears in the context of nearly every single initiative dedicated to a Jewish future in Palestine. Frank Schlöffel, in his study *Heinrich Loewe. Zionistische Netzwerke und Räume,* made an enormous effort to reconstruct all these initiatives and to tell the story of Loewe's life, from a childhood in Magdeburg and a professional career as a librarian at Berlin's Friedrich-Wilhelm-Universität to the position of director of Tel Aviv's municipal library.[5] And there, in Beit Ariela, an important part of Loewe's papers (which had not gone to the Central Zionist Archives) were kept in bad condition without a secure future. Now they have been preserved and can be made accessible. These papers contain life stories, "traces," that led from Germany to Palestine and Israel, and they reflect individual experiences of emigration and immigration, feelings of a *Heimat* lost and a new life gained.

They are indeed "treasures." To have this knowledge is important both for the self-understanding of the Israeli society and its relationship to the diaspora and for our understanding of a German and German-Jewish culture that has partly been destroyed and lives on—in fragments. These documents show, as Caroline Jessen put it in an interview, "how deeply Israeli history is connected to German-Jewish history" and that "the work of German Jews has become a part of Israeli identity."

In the second part of this contribution, I would like to open our perspective and look at other forms of dialogue between German-Jewish émigrés and their former home, with a specific focus on the city of Berlin on the one hand, but on a worldwide connectivity at the same time. Questions relating to the fate of German-Jewish cultural property after 1933—from the initial "loss" to eventual restitution—are generally addressed within the framework of the state or other official institutions. Yet there is a further dimension to both the historical events and current debates about them, namely that of the individual and personal experience. "Aryanization," theft, confiscation—these impacted individuals and families first of all. Those who were able to flee from Nazi persecution and emigrate to places all over the world were forced to leave property behind, to sell art collections or furniture for the lowest prices, or to hand over their firms and stores to whoever profited from their loss. During my current research on family letters and testimonies written during the process of emigration (and over ensuing decades), I have come across numerous sources that have rarely been used in this context: Family members and relatives exchange information about the loss of material objects in documents that are, perforce, of a transnational character, while at the same time they refer to the former *Heimat*, their *home*—the place of departure. These documents afford us a valuable insight into the meaning of *things* for families and individuals.

A first source that demonstrates this importance of property to the emigrants and survivors is a letter written by Walter M. Danziger, 2907 Fallstaff Road, Apartment T5, in Baltimore, Maryland, on April 29, 1991. The letter is addressed to Dr. Klaus Sühl, Freie Universität Berlin, who had been commissioned by the Senate of Berlin to prepare the publication of the *Gedenkbuch der ermordeten Juden Berlins* (Memorial Book for the Murdered Jews of Berlin). Walter Danziger writes as follows:

> *Dear Dr. Suehl,*
> *With regard to your appeal in Aktuell-Berlin, I wish to inform you of what we went through in Berlin before we were finally permitted to emigrate to America. We also sadly lost many relatives in concentration camps, even entire families. My*

parents owned a department store in the Schlossstraße in Berlin-Koepenick, called Lichtenstein Nachf. D. Cohn. The building in which the store was based and where we lived belonged to my grandmother Emilie Cohn. Behind the building there was also a very beautiful garden, with a view over the Dahme, which also belonged to my grandmother Emilie Cohn.

In 1938, my father was forced by a Nazi called Ahrendt to sell the store. This Nazi also bought all the other Jewish stores in Koepenick and took over our apartment. The City of Koepenick bought the building at a very low price. Life in Koepenick became very uncomfortable in 1939. Jewish families were taken out of their houses at night and led through the entire city accompanied by ugly taunts. Thus my parents decided to move to West Berlin, where we managed to get an apartment in Schaperstraße 8, near the Kaiserallee. Our friends were called Loewe. Our host owned a publishing house. His wife was descended from one Professor Abraham Geiger, who had founded Reform Judaism.[6]

This source forms part of a large body of correspondence that has not been accessible so far and which I was permitted to view in the archives of the Stiftung Neue Synagoge—Centrum Judaicum in Berlin's Oranienburger Straße. The task assigned to Klaus Sühl and his colleagues, Ulrich Schulze-Marmeling and Rita Meyhöfer, was—as the correspondents frequently note—immense. They attempted to list all the Jews who had been deported from Berlin and murdered in the Holocaust, along with the dates of their deportation and the dates of their death, and any further information that could possibly be found.[7] What the researchers had not foreseen was that those who responded to the appeal titled "Aufruf an alle ehemaligen Berliner Juden" (call to all former Berliner Jews), advertised in *Aufbau, Mitteilungsblatt, Semanario Israelita, AJR Information,* and many other newspapers and journals of German-Jewish émigrés worldwide, wished to tell—indeed *had* to tell—their own stories: stories of survival in concentration camps or living "illegally" on the streets of Berlin; tales of migration, of the many different ways in which their life in Berlin came to an end and how they began to build a new life elsewhere; and accounts of the material objects they were able to take along or were forced to leave behind.

This collection, originating in the idea to document the circumstances of death, has evolved into a reservoir of stories of survival. *Berlin-Aktuell* is the name of the journal—which appeared in print for many years, and today is mainly accessible online—founded by the so-called *Emigrantenreferat* of the Berlin Senate, whose main task has been, since 1969, to maintain the numerous forms of contact between the city and its former inhabitants, most importantly the regular visits of groups of "former Berliners."[8] Letters addressed to and sent by *Berlin-Aktuell* and the *Emigrantenreferat* form a further body of sources, stored in the upper floor of Berlin's Rotes Rathaus. Together these two sets of sources, which comprise thousands of letters, provide insight into the multiple forms of relationships among the Berliners who now reside (or, as many have since passed away, resided at the time) in Baltimore, Maryland and in so many other places around the globe. They provide an idea of the relationship between owners and their property as well as their sense of loss and hope for restoration.

What became of the house and the garden in Köpenick? Which parts of the family property were those who emigrated able to take along with them when they left? (Walter came to England with the *Kindertransport*.) What role did the former property play in the subsequent lives of those who managed to escape? Did the emigrants try to retrieve it? Did they talk about it during family meetings? When we think of all the human lives destroyed by the Nazis, writing about material objects, from houses to children's toys, may seem trivial. Yet the letters show that this is not the case. Another former Berliner, Walter Lachman, wrote as follows from Longmeadow, Massachusetts in the 1990s:

I am still suffering today from a terrible fear that I will again lose the tangible properties I have been able to amass in this world, and even more, that I will again lose my decent human instincts and cultural values.[9]

The loss of property is an ever-present event in the lives of those who remained, and for those who emigrated. These events mark the steps of persecution and marginalization. The experiences noted in the letters directed to the city of Berlin illustrate Walter Danziger's assertion that the loss of property was no less significant than his memory of the loss of human dignity. This was equally true for those who managed to emigrate. Leo Eisenfeld writes as follows in his *Erinnerungen*, a report that he submitted to the *Gedenkbuch* team:

From January to July 1939, after I had to leave my mother alone in Berlin, she began wandering around Berlin in ever-greater desperation, bullied terribly at the police precinct, to try nevertheless to obtain something in return for her apartment furnishings, to try nevertheless to obtain certificates for Palestine or quotas for America. The little that she managed to get for her things she of course had to spend on her upkeep, to meet the emigration expenses, etc.[10]

The emigrants take stock of their belongings and their meanings, as Vivian Jeanette Kaplan observed: "Sitting cross-legged on the ground beside the empty overseas bag, I wonder what, among the inventory of my previous life should go into this container and what should go onto the large pile of things that I have to leave behind."[11] The objects become travel companions whose presence is described in memoirs: "I also recorded in the text descriptions of mementos among my items, of objects to which I was attached, because they remained with me on the entire journey described here."[12] The many practical steps needed to prepare for emigration often led families to reassess their material possessions and to discuss their use and value.

Exile research has recently begun to focus increasingly on the place of things, of material objects, in emigration. Objects are manufactured from particular materials; they are used during the course of everyday cultural practices in the context of work or home life; they are repaired (as part of a "makeshift economy"), inherited, rededicated, dug out again, forgotten, and then remembered once again. However, cultural anthropology has tended to focus on the objects that remained in place rather than on those that went "on a journey." But what happens when the "domestic environment," the home, is threatened, confiscated, destroyed? What happens to belongings and to their significance? Jewish families that decided to emigrate in the face of Nazi persecution were obliged to reexamine their belongings, assess whether they could be used in a different location, itemize them for the purpose of taxation, pack them, and ship them.[13] British legal theorist Jeremy Bentham highlighted the importance of the relationship between an object and its owner as early as the end of the eighteenth century, observing that ownership is the basis of hope. Only the law can ensure that the relationship can endure into the future for the next generation, to provide "an assurance of future ownership." Should this security be attacked or threatened, more than the object itself is at stake: "Every attack upon this sentiment produces a distinct and special evil, which may be called a pain of disappointment."[14]

Objects make the world comfortable and homely by creating relationships between people who pass them on to one another and who leave personal traces on them, which later owners can come to know and love. Exile—the (violent) expulsion from one's familiar life environment—destroys this familiarity with objects and the communicative and mediatory function they perform within the close-knit world of owners of the same house—in both a literal and in a figurative sense.[15] As soon as the surviving family members and friends were able to get in touch with one another again, the topic of "things," of property once owned and then lost, resurfaces in the letters they write to one another. The correspondents do not simply bemoan the loss of some material object or another—they use the objects as symbols of what they went through. The restitution they would claim was no doubt financially important but beyond this restitution possesses a far broader dimension.[16] Talking and writing about a lost house or stolen furniture becomes a means of reassertion, enabling exiles to grapple with questions such as "Who are we now?" or "Who is still here to share the memories of things once owned and then lost?" When the city of Berlin (like many other cities in Germany), with the best intentions, began to contact those who emigrated, the lost houses and the lost possessions became topics of discussion and means of negotiation:

about money, about status, but also—to return to Walter Danziger's phrasing—about "cultural value" and human dignity.

The Berlin archives I consulted comprise 31 folders—*Ordner*—that contain thousands of letters. And even this constitutes only a tiny part of the immense project of retrieval of personal memories undertaken by these German-Jewish families that represent the fragmented world of German Jewry on a worldwide scale. Interestingly, social media has created new forms of networking between descendants of such families—their exchanges about trips to Germany, the laying of *Stolpersteine*, questions of genealogy and about material objects such as paintings, books, or manuscripts form a new set of sources for the study of the continuity of German-Jewish history and culture outside Germany.[17] Most of this virtual collection has been lost. What remains should be considered a telling and significant element of German-Jewish cultural property. I find it so important because these sources possess a narrative dimension that is sometimes lacking in better-known cases of looted art or book collections. As Rom Harré argued, "What turns a piece of stuff into a social object is its embedment in a narrative construction. The attribution of an active or a passive role to things in relation to persons is thus essentially story-relative: nothing happens or exists in the social world unless it is framed by human performative activity."[18]

This view corresponds with the concept of culture as process and practice that has evolved in the fields of European ethnology and cultural anthropology. Harré's insistence on the importance of the narrative helps us appreciate the significance of the letters stored in Centrum Judaicum and in Berlin's Rotes Rathaus and treats them with the same respect and scholarly interest as the papers collected in the "Traces and Treasures" project: there are still so many stories waiting to be told.

NOTES

1. This report is based on two earlier contributions. The first part has been published in German as "Heimat auf dem Balkon. Zur Erschließung deutsch-jüdischer Nachlässe in Israel," in *Jüdische Geschichte und Kultur. Magazin des Dubnow-Instituts* 2 (2018): 60–61; the second part has been published as "Reflections on the Loss: Objects in the Correspondence between Former Berliners and Their Hometown," in *Contested Heritage: Jewish Cultural Property after 1945*, ed. Elisabeth Gallas, Anna Holzer-Kawalko, Caroline Jessen, and Yfaat Weiss (Göttingen, 2020), 195–203, https://doi.org/10.13109/9783666310836.195.

2. See Arnon Goldfinger's film *The Flat* (2013 edition Salzgeber, Berlin).

3. Unfortunately the museum closed in August 2020 after the Wertheimer family withdrew their financial support. Ruthi Ofek, with the support of the Irgun Jozei Merkaz Europa, is looking for a new location.

4. https://rosenzweig.huji.ac.il/book/traces-german-jewish-history [July 18, 2018].

5. Frank Schlöffel, *Heinrich Loewe. Zionistische Netzwerke und Räume* (Berlin: Neofelis, 2018).

6. "Sehr geehrter Herr Dr. Suehl, Im Bezug auf Ihren Aufruf im Aktuell-Berlin moechte ich Ihnen mitteilen, was wir in Berlin durchgemacht haben, bevor wir dann endlich in Amerika einwandern durften. Auch haben wir leider viele gute Verwandte in Konzentrationslagern verloren, sogar ganze Familien. Meine Eltern hatten ein Kaufhaus in Berlin-Koepenick in der Schlossstr. mit dem Namen Lichtenstein Nachf. D. Cohn. Das Haus, in dem das Geschaeft war und in dem wir wohnten, gehoerte meiner Grossmutter Emilie Cohn. Hinter dem Haus war noch ein sehr schoener Garten mit dem Ausblick auf die Dahme, welcher auch meiner Grossmutter Emilie Cohn gehoerte. Im Jahre 1938 wurde mein Vater von einem Nazi mit dem Namen Ahrendt gezwungen, den Laden zu verkaufen. Der Nazi kaufte auch alle anderen juedischen Laeden in Koepenick und uebernahm unsere Wohnung. Die Stadt Koepenick kaufte das Haus fuer einen sehr geringen Preis. Das Leben in Koepenick wurde im Jahre 1939 sehr unangenehm. Man hat juedische Familien nachts aus ihren Haeusern geholt und sie durch die ganze Stadt mit haesslichen Beschimpfungen gefuehrt. So haben sich meine Eltern entschlossen, nach West Berlin [*sic*] zu ziehen, wo wir eine Wohnung in der Schaperstr. 8 in der Naehe von der Kaiserallee bekamen. Die Freunde hiessen Loewe. Unser Wirt hatte einen Buecherverlag. Seine Frau stammte von einem Professor Abraham Geiger ab, der das Reformjudentum gegruendet hat." All the letters I refer to here are kept in the Centrum Judaicum—Stiftung Neue Synagoge Berlin—Archiv (CJA), Sig. 5C2, where they are alphabetically arranged.

7. *Gedenkbuch Berlins der jüdischen Opfer des Nationalsozialismus: Ihre Namen mögen nie vergessen werden! Freie Universität Berlin. Zentralinstitut für Sozialwissenschaftliche Forschung* (Berlin: Edition Hentrich, 1995).

8. See Lina Nikou, *Zwischen Imagepflege, moralischer Verpflichtung und Erinnerungen. Das Besuchsprogramm für jüdische ehemalige Hamburger Bürgerinnen und Bürger* (Munich: Dölling und Galitz, 2011). Lina Nikou, *Besuche in der alten Heimat. Einladungsprogramme für ehemals Verfolgte des Nationalsozialismus in München, Frankfurt am Main und Berlin* (Berlin: Neofelis 2020); Gad Engelhard (University of Haifa) has written a comparable dissertation on organized visits in Leipzig, Nürnberg, Halberstadt, and Rexingen.

9. CJA, 5C2, Correspondence Lachmann.

10. "Von Januar bis Juli 1939, nachdem ich meine Mutter allein in Berlin lassen mußte, war sie in immer größer werdender Verzweiflung in Berlin herumgelaufen, vom Polizeirevier grausam gebullied, um vielleicht doch etwas für ihre Wohnungseinrichtung zu erhalten, um vielleicht doch noch Zertifiklate für Palästina oder Quoten nach Amerika zu erhalten. Das Wenige, welches sie für ihre Sachen erhalten könnte, mußte sie doch

für ihren Lebensunterhalt, für die Ausreisespesen u.s.w. ausgeben." CJA, 5C2, Correspondence Eisenfeld.

11. "Im Schneidersitz neben dem leeren Überseekoffer auf dem Boden sitzend, überlege ich, was von dem Inventar meines bisherigen Lebens in diesen Behälter wandern soll und was auf den großen Haufen der Dinge kommt, die ich zurücklassen muß." Vivian Jeanette Kaplan, *Von Wien nach Shanghai. Die Flucht einer jüdischen Familie* (Munich: dtv, 2006), 93.

12. "Ich habe in den Text auch Beschreibungen von Erinnerungsstücken aus meinem Besitz aufgenommen, von Gegenständen, an denen mein Herz hängt, weil sie auf dem gesamten Wanderweg, der hier nachgezeichnet wurde, mit dabei waren." Ibid., 10.

13. Joachim Schlör, "'Take Down Mezuzahs, Remove Name-Plates': The Emigration of Material Objects from Germany to Palestine," *Jewish Cultural Studies* 1: *Jewishness: Expression, Identity, and Representation* (2008): 133–150.

14. Jeremy Bentham, *The Theory of Legislation*, 2nd ed. (London: Trübner, 1871), 111.

15. Joachim Schlör and Doerte Bischoff, eds., "Dinge des Exils. Eine Einführung," *Exilforschung. Ein internationales Jahrbuch* 31 (2013): 1–8.

16. For a comparative analysis and an important interpretation, see Leora Auslander, "'Jewish Taste'? Jews and the Aesthetics of Everyday Life in Paris and Berlin, 1933–1942," in *Histories of Leisure*, ed. Rudy Koshar (Oxford: Berg Press, 2002), 299–318.

17. Joachim Schlör, "'Irgendwo auf der Welt': German-Jewish Emigration as a Transnational Experience," in *Three-Way Street: Jews, Germans and the Transnational*, ed. Jay Geller and Leslie Morris (Ann Arbor: University of Michigan Press, 2016), 220–238; see the Facebook group JEWS—Jekkes Engaged in Worldwide Social Networking, created by Vera Meyer from Boston, with more than 1,500 members.

18. Rom Harré, "Material Objects in Social Worlds," *Theory, Culture & Society* 19, no. 5–6 (2002): 23–33.

FROM OBJECT TO SUBJECT

Representing Jews and Jewishness
at the Jewish Museum Berlin

MICHAL FRIEDLANDER

W HEN WALKING PAST a Berlin Oxfam store, I noticed that they were holding a one-euro book sale and paused to burrow through the rows of boxes
laid out on the pavement. I saw no books on Jewish themes and asked
a shop assistant if he could point me in the right direction. We fell into conversation
and the man told me that he was a Berlin schoolteacher who volunteered at the shop
when he had time. He confided that they did have one relevant book for me, a guide-
book to Jewish Berlin, and while he couldn't place his hands on it directly, if I came
across a book called *Neger, Neger, Schornsteinfeger* (Nigger, Nigger, Chimney Sweeper)
I would find it. He had grouped them together himself.

Jews, alongside people of color, still have serious image problems in Germany.
Viewing the Jew as "other" in Germany is hardly a new theme and planting the history
of Jews in Germany firmly in the box for oppressed minorities, rather than in the broad
scope of general German history, is not new either. Even today, Jews in Germany are
largely defined by the Holocaust in the popular imagination. Widespread ignorance
continues to fester as Jews are envisaged as protagonists in improbable mythic tales,
and the age-old conviction that Jews are a group of people that belongs elsewhere holds
strong. How then should a national museum of German-Jewish history attempt to
open the minds of its visitors to alternative narratives about Jews? How should Jews
be presented? Whose perspective(s) should be heard? Can a museum experience play
a role in shifting anti-Jewish paradigms and quelling stereotypes? And who should
determine Jewish museum narratives, both now and in the future?

These questions are part of the many ongoing discussions that have been preoccu-
pying staff at the Jewish Museum Berlin (JMB) as they look toward the future. This

federal institution stands alone and is not incorporated into a national German history museum (such as the German Historical Museum), which is a double-edged sword. German-Jewish history is set apart and ghettoized rather than being naturally integrated into Germany's historical narrative. Through the institution's splendid isolation, however, the state attests to the great importance of German-Jewish history and culture and maintains the public memory of the Holocaust. But for how long? What subjects will federally funded museums prioritize in their national narratives in twenty, or even fifty years? Public policies shift and the politics of remembrance is fickle, as is the celebration of minority cultures. Will future German governments still feel committed to maintaining the JMB as a significant platform for German-Jewish history and Holocaust remembrance?

Since it opened in 2001, the Jewish Museum Berlin continues to be a magnet for tourists and school groups. Having chalked up close to twelve million visitors, the museum has spent the past few years developing a completely new core exhibition. A project of this size (3,300 square meters) is a tremendous financial investment for a museum and the permanency of the exhibition inherently implies a committed approach to German-Jewish history that, if judged correctly, should remain relevant for the next decade or two.

MINORITY AS CURIOSITY

Looking back to the early days of presenting "Judaism" in German collections, one encounters the "*Wunderkabinett*" or "Cabinet of Curiosities," a prototype museum where the mysterious and exotic were displayed, examined, and interpreted from the seventeenth century onward. This was the place to marvel at unicorn powder. In the spectacular palatial galleries of the Zwinger in Dresden, a traveler's account of 1735 reveals a specific encounter with another exotic creature:

> Each room (in the Zwinger) contains in itself special rarities, which together are known as the Curiosity Cabinet. The name is apt, for one sees here every curious and seldom-seen thing that the world has brought forth. . . . The Juden-Cabinet displays all manner of rarities. Here there can be found a life-sized stuffed rabbi (*ausgestopffter Rabine*) [*sic*] who has a hat on his head, spectacles on his nose and a coat on. One sees him standing at a lectern on which a Talmud is lying, which he is touching with several of his fingers. Anyone entering this Cabinet for the first time and without prior knowledge would swear that this is in reality a live rabbi, on account of the accuracy and lifelikeness of the presentation. Inside are also shown the instruments used for circumcision and other Jewish rituals.[1]

Arriving in Berlin in 2001, it didn't feel as though much had changed with respect to exoticism or sensitivity to "otherness" and I felt a marked lack of sensibility for cultural difference. I was relocating from Berkeley, California, where I experienced ethnic, religious, cultural, and gender diversity as a norm. It was beyond my comprehension that the Sarotti "Moor" figure, used to market a chocolate brand since 1918, was still regarded as "cute" and "harmless" by people whom I thought I liked.[2] And how was it possible that dark brown "Othello" cookies were still marketed—feted as a classic cult snack in waves of spirited "*Ostalgia*" for products of the former German Democratic Republic?[3]

While a strong Turkish presence in Berlin was palpable in 2001, there was no Museum of Turkish-German history on the horizon in the nation's capital.[4] There were remarkably few black faces on the streets to build a political lobby and put an end to Othello cookies or "the Moor" found on chocolate boxes, in street and pharmacy names, and beyond.[5] Germany was still very much preoccupied with a different minority group: the silent Jewish minority—the murdered, dead Jews of the past. There was in fact a small Jewish minority present in Germany at the time, but they were essentially invisible. Paradoxically, Jews who were in the public eye attracted exceptional attention, should they put a foot wrong.[6] German museums were, and are, far behind in the discourse surrounding identity and representation that permeates social history and cultural heritage museums in other countries. The questions that are normative in similar institutions, in the United States, or in Australia, are still regarded with apprehension in German museums, if considered at all. These questions are simple but pivotal: Whose history? Whose narrative? Whose voice?

"JEWISHNESS" IN THE FIRST CORE EXHIBITION OF THE JEWISH MUSEUM BERLIN

In 2001, the Jewish Museum Berlin opened its doors and core/permanent exhibition, which was entitled "Two Millennia of German-Jewish History"—a bold assertion that has been debated ever since. The project was spearheaded by Ken Gorbey and the late (and sorely missed) Nigel Cox, who were the innovative spirits behind the Te Papa national museum in New Zealand. The pair introduced refreshing ideas that diverged from the norm in German (-Jewish) history museums of the time. They included short text labels in both German and English, accessible informal language, a training program that transformed gallery guards into "friendly hosts," and an emphasis on a family museum experience, to name a few highlights. Yet, in contrast to their approach in New Zealand, a partnership with the community whose history was being presented was absent. While one might argue that the postmillennial Jewish community in Germany has little connection to the pre-1933 community, this is in itself an interesting phenomenon that could have been explored in more depth.

The permanent staff of the Jewish Museum Berlin includes many highly qualified, talented, and exceptionally dedicated museum professionals, few of whom are Jewish. Their commitment and vigor is the power behind the success of the institution. However, the question of "Who is speaking about, and for whom?" was not given due consideration by the exhibition team during the conception of the first core exhibition. The exhibition was therefore driven by the traditional narrative form of an omniscient narrator: an authoritative (non-Jewish?) curatorial voice that neither questioned itself, nor attempted to engage the visitor in the discourse, but peered down on its subject from a bird's-eye perspective.

In the chronological dramaturgy of the exhibition, the emancipation and subsequent enlightenment of Jews were strongly featured. It showed how Jews became assimilated, bourgeois Germans with secular educations during the eighteenth to nineteenth centuries, and stressed the significant contributions of such Jewish citizens to business and cultural life in Germany in subsequent generations. This was a story of successful integration—a happy German paradigm where Jews finally acculturated and became exemplary citizens and actors in the German *Leitkultur* (predominant culture).

As Jews became Germans, synagogue life was reformed and sanitized, and no antiquated or troubling religious practices were addressed for the remainder of the exhibition. There was in fact only one space in the entire exhibition that made a focused attempted to present Judaism, through Jewish life cycle events, kosher food, and the Sabbath. This gallery, entitled "Tradition and Change," was awkwardly sandwiched between the enlightened world of Moses Mendelssohn and the material comforts of the Jewish bourgeoisie. For the subject of childbirth in Jewish culture, it devoted a large showcase to the theme of circumcision. Rather than learn about the joy and importance attached to welcoming a new child into the Jewish community, the visitor could appreciate that Jews had transitioned from rusty double-edged circumcision knives in the eighteenth century, to an entire set (around twenty pieces) of modern hospital medical instruments. These were all neatly laid out on a sanitary, disposable blue cloth that covered a hospital trolley. What did these eye catchers transmit to the museum visitor and how distant was this installation from the eighteenth-century voyeurism of the curiosity cabinet?

To add insult to injury, a showcase on the opposing gallery wall gave visitors the opportunity to feast their eyes on more old knives, as part of an installation on the subject of *kashrut* (Jewish food laws). These large knives were intended for kosher butchering, a Jewish ritual that is contentious in Germany today, just as it was in the past. Antisemitic rhetoric has often advanced the theory that Jewish religious rituals involve severe brutality and that Jews intentionally inflict pain on children and animals. In a thoughtful and nuanced study, Robin Judd has written about German antisemitic campaigns against Jewish ritual during the mid-nineteenth to early twentieth centuries and how Jewish ritual behavior was characterized as being cruel and "knife-centered."[7] The association of Jews, knives, and blood has negative connotations that go all the way back to the medieval period and the often repeated, but unfounded, accusations that Jews performed acts of ritual murder and host desecration. Antisemitic blood libel propaganda is still circulated in the twenty-first century and a museum's choice to represent Jewish ritual and "Jewishness" through knife displays is questionable, to say the least.

EXPERIMENTATION WITH JEWISH REPRESENTATION

The core exhibition of the first Jewish Museum Berlin was not conceived with flexibility and future revisions in mind. While criticism was accepted and some exhibition sections were reworked over the years, it was difficult and expensive to incorporate major conceptual changes. This limitation was countered by the introduction of a creative and experimental temporary exhibition program. Some of these exhibitions were notable for challenging received wisdom and addressing taboos, using intelligent argumentation and original forms of presentation. I had the good fortune to be a curator for several temporary exhibition projects and was part of the curatorial team for the 2013 exhibition "The Whole Truth—Everything You Always Wanted to Know about Jews."

Over the course of time, I developed sharply attuned antennae for the public image of Jews and Judaism in Germany. It seemed that Jews in the German media were primarily shown as Chassidic men and Israeli soldiers, or illustrated using a snapshot of a random man's head, from behind, on which a skullcap (*kippah*) is perched. I had meanwhile received enough philosemitic attention and special interest as a "Jewish specimen" to last me a lifetime and dearly wanted to invert the "stuffed rabbi" museum prototype. For the JMB's "Whole Truth" exhibition, I suggested that one of the exhibition stations should include an open showcase where a different Jew could sit for an hour every day. Participation would be on a voluntary basis, with the prerequisite that guests needed to be part of the German-Jewish experience (no American-Jewish tourists, for example). The participants could define their own "Jewishness" in whatever way they chose to frame it. They were free to do what they wanted in the showcase— to interact with museum visitors, or to ignore them. There would be no censorship and the participants could respond as they wished to any questions that might be posed to them. We would only ask for their name and place of origin, if they wanted to give one, as well as the languages that they spoke. This information would be handwritten by the participant as a showcase label.

It must be said that this idea was greeted with some skepticism. There was considerable doubt that we would succeed in finding enough volunteers to sit in a museum showcase wearing a bold pink badge that was emblazoned with the words: "Ask me, I'm Jewish." But we did. We were swamped with volunteers for the complete run of the show. A report by the Associated Press news agency, focusing on this exhibition element, was picked up internationally and widely distributed.[8] The story used the term "Jew in the Box" and quoted several statements made by showcase volunteers, including:

> I feel a bit like an animal in the zoo, but in reality that's what it's like being a Jew in Germany. You are a very interesting object to most people here. (Ido Porat)

> They associate Jews with the Holocaust and the Nazi era. Jews don't have a history before or after. In Germany, Jews have been stereotyped as victims. It is important that people here get to know Jews to see that Jews are alive and that we have individual histories. I hope that this exhibit can help. (Dekel Peretz)

The news story sparked international outrage, feeding on the perception that Germans were putting Jews on exhibit. These protestors had completely missed the point: a cornucopia of Jewish people, from Holocaust survivor to punk, were *choosing to put themselves on exhibit in Germany,* to make themselves visible in numerous acts of self-assertion and pride. This, I think, was a radical subversion of the stuffed rabbi model of the past and, as such, an important moment for a Jewish museum in Germany.

GETTING IT RIGHT? REPRESENTATIONS OF JEWISHNESS IN 2020

Jews remain a very small minority in Germany, despite the touted recent influx of Israeli immigrants. Not all Jews in Germany are registered with the official Jewish community, and a generous figure for the current (ageing) Jewish population would be 150,000 people within a total population of nearly 84 million. By way of comparison, the 4,000,000-plus Muslim population makes up over 5 percent of Germany's total population. This means that it is quite unlikely for a German non-Jew to encounter someone Jewish in their daily lives and they might not "recognize one" if they did. Specific forms of head coverings (*kippot*), sidelocks (*payot*), and visible fringes (*tzitzit*) that are attached to undergarments are understood to be the Jewish markers of identity. They are markers of "strangeness" and "foreignness," although most Jews in Germany cannot be identified using these visual codes. The majority of Jews are not only invisible; they don't even reach the critical mass necessary to be viable for targeted marketing. In 2018, the German confectioner Katjes ran an advertising campaign for vegan sweets made without animal (pig) gelatin. There was much discussion when they featured a woman wearing a hijab in their advertisements, although the word "halal" was never mentioned. Interestingly, the model who was employed for this "Muslim role" in the campaign was an Orthodox Christian with a Serbian background. When I contacted the company to ask if kosher certification was under consideration, I was informed that this idea was "not part of any future agenda." It was obvious that the idea had not even occurred to them—a marketing campaign embracing "racial capitalism" needs a commercially feasible target group in order to function.[9]

While most Germans have little or no contact with today's small German-Jewish community, there seems to be a public desire to understand Jewish particularity, although the Jewish Museum Berlin's first permanent exhibition chose to focus on similarity. From the frequency of questions received by JMB guides, it appears that this desire is expressed in the wish to be able to define and "recognize" Jews. Even in my daughter's seventh-grade social studies class, when learning about Judaism, the first question that was posed to the students was "What does a Jew look like?" The children were rather puzzled, until one bright spark broke the silence by pointing at my daughter, and the class broke into laughter.

The representation of Jews, for consumption by museum visitors, is a daunting task. The vast majority of visitors to the Jewish Museum Berlin are non-Jewish and many carry visions of imagined Jews in their heads. The initial curatorial team for the new permanent exhibition comprised a chief curator, eight in-house JMB curators, and five academic specialists who were brought on board for the project; only three members of this content team had worked on the 2001 exhibition. In an associative use of the Pareto principle, the team was given an 80:20 model to consider. The premise was that if (for the sake of argument) Jews are 80 percent like anyone else, what defines the remaining 20 percent? What is distinctly Jewish and remains so over time? What are Jewish belief systems and what is Jewish thought and practice? We had arrived at an awkward and uncomfortable moment for the team—were bearded rabbis and circumcision tools back on the agenda? Much discussion ensued, with the Jewish curators taking the lead. Surely we wouldn't pander to voyeuristic curiosity and show Jews enacting religious rituals? Please—no interactive visitor activities involving prayer shawls and head coverings! We unanimously agreed to discard the tried and tested method of showing Judaism through life cycle and holiday objects, so popular in Jewish museums around the world. This is a tired format and it is easier to reject old forms of presentation than to create something new. Daunted, we took up the self-imposed creative challenge. As Edward Rothstein wrote in his searing critique of "Jewish identity museums":

There is much more to Jewish identity than its secularised and politicised incarna-
tion now prevalent in the museum world: something deserving of the deepest pride
and most scrupulous study.[10]

In the end, we went back to the heart of it all: the Torah, the most Jewish of narratives.

Judaism is an integral part of Jewish life and is given considerably more space in the
new Jewish Museum Berlin core exhibition than it was in the past. While the primary
historical narrative is chronological, the chronology is intermittently interrupted by
galleries that focus on a particular theme. These thematic spaces are not restricted to the
German- Jewish experience, but are broadened to include international Jewish perspectives. The first galleries encountered by visitors are dedicated to the written and oral Torah
and unapologetically stress the centrality of the Torah for Jewish life in the past and the
present. Jewish continuity is emphasized and the joy that is intrinsic to Judaism is celebrated. No single normative form of Jewish religious life and expression is championed,
and Jewish choices, whether living as a Jewish atheist or according to an Orthodox Jewish
tradition, are not judged. In a film installation, for example, a number of Jews speak about
the role of Jewish law (*halachah*) in their lives and how they are either guided by it, or
choose not to follow it. The exhibition also presents Jewish ceremonial objects in a novel
manner, using a traditional Jewish taxonomy that classifies ceremonial objects in terms of
their levels of "holiness" or "sacredness" (*kedushah*) and grouping the objects accordingly.

It will be interesting to see if any Jews will consider the exhibition as "too Jewish"
because of this new emphasis. However, this may be preferable to the museum's nick-
name in some German-Jewish circles: "The Non-Jewish Museum," or more recently
the "Anti-Israel Jewish Museum"—a position that is addressed in more detail below.

THE JEWISH VOICE

Another significant change in the new exhibition is the decision to use many more
"Jewish voices," thus giving more weight to "Jewish perspectives" in the narrative.
The technique of incorporating Jewish voices, in particular the inclusion of quota-
tions from historical figures, is used extensively in Polin, the Warsaw Museum of the
History of Polish Jews, which opened in 2014 under the conceptual leadership of
Barbara Kirshenblatt-Gimblett. The strategy found both resistance and acceptance in
the Berlin curatorial team. Team reactions ranged from discomfort and stonewalling
("I can't use a Jewish voice, I'm not Jewish") to positive and excited responses. A few
non-Jewish colleagues said that using "internal Jewish voices" resolved a dilemma for
them and gave them a new sense of freedom. This exhibition strategy also presented
them with the welcome challenge of finding creative ways to incorporate these voices.

One of the most consistent uses of a Jewish narrative approach in the new exhibition is in the section dealing with the period from 1930 to 1945. Here, attempts have been made to use photographic and documentary film footage from Jewish sources, where possible, rather than material that was produced by the National Socialist regime. This approach continues in the postwar period of the exhibition, which has been assigned far more gallery space than in the 2001 exhibition. This section focuses on the postwar Jewish communities in Germany, integrating Jewish home movies as a source. Unlike the 2001 exhibition, a place is given to the voices of immigrants from the former Soviet Union (the "*Yevrey*") in the late 1980s and early 1990s, through quotations and a colorful "carpet" of literary works. The exhibition concludes with a riveting video installation, with a bonanza of contemporary Jewish voices, speaking for themselves, but you shouldn't expect to find any spoilers here.

WHOSE JEWISH MUSEUM?

While the new exhibition was still in the planning stages the Jewish Museum Berlin found itself, from December 2018 onward, at the center of an extensive public debate. The discussions raised the issues of the nature and purpose of a Jewish museum in Germany today—the museum's approach to taboo subjects, as well as the control of the museum's content. A large exhibition on the incendiary topic of "Jerusalem" had opened at the JMB in December 2017. It considered the holy city as an important center of faith for different religions and as a place of extreme political tension. These conflicts were neither whitewashed nor ignored, which inevitably triggered strong reactions. In an extraordinary step, Israel's prime minister, Benjamin Netanyahu, requested that the German chancellor, Angela Merkel, cut government funding to the JMB for perceived "anti-Israel activities."[11] This incident and subsequent events led to a barrage of verbal attacks against the museum in the media, as well as from the Central Council of Jews in Germany, whose president suggested that the word "Jewish" should be removed from the name of the institution.[12] It should be noted that the museum does not operate in a vacuum and a board of trustees oversees its projects—a board that includes a Jewish community delegate.

The critical onslaught against the Jewish Museum included various "external Jewish voices," which prompts elemental questions about narrative control in such an institution. Is it appropriate for the content of a Jewish museum in Germany to be dictated by the demands of an Israeli government, a political lobby, or by the representative of a Jewish community? Then again, can a federal museum of Jewish history in Germany afford to alienate segments of the Jewish population? Jewish voices and Jewish involvement are naturally of great importance for the Jewish Museum Berlin. Non-Jewish professionals are, of course, invaluable members of the Jewish Museum Berlin team, but I believe that the museum would benefit from employing a greater number of qualified Jewish members of staff in content areas. More Jews would surely enter this field if there were training and job opportunities and if potential international candidates were encouraged to apply.

The Jewish Museum Berlin is a state-funded, scientific institution with an educational function, and it exists to serve the public. One of its goals is to provide a forum for open discussion and debate on difficult topics, to be a "space for critical dialogue" as described in a new definition of a museum that was proposed by the International Council of Museums in July 2019.[13] These are brave aspirations at a time when fierce polemics rage and diametrical political positions become hardened and immutable. Subjects that are pertinent (and touchy) for the JMB include antisemitism, the Middle East conflict, and intercultural relationships. A well-formulated response to the Jewish critics of the JMB came from Dr. Hanno Loewy, director of the Jewish Museum Hohenems, who wrote in the *Frankfurter Allgemeine Zeitung*:

> The current tabooing of any open discussion about Israel or about contemporary antisemitism which has found its fatal expression in the campaign against the Berlin Museum, hits above all: Jews. If Jewish voices that do not want to bow to such prohibitions of thought are silenced with hidden and open threats, then Jewish museums that offer a stage for this diversity are apparently more necessary than ever.[14]

REPRESENTATION SHIFTS

In 2004, the Sarotti chocolate brand exchanged their trademark "Moor," who carried a tray and later a flag, for a "golden-skinned" magician, who stands on a crescent moon and juggles stars.[15] How has the Jewish Museum Berlin adjusted its representation of Jews in its new permanent exhibition? To what extent have Jewish historical sources been implemented? Ultimately, are the historical Jewish voices and faces that are presented dominated by nostalgic reviews of a (nonexotic) Jewish bourgeoisie, or are the cultures of rural cattle dealers and impoverished Eastern European immigrant Jews highlighted? Have we reached a time in Germany when we no longer need to disproportionately proclaim the great achievements of Jews, as if to prove that the destruction of the community was really quite a bad loss? Can we talk about the lives of the majority of Jews, which are just as banal or interesting as anyone else's, or must Jews always be "special" and "other"?

The relevance and purpose of the Jewish Museum Berlin should be, and will be, reassessed regularly from within and without, and its path will shift according to the political and social climates of the time. It is inevitable that exhibition content relating to Zionism, Israel, antisemitism, and the Holocaust will be subjected to external criticism, decontextualized, and used to serve different agendas from all sides of the political spectrum. An academic advisory board was therefore formed in June 2019 to review such exhibition content and to counsel the exhibition team. Critical voices are not ignored and are essential for the museum to stay alert, self-reflective, and to maintain an open dialogue with the diverse communities, both Jewish and non-Jewish, that are invested in the institution. The challenging period that the museum recently faced may even help to clarify its future path, as it must ensure that its many groups of stakeholders are heard. A clearly defined mission, alongside strong leadership and management are required to determine *how* Jews are represented and *who* is representing Jews in this museum of German-Jewish history.

The role and content of the Jewish Museum Berlin will continue to be discussed and contested. Meanwhile, significant shifts have quietly taken place in the museum's approach to representing Jews and Jewishness in its core exhibition. A major goal of the exhibition is to highlight plurality and diversity within Jewish culture and in the German-Jewish experience in particular. A heterogeneous Jewish culture is celebrated in which questioning and debate are intrinsic as are multiple, concurrent, different schools of Jewish religious thought. The exhibition makes evident that, likewise, contradictory, secular Jewish viewpoints coexist. The exhibition also demonstrates the entangled histories of German Jews and non-Jews over time, rather than presenting Jewish life as isolated, and it attempts to break away from a singular, authoritative (non-Jewish) curatorial voice. It deals with the Holocaust and other periods of Jewish persecution, but does not show the history of a minority group that is dead and extinct. There are neither stuffed, nor living, nor holographic Jews in the galleries for the curious spectator.

IN THE END, it was decided that two seventeenth-century knives would be displayed in the medieval Ashkenaz gallery. For centuries, these knives were attached to the legend that they had been used by Jews for host desecration. It remains to be seen if presenting Jews in association with a different genre of rusty knife will undermine, or reinforce, anti-Jewish "knife-centered" myths and preconceptions. Exhibition goals are all theoretical until visitors interact with and respond to a presentation, but a new core exhibition is not rigid—it is a work in progress that is continually tweaked. The doors to the new core exhibition of the Jewish Museum Berlin opened on August 23, 2020 and visitation began under the hygiene regulations that were implemented due to the Covid-19 pandemic. These new restrictions impacted many of the "hands-on" interactive stations. Nevertheless, within the JMB's core exhibition galleries, you will see and hear many more Jews talking and defining themselves, rather than being talked about and defined by non-Jews. And this, my fellow non-Jewish and Jewish world citizens, is progress.

NOTES

1. Cited in Michael Korey, "Displaying Judaica in 18th-Century Central Europe: A Non-Jewish Curiosity," in *Visualizing and Exhibiting Jewish Space and History*, ed. Richard I. Cohen (Oxford: Oxford University Press, 2012), 29.

2. People are still inhibited to dress up as the "Sarotti Mohr," in full blackface, for the Fasching carnival festival that precedes Lent. Costumes can be bought online. Incredibly, even the model in the costume catalogue is blacked up. See https://www .karnevalswierts.com/de/product/ergebnisse/mohr-sultan-scheich/3563; http://www .nnp.de/lokales/limburg_und_umgebung/Spass-off-der-Gass;art680,1267443 (accessed October 18, 2020). Other offensive racist costumes and accessories (such as for "Bush man," an inflatable "Hawaiian Hula girl," "Native," "Sioux woman," Eskimo child," "Sexy Massai," "Gypsy," and "Rasta King") continue to be widely available on German websites, such as Buschmann Afrikaner-Kostüm in dunkelbraun mit Leoparen Slip & Penis (accessed October 18, 2020).

3. The Othello cookie is still being manufactured in 2020: "Thanks to its traditional original recipe, with lots of cocoa, and characteristic shape, it has always been unmistakable and unique in terms of both flavor and appearance" (author's translation); https:// www.wikana.de/produkte/othello_keks/ (accessed October 18, 2020).

4. There have been various initiatives to create a museum dedicated to immigrant history in Germany (e.g., in Essen, DOMiT, the Dokumentationszentrum und Museum über die Migration aus der Türkei e.V was founded in 1990, later merging and moving to Cologne; see https://domid.org; a Museum of German Immigrant History opened in Munich in 2015, etc.). However, there is still no museum devoted to this subject in Berlin.

5. This essay was originally written in 2018, prior to the wave of antiracist demonstrations and debates about structural racism in Germany that followed the murder of George Floyd in Minneapolis on May 26, 2020. The Berlin transport authority officially announced in July 2020 that the name of the train station, Mohrenstraße, would be changed to Glinkastraße. Mikhail Glinka was a nineteenth-century composer who expressed antisemitic views, which led to renewed criticism (see https://www .theguardian.com/world/2020/jul/07/blm-inspired-name-change-for-berlin -metro-station-mohrenstrasse-fails-to-end-controversy, accessed October 18, 2020). The street has since been renamed for Anton Wilhelm Arno, Prussia's first black academic. Such public discussions are giving momentum to activist movements demanding that Germany openly confront its colonial past and structural racism today.

6. Note, for instance, the media attention in 2003 that surrounded the spectacular fall of Michel Friedman (lawyer, television presenter, deputy chair of the Central Council of Jews in Germany from 2000 to 2003, and president of the World Jewish Congress

from 2001 to 2003) in an affair involving prostitutes and drugs. See Robin Detje, "Im freien Fall," die Zeit, June 18, 2003, https://www.zeit.de/2003/26/Friedmann (accessed October 18, 2020). This article asked what was permissible or acceptable behavior for a Jew in German society.

7. Robin Judd, *Contested Rituals: Circumcision, Kosher Butchering, and Jewish Political Life in Germany, 1843–1933* (Ithaca and London: Cornell University Press, 2007), 107–110.

8. Kirsten Grieshaber, Associated Press, March 29, 2013; see for example: https://www.cbsnews.com/news/jew-in-the-box-exhibit-raises-interest-ire-in-germany (accessed October 18, 2020).

9. For a satirical take on marketing gelatin-free sweets to religious groups, the "ethno-satirical" group Noktara designed an advertisement with an apparently Jewish man holding a bag of "kosher" Katjes, pig-shaped sweets: https://noktara.de/katjes-halal-koscher (accessed September 12, 2018).

10. Edward Rothstein, "The Problem with Jewish Museums," in Mosaic, February 1, 2016, https://mosaicmagazine.com/essay/2016/02/the-problem-with-jewish-museums (accessed September 12, 2018).

11. See https://www.faz.net/aktuell/politik/ausland/netanjahu-verlangt-einstellung-der-foerderung-fuer-das-juedische-museum-15946640.html (accessed August 4, 2019).

12. See https://twitter.com/zentralratjuden/status/1138364310294540288 (accessed August 4, 2019).

13. See https://icom.museum/en/activities/standards-guidelines/museum-definition (accessed August 4, 2019). In 2020, agreement on this highly contested definition had still not been reached.

14. See Loewy's article in the Frankfurter Allgemeine of June 26, 2019: https://www.faz.net/aktuell/feuilleton/debatten/ein-juedisches-museum-was-ist-das-ueberhaupt-16253726.html.

15. The "modernization" of the Sarotti trademark is referenced on the company's website: https://www.sarotti.de/historie (accessed September 12, 2018).

PAST IMPERFECT, FUTURE TENSE

A Mother's Letter about Loss, Storytelling, and the Profound Ambivalence of the German-Jewish Legacy

NICOLA GLUCKSMANN

TRY TO IMAGINE Christmas Eve, 1934. A large carp is swimming up and down the length of the family bath at the Berlin apartment, real candles are burning on the fir tree in the drawing room, and wrapped presents are piled in front of the fireplace. Helene, a young twice-widowed mother, is elegant and cultured. The household is well staffed, which allows Helene the leisure to take to her bed for a few days each month; a masseuse regularly comes to the apartment. Helene's only daughter, Lilly, your grandmother, is a pretty but plump child, and this worries Helene, who asks her masseuse to massage her daughter's tummy.

I have no idea if any of this is true. In every family history even the simplest facts are disjointed and vulnerable. As a child, I delighted in the story of my roly-poly mother but, as an adult, the same story about maternal discomfort with a child's weight jars.

This is how stories change. One day you'll want to tell your own children my stories about your German-Jewish family and, in the very act of telling, tiny reworkings will slip through the fissures of space and time. In this way, each generation in turn leaves their own mark on the narrative. Every slight shift of emphasis, tiny tilt and tamper, each careful or careless omission will excise or amplify. My story, then, is no more than that, a story. The past is not immutable. Like the future, it's a heady cocktail of interpretation and imagination, and anticipating the future of that past is an impossible task.

This is what I think I know: that your grandmother, Lilly, died before any of you were born is a fact. She was a German Jew, who came from what was described to us as children as a "completely assimilated" middle-class Berlin family. I realize now that I didn't know what that meant but I understood, even then, that it was important.

The family lived in Charlottenburg. They saw themselves as the professional middle class, urbane, cosmopolitan, besuited like other Germans, and, in their minds, a million miles away from the bearded religious Jews arriving from the East. Life was aspirational and comfortable. But, as it turned out, what Helene or her family thought didn't matter. Their secular "German" lifestyle counted for nothing in Nazi Germany and, whether they liked it or not, their story, your story, would soon become one of a German-*Jewish* past. That's the story that you've inherited. It's a proud, secular, and persecutory narrative, but soon it'll be your turn to decide how to tell your children the story that is peculiarly yours.

My mother told me that the first time she remembered finding out she was Jewish was when Hitler made her change schools in 1935. By 1937, the younger of her brothers had already been sent to England. Then, in August 1939, at barely thirteen, she too was sent to England, arriving at Liverpool Street Station on one of the last *Kindertransports*. Lilly's goodbye to her mother took place in in a psychiatric hospital in Berlin. Helene had collapsed with a nervous breakdown and my mother knew even then, so she told me later, that it was the last time she would ever see her. In 1946, the names of both her mother and her older brother appeared on the lists compiled by the Red Cross of those who had died in the camps.

That story of a moment of traumatic and finite separation from her only living parent is an important part of your legacy because it haunted your grandmother and it was raw and inescapable in the way that she mothered me, her younger child. Her emigration was organized by Helene's cousin, Otto Kahn-Freund, a young German-Jewish judge who had been blacklisted by Hitler in 1933 and who'd been living in the UK since then. He and his wife were my surrogate grandparents; we celebrated Christmas and Easter with Otto, his wife, Liesel, and their daughter, Sylvia. Our refugee heritage was ever-present in the conversation, the German cooking, and the music but our Judaism was conspicuously absent. Things, though, are never quite what they seem.

"The single most important fact about my life is that I was born a Jew," wrote Otto in his unfinished personal memoirs of 1979. Not "am a Jew" but "*born* a Jew." Despite his choice to live in a determinedly secular world, here by Otto's own admission was acknowledgment that his life was nevertheless defined by this one fact. The precision of his language was less of a surprise. Distancing himself from the idea of an active Jewish self-affirming personal identification was important to Otto. Being German was easy to own, but being born Jewish, rather than simply being Jewish, suggests only an accident of birth. Otto wasn't trying to deny that he was Jewish, but he did want to be sure that his Jewishness could not be co-opted by a religious Jewish community with whom he didn't identify.

Your grandmother studied at the London School of Economics where she was one of a group of young German-Jewish refugees who used to echo this distinction. She would say she was Jewish not by religion but "by *race*." Like Otto, she couldn't simply tick the box marked Jewish. It was a matter of core identity to her *not* to do so. Not to be Jewish in the way she thought *they* meant. This dissociation, like the curiosity of being "completely assimilated," is an important piece of the disconsolate past that you've inherited.

For your grandmother, joining a synagogue hadn't ever been an option. I was led to believe that it wasn't a world that she knew. She saw organized religious Judaism as fundamentalist and separatist. Her life had been shattered by being Jewish and whatever identity she had managed to hang onto was still vested in being on the outside. Anything else was Hitler's classification system, not hers.

Instead, she was intent on creating a world where what had happened to her could never happen again, to anyone, of any faith. And it is the failure of that postwar dream of international socialism, and more recently the resurgence of antisemitism, that perhaps best explains some of the legacy of family ambivalence and alienation that you've inherited. It has created a vacuum and vacuums are seldom left unfilled.

Your grandparents met at a boarding school for Jewish refugee children. Your grandfather had emigrated from Berlin together with his family. After marrying in their early twenties, they bought a Victorian house in Finchley, in northwest London, together with some left-wing non-Jewish friends, and converted it into two flats.

Finchley had a conspicuous share of comfortable British Jews. But there was no common language of dislocation between these Jewish neighbors and ourselves. The values with which we were raised had become so completely alienated from their distant roots in the same religious teaching that their shared origin never ever occurred to me. My parents' emphasis was on education and intellectual life—those things that no one can take away. Social responsibility and compassion for the outsider and the underprivileged were paramount principles. Prioritizing your own community was unthinkable.

While she felt no affinity with the established United Synagogue Finchley Jews, your grandmother was even more uncomfortable driving through Golders Green. She saw the ultra-orthodox as backward-looking fanatics whose culture was as far removed from us as that of the Asians on Brick Lane. If anything, she felt closer to the Asian community—they at least basked in the warm glow of her committed multiculturalism. Your grandmother's discomfort with orthodox Jews was perhaps learned behavior. It echoed her own mother's reaction in the 1920s to the "Shtetl Jews" arriving from the East.

I'm aware that I'm writing more about your grandmother than about your grandfather. Despite their shared history as German Jews, your grandfather was more fortunate and lost fewer family members. Perhaps there was something about the scale and depth of the losses that your grandmother suffered that found its way into me both consciously and unconsciously. Or perhaps your grandfather was simply damaged in a different way. He was insecure and in need of constant validation. In search of that validation, he spent his life telling jokes. He was her hope of laughter while she was his hope of understanding.

In my childhood home in North London, perhaps just as in my grandmother's in Berlin, assimilation was something to be proud of. It was proof of newfound and hard-earned professional success, which relegated "the ghetto" to someone else's history. My own family was completely out of step with affiliated British Jews. I once attended a conference on assimilation organized by a university Jewish Society—thinking that here at least would be common ground—and it was only after half an hour that I understood that they were talking about assimilation as a bad thing. I know I instinctively react with the same irritation as your grandmother to men in fur hats and stockings and young mothers in wigs and I wonder if I've passed on that same visceral intolerance to you.

The religious Jews were the only minority for whom my mother made no allowances. In effect, her silence dehumanized a community and perhaps that's the worst kind of prejudice. This aversion to people she didn't even know was unlike her attitude to any other minority. It contradicted her politics and did not reflect her usual sympathies, but it is a measure of how deep these conflicted feelings of willful "not belonging" ran. And perhaps portrayed how deeply her unconscious perceived the threat to be. Without her identity as an outsider, who was she?

For motherless refugee children like my mother, forced to confront the reality of loss and terrifying feelings of abandonment, there were very few choices if she was not to break down. In order to survive an unbearable intensity of anger and despair, she had to "murder" a part of herself, to cut herself off from feelings that were too agonizing to bear. Only then could she comply and adapt to new institutions. In this way, she severed contact with the rage inside her and projected her own destructiveness onto a group she identified, mistakenly, as inferior and threatening. Perhaps she unconsciously held them responsible for what had happened to her and other assimilated Jews. She would, I suspect, be horrified by this idea but without doubt she'd be brave enough to confront it.

So there you have the paradox. Our family always came in at an oblique angle. Whereas both the orthodox and even the affiliated Anglo-Jews were "nothing to do with us," the Nazi mind seemed to have everything to do with us. It was never discussed without some analysis of the German psyche and the power of popularism. In this way, a delusion of control over the persecution was maintained by intellectual rhetoric. If it could be explained, it could also be prevented. Or so we thought. It was only the unassimilated Anglo-Jews who were singled out as the alien experience. Their politics, their conspicuous consumption, and their closed communities were never counterbalanced by compassion for their insecurities and fearfulness. Quite extraordinarily, around our family dining table even those Germans who collaborated had an easier ride.

Ownership of the Holocaust by Anglo-Jewish communities, whose own immediate families were untouched, still grates with me today. It feels as if the real trauma that your grandparents experienced is being hijacked for someone else's proxy agenda. How do I reconcile that this is being done by strangers "in my name" but in the service of politics diametrically opposed to my own and to those of my parents?

But I'm horribly inconsistent. In imposing this particular hierarchy of suffering, I do the very thing I'm complaining about. I get to be the special one. But only narcissistically, as an individual, never as a member of an identified Jewish group. In recent months you've seen my discomfort about so much talk of antisemitism and you've seen me attempt to dismiss it as Jewish paranoia. The Jewish preoccupation feels too self-regarding and I fear it'll be self-fulfilling. But perhaps I don't allow myself to see antisemitism where others do. I also know that my inherited reactions and defenses are primitive and unprocessed because I can't translate them into rational thought. I involuntarily physically clench or squirm a little instead. I see other Jewish friends from a similar background do the same thing.

Relinquishing any defense means facing the pain it protects you from, so the disincentive to change is very strong. I can only suspect that I fear finding out that I am not so different. Perhaps I'm that very imposter I denigrate—the person who claims the trauma as my own in order to be special. My inner-world apartheid is of course mirrored by projected fantasies about the attitude of orthodox Anglo-Jews to my secularism and to my lack of religious knowledge. They're not "my kind of Jews" but nor am I theirs. I'm the reason their messiah doesn't come. This insistent conflicted disidentification with the modern affiliated Jewish community is peculiarly German-Jewish and it's not good.

It is elitist, full of bitterness and disdain. It's too hot to be rational. And it holds us back. Extreme disidentification still means that you're defined by the very thing you want to escape—just in reverse. The very identity we're consciously trying to avoid is unconsciously calling the shots. We may not want to be "that" but by defiantly being "not that" we're no closer to being who we really are. And that's the difficult question for the future.

The German-Jewish past you inherited was both Jewish but not Jewish. It was intellectual, psychoanalytic, and cultural. The Holocaust that disrupted that past was to be understood as a fault line in humanity, and the safeguards that had to be put in place to prevent a repetition were deliberately nonpartisan. But now, one generation on, we're members of a synagogue. An access we'd never had before was offered by your stepfather and I didn't fight it.

I wasn't sure that the inverted "badge of honor" associated by my own family with "not belonging" was a legacy that I wanted to pass on to you. I remember seeing Jewish families walking to synagogue on Yom Kippur, when I was small, and feeling quietly wistful. I didn't want you to feel the same. But, just as I questioned imposing my ambivalence on you, I worried that embracing something which, to the best of my knowledge, my parents and grandparents had rejected was inauthentic. What I really wanted for you was the choice and a privilege that I'd not had, to be able to embrace or reject your lost heritage from the inside.

The remaining members of my maternal German-Jewish family were intensely uncomfortable with my joining the synagogue, and perhaps it's significant that by the time you first went to *cheder* both my parents had died. My only sister and her family came to Louis's bar mitzvah but declined the invitation to Lilly's bat mitzvah a year later. But even coming to one can't have been easy. My mother's only nephew, her brother's son, John, carried the Torah, in the face of his Viennese mother's vocal disapproval. It must have also been difficult for him.

I weighed up every decision connected with the event in an effort to stay true to my own values. You, Louis, didn't get presents but you did raise money for a Ugandan orphanage. In the end, you emerged as someone comfortable in both the world of ritual and faith and the world of ideas and secularism. Whether this would have happened anyway, I don't know. But a tiny piece of our collective Jewish past was recovered in the face of the loss of the political optimism of the postwar period, the intermarriages, and our family's deeply felt and unresolved ambivalence about organized religion.

As the second child, Lilly, you were spared much of this recalibration. Your bat mitzvah came organically from *within* the synagogue and was borne out of the community. You encapsulated "Why not?" and this too was a sea change in the family. One secular generation earlier we'd only ever have asked "Why on *earth*?" On that day, it was hard for us all not to think about what the other Lilly had faced at the same age. She too had two brothers but, by the time she was thirteen, she had been issued an identity card giving her the mandatory name of Sarah, heard the shattering glass of *Kristallnacht,* and seen the friendly beer halls of her childhood neighborhood turn into fascist drinking haunts.

My aunt translated some of the letters Lilly wrote to her older brother in those first few weeks after leaving Germany. Her account of crossing the channel on a ferry subcontracted by the British government to bring the last transports of children over here is all about being thirteen. "We danced the whole way across the Channel," she wrote excitedly. As the band played, grief was temporarily suspended. In a later letter, she describes how, upon hearing of the outbreak of war, she turned her rage at the world inward and attacked herself as if she were somehow responsible. She hacked away at her own hair and from that day forward never wore makeup. Unlike your namesake, Lilly, you've not had your Jewish identity forced upon you; you've chosen it and now, true to your grandmother's humanitarianism, you're in the West Bank trying to build bridges between Israelis and Palestinians.

And then, Harry, there's you. You didn't want a bar mitzvah at the time but three years later you chose to go on tour with B'nei Akiva. I'd never heard of B'nei Akiva but I loved the friends you wanted to go with. To our surprise and despite your atheism, you celebrated your bar mitzvah with your friends in Jerusalem. I don't think B'nei Akiva had ever taken someone on tour who hadn't already had a bar mitzvah—everyone said it was joyful.

A few years after these first family *b'nei* mitzvahs, the family went in yet another direction. We were invited to my niece's wedding in the beautiful Lichfield Cathedral. I probably felt less alienated than my sister had felt in a synagogue but it did give me pause for thought. Only sixty-five years after the Holocaust, my mother's granddaughter was promising to raise her children as Christian. Kind, unentitled, a serving Metropolitan Police detective, Laura nevertheless defines the very best of Jewish values as defined by her grandparents.

My Viennese aunt, the only one of the first generation of German-speaking Jewish refugees present, had hated the bar and bat mitzvahs, but she never complained about the cathedral. Nor did she blink an eyelid when pork appeared on her plate at the reception. But she was appalled when you and I didn't eat it. Her discomfort was still with the Jews. She had always believed that in sending my children to *cheder* and, in Harry's case, on tour to Israel, I was subjecting them to brainwashing. I think that she felt that I was attacking hard-won territory and she was fighting fiercely to defend her secular identity. But, in so doing, she was also betraying an almost existential fear of confronting something else. Something that she wanted no part of. Her own ambivalence ran so deep that she even used to pursue a contrary passion and visit medieval churches wherever she went. I can't put into words what frightened her. We couldn't discuss it. It was simply too painful.

My attempts to reconcile this legacy of my German-Jewish secular past with different, but not necessarily better choices for the three of you risked violent clashing of family values. Positions that I feel were so fiercely defended, not out of ideology, but out of abject fear borne out of Holocaust trauma. If my Jewish family didn't assert their secularism against my apparent wobble, who were they?

My mother, whose LSE peer group equated Zionism with racism, once mischievously admitted that she didn't dare go to Israel in case she really liked it. Like my sister, my Torah-carrying cousin married a non-Jew. His children will not even be secular Jews. But he is currently organizing the translation of the German-Jewish family archive, including our grandmother's letters written from a concentration camp, so that you and your children can read them.

My mother's cousin, another German-Jewish refugee in London, also raised her children in the secular world, but both of her daughters have married observant Jewish men—one has a kosher home in North-West London and the other has moved to Israel. People find their own way.

So there you have it. On the one hand you have a new generation of observant Jewish family members and, on the other, our secular Jewish family whose Jewishness, by most definitions, is likely to become nothing more than a quirky memory. For reasons I can't defend, given everything else I've said, I'm not indifferent to that. I feel sad about it. But I still have many of the ambivalent feelings about any affiliation that they do. For the Berliners, being Jewish was at first a handicap and then, at the end, a death sentence and so, for me, survivor guilt may well still play a part. I don't know whether these tensions will affect you too. I never wanted it to be an either/or and perhaps, if the family had been closer, I wouldn't have considered breaking ranks.

The least complicated family members are our non-Jewish cousins on my father's side (my father's brother married a practicing Christian) who have delighted in the introduction to the Belsize Square synagogue and to family shabbats. For them, something lost was being recovered and, unlike those of us with two Jewish parents, this did not raise the same complicated questions of belonging. Along with all of you, my non-Jewish cousins now have their German passports. Curiously, my sister and cousin who both had two German-Jewish parents haven't yet applied.

It's the issue of group membership that divides us more than any other. But just as I was raised to be scared and critical of anything that reinforces tribalism, I'm also envious of people for whom being primarily identified as a member of the group is easy and irresistible. I'm not even sure why I still stand back, but I know I can't step forward. And I'm not alone. From the air, it would look as if our half of our North London German-Jewish friends were doing a curious hokey cokey: "In out, in out, shake it all about." It's not a restful life but perhaps in itself intrinsically Jewish.

The longing to belong is universal but the central Judaic idea of being "chosen" or of being special is fundamentally at war with my refugee DNA, and I know you must have picked up on that too. I fuss every Passover. It can't be my noble egalitarianism. It must have everything to do with my own disowned terror of antisemitism. If anyone tells you they're special, a part of you will want to take them down.

So where does this leave you? Your mother and her friends recoil at anything "too Jewish" but nevertheless, despite our self-belief that we are more liberal and more tolerant than the other group, that very same indefensible superiority—that unworthy "specialness"—still creeps in.

You see us laugh at Jewish jokes, enjoy the idea of a Jewish way of thinking, find comfort in our neuroses. We're a bit nostalgic about "tradition" even if we never had it at home. I can watch *Fiddler on the Roof* and recognize something familiar in Topol's smile. I like it.

The irony is everywhere. We claim not to be "joiners" but you can't have missed the shorthand of cultural affirmations and dissociations that we all understand. In some circles we're proud to be Jewish. In relationships with non-Jewish refugees, we use it to shore up our credibility as fellow travelers. In other circles, we're wary and say suspiciously quickly: "But I don't practice," even when no one has asked if we do. "Are you a Zionist?" decisively separates the men from the boys. We're no less bound by the handbook for nonjoiners than congregants are bound by the Torah. We're a community, but one of outsiders by unspoken collective design.

Circumspection perhaps gives you something that only the ever-watchful outsider will have: a survivor's sensitivity to the nuances of language and to what's implicit rather than owned. Our enduring sense of not really belonging affects everything we see; it both diminishes us and simultaneously elevates us. But when we equate the perspective of the outsider with a heightened empathy and understanding, we also accept a heightened sense of responsibility.

The secure insider doesn't need to be so watchful but, for us, nothing is ever to be taken at face value. Perhaps only someone who's been on the outside feels as acutely the determination to make a difference? In the end, their description of themselves as "completely assimilated" didn't make your German-Jewish grandparents any safer. In order to feel at *all* assimilated, they had to work very hard to hold positions of power, to be part of an educated elite that represented all the trappings of being in control. Something that, as it turned out, they weren't. The shadow side—those truths about ourselves that we deny—was always there. Are we really meant to believe that there was a day when their assimilation was complete, when there was nothing left in their lives to suggest any difference from non-Jews?

I don't believe it. People don't work like that. "Completely" is an adverb. Its real meaning lies in the reinforcement of the opposite. Even as a teenager I knew that it was meant to describe not what we were but everything we weren't.

For my parents, the refugee drive for recognition and professional influence in the secular world were powerful displacements of potentially paralyzing grief, an unconscious splitting in order to deny the vacuum left by the loss of family, culture, and community. They prioritized their work and their politics in order to maintain an illusion of meaning and order where they had experienced only chaos. My generation could not fail to take those values forward. But whatever they did, our grandparents and parents remained outsiders and we take that past into the future. Some might have achieved more assimilation than others, either in pre-Hitler Germany or in new countries after the war, others might have retreated into a religious community, but every group has suffered. And that past has bequeathed an acute watchfulness on the next generation borne out of the constant awareness of something withheld.

The emotional legacy of separation, murder, and displacement is what dominates everything in our family. Being raised by a mother who had lost everything except the one brother who arrived in the United Kingdom ahead of her is different from being raised by a mother who can rely on her own mother to help. The world is not as safe, death is ever-present, and a fear of violence and fracture is everywhere. Separations are poorly negotiated, mental health is delicate, and pathology is both literally and metaphorically never far away. In trauma work, the body is the self and we have to ask what stories our symptoms are telling. You have inherited multiple unconscious traumas of denial, loss, and fragmentation and you're going to have to work with the pieces.

But, unlike the German Jews of your "completely assimilated" past, you know Hebrew, you understand the synagogue service, and maybe those childhood experiences of integration will mean that you don't need to be defensive. Perhaps as their trauma fades you'll be able to live less risk-averse lives. You can, if you want to, identify from within, something your German-Jewish ancestors resisted, and I hope you'll do it on your own terms, whatever that might mean and however conflicted you might still be. In the absence of the same options, your grandmother spent her life searching for spiritual meaning in everything while your grandfather spent his life searching for humor in that meaning. Both lessons are invaluable but arguably both functioned to distract from the emptiness of being on the outside of a community and the timeless and universal pain of not belonging.

The important thing is to honor the German-Jewish intellectual tradition and to keep questioning everything, including what it means to be Jewish, and that, as the hokey cokey says, really is "what it's all about."

Perhaps in time, if you decide against synagogue affiliation, that Jewish heritage will dissolve, but I believe that there will be other heritages in the intervening years that may inject the same values with new life. And if the persecution and displacement of the past does make you "special," then it's only as special as others with a refugee past. You can be proud to call yourselves their equals.

Looking Back to Future Visions
of the German-Jewish Past

THE EVER-DYING JEWRY?

Prophets of Doom and the Survival of European Jewry

MICHAEL BRENNER

I N 1948, THE philosopher Simon Rawidowicz published a Hebrew essay under the title "*Am ha-holekh va-met.*" It served as the basis for his posthumous English publication "Israel: The Ever-Dying People." These could have been appropriate titles for this volume as well.

"The world makes many images of Israel, but Israel makes only one image of itself: that of being constantly on the verge of ceasing to be, of disappearing. The threat of doom, of an end that forecloses any new beginning, hung over the people of Israel even before it gained its peoplehood, while it was taking its first steps on the stage of history." Thus begins Rawidowicz's essay, which was written—as we should keep in mind—in the shadow of the annihilation of most of European Jewry. "He who studies Jewish history will readily discover that there was hardly a generation in the Diaspora that did not consider itself the final link in Israel's chain," Rawidowicz reminds his contemporaries who were standing at the abyss of the greatest catastrophe in Jewish history. He tells them that "in the centuries following the destruction of the Second Temple, almost every leading Jewish poet and scholar considered himself the last— the last poet, the last scholar."[1]

BEFORE CATASTROPHE

Among German Jews, such threats of doom were widespread from the beginning of the twentieth century. Obviously, none of them predicted the real catastrophe that would soon befall European Jewry. Their prophecies were based mostly on demographic data and sociological developments. In 1911, the Berlin Zionist Felix Theilhaber published his widely discussed book *Der Untergang der deutschen Juden* (The Decline of German Jews), while two decades later the Communist Otto Heller wrote his *Der Untergang des Judentums* (The Decline of Jewry).

Both accounts, which were deeply inspired by a more general "Decline and Fall" discourse culminating in Oswald Spengler's classic *Der Untergang des Abendlands* (The Decline of the West, 1918–20), carried a clear message: European Jewry, in its present form, was doomed to disappear. While the physician Theilhaber's prescribed treatment against this diagnosis was immigration to Palestine and the building of a "normal, healthy" society, Heller, who was also the author of a book called *Siberia: The Russian America,* advocated total assimilation as the only option for the future.[2] His solution was the classical communist one. As he claims, his books analyze the "Jewish question" and its "solution through the proletarian Revolution."[3] For Heller, traditional Judaism as well as Zionism were not options and only the Soviet Union and especially Stalin's Birobidjan project represented the future of a de-Judaized Jewish population in a classless society.

Theilhaber's book received considerable attention and was published in a second edition, in which he refuted all arguments brought forward against him in the preceding decade and even sharpened his tone. The critics, he argued, closed their eyes in front of the unpleasant facts, which, in his opinion, spoke a clear language—a language of gradual dissolution of Jewish life. And, he would argue, this was nothing unique in Jewish history: integration led to assimilation, which led to disappearance. Chinese Jews had shown us that it was possible to disappear, as had the original Italian-Jewish community and the Sephardic population of Holland.[4] Providing evidence of low birth rates, increasing mixed marriages, and declining religious practice, his conclusion was crystal clear: German Jews will follow in the footsteps of the lost Jewish tribes. "All conditions, preconditions and processes which contributed to the systematic dissolution, are existent for Germany's Jews. The Jews are caught in a net, which is tied with all its parts to this development."[5]

What, he asked, should be the remedy for this deadly disease? "Teach them Hebrew language and culture, their own customs and laws, and force even the last Jew . . . into a viable whole. Create first and foremost a healthy *Volkstum*, possibilities of normal love life, an economic basis—just become Jews like in earlier times."[6] Theilhaber, the physician, is prescribing a bitter medicine to his patient: overcome the dream of assimilation and you will survive. It is a radical treatment that seems to contradict any law of history: recreate the Jew of the past. Clearly, his writings not only reflected the language of a national movement, but also the racial discourse of the time. A "healthy *Volkstum*" and a "normal" love life, which means to abstain from sexual contact with people outside the group, would destroy any individualism and bring the people back to the collective. It is unsurprising to learn, as John Efron has shown, that Theilhaber became a leading promoter of a racial, though not racist, science of the Jews.[7]

Theilhaber found an ally in the person who established the field of Jewish demography, the German Zionist Arthur Ruppin. In 1904, he had published the first edition of his account, *Die Juden der Gegenwart* (The Jews of Today), which appeared in a second edition the year that Theilhaber's prophecy of doom was published. Already, in the preface, Ruppin makes clear that, as someone "to whom the fate of the Jewish people is more than a purely scientific question, I could not abstain from drawing conclusions of the facts and express my attitudes and hopes towards the future."[8]

Ruppin's first sentences are an analysis of a society in the process of dissolution: "Before our eyes stone after stone is loosening from the once so firmly built construction of Jewry. Conversion and mixed marriage lead to significant losses and the enormous decrease in births will make it more difficult to close the gap in a natural way."[9] This process was no longer restricted to Western or Central European communities, but, Ruppin argued, was already visible in Eastern Europe as well. Thus, his book *Die Juden der Gegenwart* concentrates in its first part on the problems of his time. Its chapters have gloomy titles, such as "The Reduction of Births," "The Loss of Meaning of Religion," "Mixed Marriage," "Conversion," and "Antisemitism as Insufficient Barrier to Assimilation." The second part of the book, entitled "Jewish Nationalism," then points to the solution. Its chapters discuss the strength of the "Jewish race" and its viability: "The Racial Value of the Jews," "The Cultural Value of the Jews," "The Creation of a Closed Jewish Economic System Through Return to Agriculture," and "The Revitalisation of the Hebrew Language." No wonder that the last chapter, its apotheosis, is called "Zionism." The book, whose author had emigrated to Palestine between the first and second editions of its appearance and who was a chief engineer of the new Jewish society, ends on an optimistic note about Jewish survival outside Europe—the hope of "the national rebirth of the Jewish people in Palestine."[10]

POSTMORTEM

There was no time left to prove Ruppin's or Theilhaber's visions right or wrong. The dissolution of the Jewish communities of Europe came faster than any of them had predicted, and in quite another fashion than they could have imagined. When the heavens darkened over European Jewry, collective survival on the bloodstained soil of Europe seemed a distant thought for the few who had escaped hell. In the imagination of most Jews, both the remainder in Europe and the vast majority outside, the old world seemed nothing but a huge Jewish cemetery. As one of the leaders of the surviving Jews, the *she'erit ha'pleita*, Samuel Gringauz, put it: "After the catastrophe,

Europe was no longer characterised for the Jews by Westminster Abbey or Versailles, nor by Strasbourg Cathedral and the art treasures of Florence, but by the violence of the Crusaders, the Spanish Inquisition, the pogroms of Russia and the gas chambers of Auschwitz." His only conclusion was: "Adieu Europe!"[11]

And still, not only in the communities of Western Europe that were spared the worst fate of European Jewry but also in other parts, where political circumstances allowed it, Jews reconstituted Jewish life immediately after the war. This can be seen nowhere more clearly than in Germany itself. There are even cases where a new Jewish community was reconstituted before the official end of the war, as was the case in Cologne in April 1945. The few surviving German Jews were joined by around a quarter million Eastern European Jewish displaced persons who all hoped to leave the then-occupied Germany when the Jewish state was founded and U.S. immigration restrictions lifted. But again, despite all prophecies to the contrary, even after 1950 the German-Jewish community survived. To be sure, it remains a shadow of its prewar existence but, due to immigration from the former Soviet Union, it grew to over 100,000 in over 100 organized communities by the beginning of the twenty-first century. In France, the Jewish community drew from immigration from Northern Africa and became larger than ever before.

How should one view such a development? There was the classical Zionist interpretation, which regarded *any* diaspora existence as fragile, and a post-Shoah one in Europe as pathetic. This view is represented by Israeli historian David Vital, who in 1990 made this utterly clear: "It must be said that there are communities in contemporary Europe which can only strike one with dismay. How *can* there be an organized Jewish community in Germany in our time? Or in Austria? There are aspects of the modern history of France, too, which prompt one to ask whether the Jews, of all peoples, have not lost their historical memory and much else besides. . . . The major communities in central and Eastern Europe are gone, of course, and are no more than subjects for academic research, much too much of it vitiated by nostalgia and vulgar sentimentality." Even the British and French Jewish communities, in Vital's opinion "manage to do no more than persist. . . . In any event, to a traveler like myself, the Jewries of Europe cannot fail to seem subject to steady erosion, if not decay. They are too small to be culturally self-sustaining." Only "a form of re-entry into the ghetto" could save their future, according to Vital.[12]

A few years later, British historian Bernard Wasserstein published a book that earned him a place of honor in the niche of the prophets of doom of European Jewry. He called it *Vanishing Diaspora*. Like Theilhaber, he predicted for European Jewry the same fate as for Chinese Jewry, which had disappeared because of assimilation. What the Nazis did not manage by mass killings, the friendly integrationism of Western Europe would finally achieve: a *judenfrei* Europe, with the exception of a few insignificant and marginal ultra-orthodox islands in London, Paris, and Antwerp: "a picturesque remnant like the Amish of Pennsylvania."[13]

Wasserstein's conclusions are clear: "The dissolution of European Jewry is not situated at some point in a hypothetical future. The process is taking place before our eyes and is already far advanced on at least three fronts. 1. We witness now the last scene of the last act of more than a millennium of Jewish life in Eastern Europe. . . . 2. We witness now the withering away of Judaism as a spiritual presence in the daily lives of most Jews in Europe. . . . 3. We witness now the end of an authentic Jewish culture in Europe."[14]

Wasserstein's analysis, in its last consequences, holds true for the American diaspora as well, with the significant difference that it is a much larger community, concentrated in a few centers, and still being held together by substantial centers of learning. In general, though, American Jews, according to this analysis, will be hit by the same fate. Wasserstein's European patient suffers from the same disease as American Jewry, according to Alan Dershowitz (who in 1997 published a book called *The Vanishing American Jew*), with the only difference that he is in a more critical and lethal state. In this respect, there is a direct line from Ruppin and Theilhaber via Vital to Wasserstein and Dershowitz and most Israeli demographers who have no doubt about the dissolution of European Jewry and little doubt about the predictable end of the Jewish diaspora as such. Even more radical was French sociologist Georges Friedman's 1965 analysis, *Fin du Peuple Juif?* (The End of the Jewish People?), in which he suggested that the increasingly Western materialistic culture of Israel will ultimately lead to a collective assimilation and transform Israelis into "Hebrew-speaking Gentiles."[15]

In Israel, the opposite argument can be heard: that the survival of Jews and Judaism is possible only in a Jewish state. As renowned journalist Amotz Asa-El wrote in 2004, all attempts to construct Jewish life in the diaspora are suicidal: "Today, there are still, around the world, many Jews unwittingly nurturing national suicide, from Russian Jews flocking to Germany to Lubavitch Hassidim opening up yeshivot, mikvas and kosher butcheries in Crimea, Siberia and Kalmykia. These Jews are still in the business of feeding future generations of antisemites with vulnerable communities to prey on."[16]

FROM REQUIEM TO REVIVAL

The first major voice of dissent in this choir of doom was that of a novelist. Philip Roth's *Operation Shylock*, published in 1993, contained a shocking message: the return of Israeli Jews to the Europe that had killed their families. "The so-called normalization of the Jews was a tragic illusion from the start. . . . The time has come to return to the Europe that was for centuries, and remains to this day, the most authentic Jewish homeland there has ever been, the birthplace of rabbinic Judaism, Hasidic Judaism, Jewish secularism, socialism—on and on. The birthplace, of course, of Zionism too.

But Zionism has outlived its historical function. The time has come to renew in the European Diaspora our pre-eminent spiritual and cultural role."[17]

The character Philip Roth, author of *Portnoy's Complaint*, in Philip Roth's novel, says those words to the character Aharon Appelfeld in a suite of the Jerusalem King David Hotel. Just as in his novel about the Nazi plot against America, reality and fiction are interwoven. In *Operation Shylock* Roth wants to save Israeli lives by directing Jews out of their endangered states. For this purpose, he even meets Polish Solidarity leader (and later president of Poland from 1990 to 1995) Lech Walesa to discuss a large-scale resettlement of Polish Jews.

Operation Shylock can be read as a counter-novel to Leon Uris's *Exodus*. Roth's diaspora Jews are the mirror image of what he depicted already in a 1961 speech as "the image of the Jew as a patriot, warrior, and battle-scarred belligerent" as depicted in *Exodus*. Israeli writer Yitzchak Laor noted that "Israelis cannot read this corpus without being threatened by yet another complicating question posed in front of our Imaginaire.... Roth's project is too big for public discourse, for tastemakers to discuss."[18]

It is significant, of course, that Roth lived in the United States. He may have shared the thought not only of a grand European Jewish past but also of a possible Jewish future in Europe, but he was no part of it, was not contributing to it, not drawing inspiration from it. Similarly, in a relatively recent attempt to reinterpret Jewish history in a grand manner, David Biale's *Cultures of the Jews* does not deal at all with post-Shoah European Jewry, while containing chapters on contemporary American and Israeli Jews. Only one of its twenty-three contributors is based in Europe.[19]

Is Europe then, as Vital and Wasserstein argue, utterly marginal in the Jewish world? Or are there any Jewish voices in Europe that may apply Rawidowicz's thesis of the ever-dying people so apt to survive to Europe? The most eloquent voice promoting a new European Jewry has been that of the Italian-Jewish historian Diana Pinto, educated at Harvard and living in Paris.

In several essays and numerous speeches, mostly written around the turn of this century, Pinto argues for the construction of a new European Jewry within the New Europe, for a third pillar of world Jewry next to America and Israel. European Jews, she writes, "must have the intellectual vision to realize ... that Judaism recovered from other devastating historical experiences: the Spanish expulsion, for example."[20] Europe today, she wrote in the mid-1990s, offers the unique chance of a new postnational identity: "Jews can and should take advantage of this new paradigm and create a European identity for themselves.... For Jews, Europe is newly emerging. It is not a finished product." They can, and should, create a "Jewish space" fifty years after the Holocaust and revive a positive Judaism. And while Wasserstein's account ends with a comparison of European Jews to Chinese Jews who disappeared as well, Pinto's conclusion is optimistic concerning the survival of European Jewry: "Europe is not Australia.

It is a place where Jewish history, culture and creativity have been rooted for more than two thousand years. That history cannot be reduced to a mere episode of colonization in an Israeli rewriting of history; nor should it become a latter-day version of post-1492 Spain in which Jews exist primarily as a symbolic memory. It is up to us, as Europeans and Jews, to turn Europe into the third pillar of a world Jewish identity at the cross-roads of a newly interpreted past, and a pluralist and democratic future."[21]

Between those contradicting visions, what then is the future of European Jewry? Historians are no prophets, and instead of predicting the future we analyze past developments and draw conclusions from them. Our conclusions of these analyses are less based on objective facts than on our own biases; they grow out of our personalities rather than of indisputable truths. How else can we explain that Israeli demographers continue to predict the slow decline of the Jewish diaspora, while some of their American Jewish colleagues see a more rosy picture of their own future? The disputes begin with very different notions of "Who is a Jew?" For example, the number of Jews in post-Communist communities like Hungary or Poland vary a huge amount due to differing definitions and they end with basic disagreements over the definition of Jewish culture. It matters if we look at the world from a Zionist or a diasporist point of view; it matters if our personal inclination is that of an optimist or that of a pessimist. And none of us can predict how the State of Israel and the Middle East will look in one generation, even ten years from now; none of us can predict how much longer feelings of ethnic pride will continue to exist in America, or how antisemitism will develop in Europe. Those are just a few of the factors that will influence Jewish life in Europe and beyond in the next decades.

I would distinguish between two parallel and seemingly conflicting developments: on the one hand, a progressing assimilation, and on the other hand, a strengthening of Jewish identity and knowledge. The first, we may call Wasserstein's Europe; the second, Pinto's Europe. Both of them exist, and both exist at the same time. The first reflects the situation of the majority of European Jews. If we consider any practice or positive commitment to Judaism as relevant, the European Jewish community is further diminishing. Their children and grandchildren may be regarded as Jews or of Jewish descent by their non-Jewish neighbors, but many European Jews won't know anymore what it means to be Jewish other than being regarded as such by others. Intermarriage is one strong factor in this development—the other one is the ease of integration and the secularization of European society, not comparable to an American society in which God and religion still play a major role.

While this development concerns the majority of European Jews in the next generation, a contrasting tendency cannot be denied. The margins are drifting away, but the center may gain strength. During the last decades the number of Jewish children attending Jewish schools all over Europe has grown, especially due to a certain kind of Jewish revival in Eastern and Central Europe: a few innovative institutes of adult learning have opened their doors; Jewish studies at universities have been strengthened; the attractiveness of Jewish culture by non-Jews has had its impact on Jews as well; and the diversity of religious life ranging from the Reform movement to Chabad has become notable. Again, those developments may only be relevant for a minority of European Jews, but this minority may indeed prove big enough to survive.

Three examples may provide some background to this development. In Great Britain, *Limmud* has proved an enormously successful innovation to Jewish learning. What started as a happening and learning event has become a movement. Besides the *Limmud* meeting around Christmastime, where thousands of British Jews gather to study and discuss a broad variety of aspects of Judaism, there are many smaller *Limmud* learning days all over Great Britain, and now also in other parts of Europe. In Germany, a similar event called *Tarbut* for Jews from German-speaking countries has proven an unforeseen success with hundreds of Jews from Germany, Austria, and Switzerland gathering regularly to discuss all aspects of Jewish life, to learn, and to meet a broad range of German-Jewish writers, politicians, and religious leaders. Another, much smaller, but more substantial enterprise is *Paideia* in Stockholm. Founded by an American, *Paideia* brings together young Jews from all over Europe for one year to teach them Jewish texts and create a solid basis of Jewish knowledge for people who then can transmit this to their own communities.

Enterprises such as *Limmud*, *Tarbut*, and *Paideia* are by no means guarantees for the survival of European Jewry. They are, however, signs that a substantial number of European Jews are ready to invest their time and money for a Jewish future in Europe. More than that, they underline that the memory of Europe among Jews is no longer exclusively defined by the Crusaders, the Inquisition, and Auschwitz, but also by reclaiming the diverse heritage of Rashi, Mendelssohn, Kafka, Freud, and Einstein.

Anthropologically speaking, we deal more with a thin than with a thick culture. The last generation of Jews who grew up in the shtetl, in a Europe in which being Jewish meant an everyday culture distinguishable by cloth, language, and religious practice, is no longer. The majority of the European Jews of the next generations are not willing to invest on an everyday basis. Their commitment to Judaism and Jewish culture is restricted to occasional activities, but many of them still have a social life that is primarily Jewish; they undertake efforts to find a Jewish partner and provide their children with, at least, a minimal Jewish education. They will remain tied to Israel to a greater extent than American Jewry because of their small size, their close proximity to Israel, and also, perhaps, due to their bad conscience about living on a continent many in Israel and America consider to be a large cemetery.

The development of religious life in Europe is another factor not to be overlooked. In recent years, both Chabad and Reform as well as Conservative movements have made large inroads. In Eastern Europe, Lubavitch has more or less taken over large parts of Jewish life and, even in Western Europe, religious life may become dominated by Chabad to a large extent in another generation. In Germany the first Chabad rabbi arrived in the 1980s—there were only three Chabad rabbis until the influx of Russian Jews, and now their number has grown to over twenty, which comprises a third of the total number of rabbis in Germany. In Berlin, where both Reform and Orthodox movements have established rabbinical schools and now educate German-speaking rabbis, the Chabad community has laid the foundation for a modern educational campus in 2018.[22] While many Orthodox (and non-Orthodox) rabbis disagree with their ideology, almost no one dares to raise the issue, partly because the communities themselves would not be able to fill the gap caused by their retreat and partly because they are afraid of splits within the communities.[23] It should be added that the Ashkenazi chief rabbi of Israel leaves no doubt about his support of Chabad activities in Germany and other parts of Europe. On the other hand, non-Orthodox religious activities are growing. The first female rabbi was appointed to a German-Jewish community in the 1990s and in Berlin and some other communities, egalitarian services are no longer a provocation as they were for many decades.

Those tendencies might help to build up religious Jewish life in Europe, but they also have another consequence. Whatever remained of the indigenous European-Jewish culture is about to disappear. Basically no Jew in Germany today is familiar with traditional Ashkenazi *minhagim*; the Italian Jewish rite is dying out; Hungarian Jews may call themselves Neolog or Status Quo but they have little idea what those notions really mean. European Judaism is about to be replaced by the import of Israeli and American notions: the melodies heard at a wedding in Afula or Bat Yam are the same as those heard in Milano or Manchester. The *shaharit nussah* heard in a conservative synagogue in Los Angeles soon will also be heard in Berlin or Budapest. The school curricula are not giving much emphasis to any particular local or regional traditions and most students don't know much of the Jewish histories of the places in which they grow up. Despite new home-grown institutions, Judaism in Europe today rests on the import of leaders and ideas. There will be Jews in Europe, there will be Judaism, but one does not have to be a prophet to predict that this is no longer a European Judaism with its own traditions and rituals.

A VIRTUAL EUROPEAN JUDAISM?

As for secular Jewish culture, another phenomenon is palpable. We may soon encounter a Jewish culture in Europe that is neither Wasserstein's nor Pinto's Europe, but Gruber's Europe. The American journalist Ruth Gruber, who resides in Italy, has analyzed what she calls "Virtual Judaism," a non-Jewish Jewish culture based on klezmer music, Jewish museums, cultural festivals, and academic study of Judaism.[24] Much has been written on this phenomenon, including a large amount of ridicule and cynicism. This is understandable for anyone confronted with this phenomenon. Still, one may add one more aspect: this unpredicted interest in Jewish culture might have unpredictable positive effects on Jewish life. As some Jews begin to realize: if so many non-Jews like Jewish culture, maybe there is actually something to it. Some Jewish museums have begun to develop programs for Jewish schools and others inspire Jewish artists. The Rothschild Foundation in London has developed significant programs to support both Jewish cultural creativity and Jewish studies. Some of the beneficiaries of those programs are non-Jews but there are also many Jews who will contribute to a more creative world of Jewish culture in Europe in the generations to come.

One may argue that Jews in the twenty-first century do not need Europe, but Europe needs the Jews. A *judenrein* Europe a few generations after the Shoah would be conceived as the ultimate posthumous defeat of liberal and democratic values by the forces of totalitarianism. Therefore, even European states with the tiniest Jewish communities are well prepared to preserve and cultivate Jewish existence. Is the Jewish presence, then, to become a merely symbolic one, an exhibition of exotic animals in the European zoo? While this danger cannot be neglected, one could argue that even though Jews may not need Europe, Jewish culture would lose a significant dimension without a European presence. After all, Jews did not stay as tourists in this continent over two millennia, but were shaped by their European surroundings in all possible ways, just as they influenced their non-Jewish environment. Thus, asked for the reasons why Jews remain in Europe after all that happened, one might add to the "fleshpot" argument (to secure their economic well-being) and the "*davka*" argument (not to grant Hitler a posthumous victory), the "culture" argument: they feel part of either the particular French/German/Italian culture or of the more inclusive European culture.

One factor that seemed rather marginal to the future of Jewish life in Europe in the late twentieth century, but which has gained momentum as an argument among modern-day prophets of doom, is antisemitism. The second decade of the twenty-first century has seen a significant rise of verbal attacks against Jews and of actual violence against Jewish institutions in almost all European countries. While one cause for this development is the transmission of the Middle East conflict into European territory with its side-effect of the growing presence of radical Islam, another troubling development is the revival of right-wing nationalist parties. Their rhetoric is nowadays often friendly toward Jews and especially toward Israel, and their anti-Muslim agendas even appeal to some Jewish voters, but their xenophobic ideology will ultimately be counterproductive to any revival of Jewish culture in Europe.[25] As always, though, the rise of antisemitism not only has the effect of Jews hiding their Judaism or leaving for other places: even if one disagrees with Jean-Paul Sartre's thesis that antisemitism creates the modern Jew, there can be little doubt that, among many Jews who otherwise might have assimilated, it involuntarily strengthens a sense of solidarity.[26] Thus, antisemitism works both to weaken and to strengthen Jewish identity.

It is impossible to know if the numbers are substantial enough and the creativity sufficiently strong to lay the foundations of a future European-Jewish life. But synagogues are being built, new Jewish community centers are opening, innovative operations are beginning their activities, schools are increasing the number of students, and ideas about a new "European Jewry" are floating around. So, at least for the short run and contradictory to all prophecies after the Shoah and to all appeals of Israeli prime ministers and chief rabbis to emigrate, European Jews will be around for some time. In fact, in recent years more Israelis have emigrated to Europe, with Berlin as a new hub, than European Jews to Israel. More former Soviet Jews have settled in Germany in the early 2000s than in Israel. Those facts also have some impact for a future Jewish world.

European Jewry is the smallest pillar in the Jewish world next to North America and Israel, but it is still here to stay as long as the economic conditions remain stable and antisemitism is not an everyday experience. Individual Jews will always opt for other options, such as remaining Jews outside Europe or remaining Europeans without Judaism. The majority will not disappear that fast.

Two countries with small but lively Jewish communities prove the notion of the ever-dying people: Spain and Germany. Five hundred years after the expulsion, fifty years after the Shoah, Jewish communities are existent in both places, have been growing in the last generation, and—whether one likes it or not—will be there for the next few generations. If those countries have Jewish communities after their respective experiences, then how can we predict the decline of any Jewish community?

Let us then, in conclusion, return to Simon Rawidowicz. "When we analyze somewhat more deeply this constant dread of the end, we discover that one of its decisive psychological elements is the general, not particularly Jewish, sense of fear of losing ground, of being deprived of possessions and acquisitions—or, still deeper, the sense of fear that came over man when he first saw the sunset in the west, not knowing that every sunset is followed by a sunrise, as the *midrash* so beautifully described Adam's first great shock." That the sunrise is also there for the Jewish people is Rawidowicz's point in a post-Shoah world. He regards the fear of cessation as a "protective individual and collective emotion. Jewry has indulged so much in the fear of its end that its constant vision of the end helped it to overcome every crisis, to emerge from every threatening end as a living unit, though much wounded and reduced. In anticipating its end, it became its master. . . . There is no people more dying than Israel, yet none better equipped to resist disaster."[27]

NOTES

1. Simon Rawidowicz, "Israel: The Ever-Dying People," in *State of Israel, Diaspora, and Jewish Continuity*, ed. Benjamin C. I. Ravid (Hanover: New England University Press, 1998), 53–54.

2. Otto Heller, *Sibirien: Ein anderes Amerika* (Berlin: Neuer deutscher Verlag, 1930).

3. Otto Heller, *Der Untergang des Judentums: Die Judenfrage/Ihre Kritik/Ihre Lösung durch den Sozialismus* (Vienna and Berlin: Verlag für Literatur und Politik, 1931).

4. Felix Theilhaber, *Der Untergang der deutschen Juden. Eine volkswirtschaftliche Studie* (Berlin: Jüdischer Verlag, 1921), 32–33.

5. Ibid., 153.

6. Ibid., 157–158.

7. John M. Efron, *Defenders of the Race: Jewish Doctors and Race Science in Fin-de-Siècle Europe* (New Haven: Yale University Press, 1994).

8. Arthur Ruppin, *Die Juden der Gegenwart. Eine sozialwissenschaftliche Studie* (Cologne and Leipzig: Jüdischer Verlag, 1911), iii.

9. Ibid., 3.

10. Ibid., 302.

11. Samuel Gringauz, "Jewish Destiny as the DPs See It," *Commentary*, December 1947, 505. On the context, see Michael Brenner, *After the Holocaust: Jews in Postwar Germany* (Princeton: Princeton University Press, 1997).

12. David Vital, *The Future of the Jews: A People at the Crossroads?* (Cambridge: Harvard University Press, 1990), 104–107.

13. Bernard Wasserstein, *Vanishing Diaspora: The Jews in Europe since 1945* (Cambridge: Harvard University Press, 1996), vii.

14. Ibid., 283–284.

15. Georges Friedmann, *Le fin du peuple juif?* (Paris: 1965). (English transl. by Eric Mosbacher: *The End of the Jewish People?* [London: 1967].)

16. Amotz Asa-El, "Letter to a Palestinian Colleague," *Jerusalem Post*, December 31, 2004, 20.

17. Philip Roth, *Operation Shylock* (New York: Simon & Schuster, 1993), 32.

18. Yitzchak Laor, "From Exodus to Operation Shylock: Who Is Philip Roth in Israel," *Du 740: Philip Roth. Inventing America* (Zurich: October 2003), 80.

19. David Biale (ed.), *Cultures of the Jews: A New History* (New York: Schocken, 2002).

20. Diana Pinto, "A New Jewish Identity for Post-1989 Europe," *JPR Policy Paper* no. 1 (June 1996), 2.

21. Ibid., 15.

22. "Baubeginn für Jüdischen Campus in Wilmersdorf," *Berliner Mogenpost*, May 23, 2018. https://www.morgenpost.de/bezirke/im-westen-berlins/article214359891/Baubeginn -fuer-Juedischen-Campus-in-Wilmersdorf.html.

23. An exception to this rule is the Frankfurt community, where the dispute between the community and Chabad led to an open break in 2017. See "Zwist in der jüdischen Gemeinde," *Frankfurter Rundschau*, March 28, 2017. http://www.fr.de/frankfurt /frankfurt-zwist-in-der-juedischen-gemeinde-a-1250418.

24. Ruth E. Guber, *Virtually Jewish: Reinventing Jewish Culture in Europe* (Berkeley: University of California Press, 2002).

25. The most recent attempt to embrace Jews by a right-wing party is the establishment of a group called "Juden in der AfD" in Germany. See *Jüdische Allgemeine*, October 7, 2018.

26. Jean-Paul Sartre, *Anti-Semite and Jew: An Exploration of the Etiology of Hate* (New York: Schocken, 1948).

27. Rawidowicz, "The Ever-Dying People," 60–61.

THE THIN CRUST OF CIVILIZATION

Lessons from the German-Jewish Past

MATHIAS BEREK

IT HAPPENED MORE than once. Sitting in a bar after a conference, Jewish colleagues asked me why I, as a non-Jew, would be interested in German-Jewish history. I could never answer in one sentence, but the response always had a connection to the present and how today's societies could develop further. Every question led me to think more about it, many elements of my answer changed, but at its core it still is related to present-day German and European societies. In the German-Jewish past we find Jewish visions for a modern society, as well as Jewish answers to modernity's challenges, which individuals and groups face in the contemporary age. In the very same past we can also find non-Jewish perceptions of these visions and attitudes as well as actions toward Jews as such. The Swiss writer Gottfried Keller succinctly depicted the relevance of the German-Jewish past for the present and the future. In a letter to the German-Jewish philosopher Moritz Lazarus, dated December 20, 1881, Keller drew a picture of "the thin crust of civilization that only scantily separates us from the animals burrowing and howling in the abyss and which can collapse with every occasional vibration."[1]

The visions of culture and society to which I am referring by no means belong exclusively to German Jews, or Germans or Jews alone. But the particular situation many German Jews found themselves in during the nineteenth century led quite a few of them to develop progressive and modern ideas of society. These visions comprised pluralism, humanitarian universalism, constructivist and voluntaristic concepts of belonging, high esteem for knowledge and education, and cosmopolitanism. They included the insight that every culture and every society was basically dynamic, a product of action, history, exchange, and migration. To put it bluntly, the opposite of these ideas gained control over Germany at the end of the nineteenth century: ideas of homogeneity, nationalism, biologistic or otherwise essentialist definitions of belonging, and a static concept of culture firmly grounded in an imagined distant past. Exploring the German-Jewish past offers insights into what today would probably be termed emancipatory ideals of a society based on principles of plurality and equal rights. It is, however, also a story about how such ideas failed.

In this essay, I will draw on my research on the impact of a prominent German-Jewish intellectual, Moritz Lazarus, in nineteenth-century Germany. What I find so intriguing about the nineteenth century is that many of the unanswered questions about modern society were raised at that time. I chose Lazarus because he was a prominent German-Jewish intellectual who dedicated most of his work to understanding life in modern society. The thinker Lazarus was highly influential for sociology, social psychology, (cultural) philosophy, and anthropology, although mostly neglected until recently. As early as the 1860s, for instance, he developed a broad, pluralist, dynamic, and subjectivist understanding of culture (the "objective spirit" that formed the subjects and was formed by them), which comprised every outcome of human action, even the most mundane like the farmer's market. And he sought to put into practice his conceptual insights of social psychology and philosophy. I will mainly concentrate on the second half of the century, a very special period for German Jewry and for Lazarus in particular. It was the time of Jewish emancipation becoming a reality, when Jews could play a "co-constitutive" role in the newly founded nation-state and the majority of Jews could finally advance into the midst of German society.[2] This period began to draw to a close in 1879 as German-Jewish optimism faltered with the emergence of a new modern, racial antisemitism and its dissemination among the educated middle classes.

The life and work of Moritz Lazarus is paradigmatic for German Jews in his era—in the success he had and the disappointments he experienced.[3] Of course, he is not the only German-Jewish thinker envisioning a society based on plurality and equal rights for all. Gabriel Riesser (1806–1863), Ludwig Bamberger (1823–1899), and Berthold Auerbach (1812–1882) are just a few other prominent examples. One could also refer to Joseph Lehmann (1801–1873), the founder and lifelong editor of the *Magazin für die Literatur des Auslandes*, one of the most important German review magazines, published from 1832 to 1905. The position the journal took against antisemitism largely represented the views of contemporary Jews in Germany: "In keeping with the spirit of our magazine, we have hitherto abstained from saying a word about the abuse of German honour in the form of incitement against all German citizens of Palestinian origin by a few German citizens of Indian descent. We consider such publications as nothing more than banal vulgarity, ambition, stupidity, and greed, that utterly lack *literary* value."[4] In what follows I will elaborate on this so-called thin crust of civilization by discussing five aspects of the German-Jewish experience: education, religion, nationality, liberalism, and exclusion. This discussion will show how these German-Jewish visions of a just and diverse society found a selective reception among non-Jews and that the nation and liberalism are basically incapable of overcoming exclusionary hatred such as antisemitism.

EDUCATION AND *BILDUNG*

The high esteem in which education is held in Jewish life is common knowledge. In nineteenth-century Germany both Protestant as well as Jewish reformers struggled to make *Bildung* a basic right for every member of society. It was part of the project of Enlightenment, idealism, and scientific modernity that drove the progressive movements in both religions (and in socialism, too). But, at least from the Protestant side, the commonality of this cause has not been acknowledged. In the end, even progressive Protestant liberals refused to desist from their exclusionary attitudes toward the Jews—so long as they were considered Jews they were not regarded as true Germans, notwithstanding how educated they might be.[5]

But the rather pessimist outlook of the fin de siècle was not the typical Jewish perspective throughout the century. Coming back to Moritz Lazarus, education was a central part of his work from the beginning. He discussed it in his philosophical as well as in his political texts, even proposing a reform for the education system of the canton of Bern when he was dean and rector there between 1860 and 1866.[6] A condensed form of his approach to education can be found in a small article to which I will refer to here. In this essay he combined classical Humboldtian education ideas with Jewish ideals of bettering the world. The influences of reform Protestantism, Kantian Idealism, the pluralistic experience of Jewish emancipation, and German nationalism with its cultural-nationalist foundations are clearly noticeable. His goal was to create modern humanist ethics based on *Bildung* and on Jewish as well as Protestant ideas.

The piece appeared in 1886 in Paul Lindau's cultural journal *Nord und Süd* and described Lazarus's vision of a Sunday celebration.[7] He depicted a community building reminiscent of Socialist houses of culture or Zionist kibbutz clubs. There, on Sunday afternoons, after the religious gathering, the community would get together for education in its broadest sense, as *Bildung*: lectures, music, sports, games, discussions, or plays. Every village would employ a teacher who prepared the activities for the Sunday gathering during the week. The fundamental principle of Lazarus's vision was the right for everyone to enjoy leisure time. In capitalism, according to Lazarus, labor dominates life; and the spirit, even religious spirit, was in need of leisure time in order not to degenerate. "The world of labor has created conflict, education has generated awareness of that conflict; the world of leisure has to bring back peace and it alone will be able to do so."[8] Leisure, as Lazarus understood it, consisted primarily, but not only of aesthetic and scientific *Bildung*. Sports, games, socializing, lectures, discussions, drama, music, or poetry, in active or passive roles: "All the rivers run into the sea; the earth shall become full of understanding, of inner culture, than it will also be full of morals and morality."[9]

The article appeared in a journal that claimed to represent "German education" and it attracted contributions from important writers such as Paul Heyse, Berthold Auerbach, and Theodor Fontane. Paul Lindau, in his time, was one of Berlin's most famous critics and journalists.[10] Within this context, Lazarus's vision reached a wide audience. At the same time, if we look at German society of the time more broadly, it is more than questionable whether he was able to assert any significant influence with his vision—on the nation as a whole, or on its morality, in politics or in the education system. Lazarus's article is an example for the *possible* influence of his work, but even more so a paradigm for the reform ideas of German Jews and the lack of their impact.

At most, Lazarus's influence was that of a selective perception: as in other areas of his work, only those of his thoughts about education that suited the *Zeitgeist* were welcomed in public. For instance, male reviewers applauded his views about women's education only where they confirmed their own point of view that women per se were not fit for many jobs.[11] They ignored Lazarus's arguments that differed from their worldview, for example the observation that it was social circumstance that made women lack the knowledge required for certain occupations. Lazarus was too early for many when he demanded equal education for men and women.

RELIGION

As a parallel movement to Protestant reformer groups such as "*Lichtfreunde*" or "*Protestantenverein*," Jewish reformers like Lazarus sought to strengthen inner religiosity rather than religious institutions or rules. The most important juxtaposition of nineteenth-century German-Jewish reform was that of the opposition of the halakhic, traditional-rabbinic, orthodox *shell* versus what reform thinkers saw as the prophetic, individualistic-confessional *core* of Judaism. It was a specifically Jewish debate whether, and how, traditional rules and laws should apply to modern everyday life—whether only biblical and Talmudic laws or also rules from the Middle Ages like the *Shulchan Aruch* should be relevant. In addition, liberal German Jews were discussing other broad questions about religion in a modern bourgeois society: Should the modern state be laicist, secular, neutral, or affiliated to religion? How far should religious law influence everyday life? Which parts of religious tradition were to be considered as divine revelation and which as historical, human products?

Another commonality between Protestant and Jewish reform was in the effort to comprehend the nature of religion as ethics, and the attempt to ground religion as well as religious ethics in reason. When Lazarus published his *Ethics of Judaism* in 1898 he met with almost unanimous approval from the liberal German-Jewish public.[12] His Kantian definition of the autonomous nature of moral laws in Judaism seemed to give voice to a widespread conviction of the liberal, moderately reformed majority of German Jews in his time: "not because God has ordained it as moral law, but because it is moral, therefore God has ordained it." Hence, "the moral law is autonomous, because it originates in the nature of the human mind alone."[13] Also, most of the Christian commentators acclaimed his reading of Jewish ethics. Conservative or neo-Orthodox Jews, not surprisingly, rejected this foundation of moral law on reason alone. They insisted on the primacy of theology over philosophy, at least when it came to matters of religion.

NATION

German Jews were significant proponents and supporters of the cultural-nationalist movement in Germany before the foundation of the Wilhelmine nation state in 1871.[14] They were part of the process of the nation's construction and among them quite a few, including Lazarus, supported the Prussian, lesser Germany (*Kleindeutschland*) version of unification. This is what Lazarus, Riesser, Bamberger, and others were striving for, on the assumption that a pluralistic, emancipatory nation without exclusionary tendencies could exist. It was the experience of emancipation, upward social mobility, and support from prominent non-Jews that fostered their optimism and their belief in the state and the German nation.

Lazarus commenced his career as a writer with a political rather than a scholarly book when he published his *Sittliche Berechtigung Preußens in Deutschland* in 1850.[15] The volume combined Enlightenment's ideals with ideas about international law as well as a view of Prussia as the most cultivated and civilized German state and therefore the legitimate power to lead German unification. Lazarus's idea of a nation built on the action and commitment of its members was fortified during his five years as professor in Bern, Switzerland in the early 1860s. At its core was the voluntaristic, subjectivist concept of belonging, which he laid out in his *Völkerpsychologie:* "That which constitutes a people does not lie fundamentally in certain objective circumstances, such as descent, language etc., in themselves, but rather only in the subjective perspective of the parts of the people who all together *regard* themselves as belonging to one people. [...] A people is a spiritual product of the individuals who belong to it; they are not a people, they just produce it perpetually."[16] One belonged if one saw oneself as a member and participated in the activities that were demanded by the collective. In this under-standing of belonging, there was no place for biologistic, racist, or other essentialisms. It was solely based on individual choice and action. Undoubtedly, this conception corresponded to the way many patriotic German Jews, like Moritz Lazarus, saw their own situation—as members of the common project to create a German nation state. What they did not, and probably could not, anticipate was that the nation-state was not the ideal form of society to secure emancipation, inclusion, and plurality. As a constructed collective based on narratives and stereotypes that sought to homogenize society, exclusion was built into the notion of a nation-state. It was the tragedy of the German Jews that they, despite their majority embracing the German nation so enthusi-astically, would become the group most brutally excluded from the German collective.

LIBERALISM

The optimistic view that history, and especially German history, would always progress toward a better future was not only a German-Jewish but also a liberal trait. Until the end of the 1870s, after the first economic depression and Bismarck's turn to the conservatives, this was a prevailing approach. For German Jewry, at least for a number of German-Jewish intellectuals, the end of the 1870s was marked by events that shook their belief that emancipation and civilization would prevail: the propagation of modern antisemitism within the educated bourgeoisie.

Within academic circles, modern antisemitism was popularized most successfully by the renowned historian Heinrich Gotthard von Treitschke (1834–1896), whose infamous essay "Unsere Aussichten" had provoked the "Berlin antisemitism dispute" in 1879.[17] He was a liberal. One could object that he was a member of the *national* liberal faction, but also his famous *left*-liberal opponent in the dispute, Theodor Mommsen (1817–1903), another prominent German historian, in the end did not accept Jewish presence in German society without baptism. This failure of liberal-ism to be a stronghold against antisemitism is the first of three lessons that should be learned from the German-Jewish past: liberalism is no vaccine against antisemitism. Second, unrestrained *economic* liberalism, in its production of inequality and injustice, can prepare the ground for fascism. At the present day the correlation can be seen in the Europe-wide, if not global, success of far-right movements and parties following decades of neo-liberal destruction of the welfare systems, union power, state property, and other limits to the forces of capitalism. Third, the inclination to conflate politi-cal and economic liberalism proved to be misleading. As at the end of the nineteenth century, today's political liberalism is rejected together with neo-liberal capitalism as if they were one. I doubt if they really cared, but this is quite the opposite of what

Friedrich August von Hayek and Milton Friedman claimed: democracy and political liberalism are not an automatic outcome of unregulated markets; capitalism does not need individual freedom to exist. Liberal Jews in nineteenth-century Germany were possibly the first liberals to face the consequences that uncontrolled economic liberalism could have for liberal political ideals.

That said, it seems that the majority of Jews did not realize the implications of this development at the time. In fact, perhaps liberal German Jews were the only liberals who, due to their personal circumstances, took the political promises of liberalism seriously. One of their prominent intellectuals, Moritz Lazarus, stated in 1887 that in Germany the liberal parties should be the real conservative ones. Asking whose ideals were fulfilled here, Lazarus reminded his readers that it had been conservative politicians who had opposed the creation of a unified Germany with Prussia at its head, as well as a *Reichsparlament* elected through universal suffrage, a single law for all Germany, equality for all religions, and so on.[18] "But we, all we liberals, and mostly we liberal Jews, should support the government, should be its strong pillar, in order to save our *ideals—that are realised in all their essentials—*and to extend them"—an economic-liberal blasphemy.[19]

EXCLUSION

The pluralist Enlightenment ideals of German-Jewish thought of the nineteenth century notwithstanding, the modern humanitarianism behind it had its limits. Gender equality, for one (or thinking beyond gender duality), was far from the imagination of most of the Jewish and non-Jewish proponents of liberal humanism at the time. And as we know, many of today's structures to enforce this duality and to suppress women are a product of this very enlightened modernity. Moreover, even the most liberal thinkers of the nineteenth century would not generally question white European supremacy. Even Lazarus, who categorically rejected any racial ideas, spoke of higher (advanced) and lower (primitive) *Stämme* or cultures. He considered a non-European culture, such as ancient Jewry, one of the higher ones but what he wrote about people from sub-Saharan Africa hardly differed from the racist mainstream of his day. In short: German Jews pleading for a nonexclusionist society left some exclusions untouched.

There is much to learn for the future from the exclusion that affected Jews, namely: antisemitism. In my view the emergence of modern antisemitism can tell us a lot about most current forms of racist and culturalist exclusions. Its structure has been copied in many other cases. And from the fight against antisemitism there is much to learn for the fight against all forms of group-related enmity. Of course, there are differences between antisemitism and racism in particular. To sum up some strands of research on antisemitism: not only is antisemitism older, it also is inherently antimodern, whereas racism always refers to modernity or at least modern ideas with positive connotations; antisemitism is based on narratives of power and conspiracy, it constructs the total other, the non-nation, even non-race, and it has led to industrialized mass murder.

Parallels can definitely be found in the perspective of the victims, at least before the stage of mass murder. Liberal German Jews in the nineteenth century found themselves in many ways in a similar situation as other minorities today: they were members of their society since birth but nevertheless regarded as not belonging to it by the majority. They were wedged between the exclusionary violence of the majority of society and the rebuke of being assimilationist by orthodox fundamentalists or nationalists of their own group. And in the way that antisemitism has been identified as a cultural code representing a larger set of traditionalist and authoritarian beliefs, present-day animosities against Muslims or immigrants could be depicted in a similar manner.[20] Finally, future struggles against antisemitism can learn one thing from the past: they must be based on emancipatory ideals. They will be futile if the critique of antisemitism is used for other purposes, especially if they are antiemancipatory. The histories of nationalism and liberalism in a German-Jewish context provide more than enough material for this insight.

ALMOST TWENTY YEARS into the twenty-first century, the crust of civilization is still thin—or thin again. The animals in the abyss are howling louder than at the beginning of the millennium. Lessons from the German-Jewish past could help to stabilize this frail crust.

NOTES

1. Gottfried Keller, "Das Vorwort erinnert mich freilich an die dünne Kulturdecke, welche uns von den wühlenden und heulenden Tieren des Abgrundes noch notdürftig zu trennen scheint und die bei jeder gelegentlichen Erschütterung einbrechen kann" (my translation, M.B.), in Franz Kobler, *Jüdische Geschichte in Briefen aus Ost und West. Das Zeitalter der Emanzipation* (Wien: Saturn, 1938), 436; Keller referred to the foreword in Moritz Lazarus, *Das Leben der Seele in Monographien über seine Erscheinungen und Gesetze. Dritter Band*, 2nd ed. (Berlin: Ferd. Dümmler/Harrwitz and Goßmann, 1882). There, Lazarus positioned his philosophy, psychology, and ethics against the antisemitic trends of the 1880s in Germany, particularly within the "Berlin antisemitism dispute."

2. Steven E. Aschheim, "German History and German Jewry: Boundaries, Junctions and Interdependence," *Leo Baeck Institute Year Book* 43 (1998): 317.

3. Mathias Berek, "Neglected German-Jewish Visions for a Pluralistic Society: Moritz Lazarus," *Leo Baeck Institute Year Book* 60 (2015): 45–59.

4. My translation (M.B.), emphasis in the original. Some of the wittier wording in this text is hard to translate. Full quote: "Wir haben uns, der Natur unseres Blattes entsprechend, bisher enthalten, über die Schimpfirung der deutschen Ehre in Form der Hetze gegen alle deutschen Bürger palästinensischer Herkunft durch wenige deutsche Bürger indischer Herkunft ein Wort zu verlieren, weil wir in den gedruckten Veröffentlichungen über jene sogenannte Frage entweder platteste Gemeinheit, Strebertum, Langweiligkeit oder—Reptilienfonds, immer aber einen vollständigen Mangel an *literarischem* Werte entdeckt hatten." "Kleine Rundschau: Zur Judenfrage," *Magazin für die Literatur des In- und Auslandes* (July 2, 1881): 409. "Reptilienfonds" means a fund used by Bismarck to unofficially exert influence on the press.

5. Uffa Jensen, *Gebildete Doppelgänger. Bürgerliche Juden und Protestanten im 19. Jahrhundert* (Göttingen: Vandenhoeck & Ruprecht, 2005).

6. See Kommission für Bernische Hochschulgeschichte, ed., *Hochschulgeschichte Berns 1528–1984. Zur 150-Jahr-Feier der Universität Bern 1984* (Bern: Universität Bern, 1984), 700; Nahida Lazarus, *Ein deutscher Professor in der Schweiz. Nach Briefen und Dokumenten im Nachlass ihres Gatten* (Berlin: Dümmler, 1910), 128–133.

7. Moritz Lazarus, "Die Sonntagsfeier. Eine Vision," *Nord und Süd. Eine deutsche Monatsschrift* 37, no. 109 (April 1886): 70–87.

8. My translation (M.B.). Original quote: "Die Welt der Arbeit hat den Widerstreit erzeugt, die Bildung hat ihn zum Bewußtsein gebracht; die Welt der Muße muß und sie allein kann den Frieden wiederbringen." Ibid., 85.

9. My translation (M.B.). Original quote: "gymnastische Übungen und erheiternde Spiele, freie Geselligkeit und zweckbewußte, z. B. pädagogische Besprechung, Schauen und Vernehmen oder Vortragen und Darstellen dramatischer oder musikalischer Werke, klärende und erhebende Belehrung und ergreifende Dichtung: alle Ströme gehen in's Meer; die Erde soll voll werden von Erkenntnis, von innerer Cultur, dann wird sie auch voll sein von Sitte und Sittlichkeit." Ibid., 87.

10. Hans-Manfred Bock, "Vom europäischen Panoptikum zum europäischen friedenspolitischen Forum.—Die Kulturzeitschrift Nord und Süd im Kaiserreich von 1877 bis 1914," in *Le discours européen dans les revues allemandes, 1871–1914,* ed. Michel Grunewald (Bern: Peter Lang, 1996), 129–131.

11. Moritz Lazarus, *Das Leben der Seele in Monographien über seine Erscheinungen und Gesetze. Erster Band,* 3rd ed. (Berlin: Ferd. Dümmler / Harrwitz und Goßmann, 1883), 40–42.

12. Moritz Lazarus, *Die Ethik des Judenthums* (Frankfurt am Main: Kauffmann, 1898), in English: Moritz Lazarus, *The Ethics of Judaism. In Four Parts,* transl. Henrietta Szold (Philadelphia: Jewish Publication Society of America, 1900/1901).

13. Ibid., part I, pp. 111f., 134f.

14. Since the formation of Germany as a nation state seemed far from accessible in the first half of the nineteenth century, German nationalist movements mostly favored the cultural approach: searching for national unity and identity through language, literature, and tradition.

15. Moritz Lazarus, *Die sittliche Berechtigung Preußens in Deutschland* (Berlin: Carl Schultze, 1850).

16. My translation (M.B.). Original quote: "Das, was ein Volk zu eben diesem macht, liegt wesentlich nicht sowohl in gewissen objectiven Verhältnissen wie Abstammung, Sprache u. s. w. an sich als solchen, als vielmehr bloß in der subjectiven Ansicht der Glieder des Volkes, welche sich alle zusammen als ein Volk *ansehen*. [...] Volk ist ein geistiges Erzeugniß der Einzelnen, welche zu ihm gehören; sie sind nicht ein Volk, sie schaffen es nur unaufhörlich." Moritz Lazarus and H. Steinthal, "Einleitende Gedanken über Völkerpsychologie, als Einladung zu einer Zeitschrift für Völkerpsychologie und Sprachwissenschaft," *Zeitschrift für Völkerpsychologie und Sprachwissenschaft* 1, no. 1 (1860): 35–37, emphasis in the original.

17. The debate lasted from 1879 to 1881 and took place in journals, papers, and books. In the first year, almost exclusively Jewish intellectuals, one of the first Moritz Lazarus, attacked Treitschke for his attempt to construct an essential difference between Jewish and German. For the sources and an introduction see Karsten Krieger, *Der "Berliner Antisemitismusstreit" 1879–1881. Eine Kontroverse um die Zugehörigkeit der deutschen Juden zur Nation. Kommentierte Quellenedition* (München: Saur, 2003).

18. Moritz Lazarus, *An die deutschen Juden* (Berlin: Walter und Apolant, 1887), 26, my translation (M.B.). Original text: "In diesem Deutschen Reiche nun sollten die liberalen Parteien die eigentlichen conservativen sein. Denn wessen Ideale sind in demselben erfüllt? In den Wünschen der hochconservativen Partei hat es doch wahrlich nicht gelegen, ein einiges Deutschland, mit Preußen an der Spitze, ein Reichsparlament aus allgemeinem Wahlrecht, ein einheitliches Recht für Alldeutschland, die bürgerliche Gleichstellung aller Confessionen u. s. w. zu schaffen."

19. "It is first and foremost us [Jews] who have to strive for the strength of the Empire, the strength of the government." Ibid., my translation (M.B.), emphasis in the original. Original text: "Wir aber, wir Liberalen alle, und die liberalen Juden zumeist sollten mit der Regierung gehen, sollten ihre feste Stütze bilden, um unsere *in allem Wesentlichen erfüllten Ideale* im Bestande zu sichern und den weiteren Ausbau zu ermöglichen. Uns am meisten muß die Stärke des Reichs, die Stärke der Regierung am Herzen liegen, unter deren Führung die deutsche Nation in einem Menschenalter erreicht, was sie durch Jahrhunderte vergeblich ersehnt hat."

20. Shulamith Volkov, "Anti-Semitism as a Cultural Code," *Leo Baeck Institute Year Book* 23 (1978): 25–45.

THE DIALECTICS OF TRADITION

German-Jewish Studies and the Future

GALILI SHAHAR

T HE FUTURE OF Jewish studies, including research of German-Jewish history, literature, and the arts, depends upon the interpretation of their past. The study of German-Jewish literature is committed to enterprises of this kind: we are not able to tell the future, but through learning, readings, and interpretations, we can attest to its possibilities. In asking about the future, we are called back into the realm of the past. In this dialectic lie the real possibilities of interpretation, which are of future value. In our own study of German-Jewish worlds, in looking for their future, our research itself turns into an act of witnessing.

What does that mean? Literary studies are committed, as are other disciplines, to perspectives and reviews of their subject matter. This is what we call "theory," from the Greek *theoria*, namely looking at—contemplating. Studies often mean to "review," which implies also a return, a step back.[1] Our interpretations of Jewish literature demand grand visions and perspectives. These insights are also acts of eye-witnessing. Every act of learning (in Hebrew/Aramaic: *Talmud*), every effort of research is an attempt of witnessing. In asking about the future of our studies we are always wrestling with the leftovers of our traditions. Our interpretations, our own readings and acts of writing, our research for new visions, imply a step back into the fields of tradition.[2] These paths of learning are difficult to cross and too often lead to detours and dead ends. These reviews and insights of the past involve blindness too, as witnesses are often engaged through acts of silence. German-Jewish studies are complicated by these tensions, bearing the dialectics of tradition.

DIALECTICS OF TRADITION

German-Jewish literary study provides us with insights into this experience: in its most modernist, futuristic visions, German-Jewish writing returned and reviewed its past form and sought to redefine its own heritage. One has to recall, in this context, the contributions of German-Jewish authors in the anthology *Die Menschheitsdämmerung*,[3] edited by Kurt Pinthus, and to read again poems by authors such as Else Lasker-Schüler, Franz Werfel, and Iwan Goll and others, performing acts of return into biblical and Talmudic traditions, imagining in them the visions of a future. One has also to review the role and engagements of writers such as Carl Sternheim, Walter Hasenclever, and Walter Mehring in Expressionism and the Dada movement during the early decades of the twentieth century, in acknowledging how deeply the futuristic texts involved reviews of tradition and a poetic search for a past. Whether it was biblical or Talmudic, influenced by Chassidic sources or flooded by major streams of the Kabbalah, the reinterpretation of tradition was one of the major futuristic acts of German-Jewish literature.

Through radical readings of the biblical and the rabbinical sources, through deconstructive gestures, misinterpretations, and ironic play in the field of tradition—both the Halachic literature and the *Aggadah*; one must recall Kafka's versions of the Genesis stories and his esoteric Talmudic readings—German-Jewish writing created its most original contributions. Through transformation and adaptations of classical poetical forms, through inversions of sex and of gender and great maneuvers and U-turns between "West" and "East," we recall in this context Else Lasker-Schüler's "biblical" poems and her short Orientalist stories entitled "Yusuf" and "Tino of Bagdad." [4] German-Jewish literature reoriented itself in space and time. Through acceleration and collapse of eschatological figures, one remembers Walter Benjamin's new angels and his acts of messianic writing, German-Jewish authors engaged anew with the question of future.

In asking about the future of our own realm of studies, in asking how to bring together its major curricula, its theories and methods, its heritages and traditions, we are first asked to recall the core experience of the German-Jewish projects of modernity. As students of German-Jewish studies, we are called also as witnesses, we are called to review and to retell. The future of this realm of study depends upon the possibilities of return. Yet, the question stands, and much is at stake: where to?

WHAT IS LEFT FOR THE FUTURE

We argued first: the question concerning the future of German-Jewish studies depends on the unfolding of its past forms, the interpretation of tradition is the subtext of possibilities. German-Jewish literature itself is one of the greatest examples for such an attempt: in asking about its future we learn to ask what the past comprises, we learn to ask what is being left for us, and we begin to review what is being hidden in the realm of tradition. However, German-Jewish literature signifies not only the possibilities of the past, namely the unfolding of what is left for the future, but also hints at its failures and impossibilities and admits its disorientations and dead ends. It is, if one recalls Franz Kafka's famous letter to Max Brod from June 1921, dealing with the nature of the "minor German-Jewish literature," rather the impossibility of writing, the failures that become essential for understanding the experience of the German-Jewish author.[5] Kafka describes in his letter "three impossibilities" (*drei Unmöglichkeiten*) German-Jewish authors of his age are suffering from the impossibility not to write, the impossibility to write German, the impossibility to write differently.[6] The only possibility of writing that is left to the German-Jewish author of his generation thus depends on the experience of major impossibilities. The essence of German-Jewish writing, to follow Kafka, expresses its impossibilities.

What Kafka teaches us (Kafka, a teacher?) is that the unfolding of the past seems rather to attest to no future, to promise no progress and no production, but to reveal disabilities and crises time and again. German-Jewish authors asked a challenging question—where to? However, too often, these authors lost their own way and found themselves in states of crisis. German-Jewish writing so often tells of terminal failures, attesting to crucial interruptions in being. When we ask about the future of German-Jewish tradition we have to reconsider their dead ends.

One is not wrong to argue that Jewish writing in German, at least in the modernist circles of the twentieth century, defined itself through radical deformations of the European literary tradition and through interruptions of its major movements. The act of Jewish writing in German was also an act of resistance; it was, to quote one of Paul Celan's remarks from his *Meridian* (1960), an expression of a *Gegenwort*, a word that is being written and sent toward the other shore.[7] The word is written and sent against the major streams, against the flow of language itself. The word is also sent "toward" the other, who was left behind—on the denied, forgotten (historic) shore of the German language. The word in Celan's poetry that is written "against," written in a foreign syntax, in deformed German verses, fragmented sentences, performs resistance in language, yet it also implies an act of witnessing. To write against the stream (in Hebrew: *Shibboleth*) means to write for (and on behalf of) those who were forgotten. The question concerning the future demands certain poetics of memory, in which the past is recollected, yet against the false structure of time, against streams of forgetfulness.

Once we ask the question concerning the future of our realms of study, we must question its past. In past forms one is to find the subtexts for a proper unfolding of possibilities, which are to be named the "future." However, the German-Jewish past, at least in its radical, modernist experience, not only attests to possibilities and projects of futuristic values, but rather voices interruptions and crisis, ruptures and acts of resistance, standing against major streams and false visions of the future, against the illusions of the "new." In thinking and writing about the futurities of the German-Jewish past we also recall these countermovements and acts of resistance. It is well known that Walter Benjamin sought to find in these moments of standstill, in acts of return, and in the resistance to the empty, homogeneous stream of time (being signified by the mechanical clocks of the modern era), the radical possibility of all future forms, namely, the pure form of the messianic impossibility.[8] For the messianic, at least in its Talmudic sense, is not merely a figure of what is yet to come—a celebrated, mighty figuration of the last day (a day of judgment), but rather a poor, forgotten man, who never arrives at time, but only later, on the day after.[9] However, this belated, irritated, impossible arrival creates the time space (the interval) of return (in Hebrew: *Teshuva*, repentance).[10] Acts of resistance, interruptions, gestures of return, and moments of standstill produce poetics of memory, signifying a path of reparative actions. The radical possibilities for the future, we learn, depend also on these impossibilities of the past.

LEARNING FROM AN IMPERFECT PAST FOR A TENSE FUTURE

In asking about the future we learn first how to ask properly the question of the past, that is—to ask in re-turn, to ask in review. However, this brings us, once we engage the core of German-Jewish literary tradition, to disorientation and dead ends. The path of studies itself attest to broken experiences, failed projects, skepticism, and radical critique. What German-Jewish authors found in their own detours, in their own researches of the past, were not only futuristic values (progress, production, projection, timing), but rather esoteric time concepts, acts of suspensions and moments of delay, interruptions of labor, deformation of forms, and the collapse of all vision. What does it tell us? How should we rethink our own future, once it is based on traditions of interventions? What future is to be imagined through a broken prism of a past and via a deformed view of being? What kind of tracks of studying can be offered, founded on detours and disorientation?

We thus have to understand these paths of study as being based on interruptions and acts of resistance in which tradition had to play an essential role. Acts of return in the realm of German-Jewish writing, the step back into the worlds of biblical, Talmudic, or Kabbalistic knowledge, the review of liturgical poetry, one is reminded once again of Gershom Scholem's translations and commentaries on the Hebrew lamentations,[11] redefine the idea of the future. Future is understood as a form of being founded on acts of return, which are not alone repetitive, but rather reparative, full of possibilities that were left over, in hidden, belated forms of reality. The future as such is understood in terms of realization of a past that itself never happened. Our terms of study should be related to these tensions, unsolved dialectics of tradition. In asking about the future, we are to enter a path of learning that involves irritations and estrangements. If one follows Franz Rosenzweig's thesis about *Übersetzung*, we are asked to be lost in translation.[12] For this word, *Übersetzung* (translation), implies a journey, the path of a ferry, crossing the river, moving toward the other shore of language.

In other words, German-Jewish studies offer us the best teachers, thinkers, and writers to accompany us on a long path of learning. Due to their experiences of wandering, migration, and being in exile, due to their experiences of assimilation, conversion, and return, due to their understanding of writing and its impossibilities, due to their enterprises of translation, due to their own misinterpretations of tradition, German-Jewish authors teach us how to walk and how to learn properly. Yet, this also involves an experience of a lost way—paths that are hard and broken.

NONBELONGING AND SELF-ALIENATION

The Jewish experience of writing in German, as it was expressed in Kafka's letter of June 1921, was not only an experience of impossibilities, acknowledging the failures of Jewish authors who found no new ground in being, while they had already lost their holding in the world of their fathers, but also became a cause for deformation and radical estrangement of the literary tradition itself. The impossibility for the Jewish author of expressing him/herself in German except in broken, deformed, foreign forms, in misinterpretations of the canonical trends, and in speech acts of self-estrangement, namely in *Mauscheln,* to quote Kafka, also became a basis for critical reflection of literature.[13] One reads and relates Kafka's impossibilities of writing as evidence for the radical possibility of the literary project, namely as evidence for the experience of literature as a foreign word: every act of literature, according to this, should be understood as being based on radical self-estrangement, as an expression of being different. What the Jewish author was doomed to experience, according to Kafka, was a groundless being (*Ab-Grund*), nonbelonging, self-alienation, becoming a ground for a reflective event in the realm of writing, which signifies a critical dimension in the history and theory of European literature.

Kafka's self-ironic comments on the German-Jewish dialect, the *Mauscheln* (this, in his view, was echoed in the literary work of the author and critic Karl Kraus), cannot be understood properly without the autobiographical context of his letter in which Kafka, a Jewish author, refers again, not without irony, to the ongoing debate around

Kraus's writings. However, another, perhaps no less significant context of Kafka's letter lies in his reference to the future of Western Jewish being in relation to its lost and denied Eastern affinities. For Jews, according to this thought, are still doomed to write in German as newcomers, who throughout their long path of conversion and adaption still preserved their (so-called original) Oriental background. When Kafka defines the core of Kraus's work and with that the main character of German-Jewish authorship as *Mauscheln*, namely as a deformed, creaturely (mouse-like) language, he also attests to a Semitic remnant, a minor yet significant difference in German language—a vocal Jewish (Yiddish-like) interruption, becoming, however, a burden for Western Jewish life and letters. Jewish writing in German signifies the unconcealed corpus of European Judaism. What the German-Jewish author suffers is this experience of permanent self-estrangement, a cause for the impossibility of writing that expresses, however, a critical, interruptive dimension in European literary and cultural tradition. The German-Jewish author is neither "Western" nor "Eastern," but rather one that suffers the being of in-between, the liminal zone of existence. Its only proper, real language is the *Mauscheln* (a mixed, deformed language—a Jewish dialect). What this language expresses is the failure of transforming the Jewish past into a contemporary experience in its European terms: a civil, secular, progressive being. The future that the Jewish past foreshadows is somewhat regressive, dubious vitality. What future, we ask again, can be or should be imagined, based on such distorted experiences of tradition and unfolding of the past by German-Jewish authors?

WHERE TO?

The German-Jewish experience of writing is defined as an effort of belonging. Its power lies, however, in revealing the impossibility of being, producing countermovements, acts of resistance, estrangement, and critical (self-)reflection. Kafka (again, not without irony) calls this experience *Mauscheln*, the language of a mouse, a Semitic remnant, a creaturely experience of language. It recalls the Eastern, Semitic resources of Judaism frequently embedded in denial in the origins of Western civilization. One can thus argue that the future of German-Jewish literary heritage lies also in the critical unfolding of its associations and affinities, maneuvers, U-turns, and moments of collapse between Western and Eastern traditions.

Let us recall in this context Franz Rosenzweig's comments on the task of translation from Hebrew into German, referring to his own efforts undertaken in the 1920s of translating Yehuda Halevi's liturgical poems. Rosenzweig discusses (in the *Nachwort*) the major challenge of translating this Judeo-Arabic liturgical poetry written in the twelfth century in Al-Andalus (southern, Muslim Spain) into modern German. Yet

Rosenzweig himself tends to reject the Arabic framework and the Islamic background of these Hebrew poems by Halevi, stressing instead parallel Christian liturgical motifs of love and grace. In referring to the task of translation Rosenzweig argues that the efforts of the translator from Hebrew are not *das Fremde einzudeutschen,* namely the Germanification of the foreign elements (Hebrew/Arabic) of the poem, but rather the estrangement of the German language, *das Deutsche umzufremden.*[14] For the foreign spirit of Hebrew should be expressed properly in German, that is, in foreign syntax and with foreign words and rhymes. The consequences of this effort, according to Rosenzweig, is a disintegration of the German language. What the Hebrew words, syntax, and metrics are to bring about in translation is new, strange music to German ears. The liturgical effect of these poems by Halevi, the expression of the messianic dimension (the hope for a radical transformation of being, recalled in the prayers and lamentation for the redemption of Zion), is based, however, on Hebrew-Arabic prosodic elements and mystical conceptions of love and devotion borrowed from Islamic poetry.[15] Rosenzweig does not deny this context (the Judeo-Arabic background) of Halevi's poetry, but does not properly acknowledge its significant role in shaping the Jewish liturgical tradition.

According to Rosenzweig, the translation of the Hebrew poem can save the German language from falling into national closure and open it into worldly, universal circles, as the Lutheran Bible translation did.[16] Yet this effort itself (translating Halevi's poetry as an act of opening the German language), we argue, depends on the unfolding of the past forms of Judeo-Arabic culture, recognizing the contexts and associations in which these liturgical poems were written and sung. What the German-Jewish enterprise of liturgical translation brings about, in its reengagement with the Judeo-Arabic (Hebrew-Arabic) tradition, is a disruption of European language, deconstructing its national, homogeneous structure, reopening it toward a radical experience of the future. This, however, lies hidden (merely hinted at) in Rosenzweig's project. In looking for an orientation, a future horizon, for his community, Rosenzweig seems to be lost in translation between German, Hebrew, and Arabic.

What Kafka calls *Mauscheln,* Rosenzweig defines, in arguing about the essence of translation, the estrangement of German (*das Deutsche umzufremden*). In his turn, the Jewish poet Paul Celan names this phenomenon *Verjudung,* albeit with a different urgency, once dealing with the poetical heritage of witnessing the Holocaust. We recall these lines from his drafts to his *Meridian* (1960):[17]

Verjudung: Es ist das Anderswerden. Zum-anderen-und-dessen-Geheimnis-stehn [...]

Umkehr—dazu scheint es ja nun doch zuviel Einbahnstraßen zu geben. Gegenverkehr und Umkehr, das ist zweierlei aber auch auf den Feldwegen scheint es, ach, wenig Gelegenheit dazu zu geben.[17]

Verjudung, making Jewish (making too Jewish), implies poetical writing that demands deconstruction of the classical syntax of the German poem, its rupture, and finally its collapse. In so doing, the poem attests to a certain historical experience, to concrete, material conditions of being, associated with what is Jewish, namely with deformations, disorders of life, with foreignness and being *other*. This is the way, the path of the poem, the return (*Umkehr*), the movement against (*Gegenverkehr*), which also implies in Celan's poetical work conversation (*Gespräch*), namely the act of language. This act of language, the encounter of *I and Thou,* is founded in resistance (in standing against). The poem turns on this path into an act of witnessing, in which one should also imagine—through the impossibilities of the poem (its radical self estrangement)—an openness, a movement toward the other, attesting, saving his/ her secret. Yet, Celan too was aware that this movement (the opening toward the other) is a movement toward the unknown. The path of the poem is not of return alone, but rather of a road of departure and of loss. The poem signifies nowhere; it gives a desperate sign for where to?

What we call the "future" bears tensions of this kind: it depends upon the unfolding of tradition, the reinterpretation of past forms, which produce a vortex, a whirlpool of names and words, places, being and time. The engagement of the German-Jewish literary tradition implies endless attempts of reorientation and disorientation, keeping the dynamic, critical experience of world-being, engaging also false attempts to return. Reading Celan today takes us *anderswo,* to other places and displaces, the exile of others. Is it still possible to read Paul Celan today without the poetry of the Palestinian author Mahmoud Darwish? The future of German-Jewish past forms, the projection of its writing of Exile, its literature of migration, its poetics of memory and witnessing should be understood as another impossible introduction for reading Palestinian poetry, engaging its own where to?

HINENI, HERE I AM

I began by asking the question concerning the future of German-Jewish studies. When asking about the learning of the literatures of Jews in the realm of German letters, one demands a review, an act of witnessing. It provides us with insights, yet it also involves spots of blindness, recollections of absence, disorientations, through which one might search for the path toward him/herself. German-Jewish tradition tells us how to read, yet differently, not without irony and acts of self-estrangement. Once we return to ask the question regarding this tradition, we recall the experience of migration, of exile, an experience of dissimilation, dislocation, self-forgetfulness, and collective amnesia, and the experience of a long journey and of no return.

Not in vain, Erich Auerbach, in the opening chapter of his seminal book *Mimesis*, tells the story of Abraham alongside the Greek poem on the return home of Odysseus, on his way to the mountain Moriah.[18] What we call "literary study" recalls these paths too, these travels, which involves inversions and transformations, moments of danger, experience of loss, and paths without return.[19] In telling about Abraham's experience, Auerbach quotes the Hebrew word *Hineni* (הנני), the word of Abraham, replying to the call of God. What the Hebrew word causes, however, in Auerbach's own book, written in Istanbul in the 1940s, namely in the years of war and destruction, on the borders of Western and Eastern cultures, is indeed an echo of a foreign word, which calls both presence and denial, being-here (Da-Sein) and omission. One should listen to this Abrahamic word in Hebrew, *Hineni*, here I am, a word that the Midrash also reads as an act of resistance, an act of absence, as saying *Eineni*, Here I am not. This word thus implies a *Gegenwort*, a word that stands against and yet stands for—the unknown.

If we are to take properly the task of rethinking the future of German-Jewish studies, we have thus to recall these acts of interruption in which the Hebrew word returns in the German language, committed and responsive, yet resisting, denying, saying *Here I am/Here I am not*.[20] We have to recall the implications of these impossible words, which are symptomatic of a certain experience and expression of being Jewish, yet become an echo of a strange dialogue that attests to the possibility of unfolding tradition into a conversation that is perhaps the hardest and longest of all.

NOTES

1. On the implications of "a step back" as an interruption in the history of Western metaphysics compare Martin Heidegger, "Der Satz der Identität," *Identität und Differenz* (Pfullingen: Verlag Günther Neska, 1986), 9–30.
2. Entering the field of tradition, realms of past forms, implies, however, creative gestures, playful and ironic maneuvers. Compare Theodor Adorno, *Ästhetische Theorie* (Frankfurt am Main: Suhrkamp Verlag, 1998), 45–48, 67–68. See also Jacques Derrida, "Structure, Sign, and Play in the Discourse of the Human Sciences," *Writing and Difference* (Chicago: Chicago University Press, 1978).
3. Kurt Pinthus, ed., *Die Menschheitsdämmerung, ein Dokument des Expressionismus* (Hamburg: Rowohlt, 1959).
4. Else Lasker-Schüler, *Gesammelte Werke*, vol. 2 (Frankfurt am Main: Suhrkamp Verlag, 1998).
5. Franz Kafka, *Briefe 1902–1924* (Frankfurt am Main: Fischer Tachenbuch Verlag, 1995), 334–338.
6. Kafka, *Briefe 1902–1924*, 337–338.

7. Paul Celan, "Der Meridian," *Der Meridian und andere Prosa* (Frankfurt am Main: Suhrkamp, 1988).

8. Benjamin develops the notion of "dialectic in standstill" as part of a discussion on the dramaturgical function of the gesture in epic theater. See Walter Benjamin, "Was ist das epische Theater? (I)," *Versuche über Brecht. Texte, Briefzeugnisse, Aufzeichnungen* (Frankfurt am Main: Suhrkamp Verlag, 1981), 19; Benjamin, "Geschichtsphilosophische Thesen," in idem., *Zur Kritik der Gewalt und andere Aufsätze* (Frankfurt am Main: Suhrkamp Verlag, 1995), 92.

9. Babylonian Talmud, Sanhedrin, 98a.

10. Compare with Gershom Scholem's remarks on the concept of return and correction: Gershom Scholem, "Über Jona und den Begriff der Gerechtigkeit," *Tagebücher* vol. II: *1917–1923* (Frankfurt am Main: Jüdischer Verlag, 2000), 522–532.

11. Scholem, "Über die Klage und das Klagelied," *Tagebücher*, 128–133.

12. Franz Rosenzweig, "Nachwort," *Jehuda Halevi, Zweiundneunzig Hymen und Gedichte* (Berlin: Verlag Lambert Schneider, 1927).

13. Kafka, *Briefe 1902–1924*, 336.

14. Rosenzweig, "Nachwort," 154.

15. On Halevi's associations with the Arabic philosophical and poetic tradition see David Yalin, "The Influence and Affinity of the Arabic Poetry to the Hebrew Poetry in Andalusia," in *Studies in Medieval Hebrew Poetry*, ed. Yonah David (Tel Aviv: Tel Aviv University Press, 1975); Joseph Yahalom, *Judah Halevi: A Life of Poetry* (Jerusalem: Magnes Press, 2008).

16. Rosenzweig, "Nachwort," 157.

17. Celan, "Der Meridian," 131.

18. Erich Auerbach, *Mimesis, Dargestellte Wirklichkeit in der abendländischen Literatur* (Bern: Francke Verlag, 2001), 3–23.

19. On Abraham's movement without return compare Levinas's remark, who reads Abraham's story as opposed to the Greek epic, in which Odysseus's return home from his travels embodies, in Levinas's view, the structure of Western philosophy—the myth of return. Philosophy is based on the "autonomy of consciousness," Levinas writes, "which finds itself again in all its adventures, returning home to itself like Ulysses, who through all his peregrinations is only on the way to his native island." Emmanuel Levinas, "The Trace of the Other," in *Deconstruction in Context*, ed. Mark C. Taylor (Chicago: Chicago University Press, 1986), 346. On the interruptive dimension of the Abrahamic gesture compare also his remarks "against" Kierkegaard; see Levinas, "A Propos of Kierkegaard vivant," *Proper Names*, trans. Michael B. Smith (Stanford: Stanford University Press, 1996, 76–77).

20. On the poetical implications of denial based on the Abrahamic acts of language compare Jacques Derrida, "Whom to Give To," *The Gift of Death and Literature in Secret*, trans. David Wills (Chicago: Chicago University Press, 2008), 56–59, 79–81.

"NOCH IST UNSERE HOFFNUNG NICHT DAHIN!"

Fritz Pinkuss's View on Germans, Jews, and the Universal Value of the German-Jewish Past

BJÖRN SIEGEL

O N JANUARY 17, 1989, Fritz Pinkuss, chief rabbi of the Congregação Israelita Paulista (CIP, São Paulo), gave a speech to his Brazilian-Jewish congregation in which he summarized his experiences during his recent visit to Germany. He had returned to his former hometown of Heidelberg in 1988 and participated in the central memorial service commemorating the *Reichspogromnacht* of November 1938. During his stay he came to the conclusion that: "everything which had been erected there— synagogues, community centres, memorial sites—is built on sand. . . . The great German Jewry, its culture and lifestyle, are gone forever."[1] His words echoed Leo Baeck's view that the epoch of German Jewry had come to an end as a result of National Socialism and the Holocaust—a view that Baeck had formulated shortly after the Second World War.[2]

Despite the negative tone of his conclusion, Pinkuss also emphasized the importance of reconciliation and commemoration. In 1988, on the occasion of the memorial service at the Heiliggeistkirche, one of the central Protestant churches of Heidelberg, he publicly lobbied for reconciliation between Germans and Jews and supported a new dialogue with the German *Volk* and especially with German youth.[3] Shortly before the crucial year of 1989, Pinkuss's visit to Heidelberg demonstrates how he, like many other German-Jewish émigrés, came to terms with the past. While a future for Jewish life in Germany remained an unrealistic option, he sought to open a dialogue with a younger generation of Germans for whom German Jews were a nostalgic relic of the past. Pinkuss could not envisage how things would change after German reunification and with a new wave of Jewish immigration to the Federal Republic as a result of the dissolution of the Soviet Union.[4] However, he was convinced that the German-Jewish past held a universal value, which had to be uncovered and used in the present.

A GERMAN PAST AND
A BRAZILIAN PRESENT

A couple of weeks after his remarks in 1989, Pinkuss inaugurated a Postgraduate Studies Programme in Hebrew language and Jewish literature at the University of São Paulo (USP). For several decades previously he had worked as an independent scholar, giving lectures and teaching Jewish studies in Brazilian universities. His lecture on the occasion of the opening of the program in 1989 reflected on the cultural heritage that he brought with him from Germany. By raising the question, "What is *Wissenschaft des Judentums*?" he offered an overview of German-Jewish history in the eighteenth and nineteenth centuries, discussing the multifaceted encounter between German Jews and modernity.[5] His reflections on Leopold Zunz, Abraham Geiger, and others demonstrated the ongoing influence of his pre-1933 education in Germany on his life and identity in his new home country, Brazil.[6]

Pinkuss, who was born on May 13, 1905, lived his first years in Egeln, a small provincial town close to Magdeburg, where he began an apprenticeship at the local branch of the Deutsche Bank.[7] In 1925 he registered at the Theological Seminary in Breslau and simultaneously at the University of Breslau (today Wrocław, Poland) and studied philosophy, pedagogy, psychology, and Oriental languages. Toward the end of the 1920s Pinkuss moved to Berlin to finish his studies and religious training at the Hochschule für die Wissenschaft des Judentums in Berlin. There, he got to know some of the prominent German-Jewish intellectuals of the time including Leo Baeck, "the leader of European Jewry" as he called him later, and also Ismar Ellbogen (history), Chanoch Albeck (Talmudic studies), Julius Guttmann (philosophy), and Harry Torcziner (Naftali Herz Tur-Sinai; philology).[8] In hindsight, Pinkuss declared the time in Berlin was the influential phase of his life, in which he studied with the "most excellent personalities of contemporary academic Jewry."[9] Thus, it is not surprising that almost fifty years later, Pinkuss chose the topic of *Wissenschaft des Judentums* and the long tradition of Jewish academic learning in Germany pre-1933 in order to reconnect with his academic career and the newly established Jewish Studies Programme at USP. He saw the new program as an important venture offering Jews and non-Jews and, in particular, young people a platform for discussions and debates. Already with his first appointment as rabbi of the Jewish community in Heidelberg in 1930, Pinkuss sought to combine academic research with an educational program that was also set to support Jewish education and strengthen Jewish and non-Jewish relations.[10] Over fifty years later he continued his efforts in the Brazilian setting, which demonstrates Pinkuss's inner connection to his German past despite his experiences of oppression and persecution.

After the first boycott of Jewish stores and companies on April 1, 1933, he realized that Jewish life in Nazi Germany was in danger and stated: "We don't know what will be rescued of German Jewry, perhaps we are the liquidators of it."[11] It took three more years for Pinkuss to decide to follow his brother Kurt and emigrate with his wife (Lotte Selma, née Sternfels) and his newly born son, Michael, to Brazil. In contrast with the pamphlet entitled *Brasilien als Aufnahmeland* (Brazil as a receiving country), which was published by the Hilfsverein der deutschen Juden in 1936, praising the good climate and the developing economy of Brazil, Pinkuss was well aware of the harsh living conditions and problematic political circumstances in the South American country.[12] He was also mindful of the Brazilian immigration laws, which had introduced a strict quota system similar to the one in the United States.[13] However, thanks to family connections with Brazil and the support of the Hon. Lily Montagu, an influential founder of Liberal Judaism in Great Britain and the World Union of Progressive Judaism, as well as the support of the Joint Distribution Committee (JDC, United States), Pinkuss's emigration was made possible.[14] On September 22, 1936, Pinkuss, his wife, son, and mother—his father had already died—arrived in São Paulo.

Despite a long tradition of Jewish immigration to Brazil, the Jewish communities had remained small: before 1933 approximately 40,000 Jews lived in Brazil, of whom 15,000 to 20,000 were residing in São Paulo.[15] Many were descendants of Jewish immigrants who had come from Eastern Europe before 1930 and had chosen Brazil due to its economic prospects as well as to avoid the increasing restrictions of other countries, for example the United States, Argentina, or Canada.[16] While Brazil welcomed experts from Germany and Europe in order to improve its educational system, modernize its economy, and enhance its industry, it was highly critical of non-Christian, and particularly of Jewish migrants.[17] After the establishment of the Estado Novo, the "new state," by the authoritarian and nationalistic government under Gétulio Vargas in 1937, the fear of "destructive, poor and undesirable elements" gained momentum, giving way to a wave of xenophobia in Brazil.[18] The Vargas regime followed the political paths of Germany, Italy, and Oliveira Salazar's corporative dictatorship in Portugal. Political parties were forbidden, the parliament dissolved, and political power centralized.[19] Gustavo Barroso, a leading mentor of the Integralist movement, a movement closely connected to Italian Fascism, even published an antisemitic book, *The Paulista Synagogue* (A sinagoga paulista, 1937): this attacked the alleged influence of Jews in São Paulo and propagated antisemitic sentiments in the city, which Pinkuss and his family had just chosen as their safe haven.[20]

Against this background Pinkuss aimed at strengthening the German-Jewish émigré community and worked for its integration into Brazilian society. The financial support of the JDC proved instrumental, enabling leading figures of the German-Jewish émigré circles, such as Luiz and Luisa Lorch, Hans and Charlotte Hamburger, and others to establish a German-Jewish community in São Paulo.[21] Pinkuss endorsed this effort and, in his memoirs, he called the foundation of the Congregação Israelita Paulista

(CIP) "one of the answers of Judaism to the challenges of destruction and barbari-ty."[22] In 1961, he stated that the characteristics of the CIP were based on European, specifically German, community traditions, calling, as a matter of duty, "to remem-ber what we originally formed."[23] Moreover, he stressed that Liberal Judaism could survive in Brazil only if its preserved traditions and practices were adjusted to the challenges of the present. For Pinkuss, the German-Jewish past was not something static but a tradition that needed to be preserved in its flexibility. He understood this legacy as the cornerstone of a vibrant Judaism, which continued to develop over time and place. In his view, change was not an adversary of traditional values and norms but a way of preserving and integrating the past into the present.[24] Consequently, under the leadership of Pinkuss, the CIP embraced several ideas that originated in pre-1933 Germany. The community was established as a *kehila* and an *Einheitsgemeinde* open to Orthodox, Conservative, and Reform groups. It offered youth and adult educa-tion programs; published a newspaper, the *Crônica Israelita*; and modernized the rites, incorporating many German-Jewish musical and liturgical elements into the service.[25] In addition, Pinkuss was a living embodiment of the German-Jewish ideal of a rabbi and scholar; thus, he was an ardent advocate of communal education and in his schol-arship he sought to advance knowledge.[26] He not only transferred ideas on community and education to the Brazilian setting but also helped people to emigrate from Nazi Germany. At the end of 1938, Pinkuss held special services to mourn the destruction of Jewish synagogues in Germany during *Reichspogromnacht*.[27] He commemorated "the victims of this modern barbarity,"[28] but more importantly he also helped others to escape, such as Heinrich Lemle, who emigrated via Brighton/Hove to Brazil, eventu-ally becoming chief rabbi of the Associação Israelita Religiosa (ARI) in Rio de Janeiro and a lifelong friend and partner in re-creating Jewish life in Brazil.[29]

PINKUSS'S MISSION AND
MODERN GERMANY

Pinkuss's attachment to Brazil notwithstanding, he continued to be highly involved with his former home country and early on he lobbied for new German-Jewish rela-tions. In 1962 he visited Germany, stating that the aim of the visit was to overcome the recent past. In 1972 Pinkuss received the Großes Verdienstkreuz, one of the high-est honors of the Federal Republic of Germany, for his lifelong struggle to reconnect past and present.[30] He also participated in several official events during the 1979 visit of the German chancellor, Helmut Schmidt, to Brazil and, in doing so, he became an important and well-connected informal ambassador of German-Jewish relations in South America.[31] Pinkuss's visit to Heidelberg in 1988, more than fifty years after his emigration, can be seen as another attempt to fuse past and present and promote knowledge and education. However, in contrast to his efforts in Brazil, his intentions in Germany were different. During his speech at the Heiliggeistkirche in Heidelberg in 1988, he described the events that took place fifty years previously as an unsolved trauma for Germans and Jews alike. He emphasized the importance of remembering the dehumanization of Jews by German society and their exclusion and extermination based on racial and antisemitic Nazi ideology. While he clearly criticized the long-lasting influence of religious antisemitic stereotypes dating back to Martin Luther, he specifically condemned the inhumanity and indifference of German society during the Nazi regime and praised several prominent figures who had raised their voices against the Nazi state and its ideology.[32] Pinkuss expressly honored Hermann Maas, pastor of the Heiliggeistkirche in Heidelberg, an early proponent of Christian-Jewish dialogue, as a guiding example for a new Germany.[33] Based on these experiences, Pinkuss clearly opted for a new beginning and a new future, one that was not guided by guilt, but by responsibility and solidarity. He joined Monsignor Beil, a Catholic pastor and eyewitness of *Kristallnacht*, who also spoke at the 1988 memorial service, in a call to German society to deal with its Nazi past.[34] Pinkuss went so far as to argue that the Holocaust should not only be understood as a crime against Jews but as a crime against humanity. In using the slogan "Every human represents humanity," he labeled the barbarity of the Nazi regime as an attack against the human race and challenged every individual, in this case every non-Jewish German, to take responsibility and fight modern antisemitism and fascism. According to Pinkuss, the non-Jewish German should acknowledge the importance of the past for the present and future. Still more importantly, Pinkuss felt that he or she should not divide German and Jewish history, but see it as one—as their history.

THE PERSONAL AND THE HISTORICAL

Pinkuss's life exemplifies the importance of biographical study for a deeper understanding of the German-Jewish experience. Such a biographical approach involves a closer look into the life stories of individuals and the variety of ways in which they coped with the challenges that the German-Jewish past presented to them. An important part of this story is the influence of German-Jewish émigrés on the recovering German society after 1945.[35] This goes beyond the so-called "émigré synthesis," a concept introduced by David Sorkin in his outline for the future of German-Jewish studies from the year 2000.[36] What I am referring to is the multilayered influence of émigrés in their new and former countries, and their role as backward-facing prophets.[37] In contrast to the focus on early modern German-Jewish history, which scholars such as Stefi Jersch-Wenzel and Robert Liberles had in mind, biographical studies in modern and contemporary history offer the possibility of making German-Jewish history more visible and accessible to Jewish and non-Jewish audiences, especially due to the ongoing relevance of questions concerning xenophobia, antisemitism, migration, and refugees.[38] In using individual histories, the role of émigrés can be illustrated and the mutual interactions and influences between Jewish communities and societies all over the world visualized.[39] Such a global approach, which not only focuses on the United States, but also takes into account other countries of immigration, such as those in Latin America, Asia, and Africa, could deepen our understanding of the international legacy of German Jewry.

At the same time, a biographical approach strengthens Christopher Browning's call for more detailed and systematic "aftermath studies," which can illustrate "the reverberations and repercussions of the Holocaust in post–World War II society, and especially the politicisation, memorialisation, representation and shaping of collective memory of the Holocaust."[40] Biographical studies offer an opportunity to deal with questions of class, gender, and power structures within the local and global context. And finally, a biographical approach to the German-Jewish past can be used to challenge the prevailing narrative that depicts 1933–1945 as the end of German Jewry. Looking at individual life stories of German Jews can illustrate the complexities but also the continuity of German-Jewish history. It can also add important voices to German-Jewish history after the Shoah—the voices of émigrés. Their lives offer a new perspective on the legacy of German Jews and its challenging, but important, ongoing influence on German society after the Holocaust.[41] In studying the lives of émigrés, scholars can offer a "bridge" between past and present for the German public and the newly flourishing Jewish communities in post 1989-Germany, beyond romanticization and nostalgia for Jewish life in pre-1933 Germany. In times of rising xenophobia, new nationalistic sentiments, and emotional discussions on migration and refugees, as well as a newly declared "Jewish renaissance" in Germany, Pinkuss's universal mandate of reconciliation and commemoration (but also solidarity and respect) seems more relevant than ever in today's world.

NOTES

1. Fritz Pinkuss, *Lernen, lehren, helfen: Sechs Jahrzehnte als Rabbiner auf zwei Kontinenten,* trans. Jutta Bretthauer (Heidelberg: Heidelberger Verlagsanstalt, 1990), 184.

2. Anonymous, "Gespräch mit Leo Baeck," *Aufbau* (December 21, 1945): 1–2.

3. Private Archive of Anita and Michael Pinkuss/São Paulo, Brazil: Fritz Pinkuss, *Speech of F. Pinkuss at the Heiliggeistkirche during the Ecumenical Service and Memorial Service Commemorating 50 Years of Reichspogromnacht in Heidelberg* (audio), Heidelberg 9.9.1988.

4. For a general discussion of the newly developing Jewish life in Germany post-1945, Michael Brenner, "Ein neues deutsches Judentum?" in idem., ed., *Geschichte der Juden in Deutschland: Von 1945 bis zur Gegenwart* (Munich: C. H. Beck, 2012), 419–434.

5. Pinkuss, *Lernen, Lehren, Helfen*, 156–166.

6. Ibid., 159–160.

7. Archive of the Jewish Museum Berlin [henceforth A-JMB], K 434 2005/50/6 Lebenslauf: masch., Heidelberg, 3.2.1936; 2x. [Handschuhsheimer Landstrasse 8], 1.

8. A-JMB K 434 2009/25/7 Rabbinats-Zeugnis: Hochschule für die Wissenschaft des Judentums, unterschrieben vom Lehrerkollegium Herry Torczyner, Leo Baeck, Julius Guttmann, Albeck, Ismar Elbogen, hs., Berlin, 2.7.1931, 1–3.

9. Pinkuss, *Lernen, Lehren, Helfen*, 24.

10. Anonymous, "Jüdische Chronik—Deutschland: Heidelberg," *Gemeindeblatt der Israelitischen Gemeinde Frankfurt am Main*, 7 (March 1932): 158. More broadly on Jewish life in Heidelberg during the NS regime, see Frank Moraw, "Die nationalsozialistische Diktatur (1933–1945)," in *Geschichte der Juden in Heidelberg*, ed. Peter Blum (Heidelberg: Verlag Brigitte Guderjahn, 1996), 440–555, here 452–454.

11. Fritz Pinkuss, *O Caminho de uma Geração* (1933/1966) (São Paulo: Fundação Fritz Pinkuss/Congregação Israelita Paulista, 1966), 23–24.

12. Maria Luiza Tucci Carneiro, "Brasil, um refúgio nos trópicos/Brasilien, Fluchtpunkt in den Tropen," in *Brasil, um refúgio nos trópicos: A trajetória dos refugiados do Nazi-Fascismo/Brasilien, Fluchtpunkt in den Tropen: Lebenswege der Flüchtlinge des Nazi-Faschismus*, ed. Maria Luiza Tucci Carneiro, trans. Dieter Straus and Angel Bojadsen (São Paulo: Estação Liberdade, 1996), 33–229, here 93.

13. Klaus Wilhelm Lege/Câmaras de Comércio e Indústria Brasil-Alemanha, *A História Alemã do Brasil: Die deutsche Geschichte Brasiliens* (São Paulo: Publicação da Câmera Brail-Alemanha, 2001), 89.

14. Walter Homolka, "Tradition und Erneuerung: Die Reformbewegung und ihre Dynamik als größte religiöse Strömung des Judentums," *Compass-Infodienst für christlich-jüdische und deutsch-israelische Tagesthemen im Web Online-Extra* 60 (2007), 1–9, here 6.

15. Carneiro, "Brasil, um refúgio nos trópicos/Brasilien, Fluchtpunkt in den Tropen," 140.

16. According to Jeffrey Lesser 32,521 Jews entered Brazil between 1925 and 1935, and 45 percent came from Poland. Jeffrey Lesser, "The Immigration and Integration of Polish Jews in Brazil, 1924–1934," *The Americas* 51, no. 2 (1994): 173–191, here 175–176; see also Robert Levine, "Brazil's Jews during the Vargas Era and After," *Luso-Brazilian Review* 5, no. 1 (1968): 45–58, here 47–48.

17. For the Brazilian immigration policy, see Rochelle G. Saidel and Guilherme Ary Plonski, "Shaping Modern Science and Technology in Brazil: The Contribution of Refugees from National Socialism after 1933," *Leo Baeck Institute Yearbook* 39 (1994): 257–270.

18. For more details, see Jeffrey Lesser, "Immigration and Shifting Concepts of National Identity in Brazil during the Vargas Era," *Luso-Brazilian Review* 31, no. 2 (1994): 23–44; Avraham Milgram, "The Jews of Europe from the Perspective of the Brazilian Foreign Service, 1933–1941," *Holocaust and Genocide Studies* 9, no. 1 (1995): 94–120.

19. See Marlen Eckl, ed., "... *auf brasilianischem Boden fand ich eine neue Heimat*": *Autobiographische Texte deutscher Flüchtlinge des Nationalsozialismus 1933–1945* (Remscheid: Gardez Verlag, 2005), 15–18.

20. Levine, "Brazil's Jews during the Vargas Era and After," 51.

21. For the role of the Joint, see Carneiro, "Brasil, um refúgio nos trópicos/Brasilien, Fluchtpunkt in den Tropen," 98. For the foundation of a German-Jewish community, see Charlotte Hamburger, "Wir lebten in zwei verschiedenen Welten," in "... *auf brasilianischem Boden fand ich eine neue Heimat*": *Autobiographische Texte deutscher Flüchtlinge des Nationalsozialismus 1933–1945*, ed. Marlen Eckl (Remscheid: Gardez Verlag, 2005), 334–354, here 345–347.

22. Pinkuss, *Lernen, Lehren, Helfen*, 14.

23. ["Wir sind hervorgegangen aus dem deutsch-sprachigen Judentum: Es ist Pflicht der Pietät, dessen zu gedenken, was uns ursprünglich geformt hatte."] Archivo Historico Judaico Brasileiro, São Paulo [henceforth AHJB-SP], FP 0012 Rabino Fritz Pinkus Caixa 1, Predicás; Sermon "Neue Wege: Zur Ideologie des Fortschrittlichen Religiösen Judentums in Südamerika—Aus Anlass des 25 jaehr. Bestehens der C.I.P.," São Paulo, 1961, 1.

24. Pinkuss, *Lernen, Lehren, Helfen*, 178–180.

25. Such a focus on German-Jewish traditions and practices also led to conflicts; see Jeffrey H. Lesser, "Continuity and Change within an Immigrant Community: The Jews of São Paulo, 1924–1945," *Luso-Brazilian Review* 25, no. 2 (1988): 45–58.

26. For his efforts in both these fields he was awarded an honorary doctorate degree by Hebrew Union College (1960) and the title of Honorary Fellow of the Hebrew University of Jerusalem (1980).

27. Pinkuss, *O Caminho de uma Geração*, 65–66.

28. ["em memória dessas vítimas do barbarismo moderno"] Pinkuss, *O Caminho de uma Geração*, 69.

29. For Lemle's emigration to Brazil, see Astrid Zajdband, *German Rabbis in British Exile: From 'Heimat' into the Unknown* (Boston: De Gruyter, 2016), 77–78.

30. AHJB-SP, FP 0012 Rabino Fritz Pinkus Caixa 1, Documentos Pessoais: Verleihungsurkunde für das Große Verdienstkreuz an Prof. Dr. Fritz Pinkuss, Bonn 7.11.1972, 1.

31. In 1979 Helmut Schmidt was invited by the military regime of Brazil under President Joao Baptista de Oliveira Figueiredo. On April 3–12, 1979 he visited Brasilia, São Paulo and other cities. Johannes Marbach and Frank Josef Nober, *Helmut Schmidt: Bibliographie 1947–2008* (Wiesbaden: Harrassowitz Verlag, 2008), 173.

32. Private Archive of Anita and Michael Pinkuss São Paulo, Brazil: Fritz Pinkuss, *Speech of F. Pinkuss at the Heiliggeistkirche during the ecomenical service and memorial service commemorating 50 years of Reichspogromnacht in Heidelberg* (audio), Heidelberg 9.9.1988.

33. Pinkuss had even asked Maas to take care of the remaining Jews in Heidelberg, just before he immigrated to Brazil. In 1964 the Israeli Holocaust memorial museum Yad Vashem decided to honored Hermann Maas as Righteous among the Nations for his efforts to save Jews. Albrecht Lohrbächer, Helmut Rupper, and Ingrid Schmidt, eds., *Was Christen vom Judentum lernen können: Anstöße, Materialien, Entwürfe* (Stuttgart: Kohlhammer, 2006), 21–24. See also http://www.yadvashem.org/righteous/stories/maas.html (accessed July 13, 2018).

34. Monsignor Beil, *Speech of Monsignor*, Heidelberg 9.9.1988.

35. Michael M. Meyer, "Future Research: The Study of Judaism in Modern Germany Some Desiderata," *Leo Baeck Institute Year Book* 45 (2000): 218–219; Michael Brenner, "The Future of German-Jewish Studies: From German Jews to the German Jew," *Leo Baeck Institute Year Book* 54 (2009): 14–16.

36. David Sorkin, "Future Research: Beyond the *Émigré* Synthesis," *Leo Baeck Institute Year Book* 45 (2000): 210.

37. Already Michael Brenner had demonstrated that modern Jewish historians have interpreted and used Jewish history in their fight for ideological and political objectives. The Jewish past thereby often emerged as a powerful weapon in their struggles and a reservoir of legitimacy. Also, émigrés gained the status of prophets of the past. See Michael Brenner, *Prophets of the Past: Interpreters of Jewish History* (Princeton: Princeton University Press, 2010).

38. For Jersch-Wenzel and Liberles, see Stefi Jersch-Wenzel, "Future Research: Future Yearbook Research Publications," *Leo Baeck Institute Year Book* 45 (2000): 210–211; Robert Liberles, "Future Research: Symposium Contribution for the Leo Baeck Institute Year Book," *Leo Baeck Institute Year Book* 45 (2000): 212–214. The Leo Baeck Institute and its attempt to write a *Gesamtgeschichte* of German Jewry also combined early modern and modern history until 1945; see Michael M. Meyer and Michael Brenner, *Deutsch-Jüdische Geschichte in der Neuzeit*, Vol. I–IV (Munich: Verlag C. H. Beck, 1996).

39. Guy Stern, "Future Research: Exile Studies and Exile Literature," *Leo Baeck Institute Year Book* 45 (2000): 227; Avraham Barkai, "Future Research: Saturation or New Venues?" *Leo Baeck Institute Year Book* 45 (2000): 207–209.

40. Christopher R. Browning, "Future Research: Future Directions in Holocaust Studies," *Leo Baeck Institute Year Book* 45 (2000): 220–222. For more detailed studies see Julie Mell and Malachi Hacohen, eds., *Central European Jewish Émigrés and the Shaping of Postwar Culture: Studies in Memory of Lilian Furst, 1931–2009* (Basel: MDPI, 2014).

41. Steven Aschheim, *Beyond the Border: The German-Jewish Legacy Abroad* (Princeton: Princeton University Press, 2007), 1–6.

German-Jewishness
and Difference

ON THE POSSIBILITIES AND IMPOSSIBILITIES OF BEING JEWISH IN POSTWAR GERMANY

SANDRA ANUSIEWICZ-BAER

HALAKHAH—THE JEWISH WALK OF LIFE—is probably one of the most distinguishing features of Judaism. It is a feature that connects the past with the present and the future. Like other legal systems, it is precedent-based and future oriented at the same time.[1] From the first revelation of laws at Mount Sinai that constituted the Jewish people to the formation of Rabbinic Judaism and the compilation of the masterpieces of legal Jewish literature until today, Halakhah, or rather the discussion about it, has been unquestionably a guiding force to define Judaism. Halakhic rulings are debates about the future of Jewish life. This is true for the early decisions of the *Zugot* and *Tannaim* (the first rabbis to define the law), for the *Amoraim* and *Geonim* who developed and expanded Talmudic law, as well as for the medieval rabbis who advanced the halakhic system further (like prominent commentators such as Rashi or the Rambam—Rabbi Moses ben Maimon, also called Maimonides), and also for the decisions of such religious ruling bodies as the Committee on Jewish Law and Standards (CJLS).[2]

Today, however, especially outside Israel, Halakhah has no day-to-day or practical relevance for most Jews. Laws are enforced by civil courts and decisions as to what to eat and when to rest are strictly personal. "Thus, Halakha as a legal system that was all-encompassing within a closed Jewish world has become limited in its scope and virtually without sanctions."[3]

Yet, there is one area where Halakhah is of importance and claims relevance: in the definition of Jewish status. In present-day Germany, Halakhah can also become a decisive factor in the rejection of a person's Jewishness, regardless of the person's own conception of his or her status, subsequently leading to a clash between the notion of "identity" and "status." This clash painstakingly reminds us of German-Jewish history and the rift that developed between the different denominations in Judaism originating in nineteenth-century Germany.[4]

HISTORICAL DEVELOPMENTS AND THEIR REPERCUSSIONS FOR JEWISH IDENTITY

A three-step transformation was triggered in the late eighteenth century and continued throughout the nineteenth century. With the Haskalah, the Jewish Enlightenment movement, questions were raised about "personal autonomy, the theological origins of Jewish law and the authority of the Jewish community."[5] Following this intellectual earthquake and the process of political emancipation, Jews in Germany started to enjoy equal rights as citizens and integrated themselves increasingly into secular society. This resulted in greater freedom for the individual and less power for the Jewish community over its members, which also meant that the rabbis' influence over their constituencies was weakened. Questions of Jewish status were transformed into questions about identity. Identity is a mixture of self-identification and acknowledgment by others, a play of actions and reactions, of revealing and hiding. One could be regarded as a Jew by one group and denied that acknowledgment by another.

All these questions of status and identity became complicated further in the course of history and taken to an extreme by the National Socialists and their racist definition of who was a Jew. The German scholar Barbara Steiner writes about the difficult legacy of the Nazi past: "The years during which racial origin ideas became intertwined with religious affiliation, forming the basis for the systematic persecution of Jews, created an uncertainty around the German-Jewish identity after 1945."[6] The aftermaths are more than palpable today and demonstrate how the German-Jewish past has a tight grip on the future of Jews in Germany.

The Shoah left the European continent depleted of Jews. In many countries, the Jewish population had diminished by 90 percent. In Germany, where displaced persons poured into the zones of the Western Allies, numbers grew shortly after the war to almost 250,000—half its prewar size. But the overwhelming number of these survivors were quick to leave "the bloodstained soil" for Israel or the United States. Those left behind were isolated by world Jewry, as shown by the discussion led in 1948 by the World Jewish Congress about Jews residing permanently in Germany.[7] In its Declaration of Montreux, the congress put "a moral stigma on those Jews who, despite the warning, remained on the 'bloodstained territory.'" Chaim Yachil (Hoffmann), the first Israeli consul in Munich, declared in 1948: "All Jews must leave Germany." He regarded those who stayed "a source of danger for the entire Jewish people."[8] Hence, a unique Jewish community developed in the sealed lands of West Germany (in the East there were even fewer Jews left; official numbers cite approximately 370 members in the late 1980s in the GDR[9]). The survivors stayed away from the gentiles and sought company mainly among fellow survivors and refugees, Jews who had shared similar traumatic experiences. Outside these circles, Germany was regarded as enemy territory and contact with Germans was limited to the bare minimum. At the same time, because so few Jews remained, relationships between Jews and non-Jews were inevitable. "More than two-thirds of the members of the Berlin-Jewish community of 1946 were intermarried or children of mixed marriages. In some smaller communities, all the members were either married to non-Jews or were Jews only according to Nazi definition."[10] It seems to me that intermarriage increased the moral obligation to remain linked to Jewish roots and heritage. Merely having survived did not permit the Jewish partner to let Judaism perish in the family. These families created their own form of Judaism based on distant memories of how the Jewish partner thought things were done or newly invented traditions that suited the couple's needs.

The establishment of the State of Israel complicated status questions even further. The rise from a persecuted minority in Europe to Jewish sovereignty in the State of Israel caused religious and secular legal opinions to clash, as demonstrated by debates around the question "Who is a Jew?" in cases of conversions and the Law of Return. Children and grandchildren of Jewish descent are entitled to citizenship in Israel even without acceptance as Jews by Halakhah. Although citizens, these people are not allowed to marry in Israel as they are not regarded as Jewish by the Chief Rabbinate, which controls all matters of personal status for its Jewish citizenry.

Half a century after the end of the Second World War and the founding of the State of Israel, the first free elected government in the German Democratic Republic of 1990 decided to grant Jews from the former Soviet Union asylum in Germany. The country thus miraculously transformed itself from a place Jews were supposed to quickly leave to a haven for many Jews. But the influx of Russian-speaking Jews brought with them the challenging question of Jewish status definition.

CREATING POST-SHOAH
JEWISH LIFE IN GERMANY

Journalists, educators, and politicians as well as historians and sociologists found the 200,000 people from the former Soviet Union who had emigrated to Germany, purporting to be Jewish, a fascinating object for observation and study. Numbers alone would not ensure the revitalization of Jewish life in Germany. Having been cut off from the religion of their forefathers, these new immigrants needed to be taught and to acculturate. Thus, in the wake of this wave of immigration, educational institutions were founded to provide the immigrants with basic knowledge of Jewish religion and tradition, history and culture. The establishment of educational institutions was often supported and facilitated by money and personnel from outside Germany—namely the United States and, to a lesser degree, Israel. That is also true for the "Jüdische Lehrhaus," a Jewish House of Learning founded in 1999 by the Ronald S. Lauder Foundation, an American-based Jewish philanthropy foundation. The first director of the Lehrhaus, an American named Joel Levy, explained: "We think those people should receive a Jewish identity, that they must be provided with a Jewish education and thus get a chance to lead a regular Jewish life here in Germany."[11] The Lehrhaus was established at the site of the former institution, which had been forced by the National Socialists to close in 1941. It stood in a building adjacent to the synagogue on Rykestraße, located in Prenzlauer Berg, a neighborhood that flourished after the Berlin Wall fell.

As always on such occasions, the opening ceremony was attended by high-ranking Jewish and non-Jewish officials, in this case the former mayor of Berlin, Eberhardt Diepgen, who called the establishment of the Jewish House of Learning "a historical moment for Jewish life in Germany."[12] Paul Spiegel, a past president of the Central Council of Jews in Germany, and Andreas Nachama, then president of the Jewish Community of Berlin, as well as Ronald Lauder, participated in the inauguration of the Lehrhaus. Spiegel stressed that for most of the immigrants, "Judaism is new if not foreign."[13] Lauder concluded: "We are rebuilding a world. Some call it a miracle. We call it the future."[14] The Lehrhaus provided classes for young Jews to learn about Judaism. They were expected to return later to their communities and to teach the people there what they had learned. It also offered a Beit Midrash Program. Students would live and learn together: yeshiva with a dormitory.

THE CASE OF JONATHAN M.

Soon after the opening the institution began to determine who was eligible to study or, in other words, who was defined as a Jew and thereby qualified to rebuild a Jewish life and future in Germany. A young Berlin Jew named Jonathan, born in 1980, knocked at the door of the Lauder Lehrhaus in 2000. He had attended all the Jewish educational institutions in the city.[15] As a toddler, he was sent to the Jewish kindergarten. Later, he became a student at the Jewish Primary School and continued his education at the Jewish High School, which had opened in 1993. He spent his afternoons in the Jewish community's youth center and the school breaks at Jewish summer camp. In the summer of 2000, Jonathan received his high school diploma as a graduate of the first class of students to attend a Jewish high school in postwar

Germany. The young man was eager to continue his Jewish education. The Jüdische Lehrhaus had opened its doors the year before he received his diploma. This, he thought, was the perfect opportunity to keep on learning, to live with Jewish peers, and to study from rabbis. The young man was interested in the Beit Midrash Program. He wanted to widen and deepen his knowledge and his understanding of the holy text and its interpretations.

The application material included a section called "Proof of Jewishness." He attached his membership document from the Jewish community in Berlin and sent it off. But instead of receiving the letter of admittance, he was asked further questions. According to Jonathan's mother, Mirjam, Joshua Spinner, Joel Levy's successor as rabbi and director of the Lehrhaus, had adopted the World Jewish Congress's dictum following the Second World War. She recalled him saying that all that had happened here after the Shoah happened outside the Jewish world because Germany was cut off from Jewish life and therefore everything that happened here must be considered dubious.[16] The implication was that claims to be Jewish needed careful scrutiny and nothing could be taken for granted.

Jonathan's maternal grandmother was of non-Jewish origin; his maternal grandfather was a Polish Jew who had survived the Shoah in Russia. In his search for family members whom he hoped might have survived, he landed in Berlin in 1945–1946. While riding the tram he met a Polish-speaking woman. They started to chat and he discovered that she rented out rooms. This seemed much more comfortable than the UNRRA refugee camp where he was staying. So, he rented a room from her and soon became acquainted with her daughter with whom he shared the Polish language. They became a couple.

The grandfather had the status of a refugee. He had no citizenship. When his girlfriend was expecting his child, they wanted to marry. But this would have turned the grandmother, as well as the unborn child, into refugees. Thus, the local municipality recommended that they not marry. Jonathan's mother was born in 1953 but her legal status was not resolved until the early sixties. Finally, in 1962, the couple had a civil wedding, followed by the conversion of the bride and their child Mirjam to Judaism before a Beit Din—a Jewish religious court. They later had a Chuppa, a Jewish wedding ceremony.

The bone of contention serves as a perfect example to demonstrate how complicated German-Jewish history had become. The Beit Din put together by the renowned Rabbi Isaak Emil Lichtigfeld (1894–1967) had been chaired by Rabbi Cuno Chanan Lehrmann (1905–1977). Lehrmann originally came from Galica and had survived the Shoah in Switzerland.[17] From 1960 until 1970 he served as the rabbi of the Jewish community of Berlin and as a board member of the Conference of Rabbis in Germany founded in 1957. The problem was that Lehrmann had left Orthodoxy and officiated at the synagogue in Pestalozzistraße, a lavishly decorated temple in Berlin Charlottenburg, built in 1912 and rededicated in 1947, which is known for its musical tradition influenced by the composer of synagogue music, Louis Lewandowski.[18] Services were accompanied by an organ and a choir. Lehrmann officiating at the synagogue on Pestalozzistraße was enough evidence to declare the conversion unhalakhic (illicit according to the Halakhah).[19]

Because Jonathan's grandmother was not regarded as Jewish, his mother's and eventually his own Jewish status were also questionable in the eyes of the Lehrhaus director. In an attempt to find a solution, Rabbi Joshua Spinner suggested that the young man undergo a so-called *Giyur Lechumra*, a pro forma conversion to erase all doubts regarding his Jewish status.[20] The ensuing tug-of-war for acceptance reveals a struggle with two historical burdens. One is related to the power games between the different denominations that emerged in the mid-nineteenth century. The other concerns the insular situation of Jewish communities in the two German postwar states.

The different attitudes toward conversions that originated within the three main denominations of Judaism—Reform, Conservative, and Orthodox—shed a light on their approach toward assimilation and acculturation. "Since Christian-Jewish intermarriages and conversions had increased considerably in Germany from the 19th century onwards, this was not the first time that a rabbi's view on this 'Gerut question' had led to a hotly debated controversy, which came to represent the view that the individual rabbi stood for with regard to the future of the Jewish people and its opening to, or isolation from, the non-Jewish community."[21] When civil weddings became more common, there was no need to convert to the religion of the partner. Thus people converting to Judaism did so in most cases simply because they wanted to. Steiner observes that for most converts, as well as rabbis, family is the most common motive for conversion, that is, to marry a Jewish spouse or to have Jewish children.[22] In the eyes of many rabbis, to convert for the sake of marriage was regarded as an inappropriate motivation and not valid. Conversions had to be "free of any ulterior motive or they are null and void."[23] The halakhic rulings on conversion must be seen as protecting the interests of the Jewish community. What these interests were, however, was interpreted differently by the various halakhic authorities. I will not now go into detail about numerous responsa from all strands of Judaism. But as a general rule, one can say that Orthodox responsa were motivated by fear and ambivalence toward the growing Reform movement. First it aimed to close the ranks among Orthodoxy and adopt a very strict anticonversion policy in order to prevent people from marrying non-Jewish people. Ellenson and Gordis assess that "the German Orthodox rabbinate had transformed conversion in cases of intermarriage into a boundary issue in their attempt to rescue Judaism from the threat of dissolution created by the events of Emancipation and Enlightenment."[24] A different attitude, marked by leniency, was applied by Orthodox rabbis who feared that if people were not allowed to convert they would abscond to Betei Din (halakhic courts) run by Reform rabbis. A prominent example for a rejecting attitude toward converts was Esriel Hildesheimer (1820–1899), founder and head of the Orthodox Rabbinerseminar in Berlin. This is of particular interest in our case as Jonathan was excluded from the Jüdische Lehrhaus on the basis of Hildesheimer's spirit, which denies the validity of a conversion performed by non-Orthodox rabbis.[25]

Jonathan's mother commented bitterly on the proposed *Giyur Lechumra* by saying: "You offer a medicine, that is the *Giyur Lechumra*. This is supposed to bring cure. But first you invent the illness and with the remedy, with the proposed medicine, you create new problems."[26] She was concerned about the Jewish status of her other children if her second-born son, Jonathan, was to convert again and particularly about the status of her daughter. The mother asked what would happen if her daughter wanted to marry a man of the status of Cohen (priest), as Jews of priestly descent are not allowed to marry converts.[27] When she asked that question the rabbis sent by the Lauder Foundation to mediate the case were clueless. This fact angered the family even more. They felt that if they agreed to Jonathan undergoing another conversion, it would be an admission of doubt regarding his legitimate Jewish status. This is reminiscent of Julia Bernstein's finding in her study of children of mixed Jewish/non-Jewish origin where she observes: "A *giyur*, too, is seen by many interviewees as an insulting demonstration that they were not Jews previously, even though they felt Jewish"[28] (emphasis in original). In Joshua Spinner's opinion, Jonathan's case was "a flare-up of the re-integration process" into a cohesive Jewish community defined by halakhic standards as opposed to an individually defined Judaism that had developed in a bubble of postwar Germany.[29]

Eventually, the Lehrhaus asked Dayan Chanoch Ehrentreu, head of the European Beit Din, for advice.[30] This too was commented on bitterly by the family. "They gave a rabbi from England the power to determine who in Germany is regarded to be Jewish."[31] Dayan Ehrentreu had been born in Frankfurt and had taken refuge in England where he became a Talmud scholar and head of a yeshiva.[32] He supported Rabbi Spinner's judgment and resolutely declared that the young man had to convert again in order to be accepted as a Jew and granted the right to participate in the Beit Midrash program. Jonathan interpreted the rabbi's severity as revealing his negative attitude toward Jews in Germany. Much like the World Jewish Congress in the early years after the war and similar to Rabbi Spinner's prevalence of qualms concerning Jewish life in postwar Germany, Dayan Ehrentreu had maintained his doubts about, and dislike of, rabbis who had served the Jewish communities in Germany in the years following the Shoah. Jonathan took the rabbi's strictness in refusing to accept his Jewishness as a way to prove his own superiority. He assumed that the stricter the rabbi handled such cases, the less his authority in legal matters would be questioned by other (Orthodox) rabbis. Jonathan called this approach the "Jew-by-me" method.[33] It justifies overturning the conversion, questioning the convert's Jewishness along with everyone else's. It requires the convert to reconvert without giving him the assurance that the conversion would be accepted by other rabbis in the world. It thus places doubt on the offspring of such converts and in doing so gives the phrase "*L'Dor vaDor*" (For all generations) a completely new meaning.

Jonathan's case also demonstrates how isolated Germany's Jewry remained for decades. Detached from the rest of the Jewish world community, it first had to prove worthy of recognition in the Jewish world after the Berlin Wall fell and the two German states were united. It is an ironic note to the story that Ronald S. Lauder not only established the Lauder Foundation in Germany and with it the Lehrhaus but, since June 2007, he has also served as the president of the World Jewish Congress, the very same organization that imposed "a spell" over Germany in the late 1940s. It is also remarkable that the Jewish establishment in Germany did not interfere and help the family. It is fair to assume that the Jewish leadership in Germany had internalized the notion of inferiority associated with all things Jewish in Germany and preferred to delegate decision-making power overseas.

In March 2018, Dayan Chanoch Ehrentreu was awarded the Order of Merit of the Federal Republic of Germany by Sigmar Gabriel, a German politician and, at the time, foreign minister.[34] Gabriel opened his speech by saying: "We are gathered here today to honour a man who has brought light into the lives of so many people. This man is not only one of the most eminent rabbis in the United Kingdom, he is also the undisputed senior authority on Jewish law in Europe."[35] Ehrentreu, who is the head of the European-Jewish Court of Law of the Conference of European Rabbis, was appointed rector of the Rabbinerseminar, the Orthodox Rabbinical College, established in 2009 in Berlin. By making Ehrentreu the founding father and director of the Hildesheimer-Rabbinerseminar, the Lauder Foundation acknowledged his previous ruling to exclude Jonathan. As Gabriel said in his speech, he might have opened many doors but he certainly closed one for Jonathan.

Jonathan remained faithful to his religion and his heritage. Much like his mother, he championed many Jewish initiatives. He became president of Limmud Germany, originally a British-Jewish initiative dedicated to Jewish learning in all its variety. It was another ironic turn in relation to Dayan Ehrentreu, who in 2013 had "issued an opinion that United Synagogue rabbis should not attend Limmud" because "spokesmen of the Reform and Conservative movements will also be present."[36] In an official letter signed by various Orthodox authorities, the rabbis state: "Participating in their conferences, events and educational endeavours blurs the distinction between authentic Judaism and pseudo-Judaism."[37]

CONCLUSION

Museums operate on a different rationale than Halakhah does but they share the same past-present-future relation. In displaying what was, they define how people will interpret the present and think about the past in the future. It so happened that the Jewish Museum Berlin acquired fifteen 8 mm films and twenty videotapes portraying Jonathan's family, starting with his mother's bat mitzvah. Tamar Lewinsky, curator for contemporary history at the museum and one of the authors of a volume on the history of Jews in Germany from 1945 to the present, has not yet decided whether to include the footage in the museum's new permanent exhibition, but she leaves no doubt about the historic significance of the material.[38] Furthermore, Mirjam has found entrance into the museum by way of her former position as a board member and head of the educational department of the Jewish Community of Berlin, where she served from January 2008 until February 2012. In this capacity she was portrayed by the museum as a representative of the community and of Jewish life in the city.[39]

Identity continues to be shaped by interaction. How Jews are perceived backlashes and influences their self-perception. We assume that being part of the Jewish Museum Berlin's collection on contemporary Jewish life in Germany, and being displayed as such in the future, reinforces the family's Jewish identity. It does not, however, alter their status in the eyes of the rabbis representing the Lauder Foundation.

In conclusion one must agree with Ellenson's and Gordis's statement that "debates about conversion are never simply about conversion, but rather about Jewish identity."[40] To broaden the scope, I dare to add that halakhic rulings (of which conversions are a part) are always debates about the future of Jewish life.

NOTES

1. David Ellenson and Daniel Gordis, *Pledges of Jewish Allegiance: Conversion, Law, and Policymaking in Nineteenth- and Twentieth-Century Orthodox Responsa* (Stanford: Stanford University Press, 2012), 149.
2. Founded in 1927 as the Committee on Jewish Law and renamed in 1948, the CJLS is the central authority on Halakhah within Conservative Judaism. https://www.rabbinicalas sembly.org/jewish-law/committee-jewish-law-and-standards, accessed September 11, 2020.
3. Jonathan Magonet. "Who Is a Jew? Conversion and Jewish Identity Today," in *Not by Birth Alone*, ed. Walter Homolka, Walter Jacob, and Esther Seidel (London and Washington: Cassel, 1997), 55.
4. Matters of determining Jewish status and identity have become complicated not only in Germany but worldwide. See Reuven Hammer's CJLS paper on the topic: https://

www.rabbinicalassembly.org/sites/default/files/assets/public/halakhah/teshuvot /2011-2020/JewishIdentity6.2011.pdf, accessed August 27, 2018.

5. Ellenson and Gordis, *Pledges of Jewish Allegiance*, 5.

6. Barbara Steiner, *Die Inszenierung des Jüdischen: Konversion von Deutschen zum Judentum nach 1945* (Göttingen: Wallstein Verlag, 2015), 107 (my translation).

7. Michael Brenner, *In the Shadow of the Holocaust: The Changing Image of German Jewry after 1945* (Ina Levine Annual Lecture: January 31, 2008; first printing: August 2010), 4, https://www.ushmm.org/m/pdfs/Publication_OP_2010-08.pdf, accessed July 11, 2018.

8. Brenner, *In the Shadow of the Holocaust*, 5.

9. Erica Burgauer, *Zwischen Erinnerung und Verdrängung: Juden in Deutschland nach 1945* (Reinbek bei Hamburg: Rowohlt TB, 1993), 358–359.

10. Brenner, *In the Shadow of the Holocaust*, 2.

11. Joel Levy, "Eine Renaissance jüdischen Lebens," in *Wir sind da! Die Geschichte der Juden in Deutschland von 1945 bis heute*, ed. Richard Chaim Schneider (Munich: Ullstein, 2000), 485 (my translation).

12. Philipp Gessler, "Ist es nicht ein Wunder?! In Prenzlauer Berg ist gestern das einzige jüdische Lehrhaus Deutschland eröffnet worden," *taz*, October 11, 1999, 22.

13. Gessler, "Wunder," 22.

14. Gessler, "Wunder," 22.

15. Philipp Gessler, "Zu wenig Jude zum Beten? Am Donnerstag beginnt am Lehrhaus der Lauder Foundation ein Intensivkurs für jüdische Studenten. Doch Jonathan soll draußen bleiben," *taz*, September 5, 2000, 19.

16. Mirjam, interview by Sandra Anusiewicz-Baer, July 2, 2018, audio, 00:09:43.

17. Reiner Strätz, *Biographisches Handbuch Würzburger Juden 1900–1945* (Würzburg: Schöningh 1989), 338.

18. The synagogue's homepage lists Rabbi Lehrmann as officiating from 1962 until 1971, accessed July 11, 2018, http://synagoge-pestalozzistrasse.de/index.php/synagoge/55 -gedenken.

19. The irony is that Lehrmann was ordained at the Orthodox Rabbinerseminar in Berlin in 1933, which is the predecessor of today's Orthodox Rabbinical Seminary, run by the Lauder Foundation and founded in 2009, Strätz, *Biographisches Handbuch*, 338.

20. Gessler, "Zu wenig Jude," 19.

21. Lida Barner, "Ehefrauen, Gottsucher, Seitenwechsler? Konversionen zum Judentum in Deutschland nach 1945," in *Treten Sie ein! Treten Sie aus! Warum Menschen ihre Religion wechseln*, ed. Regina Laudage-Kleeberg and Hannes Sulzenbacher (Frankfurt am Main: Parthas Verlag Berlin, 2012), 238 (my translation).

22. Steiner, *Die Inszenierung*, 144.

23. Ellenson and Gordis, *Pledges of Jewish Allegiance*, 25.

24. Ibid., 41–42.

25. For Esriel Hildesheimer's stance on intermarriage and conversion, see Ellenson and Gordis, *Pledges of Jewish Allegiance*, 46.

26. Mirjam, interview by Sandra Anusiewicz-Baer, July 2, 2018, audio, 00:13:38.

27. See Maimonides, Mishne Torah, 5th Book (Kedushah), Issurei Biah: forbidden sexual relations 18:3.

28. Julia Bernstein, *"Once in a While Kosher, Once in a While Shabbat": A Study on the Identities, Perceptions, and Practices of Children of Mixed Marriages in Germany* (Oxford: JDC International Centre for Community Development, 2014), 31.

29. Joshua Spinner, conversation with author, August 23, 2018.

30. See http://europeanbethdin.com/dayanim.htm, accessed July 20, 2018.

31. Jonathan, interview by Sandra Anusiewicz-Baer, June 29, 2018, audio, 00:11:56.

32. See https://rabbinerseminar.de/fakultat, accessed July 20, 2018.

33. Jonathan, interview by Sandra Anusiewicz-Baer, June 29, 2018, audio, 00:03:44 and 00:07:38.

34. See *Jüdische Allgemeine*, March 9, 2018, https://www.juedische-allgemeine.de/article/view/id/31038 and also *Jewish Weekly*, March 15, 2018, http://thejewishweekly.com/dayan-chanoch-ehrentreu-receives-order-of-merit-of-the-federal-republic-of-germany, both accessed July 20, 2018.

35. See https://www.auswaertiges-amt.de/de/newsroom/bundesverdienstkreuz-ehrentreu/16833 90, accessed July 3, 2018.

36. See https://www.thejc.com/comment/comment/the-jc-profile-dayan-chanoch-ehrentreu-1.49919, accessed July 20, 2018.

37. See Jewishnews.timesofisrael/community-leaders-abuse-strictly-orthodox-rabbis-of-shocking, accessed July 23, 2018.

38. Together with Atina Grossmann, Lewinsky wrote "Erster Teil: 1945–1949 Zwischenstation," in *Geschichte der Juden in Deutschland von 1945 bis zur Gegenwart*, ed. Michael Brenner (Munich: Verlag C. H. Beck, 2012), 67–152.

39. See https://www.jmberlin.de/en/photographic-collection, accessed July 20, 2018.

40. Ellenson and Gordis, *Pledges of Jewish Allegiance*, 108.

JEWISH STUDIES
WITHOUT THE "OTHER"

KLAUS HÖDL

I BEGIN THIS ESSAY with a brief depiction of Jewish studies in Austria. I will
point out an apparent flaw in the organization of this discipline in the Austrian
context, which has had particular repercussions on how scholars compose historical
narratives. I argue that this oversight in the field fosters the use of dichotomous
categories. Even though the employment of binaries in describing the Jewish and
non-Jewish relationship in the past as well as in the present is not restricted to Austrian
scholars of Jewish studies, indeed it is characteristic of Jewish historiography in general;
various idiosyncrasies of the Austrian academic system have produced particularly
fertile ground for the application of a pronounced Jewish and non-Jewish dualism.[1]
The main purpose of this article is to introduce an analytical concept that can be used
to replace a binary conception of Jewish historical narratives.

JEWISH STUDIES IN AUSTRIA

Jewish studies in Austria, as in most other European countries, are of recent origin.[2] In
contrast to the Institute for *Judaic* Studies at the University in Vienna, founded after
World War II, the establishment of *Jewish* studies can be traced back to the late 1980s
(Institute for Jewish History in Austria, located in St. Pölten) and the beginning of the
twenty-first century (Center for Jewish Cultural History at the University of Salzburg
and Center for Jewish Studies at the University of Graz).[3] The latter institutions have
in common that they owe their existence at least in part to a political climate that
differed from the atmosphere during the first four decades of the postwar period. The

new era broke ground after Kurt Waldheim won the 1986 presidential elections, and we must understand these shifts in the academic political climate as a reaction to his political success on the national level.

Waldheim was a controversial and divisive candidate. During his campaign, an investigative journalist brought to light that the former secretary-general of the United Nations had tried to gloss over some aspects of his activities during the Nazi period in his published biography. When faced with criticism of his tampering with his biographical account, Waldheim fixated on his version despite ample evidence to the contrary. He denied, for example, his documented membership in the National Socialist Party and steadfastly asserted that he had not been aware of the deportation of Jews from Thessaloniki/Greece while he had served there as an intelligence officer.[4]

While Waldheim was pestered by journalists, Austrians' simultaneously sloppy and shrewd handling of their past seeped into their focus as well. Following the Second World War, the country's politicians had vehemently rejected any accusations regarding Austria's complicity in the Shoah. They claimed instead that the country had been the first victim of Nazi Germany's aggression.[5] This position once served political goals, purportedly helping the country to reach independence, but was no longer tenable in the 1980s. Historians had already debunked the so-called victim myth. This myth even came to be recognized as a reason for Waldheim's electoral success in that it impeded efforts to bring the country's population to terms with their Nazi past.[6]

Although various critics of Waldheim's candidacy were vocal in admonishing Austrians not to vote for him because his election could fray their country's relations with other nations, people reacted with utmost disbelief when pertinent measures were put into practice. French, German, and other politicians shunned the newly elected Austrian president, reduced contacts with Austria's political sphere, and thus made Austrians understand that their dealing with the past was out of line with internationally acknowledged standards. This situation was only remedied by former chancellor Franz Vranitzky's visit to Israel in 1993. In a widely acknowledged speech at the Hebrew University in Jerusalem, he rejected Austria's self-deluding notion of being the first victim of Nazi Germany and admitted instead that many Austrians in fact supported, and by their own activities contributed to the Shoah.

In this context, the establishment of Jewish studies in Austria, although initiated by scholars, fits into a larger political strategy whose purpose was to rehabilitate Austria's demolished reputation. Other measures taken in this context were the restoration of synagogues destroyed by the Nazis and the opening of the Jewish Museum in Vienna.[7] Many of these initiatives were entirely, or at least overwhelmingly, funded with public money. These efforts taken to incorporate Jewish studies into Austria's academic landscape met with both approval and resistance. This push-and-pull was particularly the case in Graz where some in the university establishment initially attempted to disrupt the establishment of the Center for Jewish Studies. I wish to stress, however, that these efforts at derailing what was then a new initiative were motivated by parochial reasons, rather than by anti-Jewish sentiments.

Unlike in St. Pölten, Jewish studies in Graz and Salzburg have become affiliated with universities. This constellation has many advantages, but downsides as well. The drawbacks came to the fore in the involuntary involvement of Jewish studies in university politics and entanglement in old boy networks, as a recent job appointment illuminates. In spring 2017, the University of Graz announced a search for a new chair in Jewish studies, the purpose of which was to establish a better profile and greater international prestige for the Center for Jewish Studies. There was a stipulation, however, that eligible candidates had to be affiliated with the local university. The search committee was thus not to find the best possible candidate for the job. It became evident that the purpose of the committee was to make sure that a particular scholar from the university, to whom the new position had been previously promised, would in fact receive the appointment. This approach, a clear deviation from internationally standardized procedures of filling academic positions, nevertheless drew two applications. A top American university had also invited one of the two applicants to apply for a position in their Jewish studies department, around the time when the announcement at the University of Graz was made public on its website. The reason for the invitation, so the official letter said, was the quality of the scholar's publications. At the University of Graz, his application was rejected because of his job title. His publishing record, teaching accomplishments, and the prestigious grants that he had received throughout his career were not taken into consideration for the decision.

This is not to say that the scholar who had been promised and was finally appointed to the Jewish studies chair was not an ideal candidate. The procedure suggests, however, that conditions at the University of Graz, which are not much different from those at other Austrian universities, nurture a secluded intellectual atmosphere in which scholarly innovations occur not because of—but rather despite—given structures. The academic setting itself provides no incentive for academic achievements, but rather promotes inert stagnancy. This phenomenon came to the fore in a review of an application for a research grant drafted by an Austrian Jewish studies scholar. The proposal had been submitted to the Österreichische Nationalbank, one of the few institutions in Austria that fund basic research in the humanities. The referee reviewing the application castigated the research description by citing an irritatingly outdated and essentialist conception of Jewishness, a gesture that was in part even reminiscent of the deterministic thinking characteristic of Nazi ideology.[8] Again, this incident is not characteristic of Austrian-Jewish studies in their entirety, but indicative of an academic climate in which such drawbacks are allowed to thrive.

Essentialized thinking among Jewish studies scholars is not a necessary prerequisite for the composition of historical accounts predicated on a Jewish and non-Jewish dichotomy. There are other causes as well. But essentialist thinking always entails binary categorizations. And such binaries, I wish to argue, characterize many, if not all, Jewish historical narratives, even those on Jewish and non-Jewish entanglement or hybridity.[9] Although other academic settings may prove themselves more stimulating to innovative research, their scholars have not rid themselves altogether of the Jewish and non-Jewish dualism either. The purpose of the following pages is to present a methodological approach through which dichotomous descriptions may be abrogated. Such a new approach will hopefully be of interest to scholars of Jewish studies outside of Austria as well.

THE TENACIOUSNESS OF DICHOTOMOUS THINKING

Dichotomous thinking appears to be an anthropological constant, virtually impossible to avoid. The Harvard evolutionary biologist Stephen Jay Gould drew attention to this fact in a noted article published two years before his early death in 2002. He wrote that "we construct our descriptive taxonomies and tell our explanatory stories as dichotomies, or contrasts between inherently distinct and logically opposite alternatives." The reasons for this procedure "seem to transcend cultural peculiarities" and "may lie deep within the architecture of the human mind."[10] Rather than locating dichotomous thinking in some neural substrates, Gould draws attention to its pervasiveness and apparently ubiquitous acceptance. It is deeply ingrained in our conception of the world and therefore its cultural conditioning is almost impossible to recognize. Such recognition would be necessary, however, in order to "reject this constraining mental model."[11]

With respect to Jewish historiography, Gould's statement implies that the pronounced Jewish and non-Jewish dualism characterizing historical accounts may be less reflective of bygone life-worlds than a consequence of scholars' restricted thinking. Many research studies conducted over the last two or three decades in the field of Jewish history can indeed be read as endorsing this view: They have brought to light plenty of evidence of Jewish and non-Jewish interactions that jar with the conception, prevalent until the late twentieth century, that Jews led largely isolated lives.[12] A striking example of the discrepancy between historical accounts based on a binary division of Jews and non-Jews and their actual entanglement in the past is the history of the Polish-Lithuanian Commonwealth. With few exceptions, scholars have sketched—and in part still do[13]—a picture of historical Polish society in which, as the eminent historian Emanuel Ringelblum wrote in 1932, a "Chinese wall" seems to separate Jewish and non-Jewish Poles.[14] According to Ringelblum they are depicted as being "in a permanent state of endless conflict, if not actual war."[15] What Ringelblum wanted to convey is the fact that the particular narratives were not shaped by a lack of records demonstrating Jewish and non-Jewish togetherness; rather, they resulted from the scholars' perspective on Polish society that ignores sources contradicting their narrative.[16]

Since the turn of the twenty-first century, historians' outlook on the Polish past has changed, and considerable evidence of Jewish and non-Jewish interconnectedness has been unearthed. As is widely recognized today, Jews and non-Jews lived in close, and sometimes even intimate proximity over long periods of time. Narratives painting images of Jewish and non-Jewish relations exclusively, or almost exclusively, fraught with tensions and hostility do not correspond with actual historical life-worlds. This is not to say that the entanglement of Jews and non-Jews was free of tensions. At times, violence indeed characterized their relations. However, such conflicts frequently resulted from disagreements over quotidian issues instead of anti-Jewish sentiments.[17] Before Jews and non-Jews engaged in brawls and fights, they often ate and drank together and played cards or music.[18] Against the background of such references, the idea of a separate Jewish existence appears untenable. It is further undermined by Jewish residential patterns in the Polish-Lithuanian Commonwealth. As recent research has convincingly shown, the widespread notion of the "Jewish shtetl," that is, a town where Jews far outnumbered the non-Jewish population and consequently lived in their own microcosm that kept interactions with non-Jews restricted primarily to business matters, is largely a myth.[19] In many cases, Jews were just one of various minorities in these small towns. The administrative records of the Polish settlement of Zamość paradigmatically substantiate this view. In the mid-seventeenth century, Germans and Scots owned twenty-one houses in the town, thirty-two belonged to Armenians, twenty-three to Jews, and the majority to Roman and Greek Catholics.[20] In terms of numbers, non-Jews clearly outnumbered Jews in Zamość. Even more striking is the fact that a considerable section of the Jewish population lived among gentiles. This observation proves true for other shtetls as well. In many towns, Jewish houses were either scattered among buildings occupied by non-Jews, or Jews lived in non-Jewish households (and vice versa).[21] These findings firmly suggest that the association between small towns in Eastern Europe and isolated Jewish existence is a construct that does not reflect historical living practices.[22] Historians' dichotomous thinking apparently rendered them oblivious to evidence of a Jewish and non-Jewish co-existence. Well until the close of the twentieth century, most of them focused on demarcations and borders instead of entanglement and coexistence, and the widespread conception of the "isolated" shtetl served their purposes.

Apart from the scholars' "restricted reasoning," the selection of archival material they analyze for reconstructing the past also contributes to historical accounts characterized by a Jewish and non-Jewish dualism. It is noteworthy that pertinent records consist overwhelmingly of textual sources penned by religious authorities, more often Christian than Jewish.[23] The focus on these documents is partly due to their availability and accessibility. In addition, they easily fit into—and in turn strengthen—the concept of Polish Jewish history characterized by anti-Jewish discrimination. Aspects of the canon law and church legislation aimed at excluding Jews from society at large and relegating them to a marginal position served as evidence of an atmosphere fraught with anti-Jewish sentiments.[24]

This view is not entirely wrong, but nevertheless highly problematic. It depicts Jews merely as passive victims instead of people who helped to shape society and its culture. This is not to say that they are likewise to blame for the Judaeophobic climate in which they lived. But as some historians seeking to draw a broader picture of Polish society by taking the activities of Jews into account pointed out as early as the 1960s, rabbis also initiated measures against interreligious intermingling. Both Jewish and Christian religious authorities strove to erect boundaries between the two communities.[25] Owing to the societal power structure, however, greater blame must be assigned to the Christian side.

This new approach provided a more comprehensive understanding of the agents causing barriers between the two communities. Nevertheless, it kept the focus among scholars in Jewish studies on the rifts and demarcation lines between them. The question whether they actually determined the lives of people was hardly raised. It took historians around another two decades to concentrate on indications of entanglement rather than separation. Various developments provoked this shift in research, such as the opening of archives in Eastern Europe in the 1990s that provided historians access to a vast amount of heretofore unexplored records[26] and a new conception of the city and interpretation of people's interactions.[27] The growing interest among scholars in everyday life was also of great relevance. Its reconstruction brought to light that Jews and non-Jews displayed an astonishing degree of togetherness despite arguments to the contrary. At times, the Jewish and non-Jewish interconnectedness made it almost impossible to distinguish them from one another, be it in their behavior or outer appearances. There is evidence that Jews borrowed from and lent clothing to gentiles (and the other way around), despite the fact that this trade of apparel was strictly forbidden.[28] Such examples indicate that laws and proscriptions meant to keep the two groups apart and boundaries between them insuperable must not be taken as proof of an actual Jewish and non-Jewish separation. Ordinary people frequently defied such enactments.[29] Strict compliance with the various ordinances and decrees would probably have disrupted their habitual lives in a way that neither Jews nor non-Jews were ready to accept. In some regions and under specific circumstances, Jews in particular were able to transgress pertinent rulings by their religious elite because they could evade potential sanctions by turning to municipal courts or the jurisdiction of magnates who, at least in some cases, were more lenient.[30]

In summary, we may argue that with respect to Eastern Europe there is ample evidence of manifold Jewish and non-Jewish encounters.[31] Jews were heavily involved with non-Jews through various forms of interaction. Historians are currently investigating this interconnectedness. Yet, they continue to describe Jews and non-Jews in binary categories. A paradigmatic example of such a scholar is Gershon David Hundert, one of the trailblazers of the narrative of Jewish and non-Jewish entanglement in Eastern Europe.[32] On the one hand, he claims that there was no dichotomous juxtaposition of Jews and non-Jews. As he sees it, Polish historiography never considered Jews a "corporate entity."[33] On the other hand, and in contradiction to this assertion, Hundert subscribes to an essentialist—and therefore fundamental—differentiation between Jews and non-Jews.[34]

We may explain such perseverance in the use of binary divisions by returning to Stephen Jay Gould's reference to the restrictions of our thinking. Another reason may be linked to the lack of analytical instruments that allow the abandonment of a dualism. In further consequence, historians stick to concepts that often foreground, at least implicitly, a mutual distinctiveness between Jews and non-Jews. Such concepts are assimilation or acculturation. The terms "unassimilated" or "nonacculturated" Jews, for instance, designate those—mostly very orthodox—Jews who keep to themselves and pay heed to cultural boundaries. In a way they are seen as living "beside" or even "outside" society at large into which they integrate by adopting elements of the non-Jewish culture.[35] Jewish acculturation thus denotes a trajectory that brings Jews, understood as a distinct entity, closer to their non-Jewish surroundings. The description of the entire process departs from an assumed polarization between those who acculturate/assimilate and those who are in possession of the culture to which the former adapt. Assimilation and acculturation thus ignore the wide array of examples of Jewish and non-Jewish interconnectedness that suggests that Jews were an integral part of the social fabric of Polish society and culture and cooperated with non-Jews in their shaping. The employment of the concept of similarity, however, could overcome the Jewish and non-Jewish dualism.

THE CONCEPT OF SIMILARITY

"Similarity" is a fairly new heuristic instrument, even though studies that treat the concept of similarity were conducted in Africa and India in the 1990s.[36] Moreover, the similarity model has played a significant role in the field of philosophy. Until recently, however, this concept had not gained widespread interdisciplinary attention. Currently, this seems to be changing due to research conducted in the last couple of years, in particular at the University of Tübingen by Dorothee Kimmich and in collaboration with Anil Bhatti (New Delhi).[37]

The crux of the similarity model lies in its challenge to the binarism of identity and difference. According to the theorists of similarity, this binary not only shapes structuralist and poststructuralist theories, but it can also be located, albeit in attenuated form, in cultural studies research on postcolonialism, multiculturalism, and even hybridity.[38] The similarity model instead introduces the category of both-and-one, which withdraws from the traditional polarization of authenticity and foreignness.[39]

Thinking in terms of similarity orients us toward cultural overlapping rather than borders and demarcations. The orientation toward this kind of interrelationship is anything but unusual; rather, it is characteristic of various cultural studies approaches. At its root, it traces cultural exchanges and points of contact between individuals and/ or various groups.[40] Yet, despite the emphasis on cultural congruities, according to the pioneers in the field of "similarity," the dichotomous juxtaposition of the self and the foreign nevertheless persists.[41] The similarity model attempts to avoid this dichotomous juxtaposition by understanding spheres of cultural contact not as a space that two or more groups—conceived of at least implicitly as distinct—*negotiate* jointly; instead, they are merely a condition under which connectivity can be *perceived*. In this context, similarity represents a situational experience for which the self and the other do not form points of references. Similarity "arises in the eye of an observer and is contingent, ephemeral, unpredictable."[42] The concept of similarity thus requires, vis-à-vis other cultural studies approaches, a "changing of perspective."[43] In a concrete sense this entails a new approach to and a new understanding of cultural overlapping.

Similarity not only emphasizes the connections between Jews and non-Jews, but also allows for discussion of divisions and differences. These do not, however, form profound and fundamental differences, but rather vague and blurred dissimilarities, which emerge in different shades.[44] Contrary to other theoretical approaches, similarity thus makes it possible to abolish Jewish/non-Jewish dualism without simultaneously erasing differences.[45] The identification of similarities releases Jews from their foreignness without robbing them of their distinctiveness. An examination of similarities between Jews and non-Jews thus does not displace their mutual distinctiveness.[46] Similarity is solely intended to remove the idea of a deeply anchored and seemingly fixed otherness of Jews.

IN CONCLUSION, IT remains to be asked what sources inform us about experiences of similarity. If they are elusive and bound to the moment, where can researchers make them out and how can historians get a hold on them? In the following, I wish to list three different historical sources. The first kind of material contains "classical" sources, such as autobiographies and memoirs. They sometimes describe situations of a deeply sensed Jewish and non-Jewish connectivity. A paradigmatic example of such a memoir was drafted by Salomon I. Horowitz, a Galician Jew, and published in Lwow in 1909. In his text, Horowitz recounts his experiences during his travels in Eastern Europe. In one passage he narrates his impressions of Jewish life in Lithuania where, as he writes, a sense of togetherness between Jews and the non-Jewish rural population seems to have been extant for centuries. According to Horowitz, these largely harmonious relations find expression in people's interactions at Jewish taverns. Non-Jewish peasants and their families regularly frequent them on their way to the weekly markets. The Jewish innkeeper, his wife, and children heartily welcome the non-Jewish guests, with both parties radiating genuine joy over the reunion and exchanging gifts for the children.[47] Any sense of religious or cultural differences appear to be nonexistent or are at best secondary.

A similar feeling of Jewish and non-Jewish interrelatedness is conveyed by the memoir of Dov Ber Birkenthal (1723–1805), a Jewish businessman in the Polish-Lithuanian Commonwealth and, after the partitions of Poland, Habsburg Galicia. Birkenthal draws a vivid picture of his many contacts with non-Jews. Whereas most of these encounters are marked by religious or ethnic indifference, some of them bespeak mutual mistrust, even aversion, and a few develop into close friendship. Birkenthal thus experiences a wide range of sensations toward Gentiles; they range from dislike, and even detestation, to intimacy. What feeling actually prevails depends on the character of the individual and not on the person's ethnic or religious belonging. Some Jews, Birkenthal reports, cheated and betrayed him, and he indeed loathes them, whereas he feels much togetherness with other Jews as well as various non-Jews. For the author, there are no clear Jewish and non-Jewish boundaries when it comes to socializing.[48]

The second category of documents consists of so-called ephemeral sources, such as anecdotes. Usually, historians give them little, if any, attention, either because they mostly speak only indirectly to us, that is, must be contextualized through meticulous and painstaking work before they might make sense; or because their informative content frequently does not fit into mainstream narratives and is therefore considered irrelevant. This was the case, for example, with a brawl that took place in Vienna's city center in December 1896. A Jewish peddler who tried to hawk his wares on the street provoked the ire of an employee of a nearby store. In order to scare him away, the non-Jewish employee started hurling abuse at the Jew, and then attacked him physically. Up to this point, the incident neatly corresponds to the historical narrative of the difficulties faced by Jewish peddlers in eking out an existence in antisemitic Vienna. Yet, the occurrence took an unexpected turn at odds with prevalent narratives of Jewish and non-Jewish relations in the Habsburg capital. Non-Jewish passersby came to the aid of the Jew and severely beat the aggressor.[49] They thus displayed compassion toward a person in distress, irrespective of his religious or ethnic belonging. At this moment, non-Jews present at the scene felt more solidarity with the Jewish peddler than with the non-Jewish employee.

The third category of sources from which scholars may retrieve examples of perceived similarity are given historical accounts that must be "read against the grain." Thereby, some of the records that form the basis of the historical narrative may need to be reinterpreted. One example of such a reinterpretation concerns a brief description of a football match between the Jewish team Hakoah and its non-Jewish opponent Brigittenauer A.C. in Vienna in the 1920s. The spectators comprised both Jews and non-Jews. Many of the latter had a stake in Hakoah's win and tried to support the team by loud whooping. There was a problem, however, as they did not know how to spur on the Jewish players in a friendly manner. One of the spectators finally shouted "*Hoppauf, Herr Jud.*"[50]

So far, scholars have understood this episode as an indication of the Jewish/ non-Jewish divide in Vienna of the 1920s.[51] Non-Jews apparently did not even know how to address Jews in a nonaggressive manner. Yet, the incident can also be interpreted in a different way, namely as an instance of relatedness between the non-Jewish onlooker and a Jewish player. It is a situational experience that lasts only for the moment. But in this instant, the sensation of connectivity bridges Jewish and non-Jewish boundaries and concomitantly demonstrates the untenability of a binary categorization. Differences in fact remain, as the shouting of "Herr Jud" as a form of address indicates. However, these differences are not necessarily fundamental. "Similarity," in other words, may help to overcome the Jewish and non-Jewish binary ingrained in Jewish historiography, and thereby open up historical narratives to new readings.

ACKNOWLEDGMENTS

The research for this article was funded by the Austrian Science Fund (FWF), grant P31036-G28.

NOTES

1. See Moshe Rosman, *How Jewish Is Jewish History?* (Oxford: Littman Library of Jewish Civilization, 2007), 4.

2. Klaus Hödl, "Jewish Studies without Jews: The Growth of an Academic Field in Austria and Germany," in *Maven in Blue Jeans. A Festschrift in Honor of Zev Garber*, ed. Steven Leonard Jacobs (West Lafayette: Purdue University Press, 2009), 200–201.

3. Gerhard Bodendorfer, "Ein Forschungsinstitut für 'Jüdische Kulturgeschichte' in Salzburg?!," in *Jüdische Studien: Reflexionen zu Theorie und Praxis eines wissenschaftlichen Feldes*, ed. Klaus Hödl (Innsbruck: Studienverlag, 2003), 51–72.

4. Cornelius Lehnguth, *Waldheim und die Folgen. Der parteipolitische Umgang mit dem Nationalsozialismus in Österreich* (Frankfurt a.M.: Campus Verlag, 2013), 91–152.

5. Matti Bunzl, *Jews and Queers: Symptoms of Modernity in Late Twentieth-Century Vienna* (Berkeley: University of California Press, 1999), 30–32.

6. Richard Mitten, *The Politics of Antisemitic Prejudice: The Waldheim Phenomenon in Austria* (Boulder: Westview Press, 1992).

7. See "Das Jüdische Museum der Stadt Wien 1993/94. Chronik," in *Wiener Jahrbuch für jüdische Geschichte, Kultur und Museumswesen* (Vienna: Verlag Christian Brandstätter, 1994/95), 187–193.

8. A copy of the review can be found among my private papers, and I am happy to make it available to anybody wishing to request it.

9. Paradigmatic examples of scholarly texts in which the authors intend to go beyond the Jewish and non-Jewish binary, but are nonetheless still caught up in dichotomous thinking, are Micha J. Perry and Rebekka Voß, "Approaching Shared Heroes: Cultural Transfer and Transnational Jewish History," *Jewish History* 30 (2016): 1–13; Glenn Dynner, ed., *Holy Dissent: Jewish and Christian Mystics in Eastern Europe* (Detroit: Wayne State University Press, 2011), 1–2.

10. Stephen Jay Gould, "Deconstructing the 'Science Wars' by Reconstructing an Old Mold," *Science* 287, no. 5451 (2002): 253.

11. Gould, "Science Wars," 253. Regarding the issue of whether binary categorizations reflect people's cultural embeddedness or originate from their "neural substrate," see also Robert Sapolsky, "This Is Your Brain on Nationalism: The Biology of Us and Them," *Foreign Affairs* 98, no. 2 (2019): 42–47.

12. See Neil Asher Silberman, "Rewriting Jewish History," *Archaeology* 63, no. 4 (2010): 18, 58; Elisheva Baumgarten, Ruth Mazo Karras, and Katelyn Mesler, eds., *Entangled Histories: Knowledge, Authority, and Jewish Culture in the Thirteenth Century* (Philadelphia: University of Pennsylvania Press, 2017); Moshe Rosman, "A Jewish Guide to Medieval Domestic Europe. Review of E. Baumgarten, Mothers and Children: Jewish Family Life in Medieval Europe," *Jewish Quarterly Review* 98 (2008): 419; Francesca Bregoli, "Introduction. Connecting Histories: Jews and Their Others in Early Modern Europe," in *Connecting Histories. Jews and Their Others in Early Modern Europe*, ed. Francesca Bregoli and David B. Ruderman (Philadelphia: University of Pennsylvania Press), 10. There were, in fact, various exceptions to this view. See David Berger, "A Generation of Scholarship on Jewish-Christian Interaction in the Medieval World," *Tradition* 38, no. 2 (2004): 5.

13. Frank Golczewski, "A Jewish Space in an Extreme Context? German Ghettoes for Jews in Eastern Europe during World War II," in *Jewish and Non-Jewish Spaces in the Urban*

Context, ed. Alina Gromova, Felix Heinert, and Sebastian Voigt (Berlin: Neofelis Verlag, 2015), 102.

14. Israel Bartal and Scott Ury, "Between Jews and Their Neighbours: Isolation, Confrontation, and Influence in Eastern Europe," *Polin* 24 (2012): 3.

15. Ibid., 3–4.

16. See also Adam Teller and Magda Teter, "Introduction: Borders and Boundaries in the Historiography of the Jews in the Polish-Lithuanian Commonwealth," *Polin* 22 (2010): 3–46.

17. Eugene M. Avrutin, "Jewish Neighbourly Relations and Imperial Russian Legal Culture," *Journal of Modern Jewish Studies* 9, no. 1 (2010): 2.

18. Maria Ciesla, "Jewish Shtetl or Christian Town? The Jews in Small Towns in the Polish-Lithuanian Commonwealth in the 17th and 18th Centuries," in Gromova, Heinert, and Voigt, *Jewish and Non-Jewish Spaces*, 75–79.

19. Israel Bartal, "Imagined Geography: The Shtetl, Myth, and Reality," in *The Shtetl: New Evaluations*, ed. Steven T. Katz (New York: New York University Press, 2007), 179–192.

20. Ciesla, "Shtetl," 65.

21. David Frick, "Jews and Others in Seventeenth-Century Wilno: Life in the Neighborhood," *Jewish Social Quarterly* 12 (2005): 21–27.

22. Ciesla, "Shtetl," 63–65.

23. David Berger, "Mission to the Jews and Jewish-Christian Contacts in the Polemical Literature of the High Middle Ages," *American Historical Review* 91, no. 3 (1986): 585, 590–591. On this issue see also David Joshua Malkiel, "Jews and Apostates in Medieval Europe—Boundaries Real and Imagined," *Past & Present* 194 (2007): 32.

24. Magda Teter, "'There should be no love between us and them': Social Life and the Bounds of Jewish and Canon Law in Early Modern Poland," *Polin* 22 (2010): 250.

25. Teter, "There should be no love," 250.

26. Eric L. Goldstein, "Beyond the 'Shtetl': Small-Town Family Networks and the Social History of Lithuanian Jews," *Jewish Social Studies* 24, no. 1 (2018): 37.

27. Gill Valentine, "Living with Difference: Reflections on Geographies of Encounter," *Progress in Human Geography* 32, no. 3 (2008): 324.

28. Teter, "There should be no love," 261.

29. Teter, "There should be no love," 249–270.

30. See Magda Teter, *Jews and Heretics in Catholic Poland. A Beleaguered Church in the Post-Reformation Era* (Cambridge: Cambridge University Press, 2006), 31.

31. This holds true for other regions in Europe, but also in North Africa and the Middle East, as well. See S. D. Goitein, *A Mediterranean Society. The Jewish Communities of the World as Portrayed in the Documents of the Cairo Genizah*, vol. IV: *Daily Life* (Berkeley: University of California Press, 1999); Jacob Goldberg, "Poles and Jews in the 17th and 18th Centuries: Rejection and Acceptance," *Jahrbücher für Geschichte*

Osteuropas 22, no. 2 (1974): 259. See also Emily Gottreich, *The Mellah of Marrakesh: Jewish and Muslim Space in Morocco's Red City* (Bloomington: Indiana University Press, 2007); Nawja al-Qattan, "Litigants and Neighbors: The Communal Topography of Ottoman Damascus," *Comparative Studies in Society and History* 44 (2002): 511–533; Edward Fram, "Two Cases of Adultery and the Halakhic Decision-Making Process," *AJS Review* 26, no. 2 (2002): 277–300; Thomas V. Cohen, "The Case of the Mysterious Coil of Rope: Street Life and Jewish Persona in Rome in the Middle of the Sixteenth Century," *Sixteenth Century Journal* XIX, no. 2 (1988): 209–221; Helmut Walser Smith, "The Discourse of Usury: Relations between Christians and Jews in the German Countryside, 1880–1914," *Central European History* 32, no. 3 (1999): 255–276; Daniel Jütte, "Interfaith Encounters between Jews and Christians in the Early Modern Period and Beyond: Toward a Framework," *American Historical Society* 118, no. 2 (2013): 378–400; Eugene M. Avrutin, "Jewish Neighbourly Relations and Imperial Russian Legal Culture," *Journal of Modern Jewish Studies* 9, no. 1 (2010): 2; Thomas Cohen, "The Death of Abramo of Montecosaro," *Jewish History* 19, no. 3/4 (2005): 245–285; Ariel Toaff, *Love, Work, and Death: Jewish Life in Medieval Umbria* (Liverpool: Littman Library of Jewish Civilization, 1998); Debra Kaplan, "The Self in Social Context: Asher ha-Levi of Reichshofen's *Sefer Zikhronot*," *Jewish Quarterly Review* 97, no. 2 (2007): 210–236; Elisheva Baumgarten, *Mothers and Children: Jewish Family Life in Medieval Europe* (Princeton: Princeton University Press, 2004); Debra Kaplan, *Beyond Expulsion: Jews, Christians, and Reformation Strasbourg* (Stanford: Stanford University Press, 2011).

32. See Gershon David Hundert, *The Jews in a Polish Private Town: The Case of Opatów in the Eighteenth Century* (Baltimore: Johns Hopkins University Press, 1992), 21, 235–236.

33. Gershon David Hundert, "Polish Jewish History," *Modern Judaism* 10 (1990): 260.

34. Teller and Teter, "Introduction," 41.

35. The question of how non-Jewish culture can be defined and what it encompasses, as I wish to argue, is impossible to answer. Part of this difficulty stems from societies' heterogeneity and their cultural pluralism. This proves particularly true with the Polish-Lithuanian Commonwealth. The non-Jewish population consisted of Armenians, Germans, Poles, Ruthenians, and other groups, and each of them claimed to possess its distinct cultural profile. Vilna represents a particularly salient example of a culturally diverse city. It was home to five Christian confessions. In addition, there were Muslim Tartars and, as a matter of fact, Jews. See for example David Frick, "Jews in Public Places: Further Chapters in the Jewish-Christian Encounter in Seventeenth-Century Vilna," *Polin* 22 (2010): 215. In this context, it is unfeasible to circumscribe the non-Jewish culture to which Jews assumedly acculturate.

36. See Dorothee Kimmich, *Ins Ungefähre: Ähnlichkeit und Moderne* (Leiden: Konstanz University Press, 2017), 10.

37. Anil Bhatti, Dorothee Kimmich, Albrecht Koschorke, Rudolf Schlögl, and Jürgen Wertheimer, "Ähnlichkeit: Ein kulturtheoretisches Paradigma," *Internationales Archiv für Sozialgeschichte der deutschen Literatur* 36, no. 1 (2011): 233–247.

38. Bhatti et al., "Ähnlichkeit," 234; Gurpreet Mahajan, "Jenseits von Differenz und vollkommener Identität: Das Konzept der Ähnlichkeit in den Sozialwissenschaften," in *Ähnlichkeit. Ein kulturtheoretisches Paradigma*, ed. Anil Bhatti and Dorothee Kimmich (Konstanz: Konstanz University Press, 2015), 154–155.

39. Anil Bhatti, "Plurikulturalität," *Habsburg neu denken. Vielfalt und Ambivalenz, in Zentraleuropa. 30 kulturwissenschaftliche Stichworte*, ed. Johannes Feichtinger and Heidemarie Uhl (Wien: Böhlau Verlag, 2016), 207.

40. See for example Mary Louise Pratt, "Arts of the Contact Zone," *Profession* (1991): 33–40.

41. Dorothee Kimmich describes the preservation of dualistic categories, stating that cultural studies scholars "basically (wish to) address and resolve a self-made problem . . . but in doing so remain comparatively subcomplex." See Kimmich, *Ungefähre*, 13.

42. Aleida Assmann, "Ähnlichkeit als Performanz: Ein neuer Zugang zu Identitätskonstruktionen und Empathie-Regimen," in Bhatti and Kimmich, *Ähnlichkeit*, 168.

43. Ibid., 171.

44. Albrecht Koschorke, "Valenzen eines postkolonialen Konzepts," in Bhatti and Kimmich, *Ähnlichkeit*, 36.

45. For this point, see Rosman, *How Jewish Is Jewish History*, 4.

46. Andreas Langenohl writes in this context: "Similarity therefore does not throw difference overboard, but instead reconstructs it conceptually beyond its contrast to identity." Andreas Langenohl, "Ähnlichkeit als differenztheoretisches Konzept: zur Reformulierung der Modernisierungstheorie," in Bhatti and Kimmich, *Ähnlichkeit*, 106.

47. Salomon I. Horowitz, *Lebenserinnerungen eines polnischen Juden I. Kann ein Pole ein Antisemit sein?* (Lemberg: Verlag des Verfassers, 1909).

48. *The Memoirs of Ber of Bolechow, Translated from the Original Hebrew Manuscript by M. Vishnitzer* (London: Oxford University Press, 1922).

49. "Ein geschlagener Hausirer," *Wiener Illustrirtes Extrablatt* 23 (January 23, 1897), 8.

50. Friedrich Torberg, *Die Tante Jolesch oder Der Untergang des Abendlandes in Anekdoten* (Köln: Anaconda Verlag, 2011), 59–68.

51. Simon Schwaiadger, *Sportklub Hakoah Wien—Ikone jüdischen Selbstbewusstseins. Von der Gründung bis zur Gegenwart* (MA thesis, University of Vienna, 2008), 105–106.

RETHINKING JEWS, ANTISEMITISM, AND JEWISH DIFFERENCE IN POSTWAR GERMANY

LISA SILVERMAN

O N JULY 11, 2018, Yitzhak Melamed, a fifty-year-old Israeli professor of philosophy at Johns Hopkins University, was walking in Bonn with a colleague from the city's university, a few hours before his scheduled talk that evening. Suddenly, a twenty-year-old German-Palestinian man shouted antisemitic insults at him, throwing his kippa to the ground several times. Bystanders called the police but when they arrived, the young man ran away and Melamed chased after him. Confusing the victim with his attacker, four or five policemen then mistakenly wrestled Melamed to the ground, brutally punching, bruising, and bloodying him, as well as breaking his glasses and impairing his ability to breathe. Only after throwing more punches did they finally heed his cries that they had grabbed the wrong man and apprehend the offender.

Had this been a simple case of mistaken identity, the situation might have ended there. But as the police acknowledged their error and removed his handcuffs, one of them warned Melamed—in English—not to make trouble for the German police. To their surprise, Melamed responded that the German police had killed his grandfather, grandmother, aunt, and uncle all on one day in September 1942, and that he was no longer afraid of them. He then went to the police station to file a report about the original antisemitic incident, where he received no assistance with his wounds. Moreover, to his astonishment, the police tried to persuade him not to file a complaint about their behavior, claiming that their actions had been justified because he had resisted arrest. They told him that if he were to file such a report, they would assert that he had resisted.

Melamed then went to another police station to report the initial incident as a hate crime. There, he received friendlier treatment including expressions of regret and concern for his wounds. Hours later, Melamed managed to give his talk at the university. However, the incident was not yet over. The next morning, Bonn's chief of police visited his hotel in order to apologize in person. Nevertheless, in a subsequent statement, the police apologized for the incident but also, true to their original threat, claimed that Melamed had resisted arrest. The story of the incident went viral after Melamed posted about it on Facebook. The University of Bonn then issued a statement of outrage at Melamed's treatment and the city of Bonn organized a day of kippa-wearing solidarity for the following week.[1]

Certain aspects of this horrifying incident and the ensuing responses follow a pattern that is similar to some other recent violent antisemitic attacks in Germany. In these, a person is recognized as a Jew and attacked, catalyzing an outraged response from the German media as well as an outpouring of support for the Jewish community. If the identity of the attacker is a Muslim or associated with Muslims, that aspect is played up by the right-wing media and—in response to, or in anticipation of this display of right-wing Islamophobia—also ignored or downplayed by the mainstream German media.[2] This pattern of antisemitic incident, anti-Muslim/anti-foreigner response, and philosemitic response and counter-response is apparent here, too. Melamed's Jewishness was clearly important for his antisemitic attacker as well as for his philosemitic supporters. However, the role his Jewishness played in the German police's beating remains unclear. In brutalizing Melamed, threatening him, and lying about his alleged aggression, the police disrupted the typical pattern of events by inserting an element of ambiguity about how his Jewishness functioned in their response. Were the police indifferent to Jewishness in their eagerness to subdue an attacker and then cover up their mistake? Or were they perhaps acting on their own antisemitic impulses? Was it a mixture of the two? Whatever the case, this incident is instructive for recognizing that antisemitism and philosemitism are components of a larger ordering system of Jewish difference—by which I mean the hierarchical ordering system of constructed ideals of the Jew and non-Jew—that continues to operate as a potent ordering system in modern Central Europe.

The antisemitic impulses that drive violent attacks need to be understood as stemming from a broader framework of Jewish difference that forms not only the basis for explicit violence, but also the foundation for opportunistic support for Jews as well as moments in which responses toward Jews may be more ambiguous, displaced, or even suppressed. *All* of these responses stem from and—if not recognized and destabilized—continue to perpetuate a particular Jew/non-Jew ordering system in which the Jew functions as the quintessential Other. Recent explicit incidents of violent antisemitism, along with their accompanying philosemitic responses and blaming of, or avoiding discussion of, Muslims, highlight how the framework of Jewish difference continues to operate in Germany. In what follows, I argue that recognizing this framework's less negative and explicit iterations is necessary for understanding the systemic nature of Jewish difference and the powerful persistence of antisemitism even in the absence of explicit, violent acts.

BEYOND ANTISEMITISM

Part of the problem in distinguishing between antisemitism and the Jew/non-Jew ordering system from which it stems is that we lack a neutral term to denote the relationship between the Jew and the non-Jew. In the face of this lack, we often turn to the term *antisemitism*, even though antisemitism is only one iteration of the relationship(s) between the mutually constitutive and hierarchical ideals of the Jew/non-Jew. To be sure, scholars such as Sander Gilman have long acknowledged the historical importance of the figure of the Jew as an imagined Other in its function as part of a broader social framework.[3] And Shulamit Volkov's seminal work on antisemitism, for example, did much to advance our historical understanding of this phenomenon by showing how antisemitism functioned as a cultural code in Germany to articulate a host of other political and social tensions.[4] However, although it is not articulated as such, this scholarship, too, suggests a broader, yet unnamed, frame of constructed ideals of Jews and non-Jews from which antisemitism stems.

An analogy with gender is helpful to explain the distinction between antisemitism and the broader framework from which it stems. As Joan Scott noted, the term "gender" is readily used in part because it sounds neutral and objective: "'Gender' seems to fit within the scientific terminology of social science and thus dissociates itself from the (supposedly strident) politics of feminism. In this usage, 'gender' does not carry with it a necessary statement about inequality nor does it name the aggrieved (and hitherto invisible) party." Scott also notes that part of the strength of the term "gender" lies in its suggestion that both women and men are co-constitutive of the world they live in, and its insistence that what happens to women is completely separate from what happens to men is a fiction. Moreover, it allows us to reject essentialist, biological explanations for what women and men are, in that it instead denotes "cultural constructions" as the "exclusively social origins of the subjective identities of men and women."[5]

To articulate the Jew/non-Jew framework without automatically referring to its most negative iteration, antisemitism, we require an equally powerful term that occupies a linguistic space similar to the one gender occupies with regard to the relationship between the constructed ideals of man and woman.[6] We need this term because "antisemitism" is not equivalent to the framework that generates negative iterations of the Jew, just as the terms sexism, misogyny, and chauvinism are not equivalent to gender. Antisemitism can never be a neutral term, nor can it ever suggest that Jews and non-Jews are co-constitutive of the world they inhabit. I argue that using the term "Jewish difference" to refer to this paradigm is helpful because it opens up our understanding of the Jew/non-Jew binary as an ordering system even when its effects are not necessarily explicit or negative.[7] It also permits us to see how the categories of the Jew and non-Jew can be applied to anyone, regardless of whether they are Jewish or not. It also helps us see how this framework persists in perpetuating Otherness: while, historically, the Jew is the fundamental other, the figure of the Jew can also be replaced with a different other—such as, in recent examples in Germany, the Muslim.

Because the terms "Jew" and "Jewishness" refer only to one half of the constructed Jew/non-Jew binary that forms the basis of this analytic category, we cannot rely upon them alone to do the analytic work we need to describe these phenomena, because these terms do not indicate that the notion of the constructed Jew depends upon the notion of the constructed non-Jew.[8] Used in this manner, "Jewish difference" does not promote or celebrate "differences" between Jews and others.[9] Rather, it suggests that those differences are real only insofar as people consider them to exist, and then act upon those considerations. The word "difference" in this sense denotes the presence of the category of the "non-Jewish" and as such is analytic rather than prescriptive.

With the best of intentions, some might wish to imagine that, because it is constructed, this Jew/non-Jew binary is not so important. However, scholars have already shown the harm in downplaying the importance of difference to how people order their worlds. The work of scholars of racism who have addressed the dangers of such often well-intentioned desires to erase difference can be instructive in reflecting on the difficulties some have with conceptualizing antisemitism and Jewish difference in Central Europe. Robin DiAngelo, for example, argues that "color-blind racism," or acting as if racial differences do not exist or do not matter, ironically works to uphold the social structures that created these discrepancies by providing a convenient excuse for avoiding their discussion. In her research, DiAngelo has found that many who consider themselves to be progressive and liberal often insist "I don't see color," claiming that race only matters to racists and that discussion of racial difference is to blame for perpetuating it. However, she argues that these denials actually indicate an unrecognized preference of white people not to recognize their own role in a deeply internalized system of racism from which nobody is exempt.[10] By reducing racism to isolated incidents of violence instead of recognizing it as a larger structure in which all people hold prejudices and are affected by its forces, such individuals avoid the complicated historical and structural analysis needed to challenge the binary system of thinking from which these acts stem. As she puts it, "Differential treatment in itself is not the problem. . . . The problem is the misinformation that circulates around us and causes our differential treatment to be inequitable."[11]

Alison Bailey helpfully characterizes such refusals to recognize systemic prejudices and the avoidance of engaging ideas people perceive as threatening as "privilege-preserving epistemic pushback." Attempts to deny the inequalities produced by systemic difference can be used to guard and defend one's terrain and maintain the status quo, allowing members of groups in the dominant position to unconsciously push back against ideas that disrupt their place in that system.[12] Rejecting the binary of Jewish difference and insisting that we not focus on it, even though it deeply affected and continues to play a role in Jews' experiences in Central Europe, suggests a similar defensive response. Moreover, rejecting the broad and often unarticulated systemic effects of the Jew/non-Jew binary in favor of focusing solely on isolated, explicit acts of antisemitic violence allows often well-meaning individuals to imagine themselves as operating comfortably outside this system, instead of facing its difficult challenges head-on.[13]

THE CONSTRUCTED ANTISEMITE

It is for this reason that not only gender, but also feminism—in the sense of recognizing the constructed nature of man and woman and acknowledging the subordinate position of woman in the gender binary—is also crucial to our understanding of Jewish difference. Since the Holocaust, the constructed or figural Jew—that is, an ideal of the Jew—has been largely understood as serving as the antithesis of the figural Antisemite—a conceptual failure that obscures the true nature of the paradigm from which antisemitism stems. Jean-Paul Sartre crystallized this figural Antisemite in his influential *Réflexions sur la question juive* (1946).[14] Many quote his observation "If the Jew did not exist, the anti-Semite would invent him" to pinpoint the constructed nature of the figural Jew.[15] However, we need to recognize that according to Sartre's formulation, the counterpart to this constructed Jew is not its antithesis, but its opponent. Sartre states that the Jew is constructed in the mind of the Antisemite, but what his words *really* show is his own construction of the Antisemite: the mind of the self-proclaimed *Anti*-antisemite—that is, himself—thus allowing him to displace his own responsibility in society for the consequences of Othering.

Sartre's iteration is an expression of a broader phenomenon. As Europeans adapted to postwar conditions, they relied upon this culturally constructed category—the Antisemite—as a way to come to terms with their radically changed circumstances while absolving themselves of complicity in its disastrous effects in the Holocaust. As an easily adaptable, readily recognizable ideal figure, the Antisemite loomed large as a trope all Europeans used both to avoid responsibility for crimes committed by the Nazis and their helpers as well as to subsume Jews' experiences together with those of other victims. Decades before Jews' experiences in the Holocaust would emerge as a master moral paradigm of suffering under evil, and long before equating Jews with Nazis became a significant form of Holocaust denial, the figure of the constructed Antisemite provided a forceful narrative structure that allowed for recognizable paradigms about Jews and non-Jews to persist, even as explicit expressions of antisemitism became taboo.[16]

Given Sartre's intimate romantic and intellectual relationship with Simone de Beauvoir and their links to existentialist philosophy, it is no coincidence that Sartre's discussion of the relationship between the Antisemite and Jew bears many similarities to de Beauvoir's critique of the Man/Woman dialectic, which she outlined in her *Le Deuxième Sexe* (1949, translated as *The Second Sex*, 1953).[17] The question of who influenced whom to a greater degree is still contested.[18] But Sartre's explicit concern with antisemitism mirrors de Beauvoir's analysis of sexism on a fundamental level: the erasure of the subjectivity of the Other. Regarding women, Beauvoir posited that femininity was not a natural state, but rather a social construction according to which Man was the absolute subject—the representative of the human norm—and Woman his Other. Though scholars have often criticized various other aspects of her work, de Beauvoir's analysis of sexism represents one of her strongest contributions to our understanding of gender. Her work reveals that the relationship between the concepts of Man and Woman is an unequal dialectic, with Man signifying the universal, or human, and Woman its Other. Women have little choice but to accept—or reject—these significations; either way, they are unable to modify their terms.

Toril Moi illustrates de Beauvoir's keen identification of this paradox: To explain what she means, Beauvoir gives an example. In the middle of an abstract conversation, a man once said to her: "You say that because you are a woman." If she were to answer: "I say it because it is true," she writes, she would be eliminating her own subjectivity. But if she were to say: "I say it because I am a woman," she would be imprisoned in her gender. In the first case, she has to give up her own lived experience; in the second, she must renounce her claim to say something of general validity.[19]

Here, the impossibility of escaping the parameters of gender without erasing one's subjectivity mirrors Sartre's pronouncement that it is impossible for a Jew to choose not to be a Jew. Take, for example, Sartre's contention that "The one thing Jews can never choose is *not* to be a Jew."[20] If they do, according to Sartre, they will be in a futile position—"inauthentic Jews." For Sartre, this category is a theoretical impossibility, as a Jew who attempts this denial of subjectivity merely reinforces the terms that created them in the first place. But what his words also imply, although he doesn't say them explicitly, is that one who is not a Jew *can* deny being an Antisemite. In doing so, one can be an *Anti*-antisemite: someone who is neither Jew nor Antisemite, but—like Sartre himself—is able to reject the terms of this ordering system and float over and above the fray.

But de Beauvoir's solution—a call to action for women to demand freedom from their oppression—along with her focus on the patriarchal nature of gender and its implication of women in their own oppression, contributed to her eventual fall into disfavor. Many feminists later rejected what they viewed as her dismissal of women's agency in defining femininity, resenting the claim that women must either abandon femininity as a basis for self-identification, or remain complicit in their own oppression by accepting its terms. Yet, the notion that the categories of Woman and Man are constructions remains difficult to refute. Perhaps due to her influence, Sartre was also working with a similar binary of constructed categories, even if he mistakenly replaced the category Non-Jew with Antisemite in order to create a comfortable position for himself on that spectrum.

Hannah Arendt also reflected on the parallels between gender, Jewish difference, and subjectivity, even if she did not use these terms in the same way. In a letter to Gershom Scholem in 1963, Arendt refers to her Jewishness as an "indisputable fact in my life":

> I have never pretended to be anything else or to be in any way other than I am, and I have never felt tempted in that direction. It would have been like saying that I was a man and not a woman—that is to say, kind of insane. . . . There is such a thing as a basic gratitude for everything that is as it is; for what has been given and not made; for what is *physei* and not *nomos*.[21]

Arendt wrote defensively in order to counter Scholem's accusation that as a Jew, she should treat the extermination of Jews in the Holocaust more sensitively. Given the timing of this letter after the Holocaust, her insistence that both Jew and woman are inalienable categories is understandable. However, as sympathetic as we may be regarding her reasoning, we still cannot deny her error in refusing to recognize that society functions according to constructed ideals of "woman/man" as well as "Jew/non-Jew," and these form the basis of ordering systems that impact all of our experiences. Arendt's postwar concerns help shed light on the deficiencies of Sartre's formulation of the Jew as the product of the Antisemite's imagination, as well as his own insistence of the Jew as a natural category.

NEW DIRECTIONS

In his 2013 book *Anti-Judaism: The Western Tradition*, David Nirenberg contextualizes a wide range of negative experiences based on constructed ideas of the Jew by referring to their broader place in a "powerful theoretical framework for making sense of the world."[22] However, in labeling this framework as "anti-Judaism" and using only

explicit, negative examples, Nirenberg, too, continues to conflate the negative iteration of the Jew/non-Jew framework with the broader theoretical basis that forms this
potent, dynamic ordering system. Used in this manner, "Anti-Judaism" forecloses other
iterations of Othering as well as the possibility of an engagement with this framework
in less explicit and more nuanced forms. To name one example, in the case of Jewish
members of sport teams in interwar Vienna, researchers have shown that the degree to
which their Jewishness mattered to themselves and others depended upon a complex
structure of functions and roles depending on the time, place, and situation. Using
Jewish difference as their analytical framework, they are able better to pinpoint how
and why Jewishness mattered at certain times and became irrelevant at others—even
when not explicitly apparent—instead of relying solely on negative iterations of the
frame to prove the existence of an engagement with the Jew/non-Jew binary.[23]

Recognizing Jewish difference and the persistence of the figural antisemite can
also help us understand their links to the persistence of philosemitism in Europe. As
Jonathan Judaken has pointed out, antisemitism and philosemitism often exist side
by side, utilizing the same stereotypes, albeit for different ends.[24] The fact that the two
terms emerged almost simultaneously in Germany toward the end of the nineteenth
century helps us see how they are both belief systems that ascribe certain characteristics to Jews as part of a hierarchical ordering system. In the wake of the Holocaust, the
murder of Europe's Jews didn't eradicate the use of this powerful framework of Jewish
difference as a way to continue to order the world. Because of the murderous deeds
of the Nazis and their helpers, Jews were now largely absent, and the explicit use of
antisemitism—in both words and deeds—was now largely taboo. The postwar propen-
sity to distance oneself from public and explicit antisemitic words and deeds has been
aptly termed "antisemitism without antisemites."[25] That many remained bitter about
this new taboo on something that once featured as an integral facet of prewar culture
is clear from a common joke about how "the Nazis ruined everything—even antisemitism."[26] It is these two major changes that led to a shift in how Jewish difference was
engaged after the end of World War II. In the postwar era, it was taboo to speak negatively about Jews. But these negative qualities and essences are often evoked so that the
hierarchical framework of Jewish difference is perpetuated even in their absence. This
invisibility of the Jew also opened the opportunity for others—such as Muslims—to
take their place as an "other" as part of this system.

The notion that Jews played a major role in the creation of culture in modern
Central Europe is far from new, but we have only recently begun to probe in depth
the role of the socially constructed category of the "Jew" in that process beyond the
prejudices—or advantages—it generated. Gender studies takes it as a given that the
socially constructed ideals of the "feminine" and the "masculine" stem from, but are
not equivalent to, actual men and women, and that these ideals profoundly affect

everyone's social and cultural environment. In contrast, Jewish studies as a discipline typically deploys the idea of the socially constructed Jew only in relation to antisemitism. Thus, our study of the Jewish past remains biased in favor of the constructed Jew as a figment of the antisemitic imagination and the constructed antisemite as a convenient way to displace responsibility for the consequences of Othering.[27] The recent pattern of antisemitic attacks, philosemitic and anti-Muslim responses in Germany and elsewhere, along with their accompanying unanswered questions, makes recognizing the broader analytic system that encompasses Jews, non-Jews, and antisemites imperative.

NOTES

1. Yitzchak Melamed, "The Events at the Bonner Hofgarten This July 11th: A Letter to a German Friend," public post at https://www.facebook.com/yitzhak .melamed/posts/10204784038197204, accessed July 15, 2018. See also https://www.zeit .de/gesellschaft/2018-07/jitzchak-jochanan-melamed-polizeigewalt-antisemitismus -kippa-attacke-bonn, accessed July 19, 2018.

2. For example, see the 2017 Arte documentary *Re: Weil du Jude bist. Die Geschichte von Oscar, Opfer von Antisemitismus*, about a fourteen-year-old from Berlin who faced constant antisemitic attacks from fellow students. That these students are Muslim is suggested but not thoroughly engaged as part of the documentary.

3. Sander L. Gilman, *Inscribing the Other* (Lincoln: University of Nebraska Press, 1991). Gilman notes that this figural Jew is male, which points to the gendered nature of the framework of Jewish difference, a topic in its own right.

4. Shulamit Volkov, "Antisemitism as a Cultural Code: Reflections on the History and Historiography of Antisemitism in Imperial Germany," *Leo Baeck Institute Year Book* 23 (1978): 25–46.

5. Joan W. Scott, "Gender: A Useful Category of Historical Analysis," *American Historical Review* 91, no. 5 (1986): 1053–1075; 1056.

6. This essay expands upon arguments I presented in "Beyond Antisemitism: A Critical Approach to German Jewish Cultural History," *Nexus 1: Essays in German Jewish Studies* (2011): 28.

7. I expand on the use of this term in my book *Becoming Austrians: Jews and Culture between the World Wars* (New York: Oxford University Press, 2012).

8. See, for example, Cynthia Baker's engaging discussion of the term "Jew" and its symbolic uses throughout history in *Jew* (New Brunswick: Rutgers University Press, 2017).

9. For a critique of the use of this term, see Benjamin Baader, "Introduction: Special Issue on Gender Theory and Theorizing Jewishness," *Journal of Modern Jewish Identities* 11, no. 1 (2018): 1–4.

10. Robin DiAngelo, *White Fragility: Why It's So Hard for White People to Talk about Racism* (Boston: Beacon Press, 2018), 71–73.

11. DiAngelo, *White Fragility*, 79–80.

12. Alison Bailey, "Tracking Privilege-Preserving Epistemic Pushback in Feminist and Critical Race Philosophy Classes," *Hypatia* 32, no. 4 (Fall 2017): 876–892; 879.

13. I discuss the development of this defensive attitude toward antisemitism in my forthcoming book, *The Postwar Antisemite: Culture and Complicity in Germany and Austria after the Holocaust.*

14. See Virginia M. Fichera, "Simone de Beauvoir and 'The Woman Question': Les Bouches inutiles," *Simone de Beauvoir: Witness to a Century, Yale French Studies* 72 (1986): 51–64; here 53. See also Catherine Léglu, ed., *Les Bouches inutiles: Simone de Beauvoir* (Bristol: Bristol Classical Press, 2001); and Jonathan Judaken, *Jean-Paul Sartre and the Jewish Question: Anti-antisemitism and the Politics of the French Intellectual* (Lincoln: University of Nebraska Press, 2006), 127, 134.

15. Sartre, *Anti-Semite and Jew* (New York: Schocken, 1965), 54. It is worth noting that writer Hermann Bahr already drew this conclusion in 1894: "Wenn es keine Juden gäbe, müßten die Antisemiten sie erfinden," *Der Antisemitismus: ein internationale Interview*, in *Hermann Bahr. Kritische Schriften in Einzelausgaben*, vol. 3, ed. Claus Pias (Weimar: VDG, 2005), 2.

16. I explore the notion of the constructed Antisemite, as well as its links to Adorno and Horkheimer's concept of the "authoritarian personality," in my forthcoming book project, *The Postwar Antisemite*.

17. The most recent translation of *The Second Sex* is by Constance Borde and Sheila Malovany-Chevallier (London: Jonathan Cape, 2009).

18. Sartre based his book on his article "Portrait de l'Antisémite," which appeared in *Les Temps modernes* in December 1945 and was published by Schocken Books as *Anti-Semite and Jew* in 1948. "Portrait of the Anti-Semite," an abridged version of Sartre's 1945 article, also appeared in English in the *Partisan Review* in 1946; parts of this were also published in *Commentary* in 1948.

19. Toril Moi, "'It changed my life!' Everyone should read Simone de Beauvoir's *The Second Sex*," *The Guardian*, January 12, 2008, 3.

20. Sartre, *Anti-Semite and Jew*, 69, 89, 93.

21. "'Eichmann in Jerusalem': An Exchange of Letters between Gershom Scholem and Hannah Arendt," *Encounter* 22, no. 1 (January 1964): 51–54, reprinted in *Hannah Arendt: The Jewish Writings*, ed. Jerome Kohn and Ron H. Feldman (New York: Schocken, 2007), 465–467.

22. David Nirenberg, *Anti-Judaism: The Western Tradition* (New York: Norton, 2013), 463–464.

23. Susanne Helene Betz, Sema Colpan, et al., "Jüdischer Sport in Metropolen: Einleitende Bemerkungen," *Aschkenas* 27, no. 1 (2017): 1–8; 2.

24. Jonathan Judaken, "Between Philosemitism and Antisemitism: The Frankfurt School's Anti-Antisemitism," in *Antisemitism and Philosemitism in the Twentieth and Twenty-first Centuries*, ed. Phyllis Lassner and Lara Trubowitz (Newark, 2008): 23–46; 27–29.

25. Bernd Marin, "A Post-Holocaust 'Anti-Semitism without Anti-Semites'? Austria as a Case in Point," *Political Psychology* 2, no. 2 (Summer 1980): 57–74.

26. "'Die Nazis haben ja alles ramponiert,' raunzte ein Alt-Wiener, 'selbst den Antisemitismus.'" G. Zivier, *Ernst Deutsch und das deutsche Theater. Fünf Jahrzehnte deutscher Theatergeschichte. Der Lebensweg eines großen Schauspielers* (Berlin: Haude & Spener, 1964), 78.

27. To be sure, not all historians fall into this trap. See "Jewish Studies Meets Cultural Studies: New Approaches to the German-Jewish Past," *Journal of Modern Jewish Studies* 8, no. 1 (2009): 41–120.

NEWSPAPER FEUILLETONS

Reflections on the Possibilities of German-Jewish Authorship and Literature

LILIANE WEISSBERG

IN THE EARLY twentieth century, many prominent authors who wrote feuilleton articles for German newspapers were Jews. When and why did this genre become attractive to German-Jewish authors? And how did the place of publication influence their writing, as well as the reception of their work? This essay will explore these questions by offering some reflections on the complex history of German-Jewish literature, and some general observations that should pave the way for more detailed study and analysis.

DEFINING MATTERS

The feuilleton itself was invented in France at the turn of the nineteenth century—but such a statement speaks only to the coinage of the word and to the articles' specific placement in a news publication. It does not describe the kind of literature published as feuilletons. Articles that are similar to those published as feuilleton pieces existed before the introduction of the word; they were printed in different kinds of publications, and thus in a different context.

In early eighteenth-century Germany, book reviews and essays related to cultural events were published in journals called *gelehrte Zeitschriften* or *Zeitungen* (Learned Journals or Papers), or *Intelligenzblätter* (News and Announcement Sheets). They were seasonal, monthly, or weekly publications that were aimed at an educated audience of academics and professionals and contributed to the establishment of a new public sphere.[1] The papers represented and helped forge the German bourgeoisie, a newly emerging *Bildungsbürgertum* that prided itself not so much on inherited titles as on academic ones; these were not conveyed at birth, but after years of education, and hence a life of reading and writing. *Bildung* was not simply the same as education. It derived from a biological concept of growth and nurture, and *Bildung* was supposed to turn a human being into an enlightened person who would find self-fulfillment. By the late eighteenth century, the acquisition of knowledge would promote increasingly specialized disciplines, but general knowledge was deemed just as important. Reading a variety of books and also journals helped the new bourgeoisie to achieve that goal.

The *gelehrte Zeitschriften* evolved from earlier, simple announcement sheets that were published on the occasion of the seasonal fairs at Leipzig when new books were published and introduced. For the *gelehrte Zeitschriften*, new book publications would be news as well, albeit not necessarily political news. But any announcement published in such a journal was always also more than simply that. Christian Gottlob Heyne, the editor of the *Göttingischen Anzeigen von gelehrten Sachen* (an announcement sheet of "learned matters"), explained in 1784:

> To understand *gelehrte Zeitungen* as a collection of reviews would represent a rather narrow point of view. They are and can do much more. By virtue of these *gelehrte Zeitungen*, one will be able to judge the rise and fall of knowledge, i.e. its very progress, and gain insights; one will be able to study a country and its people.[2]

These articles did not only reflect on intellectual matters, but produced knowledge as well.

For the history of the feuilleton in France, the year 1789 serves as a crucial marker. At the time of the French Revolution, newspapers were not only eager to report on current political events, but also to expand their offerings and add print supplements. The articles published in these supplements were not only defined by their content, but also the contrast to the printed news. Like the German *gelehrte Zeitschriften*, newspapers had already begun to publish book reviews, plays, and also essays, but now, they were aiming at a larger audience. The audience of potential readers had expanded, and readers were eager to learn about current political events and new developments and welcomed editorials and reviews. There was a strong demand for newspaper fare. While the papers' news section looked to the *past* and reported about what had happened, some articles aimed to describe the *present* situation and look *forward*. These pieces were different from the news.

To implement an expanded program of publication, the political *Journal de Débats* issued articles on separate sheets that were to be inserted into the paper and could easily be removed. By 1800, the *Journal* was describing this section as one of announcements or *annonces*, and it would become a regular feature for the *Journal* as well as other French papers.[3] The innovation of printing and inserting additional leaves—or *feuillets*—led to the name *feuilleton*. And as newspapers began to offer more than just news, the name given to these additions was transferred to the German language and beyond. While the feuilleton marked a new kind of publication, it did not describe a new kind of text or even content. The feuilleton was a matter of format. Articles were simply placed as supplement. The feuilleton was the partner as well as the *other* of the political news.

In many ways, the establishment of the French feuilleton was an aftereffect of the Revolution. Very soon, however, the name feuilleton itself would prove to be technically inappropriate. For economic reasons, papers ceased to separate the feuilleton from the news via the publication of additional, inserted pages. News and non-news began to appear on the same page, but they were marked as being different from each other. A printed line would distinguish articles published above (i.e., the news) from those published below (i.e., the non-news), and thereby offer a clear and hierarchical distinction between reporting about political events and those articles that were less important and placed *rez-de-chaussée* or "below the line." News came first. Whether the feuilleton was published on separate sheets or on the same page, the newspaper's printing practice of separating items would provide the reader with some guidance as to how its content should be read and evaluated.

The *Kölnische Zeitung* (Cologne Daily) was an early German newspaper to adopt this mode of publication when it established a feuilleton section in 1816.[4] Undoubtedly, it was guided by the printing practice in nearby France. The country to the left of the Rhine had influenced German newspaper culture before the Revolution, but with the Revolution, and the ensuing French occupation of German lands under Napoleon, French influence had increased. Moving eastward, Napoleon's troops did not only introduce paper money to Germany, the so-called *Assignaten*, but also other kinds of print as well. And while the Wars of Liberation of 1813–1814 responded to Napoleon's military ventures and led to his defeat, they did not put an end to the French impact on the German press.

After the failed bourgeois revolution of 1848, German newspaper culture would evolve further and more dramatically.[5] Literacy had already spread widely in Germany, and for a time, the harsh political censorship of the press was suspended. Established newspapers would increase the rise of editions, and many new papers were founded. A good number of these endured and prospered in the years to follow. With these papers, the feuilleton was established as a mainstay of German public culture. Indeed, the feuilleton was now crafting and transmitting not revolutionary ideas, but those of a new national project. If Germany was to be united, the feuilleton would provide important support for this cause. It was to contribute to a unification of culture.

Because of the changes in press censorship, newspapers could adopt a wide array of political opinion and conservative voices were published as well as those of the left. And while all of these papers were trying to address a large audience, the authors of their articles were not always known. Many writers used initials only or did not sign their pieces. Some writers were on the newspaper's payroll, but many were not. Early on, the feuilleton section offered opportunities for freelance authors and its economic model would largely rely on them.

For Germany's Jews, the mid-nineteenth century offered great political and social changes. The newspapers' rise in the nineteenth century coincided with the move for Jewish emancipation, granted by many German states in the early to mid-century. It marked the official entry of Jews into German political life, albeit in limited ways, and writing for newspapers was one path of entry. Journalism was a new profession, and outside any established system of German guilds. Most German Jews had already abandoned Western Yiddish and were writing in German now; their voices could be heard beyond the Jewish communities addressing a wider German audience. Because of the rapid growth of the newspapers many could find employment options. Jews could join the new newspapers as editors and even owners. Newspapers offered the possibility of business ownership, of employment, and careers in writing. In general, it seemed easier to write for, and get published by papers than to break into the already established book business.

Heinrich Heine and Ludwig Börne, two of the most famous German writers of this period, wrote for the feuilleton section. Both had converted to Protestantism but still identified as Jews. They were but two of many Jewish journalists of this time, not all converts. Perhaps it was not accidental that they plied their trade as Paris correspondents, writing from a country that was regarded as the cradle of the feuilleton. "Without Heine no feuilleton," Karl Kraus would state many decades later in his very own journal, *Die Fackel* (The Torch), which attempted to enlighten its public with its fiery flame. "This is the French disease (*Franzosenkrankheit*) that he has brought to us."[6] Kraus was Jewish himself, and lived in Vienna. But for Heine or Börne, their place of residence must have had special significance as well. France had already emancipated Jews shortly after the Revolution. Yet in Paris, a city largely without Jews at the time, both could become truly German authors.

German-Jewish authors saw the newspapers as an opportunity for publication. But how desirable was such a career and how respected was the writing of feuilletons? Compared to the news section of a paper, the feuilleton was less highly regarded. Compared to book publications, particularly the traditional three-volume novel, feuilletons must have appeared less important. But the feuilleton was not just marked by a line that separated this section from the news, it seemed to have flaunted this "outsider" status. Was this a reason, too, why it had become so popular with writers who were deemed outsiders as well, and who were not yet integrated in the established businesses of literature or the academy?[7] The example of the German feuilletons would inspire Jewish authorship in Russia, Poland, and elsewhere, and influence Yiddish writing also.[8]

By the early twentieth century, an interesting situation had emerged. Many leading newspapers in Germany were now owned by Jews such as Leopold Sonnemann (the *Frankfurter Zeitung* or Frankfurt Daily), Rudolf Mosse (the *Berliner Tageblatt* or Berlin Daily), and Leopold Ullstein (the owner of the *Berliner Illustrirte Zeitung* or Berlin Illustrated News); and many writers of the articles of the section "below the line" were either known to be Jewish or thought to be Jewish. In a peculiar *mise-en-abîme*, the feuilleton became known as the "Jewish part" of a German press that was also identified as Jewish. By 1932, the *Frankfurter Zeitung* felt it had to refute a claim made in an article of the *Deutsche Allgemeine Zeitung* (German General News) that its feuilleton, and Siegfried Kracauer's handling of it, was *undeutsch*, or non-German: "'German' is just not something that happily designates something else as non-German."[9] In many readers' perception, the wealthy owners of the papers, and their all-but-wealthy feuilleton authors, were similarly defined.

NEWSPAPERS AND BOOKS

The line that separated the news from the feuilleton may have produced a hierarchical distinction. Newspapers did not only address a progressively larger group of readers in the course of the nineteenth century, but readers from diverse classes and genders. While male readers eager to read the news might venture forth to read below the line, the feuilleton attracted female readers, too. Women were becoming an important new readership for newspapers and journals, and the papers were trying to accommodate this development. By the early nineteenth century, feuilleton sections were integrated into the newspapers, but in the following decades, some would spin off and form *Sonntagsbeilagen* or weekend supplements. These would develop later into separate journals aimed at a female, or at least gender mixed, readership.

In 1801, Johann Gottlieb Karl Spazier had begun to publish his *Zeitung für die elegante Welt* (Paper for the Elegant World) in Leipzig, possibly the first paper that focused entirely on articles relating to literature and culture that had a female readership in mind. The paper did not print any news but kept the format of a political paper; it appeared several times a week and offered various supplements.[10] *Die Zeitung für die elegante Welt* continued its publication until 1859. *Familienzeitschriften* (Family Journals) such as the *Gartenlaube*, founded in 1853, attempted even more consciously to include all family members as readers, offering articles not only for women, but also for the young. *Familienzeitschriften* tried to entertain, but also to encourage domesticity.[11] *Die Gartenlaube*, as the most prominent one of this genre, bore all external traces of a newspaper as well. In many ways, it was a feuilleton writ large. The *Gartenlaube* lasted even longer than the *Zeitung für die elegante Welt*. It changed ownership during the

National Socialist regime in 1938, continued publication until 1944, and thus survived for almost a century. Not every journal or paper welcomed Jewish authors, and some changed course eventually to follow an antisemitic agenda.

By the mid-nineteenth century, the feuilleton was being compared with another institution—namely the salon, although the salon was a place for conversation rather than print. In Berlin, social gatherings that would later be described as salons already flourished in the late eighteenth century. Their hostesses were women and the comparison with the salon was due to the feuilleton's female readership. Would the feuilleton feminize its male readership? The critic Wilhelm Heinrich Riehl issued a cautionary warning in 1854, stating also the danger of distraction:

> The "feuilleton" of our literature is a similar occurrence as the salon, but the person who will predominantly read feuilletons, will not be able to read any solid book in the end. A visitor to the salon cannot do this either anymore. The real salon guest is unable to do it anymore, he does no longer read books, but only read in books. He can also only continue conversations but can't conclude any. All in all, he can only instigate, but not complete any task; he will jump around, become unstable, a broken nature. He is no longer a true and complete man, and can no longer appreciate a complete man, because in the salon, personalities only pass each other by, but they take no hold of each other. This is the state of illness of our time. In contrast to these better people, I prefer those raised in a proper *Spinnstube* (room with a spinning wheel).[12]

The perhaps most prominent Berlin salons were sponsored by Jewish women such as Henriette Herz and Rahel Levin. In his study, written around 1900, of Berlin's cultural life of the beginning of the nineteenth century, Ulrich Tadday not only refers to the popularity of feuilletons by comparing them with these salons but also highlights private music rooms. For him, the German music feuilleton emerged in Berlin in the early nineteenth century. By 1825, the Berlin critic Adolf Bernhard Marx had become the most prominent reviewer of musical events. He wrote for a journal dedicated to reviews of musical performances—the *Berliner Allgemeine musikalische Zeitung*. Marx was born Jewish and converted to Protestantism as a young man; the music journal's publisher, Adolf Martin Schlesinger, would remain a Jew.[13]

In the course of the nineteenth century, even political newspapers that offered sections "below the line" succeeded with much more diverse fare than merely book reviews and announcements. In the end, the feuilleton was not only difficult to define, but also more difficult to locate. Some articles that would have previously been regarded as part of the feuilleton would move "above the line." A good number of articles were signed by the author, who thus gained prominence and a certain literary stature. Feuilleton authors began to demand recognition for their writing.

And thus, a paradox evolved. While the feuilleton's articles were not necessarily written for the moment, they were published in newspapers nevertheless, and thus assumed the life span of news reporting. After the date of their publication, newspapers were to be discarded or used to wrap butter or cheese in grocery stores. And just like this butter or cheese, newspaper literature was to be consumed before it became old. Articles appeared with an explicit publication and implicit expiration date. Because of their brief life span, newspapers were printed on cheap paper that would turn brown and disintegrate within a few weeks. In short, the feuilleton was the fast-food industry of literature. For scholars today, it offers the same challenges as any other ephemeral object of study. There is no fixed corpus that can be established. The conditions of archiving newspaper material are not good; few of the early German newspapers are digitized.[14] This differs quite clearly from the study of books that have been meant to endure.

And just as the line between the news and non-news would become progressively less distinct, newspapers and book publishing would enter a silent or not so silent agreement in regard to the feuilleton as well. Under the line, papers began to offer fiction and travelogues that could be collected and republished in book form. Indeed, in the late nineteenth century, German feuilletons began to fulfill the task of prepublishing manuscripts by testing the success of a literary production with a newspaper readership. The *roman feuilleton*, the *Fortsetzungsroman*, or the serialized novel, became popular with the newspaper readership. A successful early run in a paper provided a certain guarantee for that of a later book publication as well. Novels were now published in multiple versions: as newspaper fiction first, and then as codices.

Writers who produced serial literature would have particular writing styles that differed from those of other novelists. Most prominent authors of the mid- to late nineteenth century who followed this course were not writing in German, but in English or French. We know of the charts that Charles Dickens produced to keep track of his characters while submitting sequels of his novels each week, or of Honoré de Balzac's outlines, offered to a writing staff that would fill in the individual chapters' plots.[15] Theodor Fontane followed these English and French examples by writing short novels that were to be published in newspapers first.

The serialized novel was literature of the production line. Editors could stop ill-fated attempts, and not every novel was completed. Only a few would end up as books. But newspaper publishing was cheaper, and thus, the serial novel was an option for lesser known authors, or for those who wanted to try out experimental writing techniques. This happened increasingly in the early twentieth century. Alfred Döblin's *Berlin Alexanderplatz* is such a case in question; the daring expressionist work was published first in newspaper format. Editors at the *Frankfurter Zeitung* commented upon readers' reactions to the novel during the course of publication.[16] As some authors gathered the sections into best-selling books, a question would arise that touched the profession of the journalist. Should journalists really become novelists, Joseph Roth would ask; should they now not write for the day, but for posterity?[17]

With these novels, the feuilleton changed again and became curiously self-reflexive. Most of Fontane's novels took information from a newspaper article as the starting point, only to rework the news into historical fiction. Just like women, Jews turned into a new reading public as well and soon, a new field of literature emerged. Heine and Börne would write for a general German audience, but others began to write for a specifically Jewish one. The newspaper became a place where authors would try out modes of new German-Jewish fiction and address a wider readership in a cost-efficient way.[18] Döblin and Roth wrote from Berlin and Vienna as Jews, but for a general readership. Georg Hermann followed the example of Fontane, on the other hand, only to become one of the most popular novelists depicting German-Jewish middle-class life, addressing the German-Jewish bourgeoisie.[19] The nineteenth-century newspaper was the birthplace of popular or middle-brow Jewish literature that would also provide its readers with the guidance expected from the feuilleton. It would define and strengthen the idea of a German-Jewish identity. These serialized novels were perhaps not avant-garde in terms of literary form and content, but in social impact.

Another literary outcome of the popularity of the newspaper fiction was the rise of the novella, perhaps the most popular genre of fiction in nineteenth-century Germany. Already understood to be the rendering of a new and unheard-of event, many novellas would refer to the newspapers in their plot and often include news items or advertisements. Included in a section earlier named *annonces*, the novellas provided another *mise-en-abîme*. And just as in a mathematical summation, everything seemed to be gathered now "below the line" in the section of the feuilleton: the novel and the novella, the *causerie* and advice, the reviews and the brief essay.

For many readers of books, the separating line on the page was familiar, for by the nineteenth century, an implicit or explicit line had become *de rigueur* for academic volumes. There was the text, and on the bottom of the page, there were footnotes, referring to sources and offering additional reading, or strengthening an argument with further evidence.[20] They were not extraneous to the content above, but were to be the anchors of an argument and evidence of a scholarly discourse. The footnote and the feuilleton became mirror images of sorts. In terms of cause and effect, the feuilleton turned the footnote's task around. It was not primary, but was regarded as secondary material.

Early definitions of the feuilleton pointed to another effect of the line and the separation of texts. The *feuilleton*, Bernd Sösemann remarked, was nothing but "politics by other means."[21] While the newspaper part above the line provided the news, the section below the line offered the news' *Kommentar* or commentary. And here, the relationship between the feuilleton and Jewish authorship or literature may go beyond a consideration of the advancement of a new medium, the development of German political life, or the social and political situation of postemancipation Jewry. The feuilleton's very form and the critics' explanation for its raison d'être is telling. As the critic Benno Reifenberg wrote in 1929, "the feuilleton is the running commentary to politics."[22]

Understood as political commentary, or general *Kommentar*, the feuilleton could easily be integrated into possibly the most important and enduring tradition of Jewish thought and practice, that is, the reading of the Hebrew Bible. Students of Jewish literature regard the Torah as a holy book that contains the law. But while the Torah does not change, the law can be commented upon. The Torah is the written law. And indeed, the relationship between the unchanging law, received from God, and the attempts of understanding and appropriating the text via commentaries, has marked the tradition of reading Torah and Talmud, the oral law that was eventually put down in print, and it would mark the reading of other Jewish texts as well. Jews are not just the people of the book, they are the people of the commentary.[23]

In book history, this tradition has led to innovations in printing. From 1516 onward, Venetian book printers rendered the Talmud pages by offering spatial separations, if not exactly lines.[24] The Venetian printers may have had Christian models for this practice, following early Bible editions with glosses, but the custom was soon adopted as a particular Jewish form of reading that would make it possible to present a discussion on the page. The separations offered by the printers distinguish the main text from rabbinical commentaries that would move the law into current debate. Commentaries that appeared in the margins of the page were highlighted by different typefaces. In a curious way, the printing conventions of the feuilleton respond to this Jewish tradition. The distinction between the law and its interpretation was exchanged by the news and a secular commentary on life's events.

TOWARD THE AGE OF THE FEUILLETON

By the turn of the twentieth century, most German papers were published in major urban centers, and Berlin became a center of German-language newspaper publication, followed by Vienna and Frankfurt. These cities also boasted the largest Jewish communities. And as German Jews would begin to play major roles in these cities' cultural lives, newspapers reflected and supported their newfound status. They accompanied Jewish urbanization. Most of the Jewish newspaper writers and readers of Vienna had moved there recently from Budapest, Prague, or small towns of the *Kronländer*, that is, the territories of the imperial crown. Many Berlin Jewish newspaper writers or readers were not born there either, but hailed from Posen or Breslau or smaller towns in

Silesia and elsewhere. Viennese and Berlin newspapers unified all dialects and served as a point of immigration.

Indeed, one can consider the newspaper to be the urban medium par excellence. The paper's daily publication schedule met with the demand for fast information and a new sense of time, brought forth by a new mobility and technological advancements. The fast writing and fast reading of the papers contrasted with the leisurely pace of the study of books. The urban readers did not have time to digest long reports or disquisitions; they wanted short pieces. They would buy papers, read them cursorily, and then discard them. But they could also borrow them. For that, however, prospective readers no longer needed to visit public libraries. Newspaper readers could frequent other places that offered the opportunity of reading as well as social gathering—primarily the coffeehouse. If the salon had provided the image for the structure and content of the feuilleton, the coffeehouse would now provide the local context of writing, reading, and discussion.

In the coffeehouses, the writers of feuilletons would write, and their readers would read, and they could meet eye to eye. As the line between the news and the feuilleton began to waver, so did the line between the public and private realms. Journalists would write about private affairs, but their desk was in the public eye. Peter Altenberg (alias Richard Engländer) was a feuilleton writer known to be a *Kaffeehausmensch*, a person whose life took place in the coffeehouse where he wrote and where he was able to consult a wide range of newspapers as well.[25]

Jewish writers and artists like Altenberg became part of the new urban coffeehouse culture and helped to define it. Many of them became *Kaffeehausmenschen* par excellence, meeting, writing, and reading in the Café Central in Vienna or in the Romanisches Café in Berlin. For that, they had to secure a chair and sit down. But the opposite was true as well. The writing and reading of feuilletons were not necessarily sedentary occupations as they could be done on the move. Feuilleton writers were known to explore the city. Indeed, writing and reading, and especially fast writing and reading, synchronized with the era of railroad travel and shortly the invention of the motorcar and commercial aviation. The erstwhile urban *flaneur* assumed an increasingly faster pace.

The Jewish journalist Daniel Spitzer became famous with his *Wiener Spaziergänge*, Viennese Walks, a series that began in 1865, moved to various papers, and was finally published in the *Neue Freie Presse* until 1892. Spitzer's articles were viewed as social events.[26] Walter Benjamin reflected on the figure of the *flaneur* in essays dedicated to Charles Baudelaire and nineteenth-century Paris, or to the childhood memories of Berlin. But conscious of the new twentieth century, feuilleton writers as commentators exchanged the walks for drives. The hero of Döblin's *Berlin Alexanderplatz*, Franz Biberkopf, would view the city from the streetcar, and Erwin Egon Kisch would write in railroad cars.[27] Karl Kraus's fascination with his motorcar was famous, even if he did not have a driver's license himself.[28] "The airship is invented and the imagination crawls along like a stage-coach," Kraus would write; "automobile, telephone, and the mass dissemination of stupidity—who can say what the brains of the next generation will be like?"[29] The newspaper was a mass medium that joined ranks and tried to keep up with these new inventions. The feuilleton writer was transgressing the city in every possible way, observing landmarks, relating incidents, and offering concentrated prose miniatures.

By the early twentieth century, the feuilleton had changed from a kind of simple text placed below the line to a proper genre. Writing for the feuilleton often corresponded to an appreciation of new music, modern art, and architecture devoid of ornament. The key to all was perhaps a changing perception of time that the new technological inventions and the new economy brought forth. Due to the possibilities of a quick turnaround, the feuilleton could be viewed as a constant intervention, and letters to the editors provided a constant feedback from the reading public.

A feuilleton article would now be more stringently defined. It was brief and reflective of the incidents or everyday events that would ultimately define modern culture. The feuilleton essay could pursue entertaining observations, such as Kurt Tucholsky's question of why the cheese had holes,[30] or philosophical reflections, such as Ernst Bloch's or Benjamin's *Denkbilder* or thought images, but it was now recognizable by its style.[31] It rejected academic rigor and preferred personal, even subjective points of view. It offered a clear alternative to the desirable neutrality of scholarship or news reporting. It took a stand. It wanted to be reflective, but also to entertain. Feuilleton essays began to pride themselves on the well-turned phrase. And while the feuilleton had become an established part of the newspaper, it was often antiestablishment in style if not in content and of particular attraction to those writers who were outside the establishment. Especially after the First World War, when book publishing became more difficult because of economic reasons, the newspaper offered publishing options that would make it possible for authors to address an even wider audience and even take a political stance. In the early twentieth century, newspapers such as the *Frankfurter Zeitung* could be discriminating in turn and choose the most interesting authors for their pieces.

What, then, was the relationship of the feuilleton to German-Jewish culture by the early twentieth century? In the Golden Age of the feuilleton, the answer had to be as complex as ever. The feuilleton provided a publication forum for those Jewish authors who had not gained an academic position or yet produced best sellers. And what had perhaps begun at the time of the French Revolution in the historical context of a political revolt at which Germans had remained *derrière-garde*, evolved in the early twentieth century into the medium of the avant-garde for which German Jews in particular developed a certain affinity. It was understood to be clearly modern.

NOTES

1. Thomas Habel, *Gelehrte Journale und Zeitungen der Aufklärung. Zur Entstehung, Entwicklung und Erschließung deutschsprachiger Rezensionszeitschriften des 18. Jahrhunderts* (Bremen: Edition Lumière, 2007).

2. Christian Gottlob Heyne, "Vorrede," in *Allgemeines Register* über *die Göttingschen gelehrten Anzeiger von 1753–1782*, vol. I, ed. Friedrich Ekkart (Göttingen: Johann Christian Dieterich, 1784), 5–6 (translation mine).

3. Almut Todorow, "'Wollten die Eintagsfliegen in den Rang höherer Insekten aufsteigen?' Die Feuilletonkonzeption der Frankfurter Zeitung während der Weimarer Republik im redaktionellen Selbstverständnis," *Deutsche Vierteljahrsschrift für Literaturwissenschaft und Geistesgeschichte* (DVjs) 62, no. 4 (1988): 697–740; and Todorow, *Das Feuilleton der "Frankfurter Zeitung" in der Weimarer Republik. Zur Grundlegung einer rhetorischen Medienforschung* (Tübingen: Max Niemeyer Verlag, 1996), 9–12.

4. Georg Potschka, "Die Kölnische Zeitung," in *Deutsche Zeitungen des 17. bis 20. Jahrhunderts. Verlag Dokumentation,* ed. Heinz Dietrich Fischer (Pullach: Verlag Dokumentation, 1972),145–158.

5. Georg Jäger, "Das Zeitungsfeuilleton als literaturwissenschaftliche Quelle. Probleme und Perspektiven seiner Erschließung," in *Bibliographische Probleme im Zeichen eines erweiterten Literaturbegriffs. 2. Kolloquium zur bibliographischen Lage in der germanistischen Literaturwissenschaft*, ed. Wolfgang Martens, Georg Jäger, Wolfgang Harms, and Paul Raabe (Weinheim: VCH Acta humaniora, 1988), 53, 69.

6. Karl Kraus, "Heine und die Folgen," *Die Fackel* 329, no. 30 (1911), 1–33, here 7.

7. Hansjakob Ziemer describes Jewish feuilleton authors as "observers of society," a term that insists not just on marginalization, but implies exclusion. Ziemer, "Der ethnologische Blick: Paul Bekker und das Feuilleton zu Beginn des 20. Jahrhunderts," in *Kommunikationsräume des Europäischen—Jüdische Wissenskulturen jenseits des Nationalen* (ser.) Leipziger Beiträge zur jüdischen Geschichte und Kultur VIII, ed. Hans-Joachim Hahn, Tobias Freimüller, Elisabeth Kohlhaas, and Werner Konitzer (Leipzig: Leipziger Universitätsverlag, 2010), 113–129, here 120.

8. See, for example, Olaf Terpitz, "Russisches Feuilleton und jüdische Selbstverständigung: Kulturgeschichtliche Annäherungen an die 'kleine Form,'" in Hahn, Freimüller, Kohlhaas, and Konitzer, *Kommunikationsräume des Europäischen*, 99–112; and see the research project on the Yiddish and Hebrew feuilleton by Naomi Brenner (Ohio State University) and Shachar Pinsker (University of Michigan).

9. *Frankfurter Zeitung*, "Literaturblatt," no. 21 (May 22, 1932); cited in Todorow, "Wollten die Eintagsfliegen in den Rang höherer Insekten aufsteigen?," 717.

10. Ulrich Tadday, *Die Anfänge des Musikfeuilletons: Der kommunikative Gebrauchswert musikalischer Bildung in Deutschland um 1800* (ser.), Metzler Musik (Stuttgart: J. B. Metzler Verlag, 1993), 223.

11. Kirsten Belgum, "Domesticating the Reader: Women and *Die Gartenlaube*," *Women in German Yearbook* 9 (1993): 93–100; Dieter Barth, "Das Familienblatt—ein Phanomen der Unterhaltungspresse des 19. Jahrhunderts: Beispiele zur Gründungs- und Verlagsgeschichte," *Archiv für Geschichte des Buchwesens* 15 (1975): 121–315.

12. Wilhelm Heinrich Riehl, *Naturgeschichte des Volkes als Grundlage einer deutschen Social-Politik* (Stuttgart: C. G. Cotta, 1854), 256.

13. Christina Siegfried, "'Das Wirken Adolf Bernhard Marx': Aspekte zur musikkulturellen Entwicklung Berlins in der ersten Hälfte des 19. Jahrhunderts," Diss. Universität Potsdam, 1992.

14. Kai Kaufmann, "Zur derzeitigen Situation der Feuilleton-Forschung," in *Die lange Geschichte der Kleinen Form. Beiträgte zur Feuilletonforschung*, ed. Kai Kaufmann and Erhard Schütz (Berlin: Weidler Buchverlag, 2000), 10–24, here 12–13.

15. See Gerald Giles Grubb, "Dickens' Pattern of Weekly Serialization," *English Literary History* (ELH) 9, no. 2 (1942): 141–156; Lise Queffélec, *Le roman-feuilleton français au XIX siècle* (ser.) Que sais-je? (Paris: Presses universitaires de France, 1989).

16. See Peter Fritzsche, *Reading Berlin 1900* (Cambridge, MA: Harvard University Press, 1996).

17. Joseph Roth, "Einbruch der Journalisten in die Nachwelt," *Frankfurter Zeitung* 945 (December 19, 1925); cited in Todorow, "'Wollten die Eintagsfliegen in den Rang höherer Insekten aufsteigen?'" 731.

18. Jonathan Hess, *Middlebrow Literature and the Making of German-Jewish Identity* (Stanford: Stanford University Press, 2010).

19. Georg Hermann wrote for about forty Berlin newspapers, predominantly those issued by the Ullstein publishing house. His novels, including his famous *Jettchen Gebert* (1906) and its sequels, depicted Jewish middle-class life. See Godela Weiss-Sussex in conjunction with the Leo Baeck Institute London, ed., *Georg Hermann, deutsch-jüdischer Schriftsteller und Journalist, 1871–1943* (ser.) conditio Judaica 48 (2004).

20. See Anthony Grafton, *The Footnote: A Curious History*, rev. ed. (Cambridge, MA: Harvard University Press, 1997).

21. Bernd Sösemann, "Politik im Feuilleton—Feuilleton in der Politik. Überlegungen zur kommunikationshistorischen Bedeutung literarischer Texte und zu ihrer medienwissenschaftlichen Interpretation," in Kauffmann and Schütz, *Die lange Geschichte der Kleinen Form*, 45. The dictum refers to General Carl von Clausewitz's statement that war is nothing but a continuation of politics with other means.

22. Benno Reifenberg, "Gewissenhaft," *Frankfurter Zeitung* no. 482 (July 1, 1929); cited in Todorow, "'Wollten die Eintagsfliegen in den Rang höherer Insekten aufsteigen?'" 697.

23. Liliane Weissberg, "Kommentar," in *Handbuch Literatur und Religion*, ed. Daniel Weidner (Stuttgart: Metzler Verlag, 2016), 231–236.

24. See David Stern, *The Jewish Bible: A Material History* (ser.), Samuel and Althea Stroum Lectures in Jewish Studies (Seattle: University of Washington Press, 2017).

25. See Victoria Lunzer Talos and Heinz Lunzer (eds.), *Peter Altenberg—Extracte des Lebens: Einem Schriftsteller auf der Spur* (ser.), Jüdisches Museum Wien (Wien: Residenz Verlag, 2003).

26. See Matthias Nölke, *Daniel Spitzers «Wiener Spaziergänge»: Liberales Feuilleton im Zeitungskontext* (ser.), Münchener Studien zur literarischen Kultur in Deutschland 20 (Frankfurt a.M: Peter Lang, 1994).

27. See Dieter Schlenstedt, *Egon Erwin Kisch: Leben und Werk* (Berlin: Volkseigener Verlag Volk und Wissen, 1985).

28. See also the photo collection at the Brenner Archives in Innsbruck, featuring numerous images of Karl Kraus in or next to an automobile.

29. Kraus, *Die Fackel* 241 (1908): 14–15, trans. Edward Timms. Cited in Timms, *Karl Kraus: Apocalyptic Satyrist. Culture and Catastrophe in Habsburg Vienna* (New Haven: Yale University Press, 1986), 150.

30. Kurt Tucholsky, "Where Do the Holes in Swiss Cheese Come From?" in Tucholsky, *Berlin! Berlin! Dispatches from the Weimar Republic, Berlin Stories from the Golden Twenties*, trans. Cindy Opitz (New York: Berlinica Publishing, 2013), 148–153.

31. See Gerhard Richter, "Thought-Images," in *Thought-Images: Frankfurt School Writers' Reflections from Damaged Life* (ser.), Cultural Memory in the Present (Stanford: Stanford University Press, 2007); Jäger, "Das Zeitungsfeuilleton als literaturwissenschaftliche Quelle," 54.

The German-Israeli Complex

NAVIGATING MYTHICAL TIME

Israeli Jewish Migrants and the Identity Play of Mirrors

DANI KRANZ

IN THE END, you cannot escape yourself and your place in the world. The way Germany perceives us [Israelis] is entirely defined by the "past". And I don't only mean the Shoah, but the long history of relations between "Germany" and "Israel"—not only the State of Israel but the Israelites. It may be trivial, but sometimes you have to remind yourself: Berlin does not love me because I am gifted, clever, or because I speak English well or because I have a hot arse. She [Berlin] loves me because of Abraham Avino and Heinrich Himmler. At the end of the day, you are just a fantasy of somebody else. It is only because of that that this whole thing happens. You can live as though none of this exists, but it seems to me that it takes a lot of effort to inhibit. (Ofri Ilany, 2015)[1]

THE TITLE OF this volume, *The Future of the German-Jewish Past*, challenges concepts that fascinate anthropologists: time, space, and memory. Various anthropologists have addressed these topics; they seep through anthropological writing and theory.[2] Scholars of other disciplines such as history, literature, or performance studies also engage with them in various ways; the titles are too numerous to list. While my own attempt is transdisciplinary, it is based on multisited ethnography and opportunistic, ethnographic data collections in Germany and in Israel/Palestine, which began in 2002 while I worked in the field as an anthropologist. Yet my ethnographic work has been informed by my lifelong personal experiences.[3] This essay looks at a specific ethno-religious group—Jewish Israelis, in a specific spatial location, Germany, at a specific time, post-Shoah—all of which relate to specific, complex, contradictory, multifaceted, and competing constructions of memories by Israelis as well as about Israelis.[4] These tie into memories of Jews, the construction of physical memoryscapes and specific performances being interpreted as Jewish, turning non-Jews into assumed Jews,[5] and in the same vein leading to specific expectations in individuals who happen to be Jews.[6] Israelis and Jews, past, present, and future are inextricably linked in the particular trope of mythical time that is at the center of this paper.

My essay entwines some approaches to time, space, and memory and relates them to Israeli migrants—immigrants, emigrants, transmigrants, returnees, sojourners, however they referred to themselves—in Germany. I attempt to link negotiations about narratives of the past; interpretations of the present and visions of the future of the German-Jewish past. I also argue for the study of German-Jewish present(s) and future(s) set against a specific, yet differently conceptualized background, which the historian Ofri Ilany depicts bluntly in the quote above—an approach that must include Israeli Jews and which must be multivocal.[7]

Pre-Shoah German Judaism might well be dead; as Leo Baeck allegedly outlined as early as 1933, the German Jewry of pre-1933 does not exist anymore, the *Requiem Germani* outlasted its final tune,[8] although it continues its existence in mythical memory.[9] Be that as it may, living Jews exist in great diversity in present-day Germany, and Israelis form part of this diversity. Jews in Germany are anything but dead. Israelis constitute approximately 10 percent of all Jews in Germany, bringing their histories, their Israeli antecedents with them—and their own heterogeneous and conflicting ideas that intersect time, space, and memories. Against the backdrop of the past, they live the present and they envisage futures that carry a Jewish-Israeli twist.[10] These Israelis are part of the future of German-Jewish studies.

The following discussion will be presented in three key sections. I open with a short overview of the approaches to time, space, and memory, which form the theoretical basis for my ethnographic vignettes, collected among Israeli migrants in Germany (not only in Berlin) between 2002 and the present. The second part of the discussion deals with Israelis living in Germany, and the third part introduces the notion of "mythical time" as a practice in which time, space, and memory collapse into a matrix that morphs and informs identities as a resource.[11] Overall this discussion demonstrates how Israelis in Germany are impacted differently by the past and how they navigate their "mythical time," forming and informing their nuances of belonging that nourish possible future scenarios.

TIME, SPACE, AND MEMORY

Nancy Munn (1992) summarized a number of issues that had been covered in temporal theory by anthropologists and sociologists and cognate disciplines such as history and literary theory. While "time" might not have been the central research agenda in specific output, it is always there—time is the movement of things in space. Standing still does not exist in physical reality. Munn argues forcefully that "we" can never escape time: ethnographic fieldwork is based in time, our observations encircle a specific temporal period, our research partners—some might remain fieldwork participants, others might become friends over time—act in time, in some way we—as anthropologists—live the moment with them, we produce temporal accounts. Based on its multiple scopes, time within anthropological writing is inextricably linked to the analysis of structures of human groups and the time of individuals. We are subjects of time and to time; we employ time to structure ourselves, our groups, our societies, and we are structured by it; we use time as a differentiation mechanism within in-groups and to out-groups: "we," "us," "other," "time" are multilectal. Among early writings about time are those of Maurice Halbwachs (1925).[12] He linked the process of remembering as a social praxis to "mnemonic agencies," which relate to landscapes as well as objects; they are not restricted to human beings.[13] Halbwachs argued in favor of understanding time, memory, and remembering, as defined by social relationships that are also informed by space, forming the triad "time, space, memories."[14]

Social relationships including intergroup relations are subject to change over time: Maurice Halbwachs was murdered, starved to death in Buchenwald in 1945, less than two months before the end of the war. In regard to his untimely death the saying "time was not on his side" takes a bitter, infuriating meaning, which directly relates to a central aspect of this essay. The before, and the after, and that in the middle, which remains subject to numerous studies covering the Nazi regime, the multiple genocides, the radicalization of masses, the trite racism of the everyday, the murder of millions, the administrative, bureaucratic support apparatus. The attempts to connect the before, the middle, and the after beg a strange comparison. In chronological order they compare to the tripartite structure of time in a ritual as stipulated by Arnold van Gennep (1909).[15] They also relate to what Yosef Hayim Yerushalmi (1982)[16] argued: that there is historic time, and that there is mythical time. In his argument mythical time relates to the praxes of passing on the Jewish Covenant that is based on Jewish scripts through historical, and thus physical time. Drawing on Yerushalmi and Jacques Le Goff,[17] who put forward the notion "of the heroic age, and beyond that, of the age of origins"[18] that form the cornerstones of mythical memory,[19] and considering the mnemonic praxes of Halbwachs and the inescapable presence of time as put forward by Munn, I argue that Israelis in present-day Germany navigate a mythical time of their own: the mythical time of the (alleged) German-Jewish symbiosis constitutes the mythical memory benchmark, coming to terms with the aftermath of utter destruction and trauma, notions of the figure of the Jew[20] are afloat, and Israelis are confronted with all this and their own personal, intimate familial memories—family myths—at the same time.

While (violent) antisemitism formed part of the everyday of the Weimar Republic, Jews had arrived at the center of society; they had risen to positions of power as epitomized by politicians such as Walther Rathenau and Kurt Eisner; and furthermore Jews intermarried with Germans in significant numbers.[21] Non-Jewish Germans were torn about the Jews in their midst. For some, Jews had shifted from alien Asiatic people to German citizens of Jewish faith. Others believed in Jews being different and in the most extreme cases saw this difference residing in their "*artfremdem Blut*" (foreign species blood).[22] Jews in pre-Shoah Germany were heterogeneous; only the superimposed, racialized Jewishness united them into a blood-bound community of fate. From 1933 onward they were targeted by increasingly discriminatory state-initiated, widely supported policies and violence, deported, and murdered.

In parallel to ritualistic time the "after" of the lives of Jews in post-Shoah Germany were irreversibly different from pre-Shoah. Times had changed in the most absolute way. I think it is possible to speak of "traumatised time": the before, the middle, and the after cannot be connected. The triad became subject to memory work, postmemories, and contaminated intergenerativity of the second generation, which duly transmitted to the third generation in Germany and beyond.[23] Only a tiny number of German Jews survived and only the tiniest number of those who had survived in exile returned. A significant number of those who returned had survived in the British mandate of Palestine and returned from there, or, post-1948, from Israel, turning these German Jews and their children into the first Israeli migrants.[24] These surviving and returning German Jews were the minority of all Jews in (West) Germany. Eastern European displaced persons (DPs) constituted the majority, which was different from East Germany where German Jews were in the majority.[25]

It was not only the decimated Jewish population that had changed irreversibly; the German population had changed too. Some had believed in Nazi ideology and experienced the downfall as a disaster, while others experienced it as liberation. Trauma and violence remained common in German family configurations.[26] Some Germans who had opposed the Nazis returned; for example, Johannes Maier-Hultschin, the first spokesperson of the parliament of the newly founded state of North Rhine-Westphalia.[27] The state prosecutor Fritz Bauer returned and resumed office, determined that Auschwitz perpetrators should be brought to trial and sentenced in Germany. After spending years in Nazi concentration camps, Kurt Schumacher (SPD) became the first leader of the opposition in the *Bundestag*, dying prematurely in 1952. Yet, these individuals were the exception and their efforts met with substantial resistance. Nazi followers and sympathizers remained in positions of power after the war and their view of the world strongly impacted public discourse.[28] Memory politics became increasingly fraught with time, or more precisely, with the second generation of postwar Germans coming of age. In part, this generation refused to accept the silence and the pleas of ignorance of their parents' generation, leading to intergenerational conflict at a societal level.[29] To date, memory and memory politics remain fraught. Irit Dekel (2013) evidences different patterns of interpretations of the Holocaust memorial in Berlin; Nina Fischer (2015) shows specific familial memory nodes within Jewish families; while Kristin Platt (2012) highlights how memories of survivors are being doubted by German bureaucrats and Henning Borggräfe (2014) analyzes the struggles concerning restitution for slave laborers as part of the process of *Selbstaussöhnung* (reconciliation with oneself) among Germans. How to deal with restitution for slave laborers came up in the case of Jan-Robert von Renesse.[30] As a judge he was allegedly too empathetic on the issue of the *Ghettorente* (ghetto pension).[31] He was subjected to disciplinary action, removed from his position as a judge, and rewarded with a number of prizes by Jewish organizations and memory activists. He was not reinstated as a judge; the final agreement between von Renesse and the Ministry of Justice of the State of North Rhine-Westphalia is classified.[32] And, to make matters worse, or more human, von Renesse's family history could be interpreted as implicating him and removing him from the alleged neutrality of the legal professions.[33] The grandfather of his Polish wife had been murdered in a camp; his own grandmother hailed from Saint Petersburg, transmitting the Russian language to him, enabling him to read correspondence from claimants in the original language and speak with them directly. Realistically, he was more than suited to deal with restitution cases due to his legal expertise and his access to discourses beyond the hegemonic German one, turning him, also realistically, into precisely the wrong expert due to too much expertise that hit too close.

Conflicts about how to remember, what to remember, and about memory landscapes replicate in material culture. Memorials exist in the shape of abstract sculptures such as *Ma'alot* (Steps, Dani Karavan, 1986) next to Cologne's main train station, or the *Denkmal der ermordeten Juden* in the center of Berlin (Memorial of the murdered Jews, Peter Eisenman and Richard Serra, 2004), but also in minor cities such as Bergheim/Erft in depersonalized, deindividualized shapes.[34] *Stolpersteine* have been laid across various German cities, reminding passers-by of those who were taken from their midst, prosecuted, brutalized, and murdered—naming the individual and supplying basic biographic data. Memorials can also take the shape of *Mahn-*[35] *und Gedenkstätten* (memorial sites), making them different in outlay from museums. *Mahn- und Gedenkstätten* might include exhibitions and they might be in buildings of specific historical significance such as the NS-Dokumentationszentrum in Cologne, housed in the former Nazi administration building, which includes the former prison of the Gestapo in its basement. Yet memory and memorialization do not end with these official spaces: memories travel in the form of objects, an issue taken up by the Historisches Museum Frankfurt that poses the uneasy question *Geerbt. Gekauft. Geraubt? Alltagsdinge und ihre NS-Vergangenheit* (Inherited. Bought. Stolen? Things of

Memorial plaque, Bergheim/Erft, Germany. (Courtesy Dani Kranz, 2018.)

the Everyday and Their NS-Past).[36] Time, memories, and space form a triad in Germany that cannot be escaped—the triad hangs in the air, it is on the ground, in the ground, in buildings, in artifacts, in personal memories, and embodied in praxes of the everyday. To inhibit it all would not only take significant willpower; as Ilany stated: "I argue that the inhibited comes out in uncanny, unforeseen ways—it is impossible to inhibit."

MYTHICAL ISRAELIS

"This train really goes to Wannsee? To *the* Wannsee?" As a German born and raised, native German-speaking, German Israeli this question surprised me during fieldwork in Berlin. Where else would this train go, is there a different Wannsee? I wondered—a thought that was cut short by the utterance: "So this is where it *really* happened." Place names and spatialities triggered specific conceptualizations for the newly arrived Israelis, living up to the "mnemonic agencies" of Maurice Halbwachs. Spatialities or memorials caused them to react differently, sometimes less than me, sometimes more. "The trains, when I see these trains [cargo trains, D.K.], they just remind me . . ." was an admission at the train station in a suburb of Cologne that I had been using my whole life and which mainly annoyed me as a commuter. The Shoah had never before crossed my mind at *my* train station. Contrary to this "trite trauma memoryscape" memorials barely created harrowing thoughts, as their scope was clear so that one could avoid them at will; they were spatially limited and detached from everyday routines. Trains seemed to be frozen in time. They were experienced as a generalized epitome of terror and genocide, an abject object of the everyday, directly connected to Israeli memoryscapes of the Shoah.[37]

Child running through the Shoah Memorial, Rabin Square, Tel Aviv, Israel. (Courtesy Dani Kranz, 2013.)

They formed part of an Israeli metanarrative that shifted the Shoah away from personal, familial memories to cultural memories, creating cultural trauma as an effect,[38] and one could add, the absolute negative version of mythical memory par excellence. Often, Israelis who came to Germany had little factual knowledge about the past of their families—an issue that came up in autobiographically infused productions such as the films *The Flat* (Dir. Arnon Goldfinger, 2011), or *Schnee von Gestern* (Dir. Yael Reuveni, 2014). During fieldwork, statements such as: "I really had thought that nobody in my family had died [murdered during the Shoah, D.K.] before I came here [to Germany]," occurred with surprising regularity, alongside impromptu insights that the Shoah played on one's mind and came up in odd situations.[39]

A decade later, the same Israeli who had assumed his family had been spared, returned to our conversation: "I really thought that nobody had been killed. I mean, I'd be the only Ashkenazi who'd not lost family." His tone of voice indicated sarcasm, how he had been affected by time and spatialities: he could not uphold his Israeli-informed denial strategy in the wake of more than a decade of familiarity with Germany. Instead, his knowledge reflected my own puzzled and highlighted field-note, jotted down all those years earlier. Despite this knowledge he remains sure that Germany is "a father-land" to him "like it is for you as well," an issue we agree to disagree upon. To him, Germany feels like home ("I came home, I fit in better here than in Israel."), while it remains a perplexing and at times an alienating and strange country to me, despite, or possibly *because of* my nativity, local knowledge, and linguistic/cultural skills.[40] Asked about reasons for migration to Germany as part of our project *The Migration of Israeli Jews to Germany since 1990*, 50.6 percent indicated that German culture attracted them to Germany specifically, 30 percent stated they held German citizenship, 70 percent self-identified as Ashkenazim, while 55 percent had surviving parents or grandparents. This barrage of quantitative data tied in with interviews and ethnographic observations. The Israeli migrants had a specific attraction to Germany and/or Europe, which had been transmitted within their families and which underpinned their identity config-urations, leading to an actual or imagined similarity to other Germans/Europeans. Germanness and Europeanness in the specific shape of *Yekkishkeit* and *Ashkenaziut* had been transmitted against the Israeli odds within families.[41]

Israelis, my research participants and I, navigate mythical time in a specific mythi-cal space infused with mythical memories, in which past, present, and future collapse and congeal, forming a sticky matrix none of us could shake off: we were impacted and implicated. But we were not only subject to our own constructions that might lead to fall-traps, we were also subject to the phenomenon "Israelis in Germany," which was guided by curiosity, wishes, and desires from the (heterogeneous) German side.[42] In 2011, the German and Israeli media picked up on the alleged mass migration of Israelis to Berlin (as opposed to Germany). Indeed, mass migration is a gross overstate-ment. Between 20,000 and 25,000 Israelis live in Germany—this figure includes dual German/Israeli citizens as well as individuals who are defined statistically as falling into the category "migration background" Israel; these "individuals with an Israeli tinge" might or might not agree to this bureaucratically superimposed category. The latest figures of the major Israeli communities indicate a plateau. Yet, these very few Israelis became subject to media scrutiny: Who were they? Why were they here? And why did they come to Germany of all places? The Israeli migrants were assumed to be Jews, an assumption that holds for the majority according to our data. Besides being migrants of identity, Israelis sought professional and educational opportunities—approximately one third migrated for family reasons. Yet, German discourse was biased toward interpreting Israelis, supporting the argument of Michal Y. Bodemann that Jews conduct ideological labor for the German non-Jewish majority.[43] Continuing Bodemann's argument, Max Czollek argued that Jews are tied to specific themes, "antisemitism, Holocaust and Israel,"[44] which is amplified for Israeli Jews, who are not only Jews, but Jews from Israel and thus "*Superwiedergutmachungsjuden*," which means Jews who were related directly to having made good (*Wiedergutmachung*) the past: all of these intersecting factors assume a specific performance of the Israelis from the German side. Whether Israelis are happy in Germany; whether they suffer antisemitism; how they deal with the past; where they stand politically on the Israeli and the German governments was of major interest in Germany. While the majority of Israeli migrants defined themselves as liberal to moderate in political terms, and while they voiced criticism, their criticism of the Israeli government was taken up and reflected through a specific German filter. Criticizing Israel remains an issue related to the German past, confirming Bodemann's, Czollek's, and my assessments.[45] Yet, not only the memory of this past is shaping German/Israeli encounters—the Palestinian/Israeli conflict is becoming more decisive[46] in this relationship as a growing number of Germans view Israel in an unfavorable light. Israel-specific antisemitism has been increasing, independently of the influx of refugees/asylum seekers/migrants from the Middle East.[47]

NAVIGATING MYTHICAL TIME IN REAL LIFE TIME

Israelis migrate to Germany and the number of Israeli migrants has increased since the early 2000s. The migration is neither a mass migration nor a reverse aliyah. Aliyah le'Berlin is not happening. Israelis move to Germany for a number of reasons ranging from economic to professional, family, identity, return, love, and culture. Whatever their individual reasons, Israelis in Germany cannot escape the past in the present and neither can Jews or non-Jews in Germany. Time, space, and memory play into their being in the country in various ways, creating a specific mythical time in which past, present, and future collapse and congeal in a particular way, supporting certain expectations, interpretations, and relations, which in turn are subject to temporal dynamics. Yet they are never independent and "beyond" the past.

While time elapses further from the Shoah and most current Israeli migrants fall within the "third-generation" age bracket, they carry specific "memory luggage," interpreting their German present(s) and envisaging their German future(s) in a specifically Israeli-inflected way. The impact of the past in the present and in the future shows by way of quantitative data and ethnographic observations and also cultural productions of Israeli or German/Israeli co-productions. To date these often maintain a Shoah focus. The recent film *Back to the Fatherland* (2017) is awash with intersections of time, space, and memory—and also fantasies, underlining the issue that one can try to inhibit, as Ofri Ilany stated, but as I claim, one is bound to fail. The poster of the film is adorned with a reversed *Nazi-Reichsadler* (Nazi eagle), which forms the base of a menorah. The base of the menorah has exactly the same pattern as the menorah on the cover of Israeli passports; its arms turn into branches of a tree (of life, *etz haim*). The poster connects past, present, and future (growth) that springs from a negative symbiosis based on the "middle" segment of the tripartite structure outlined above.[48]

Below is the emblem of the title of the film with "fatherland" in pseudo-gothic script, a script widely used by the Nazis, while at the top the poster asks: "Do you have to ignore the past to build a future?" It is not only my contention that doing so is a nonoption, but even more that it is outright dangerous. An attempt to ignore, ignores factual history. It ignores the fraught and complex past and present. It oversimplifies human relationships. The before and the after remain separated by the middle sequence, the traumatized time that thwarts the notion of "normalcy" and which, supported by mythical memories, feeds into the creation of mythical time in which past, present, and future congeal. While "normalcy" is a construct, the construction of this specific abnormality needs to be unraveled and its various nuances need to be unpacked, as these impact on individuals, families, but also the questions we tackle in research. We enter the past, present, future mythical time matrix of which we, as researchers, are also part. A future task of German-Jewish history and also of Jews in Germany, including Israelis in Germany, is to unpick this mythical time creation from their perspectives, as it cannot be escaped. Israelis who remain in Germany might find this time in their faces in the shape of their own children who beg the questions that cannot be

Film poster, *Back to the Fatherland*. (Copyright GreenKat Productions and Shani Avni, 2017. Used with permission.)

escaped by anybody implicated in the sticky matrix of time, spaces, and memories:[49] these children create their own identities, which forces parents to reflect on theirs and to enter intergenerational negotiations. The negotiations contain questions concerning what is constructed as German, what as Jewish, and what as Israeli, and how this triad—another triad—can be connected. How can it be navigated productively for the individuals concerned? This, among other topics, should be tackled in historically informed, present-centered, and future-driven anthropological and sociological research as part of the *Future of the German-Jewish Past*, present, and future.

ACKNOWLEDGMENTS

While writing this paper, my great-uncle Johannes Frankenberg entered my *pensée* time and again. A survivor of imprisonment in the Weimar Republic, Buchenwald, and the GDR apparatus, he remained a wayward beekeeper across time, space, and any German regime he encountered during his lifetime. My mother remembers her uncle as difficult and *streitbar* (argumentative). His fate is resplendent with the randomness of survival. He had been forced to dig his own grave in Buchenwald; the sole reason he was not shot was based on the fact that he was a master bootmaker. I never retrieved any official information about him. He, like so many others, live solely in the memories of their families, but as a true *nobody* he will never be subject to historical research. I wish I had had the opportunity—time—with him as an adult anthropologist. He died of natural causes when I was less than ten years old, yet he is seared into my memory as Onkel Hans, walking with my dad and me to visit his bees, and the bees crawling all over him and stinging my dad. By the same token I am grateful for the mythical time I have spent, that I am spending and will hopefully continue to spend with Emanuel Marx, who has informed my coming of age as an anthropologist in unforeseen ways.

NOTES

1. Ofri Ilany, "'We Are Just Someone Else's Fantasy': An Introduction to the New Israeli-Berlin Culture," Spitz 19 (2015), http://spitzmag.de/issues/spitz_19/7001 [in Hebrew].

2. Nancy D. Munn, "The Cultural Anthropology of Time: A Critical Essay," *Annual Review of Anthropology* 21 (1992): 93–123; Charles Stewart, "Historicity and Anthropology," *Annual Review of Anthropology* 45 (2016): 79–94.

3. George E. Marcus, "Ethnography in/of the World System: The Emergence of Multi-Sited Ethnography," *Annual Review of Anthropology* 24 (1995): 95–117; Bridget Anderson, *Us*

& *Them? The Dangerous Politics of Immigration Control* (Oxford: Oxford University Press, 2013); Dani Kranz, "Where to Stay and Where to Go? Ideas of Home and Homelessness among Third Generation Jews Who Grew Up in Germany," in *In the Shadows of the Holocaust: Narratives of the Third Generation*, ed. Esther Jilovsky, Jordy Silverstein, and David Slucki (London: Vallentine Mitchell, 2015), 179–208.

4. This chapter will use Israeli as shorthand for Israeli Jew, German as shorthand for German non-Jews; if it touches on Jews who are not Israelis or Germans who are Jews or belong to any other minority, this will be specified.

5. While it is beyond the scope of this essay, the naturalized spouses of Israeli Jews who travel to or return to Germany as Israeli citizens are a highly interesting control group. They reported in fieldwork several times about their different perceptions in Germany in terms of their "before" and "after" and after naturalization as Israelis.

6. Irit Dekel, *Mediation at the Holocaust Memorial in Berlin* (New York: Palgrave Macmillan, 2013); Michal Y. Bodemann, "The State in the Construction of Ethnicity and Ideological Labor: The Case of German Jewry," *Critical Sociology* 17, no. 3 (1990): 35–46; Max Czollek, *Desintegriert Euch!* (Munich: Carl Hanser Verlag, 2018); Dani Kranz, "Ein Plädoyer für den Alloismus: Historische Kontinuitäten, Zeitgeist und transkultureller Antisemitismus," in *Flucht ins Autoritäre—Rechtsextreme Dynamiken in der Mitte der Gesellschaft,* ed. Oliver Decker and Elmar Brähler (Gießen: Psycho-Sozial Verlag, 177–192); Nike Thurn, *"Falsche Juden": Performative Identitäten in der deutschsprachigen Literatur von Lessing bis Walser* (Göttingen: Wallstein, 2015).

7. Ruth Landes, *The City of Women* (Albuquerque: University of New Mexico Press, 1947).

8. Amos Elon, *Requiem Germani* [in Hebrew] (Tel-Aviv: Keter, 2002).

9. Jacques Le Goff, *History and Memory*, trans. Steven Rendall and Elizabeth Claman (New York: Columbia University Press, 1992).

10. Jew refers to any individual who self-identifies as a Jew. Dani Kranz, "Changing Definitions of Germanness Across Three Generations of *Yekkes* in Palestine/Israel," *German Studies Review* 39, no. 1 (2016): 99–120; idem., with Yotam Hotam and Avihu Shoshana, "Big Baggage on Small Shoulders? Children of Israeli/German Interparentage in Germany," in *Les mariages mixtes dans les sociétés européennes, XVIIIe–XXIe siècles: Pour une histoire sociale de la mixité matrimoniale*, ed. Michael Gasperoni, Cyrile Grand, and Vincent Gourdon (Rome: Vialla, 2019), 286–312.

11. Peter Rigby, "Time and Historical Consciousness: The Case of Ilparakuyo Massai," *Comparative Studies in Social History* 25, no. 3 (1983): 428–456; Geoffrey M. White, *Identity Through History* (Cambridge: Cambridge University Press, 1991).

12. Maurice Halbwachs, *Les Travaux de L'Année Sociologique* (Paris: F. Alcan, 1925).

13. Maurice Halbwachs, *On Collective Memory* (Chicago: University of Chicago Press, 1992).

14. Halbwachs, *Les Travaux.*

15. Arnold van Gennep, *The Rites of Passage* (Chicago: University of Chicago Press, 1909/1960).

16. Yosef Hayim Yerushalmi, *Zakhor: Jewish History and Jewish Memory* (Seattle: University of Washington Press, 1982).

17. Jacques Le Goff, *History and Memory*, trans. Steven Rendall and Elizabeth Claman (New York: Columbia University Press, 1992).

18. Le Goff, *History and Memory*, 54.

19. For an in-depth discussion of mythical memory, mythical time, and exile in regard to Iranian Jewry see Jennifer Langer, *Exile from Exile: The Representation of Cultural Memory in Literary Texts by Exiled Iranian Jewish Women*. PhD Thesis. SOAS, University of London (2013), http://eprints.soas.ac.uk/17841.

20. Thurn, *Falsche Juden*. Hannah Tzuberi, "'Reforesting' Jews: The German State and the Construction of 'New German Judaism,'" *Jewish Studies Quarterly* 27 (2020): 199–224.

21. Paul Windolf, "The German-Jewish Economic Elite (1900 to 1930)," *Zeitschrift für Unternehmensgeschichte* 56, no. 2 (2011): 135–162; Kerstin Meiering, *Die christlich-jüdische Mischehe in Deutschland, 1840–1933* (Hamburg: Dölling und Galitz Verlag, 1998); Beate Meyer, *"Jüdische Mischlinge" Rassenpolitik und Verfolgungserfahrung* (Hamburg: Dölling und Galitz Verlag, 2002).

22. Michal Y. Bodemann, "Between Israel and Germany from the 'Alien Asiatic People' to the New German Jewry," *Jewish History* 20, no. 1 (2006): 91–109; Dieter Gosewinkel, *Schutz und Freiheit? Staatsbürgerschaft in Europa im 20. Und 21. Jahrhundert* (Berlin: Suhrkamp, 2016).

23. Nina Fischer, *Memory Work: The Second Generation* (Houndmills: Palgrave Macmillan, 2015); Kurt Grünberg, "Contaminated Generativity: Holocaust Survivors and Their Children in Germany," *American Journal of Psychoanalysis* 67 (2007): 82–97; Marianne Hirsch, "Family Pictures: Maus, Mourning and Post-Memory," *Discourse* 15, no. 2 (1992): 3–29.

24. Dani Kranz, "Forget Israel—the Future Is in Berlin! Local Jews, Russian Immigrants and Israeli Jews in Berlin and across Germany," *Shofar* 34, no. 1 (2016): 5–28; Ronald Webster, "Jüdische Rückkehrer in der BRD nach 1945: Ihre Motive, ihre Erfahrungen," *Aschkenas* 5 (1995): 47–77.

25. Jay Howard Geller, *Jews in Post-Holocaust Germany, 1945–1953* (Cambridge: Cambridge University Press, 2005); John Borneman and Jeffrey M. Peck, *Sojourners: The Return of German Jews and the Question of Identity* (Lincoln: University of Nebraska Press, 1995); Robin Ostow, ed., *Jews in Contemporary East Germany: The Children of Moses in the Land of Marx* (London: Palgrave Macmillan, 1989).

26. Kurt Grünberg, "Bedrohung durch Normalität," in *Sozio-Psycho-Somatik: Gesellschaftliche Entwicklungen und psychosomatische Medizin*, ed. Wolfgang Soellner, Wolfgang Wesiack, and Brunhilde Wurm (Hamburg: Springer Verlag, 1989), 127–134.

27. Guido Hitze, "*Johannes Maier-Hultschin (1901–1958),*" in *Schlesische Lebensbilder*, ed. Joachim Bahlcke (Würzburg: Stiftung Kulturwerk Schlesien, 2017), 381–398.

28. Peter Longerich, "*Davon haben wir nichts gewusst!": Die Deutschen und die Judenverfolgung 1933–1945* (Munich: Siedler, 2006).

29. Ingrid Gilcher-Holty, ed., *A Revolution of Perception: Consequences of the Echoes of 1968* (New York: Berghahn Books, 2018).

30. Kristin Platt, *Bezweifelte Erinnerung, verweigerte Glaubhaftigkeit. Überlebende des Holocaust in den Ghettorenten-Verfahren* (Munich: Wilhelm Fink, 2012); Henning Borggräfe, *Zwangsarbeiterentschädigung. Vom Streit um "vergessene Opfer" zur Selbstaussöhnung der Deutschen* (Göttingen: Wallstein, 2014); Jan-Robert von Renesse, "Wiedergutmachung fünf nach Zwölf," *Zeitschrift für Rechtspolitik* (2014): 79–82.

31. Ofer Aderet, "While They Slaughtered Us, They Were Paying Our Social Benefits," *HaAretz* (February 22, 2013), https://www.haaretz.com.premium-as-they-killed -us-they-paid-our-welfare-1.5231022; Kristian Frigelj, "Ein einsamer Kämpfer für NS-Opfer," *Die Welt* (November 22, 2011), https://www.welt.de/print/die_welt /politik/article13728990/Ein-einsamer-Kaempfer-fuer-NS-Opfer.html; Kristian Frigelj, "Intrigen im Einsatz für NS-Opfer?" *Die Welt* (November 27, 2011), https:// www.welt.de/print/wams/nrw/article13737621/Intrigen-im-Einsatz-fuer-NS-Opfer .html; Julia Smilga, "Kämpfer für Holocaust-Opfer steht vor Gericht," *Deutschlandfunk* (March 3, 2016), https://www.deutschlandfunkkultur.de/land -nrw-verklagt-richter-kaempfer-fuer-holocaust-opfer.1079.de.html?dram:article _id=348742; Julia Smilga, "Richter Mundtot," *Die Zeit* (December 6, 2016), https:// www.zeit.de/2016/33/jan-robert-renesse-holocaust-ueberlebende-rente-richter /komplettansicht.

32. Land NRW. Beendigung des Disziplinarverfahrens gegen den Richter am Landessozialgericht Dr. Jan-Robert von Renesse (September 13, 2016), https://www .land.nrw/de/pressemitteilung/beendigung-des-disziplinarverfahrens-gegen-den -richter-am-landessozialgericht-dr.

33. While beyond the scope of this essay, it should be noted that law, legal terminology, and anything related to this area is not neutral; it changes over time, and it is subject to individual, and unreflected, identity investments.

34. The listed memorials address the Shoah. Other memorials that cover other groups of victims exist, of course, and they are no less contentious.

35. Both terms, *Mahn- und Gedenkstätte*, translate into "memorial site" in English. However, *mahnen* means to remind somebody of something unpleasant. The related term *Mahnung* means reminder as well as demand notice, indicating the negative connotation of the term/root *mahnen*, which is never positive in German.

36. https://historisches-museum-frankfurt.de/geerbt_gekauft_geraubt.

37. A memorial on Rabin Square in the center of Tel Aviv and another one at the corner of King George Street and Ben Tsion Boulevard contain elements of rail tracks. The memorial on Kikar Rabin is highly abstract; its content is either ignored or overlooked; it serves as an impromptu playground for children. It is fully accessible, and as I realized through my own daughter, runnable and climbable (photo by author, 2013). The memorial at the corner of King George Street is set to one side on a patch of lawn and is not accessible/climbable; five shepherd dogs, a breed used in camps, sit on top. Yad Vashem also contains various depictions of trains, rail tracks, and scenes of deportations connected to trains.

38. Carol A. Kidron, "Surviving a Distant Past: A Case Study of the Cultural Construction of Trauma Descendant Identity," *Ethos* 31, no. 4 (2004): 513–544.

39. Hadas Cohen and Dani Kranz, "Israeli Jews in the New Berlin: From Shoah Memories to Middle Eastern Encounters," in *Cultural Topographies of the New Berlin: An Anthology*, ed. Jennifer Ruth Hosek and Karin Bauer (New York: Berghahn, 2017), 322–346.

40. Other locally raised third-generation Jews replicate my sentiment, among them Yascha Mounk, who has meanwhile emigrated to the United States, and also written on his biographical background; or Lea Wohl von Haselberg, Channah Trzebiner, and Max Czollek who remain in the country. Fictional accounts or performative arts of third-generation Jews with or without (dual) Israeli citizenship indicate similar tensions.

41. Dani Kranz, "Vom Ort des Traumas zum Ort der Sehnsüchte: Anthropologische Beobachtungen zur intergenerativen Tradierung von Trauma und Deutschsein unter *Jeckes* in Israel," *Psychotherapie im Alter* 15, no. 3 (2018): 277–292.

42. Dani Kranz, "Ein Plädoyer für den Alloismus: Historische Kontinuitäten, Zeitgeist und transkultureller Antisemitismus," *Flucht ins Autoritäre—Rechtsextreme Dynamiken in der Mitte der Gesellschaft,* ed. Oliver Decker and Elmar Brähler (Leipzig: Universität Leipzig, 177–192).

43. Michal Y. Bodemann, "The State in the Construction of Ethnicity and Ideological Labor: The Case of German Jewry," *Critical Sociology* 17, no. 3 (1990): 35–46; ; Michal Y. Bodemann, *Gedächtnistheater: Die jüdische Gemeinschaft und ihre deutsche Erfindung* (Hamburg: Rotbuch, 1996).

44. Max Czollek, *Desintegriert Euch!* (Munich: Carl Hanser Verlag, 2018).

45. Dani Kranz, Uzi Rebun, and Heinz Sünker, "The Most Comprehensive Survey among Israelis in Germany Confirms the Image: Secular, Educated, and Left," Spitz (December 4, 2015), http://spitzmag.de/webonly/7238 [in Hebrew].

46. Sa'ed Atshan and Katharina Galor, *The Moral Triangle: Germans, Israelis, Palestinians* (Durham: Duke University Press, 2020).

47. Steffen Hagemann and Robby Nathanson, *Deutschland und Israel heute: Verbindende Vergangenheit, trennende Gegenwart* (2015), https://www.bertelsmann-stiftung.de

/fileadmin/files/BSt/Publikationen/GrauePublikationen/Studie_LW_Deutschland _und_Israel_heute_2015.pdf; Bericht des unabhängigen Expertenkreises Antisemitismus, *Antisemitismus in Deutschland – Erscheinungsformen, Bedingungen, Präventionsansätze*; November 10, 2011. Deutscher Bundestag, http://dipbt.bundes tag.de/dip21/btd/17/077/1707700.pdf; Bericht des Unabhängigen Expertenkreises Antisemitismus, *Unterrichtung durch die Bundesregierung*, April 7, 2017; http://dip21 .bundestag.de/dip21/btd/18/119/1811970.pdf.

48. Dan Diner, "Negative Symbiose: Deutsche und Juden nach Auschwitz," in *Jüdisches Leben in Deutschland seit 1945*, ed. Micha Brumlik, Doron Kiesel, Cilly Kugelmann, and Julius Schoeps (Frankfurt am Main: Jüdischer Verlag bei Athenaeum, 1988), 243–257.

49. Dani Kranz, Yotam Hotam, and Avihu Shoshan, "Big Baggage on Small Shoulders? Children of Israeli/German Interparentage in Germany," in *Les mariages mixtes dans les sociétés européennes, XVIIIe–XXIe siècles: Pour une histoire sociale de la mixité matri- moniale*, ed. Michael Gasperoni, Cyrile Grand, and Vincent Gourdon (Rome: Vialla, 2019), 286–312.

"THE SUN DOES NOT SHINE, IT RADIATES"

On National(ist) Mergings in German Philosemitic Imagery of Tel Aviv

HANNAH C. TZUBERI

T HE CITY OF Tel Aviv occupies a special place in German philosemitic imagery. It is a Jewish, Mediterranean, model city, a place of longing and freedom, a secular paradise. The question I flesh out in this essay is whether this image of Tel Aviv has a redemptive function within German politics of memory and embodies, to some extent, an imagined mirror-image of the ideal German state: liberal, modern, secular, and free. I argue that this image of Tel Aviv, the "White City," does not evoke alienation, but rather proximity, often accompanied by imagined physical intimacy between a feminine German and a masculine Jewish figure: an antidote to the German male soldier and the feminized Jew. I suggest that when the so-called "Berlin–Tel Aviv axis" is epitomized as a German-*Jewish* axis, it is the image of a *Tel Avivian* Jew that becomes an integral part of German national identity, history, and desire. The injured and feminized body of the European Jew is substituted with the virile body of the male, athletic, secular, Zionist Jew.

SCHLOMI AND TINA, ITAY AND HANNA, ISRAEL AND GERMANY: LONGING FOR A NATION

I began thinking about the centrality of Tel Aviv in German discourse concerning Israel while leafing through the pages of a magazine published annually by the Berlin office of the Women's International Zionist Organization (WIZO). The journal featured a travelogue by a German tourist, "Like every year, I fly to Tel Aviv" (*Denn wie immer flog ich nach Tel Aviv*), and read as follows:

> Nothing in Tel Aviv is just itself. The sun does not shine, it radiates. The sky is not cloudless, it is cobalt-blue. One does not simply go jogging in Tel Aviv—one runs as if everything was at stake.... Without a single mistake, for hours, ping-pong players (called *matkot*) on Tel Aviv's beaches hit the ball back and forth, dressed only in small bathing suits—in Tel Aviv one is not shy, in Tel Aviv one takes it all: If you wear a bikini, you wear it as low as possible. If you have big breasts, you have huge breasts. If you have long, curly hair, it reaches your butt. If you are beautiful, you are breathtaking. If you have children, you have at least three. And if a woman walks with her child, this is no reason for Israeli men not to whistle after her. . . . The portions in restaurants are never small, the cocktail glasses are always full ... the music is always loud, dancing is always wild.... Like a stormy lover, Tel Aviv holds me in its beautiful hands, flirts with me, beguiles me, sets its dark eyes upon me, courts me.... It is here where everything is possible.[1]

This text is, at first glance, about a German tourist enjoying the sight of Israeli *matkot* players and other exotic bodies on Tel Aviv's beaches. It is straightforwardly vulgar, employs sexual imagery, focuses on male and female bodily features, and takes virility as emblematic of Tel Aviv as such—the city's inhabitants' very bodies are virtual carriers of the city's spirit. I would argue, however, that this text represents more than a travelogue gone awry. It is part of an entire web of texts, a German *national* discourse, which envisions a merging (at times sexual) between Israel (specifically Tel Aviv) and Germany (specifically Berlin). This text can be read as an advertisement for the state of Israel precisely because it does *not* stand out. The German tourist, in describing her annual pilgrimage to Tel Aviv, represents a female Germany, with Israel as her virile, carnal object of desire. The feminine Germany here has a philozionist voice and it is this Germany that appears in stark contrast to the "other" Germany—the Germany of antisemitism, violence, and war, the Germany of the male soldier. Israelis, in contrast, become inversions of the feminized, prewar, diasporic Jew. *Matkot*-playing men in shorts—hassling even women with children—and women with "huge breasts in bikinis" are hypersexualized, primitively virile Orientals, rather than pale and pious *Ostjuden*.

In numerous movies, newspaper articles, and autobiographical stories, storylines concerning the meeting of a female Germany and a male Israel are reenacted.[2] In the blockbuster film *Hanna's Journey* (*Hannas Reise*), for instance, viewers follow a German social worker (a female caretaker) traveling to Israel as a volunteer for the NGO *Aktion Friedensdienste* (Action Service of Peace, referring to *Aktion Sühnezeichen*, literally: "Action Sign of Atonement").[3] While there, Hanna meets her Israeli lover, Itay, who taunts her with jokes about the Holocaust. His embrace ultimately delivers her from shame, guilt, and constraint, and in the end, he redeems not only her, but the entire German nation: he moves to Berlin to open a club together with other Israeli expatriates. Without necessarily intending to voice critique, one of the movie's reviewers aptly captures its subtext: "If, at the end of this open love story, there remains a sense of 'it is complicated,' this is not only about the relationship between Hanna and Itay, but also about the relationship between Germany and Israel."[4]

As a further example, I would like to consider the plot of a recently published German language-learning book for Israelis:

CHAPTER 1: SHLOMI AND TINA

This is Shlomi and his girlfriend Tina. Shlomi is Israeli. He was born in Petah Tiqva. Tina is German. She was born in Berlin. Tina likes to eat hummus and Bamba (peanut puffs, H. T.). She is a real Berliner! Shlomi likes sausages. He is a real Israeli! Shlomi and Tina are a couple and they live in Berlin. One day, Shlomi returns home after a long day of work and sees Tina sitting on packed bags. "I do not want to live in Berlin any longer," Tina screams. "I am done with Berlin! It is too cold here, and there is too much pork.[5] I want to live in Petah Tiqva and eat hummus and Bamba." Shlomi is shocked! He loves Tina, but he also loves Berlin and he wants to stay in Berlin. Apart from that, Shlomi likes drinking beer.[6]

The romantic relationship between Shlomi, an Israeli man, and Tina, a German woman, is simultaneously a desirous relation between nation states. "Shlomi loves Tina," as the German-born and Tel Aviv–living author of the book assures her readers, yet Shlomi also loves beer and Berlin, and Tina, respectively, Bamba, hummus, and Israel. Tina and Shlomi are a couple, as are Germany and Israel, represented here via their respective national dishes.

The mention of Bamba, a peanut butter-flavored snack produced in Israel since 1964, is particularly interesting in this context. Bamba evokes an advanced, intimate, insider knowledge and disambiguates the other dish mentioned, namely hummus. Hummus is, first of all, well known among Germans with less affinity for Israel, and could, secondly, be "misunderstood" as part of Palestinian or Lebanese cuisine. In contrast to hummus, Bamba is, in terms of its underlying semiotics, unambiguously associated with Israel, and *knowing what Bamba is* implies intimate, embedded knowledge of everyday Israel. Moreover, this kind of knowledge is, crucially, *not* articulated by Shlomi, but by Tina. Books designed for language instruction routinely convey a sense of familiarity with the everyday habits (including culinary habits) of the country in which the language being taught is primarily spoken. In a French-, Italian-, or

Russian-language book, "Pierre," "Roberto," and "Dimitri" speak about French wine, Italian pasta, or Russian vodka—in a German language-learning book, the appearance of "Tina" as a carrier of insider German knowledge is thus predictable. However, the specific kind of German insider knowledge that Tina conveys is actually *Israeli* insider knowledge, and this is not, I would argue, because the book's protagonists were accidentally mixed up. The specific German *habit* that potential Israeli clients are being taught here is German philozionism, embodied by Tina, or as the end of the first chapter puts it: "Tina likes hummus and Bamba. She is a real Berliner! Shlomi likes sausage. He is a real Israeli!"[7]

INCORPORATING JEWS

I have dwelled on the occurrence of Bamba in the above-mentioned German language-learning book because I think that Bamba here is an important signifier, one that (unintentionally) hints at the undercurrents of German postunification nation-building and the incorporation of Jews (both as German citizens and as the state of Israel) therein. I take Bamba to be a speck that marks, like an iceberg's summit peeking out of the ocean, the *conditions* underlying this allegedly apolitical text. Although it is often concealed by rhetoric striving for "normality" or calls "not to single out," I argue that, politically, the singling out of both Jews and the state of Israel is rather the perpetually enforced norm. In fact, I am suggesting that German longing for Israel—as expressed in the travelogue in *WIZO*'s magazine or the language-learning book and the absorption of Israeli insider knowledge—can be read as a micro-level representation of the German state's longing for, and absorption of, Jews into its own postwar history of national salvation. I will first sketch what I think are the major contours of the German state's incorporation of Jews into its national imagery, specifically following the fall of the Berlin wall. I will attempt to delineate German philosemitic yearning for a German-Jewish merging, that is, for a moment in which the German and the Jewish become indistinguishable—not through a dissolution of the Jewish or the German, but through an identification of the Jewish with the German and vice versa: a moment in which Germanness and Jewishness merge as one. In a second step, I will place the yearning for the state of Israel and specifically for Tel Aviv into such a German, desire-based identification with Jews and argue that the image of "Tel Aviv Judaism" solves the tensions that are inherent in the idea of German-Jewish oneness. To put it bluntly, I will attempt to explain *why* "Tina likes Bamba."

A paradigmatic expression of the German embrace of Jews after the fall of the Berlin wall can be seen in a parliamentary debate of 1990 when, following the collapse of the Soviet Union, a growing number of Russians categorized as Jews by Soviet authorities migrated to Germany, initially most via a tourist visa.[8] Responding to this migration, the German parliament set out to debate the Russian-Jewish migrants' legal status. Yet, there was, strictly speaking, no debate at all. Each parliamentary speaker, spanning all political parties, expressed an emotional, explicit, and vehement statement in favor of "Jewish migration."[9] Support even outweighed the state of Israel's opposition: despite occasional nods to Israel's claim to be the one and only homeland of the Jews, the German government did not initially heed the Israeli government's request not to grant permanent residency to Jewish migrants from the former Soviet Union.[10] Inasmuch as the wish to enable Jewish migration here also trumped legal norms— such as a prohibition on discriminating against, or privileging people based on gender, ethnicity, or religion—legal scholar Michael Demel concludes that "the attempt to re-establish flourishing Jewish communal life, and to supply the personnel for this, if necessary, also through migration cannot be depicted via the apparatus entailed in positive law."[11] The German state's policy regarding the migration of Jews is for Demel something that is "beyond the framework of regular legal thought."[12]

Whatever the legal, constitutional, or bureaucratic obstacles might have been, the political desirability of Jewish migration was non-negotiable: Germany's readmission into the circle of "civilized nations," its legitimacy as a unified nation-state in the present, required proof of having overcome the past and the "return of Jews" was thought to provide evidence of just that: If Jews today return to Germany, then Germany is no longer antisemitic, and hence, legitimate.[13] Jewish migration to Germany was thus part and parcel of a nation-building project reminiscent of the Israeli Law of Return in that it defines Jews, both absent and present, *as an inherent part of the nation*, in contrast and opposition to those who may live in the territory, and who may be given various grades of temporary toleration, but are not part of the nation's *raison d'etat*. *Gastarbeiter* (guest workers) from Turkey, who have lived in Germany since the late 1960s following agreements between Germany and Turkey, are not part of the collective, whereas Jews, even *before* they actually migrate, are "our fellow citizens" (*unsere Mitbürger*) and an integral part of the nation's self.[14]

Political scientist Jonathan Laurence has researched the differing treatment of Turkish-Muslim migrants and Russian-Jewish migrants and summarizes that "the strongly divergent bureaucratic treatment of two 'transnational' immigration groups . . . has not been influenced by overarching human rights discussions or international institutions. The outcomes are rather the resulting national debates over historical responsibility and the assimilability of immigrants in German society," an assimilability that is the result of "the projection of 'German traits' onto non-German Jews."[15] Cornelia Schmalz-Jacobsen, former federal commissioner for foreign affairs, is quoted by Laurence, musing that "when I go to a Russian migrant settlement . . . I don't feel like I'm in Germany anymore, because everyone is speaking Russian . . . but we put a template over them and say, 'These are Germans!' And we put the same template over the Jews."[16] Jews get a "German template," unlike other migrant groups who do not get this template and carry a "different religion." In the words of the commissioner of Questions of Foreigners at Berlin's Ministry of Interior Affairs: "The more different the religion, the more the religious ideas make integration harder. And, if I may say so, it is especially hard with the Muslim population, with their intellectually restricted background, because they are so traditional, they don't even accept the role of women in the same way as we do in our society."[17] Jews, in contrast to Muslims, do not have a "different religion," but are "Germans in Germany with a specific religious alignment," who "pose no problems either for security or religious tolerance."[18] The political-epistemological undercurrents that informed the differentiation of migrants from the former Soviet Union *as Jews* were thus radically different from those that directed the roughly simultaneous differentiation of another group of (post-)migrants *as Muslims.*[19]

Even though religious differentiation was applied to both migrant groups, they were seen through different lenses and kept epistemologically and politically separate: When Jews were incorporated into Germany's national imaginary they became "Germans with a specific religious alignment," whereas Muslims were framed as a threat, an element essentially foreign to Germanness.

Such differentiation, as also noted by Laurence, is unrelated to some kind of de facto greater Jewish conformity versus Islamic deviance, but has to be seen as an effect of Holocaust memory. Memory has infused *conscience* vis-à-vis Jews into Germany's national interest and impacts the way Jews are administered, discussed, and studied in political, media, legal, and academic contexts.[20] The negative views of the practices associated with Islam can be cast in the light of a legitimate and even necessary intervention that aims to liberate society from various forms of illiberal, cultural-religious deficiencies and to separate acceptable forms of religious practice from suspicious ones. However, a similarly negative view of Jewish practices would evoke the fear of antisemitism (or rather, the fear of being called an antisemite) and an undermining of the moral imperative of "never again."[21] Knowledge of what *that kind of thing* leads to makes the problematization of Jews akin to the problematization of Muslims a political impossibility. Therefore, I would argue that the protection of Jewish practices and the recognition of Jews' vulnerability in contemporary Germany is *not* related to an acknowledgment of Jews' vulnerability vis-à-vis the state *qua minority* but is rather a result of the salience of Holocaust memory, which structures the German state's relation to Jews—a relation defined by a recognition of Jews' vulnerability and need of protection as an *already historically* injured collective. Minorities that have not been annihilated by Nazi Germany, or that came under German colonial rule and genocidal violence preceding the Holocaust (such as the Herero and Nama), or even non-Jewish victims of the Nazi genocide (such as Sinti and Roma), are thus not implicated in the same way that Jews are in the normative commitment to "never again."

This is not to say that the German state's commitment to the protection and support of Jews is irrelevant as far as non-Jewish minorities are concerned, but rather that this commitment crucially *structures* the arguments non-Jewish minorities can make on their own behalf. Because political mercy in the present is *deduced* from the memory of the Nazi Holocaust, it is the association of contemporary discrimination against Islamic practices with antisemitism that is politically effective.[22] In reverse, the *dis*sociation of contemporary discrimination from antisemitism serves the intensification and legitimation of policies that aim at the restriction and/or criminalization of Islamic practice. When the contemporary "Muslim question" is made to appear historically unprecedented and an entirely *new* type of problem that pertains *exclusively* to Islam, then Muslims cannot benefit from the effective hesitation that pertains to the (renewed) injury of a Jewish body.[23]

It is thus an atoned relation to Jews, and specifically to Jews, that is a crucial ingredient of the German state's legitimation and practice of citizenship: a commitment to anti-antisemitism is a hallmark of what it means to be *properly* German, in the sense that the stance against antisemitism can be expressed not only as an empathic identification *with* Jews, but also as a standing-in *as* Jews. For instance, in the parliamentary debate discussed previously, the annihilation of European Jewry was repeatedly referred to as an act of "self-harm," an "amputation of our own limb," a "bloodletting" of the *German* nation; that is, the injury of Jews—even the Nazi genocide—can be rhetorically turned into an injury to the German state.[24] In recent years, indeed, even Jewish ritual items, primarily the *kippa*, have been increasingly made to transcend their traditional, conventional semiotics and morph from signifiers of religious practice into symbols of the tolerant, liberal state, standing in for "our democracy" and "our values."[25] If, in the words of Laurence, national debates over historical responsibility and the assimilability of immigrants in German society were structured by "the projection of 'German traits' onto non-German Jews," then I'd posit the existence of the reversed phenomenon too: Inasmuch as the "return of Jews" and "flourishing Jewish communities" became constitutive ingredients of the new, tolerant, and liberal state, the "Jewish voice" (in the widest possible sense) became a desired asset, as notions of tolerance, religious freedom, acceptable religiosity, and antisemitism became tied to the state's legitimacy and Jews' testimony thereof. Jews then inhabit a bifurcated position: on the one hand, the state's "self" and its citizens' normative commitments are being negotiated upon the question of its relation to Jews: How much weight can historical responsibility play in moments in which freedom of religion and secular norms clash? Does conscience and historical responsibility disable the criminalization of, say, ritual circumcision? Do refugees "import" antisemitism and are borders therefore to be closed, or is Germany—because of its historical responsibility and the memory of closed borders for Jewish refugees in the past—bound to "open" its borders? New Germany and its relation to Jews is, in short, where questions related to the state's national self are being negotiated, where the acceptable is marked from the unacceptable, specifically, where notions of "acceptable religiosity" can be broadened or narrowed and borders be opened or closed. On the other hand, this means that Jews and the "Jewish voice," in its broadest possible definition, becomes a signifier of new Germany, so that even the Nazi Holocaust can become an "act of self-harm," or contemporary violence against Jews an attack "against our democracy."

"WHAT IF ISRAEL WAS GERMANY?"

The demonstration of an anti-antisemitic stance through identification not with, but *as* Jews can be extended to the level of national identification, that is, to the identification of Germany *as* Israel. Thus, over the course of "Operation Pillar of Cloud" (November 2012), the *B.Z.*, a Berlin-based daily tabloid, featured on the cover page of its December 20, 2012 print edition the phrase "What if Berlin Was Israel . . . ?" illustrated with a projection of a map of Berlin onto one of Israel with red dots marking missile strikes.[26] Similarly, on August 11, 2014, during "Operation Protective Edge" (July–August 2014), *Bild*, another German tabloid, published portraits of Israeli soldiers who were killed under the header "The Fallen." "The Fallen," in terms of visual semiotics, however, conveyed (and I think was meant to convey) a sense of "*our* fallen."[27] Israel becomes *palpable* as if it were, in fact, Germany. "Tina likes hummus and Bamba. She is a real Berliner! Shlomi likes sausage. He is a real Israeli!" is a more personalized version of a longing for a national German-Israeli merging and blurring of boundaries.

It is in the context of an imagined and desired merging that the longing for Tel Aviv (or rather, an image of Tel Aviv) can be situated. Tel Aviv, I suggest, *stabilises* the figure of the Jew by normalizing Judaism, thereby effecting a separation from the figure of the Muslim *and* from memory of the Holocaust. Both these effects enable a more "easy-going," undisturbed intermingling, on both an interpersonal and a political-national level, that finds expression—to return to the text I began with—in personal and/or national embraces. To make this point, it is apt to return to the travelogue with which I opened this essay and quote part of its first paragraph:

> It is about time to see Israel without politics, but rather as that which it really is: a country full of hope, full of possibilities, full of passion, full of joy of living, and full of extremes. Tel Aviv places on top of all of this its crown, or, in politically correct terms, its *kippa*.

Notably, this call to see Israel as that "which it really is" is embedded in a section in which the travelogue's author alludes to Janosch's *The Trip to Panama* (*Oh, wie schön ist Panama*), a famous children's story.[28] In this story, a little tiger and a little bear decide that Panama must be the land of their dreams and set off on a quest to find it. Their longing is triggered by a crate floating past them that has the word "Panama" written on it and smells of bananas. The travelogue's author muses that had the crate smelled of oranges, the bear and the tiger would have picked Israel as the land of their dreams, describing it with the same words they use (in the story) to describe Panama: "In Israel, everything smells like oranges. Israel is the land of our dreams." (The original story reads "In Panama, everything smells like bananas. Panama is the land of our dreams.") However, whereas the children's story precisely highlights the *incongruence* between an object's image as created by desire and the material realities of the same object, in the travelogue, the "real Israel" is *congruent* with what a German tourist imagines it to be: a country full of hope, passion, life, and so on. The real Israel *is* what a philozionist German tourist wants it to be.

To some extent, this is not unusual in the context of a travelogue. Descriptions of Mediterranean beaches are used to sell ideas, feelings, and images to attract tourists. Yet this travelogue diverges from other standard descriptions of Mediterranean beaches: Tel Aviv has a *kippa* on its head. Akin to the specification of Bamba, this detail is crucial. Judaism here is not envisioned via cliché-laden, old-world icons, such as Hasidic Jews praying at the Western Wall, but as athletic, attractive men on a beach. Jerusalem is a land of "once upon a time," preserved and visited out of touristic duty, the way one is obliged to look at museums or ancient excavations. Jerusalem is history, yet the *new* Jewish city, what Israel "*really* is," is Tel Aviv. Tel Aviv is not a city that is simply *different* from Jerusalem, but Jerusalem's legitimate, modern, and Jewish (namely, *kippa*-wearing) heir.[29]

This travelogue then is an expression of philosemitic desire expressed in secular terms, as a desire for a Zionist, Tel Avivian Jew who can be smoothly incorporated, embedded, and absorbed into new Germany's own liberal, tolerant imaginary. Via the *kippa*, Tel Avivian Judaism can be easily differentiated as "authentically Jewish"—yet Tel Aviv is also a liberal, modern, entertaining city, associated (like Berlin) with Western freedom, tolerance, creativity, and openness. Tina and Shlomi, Hanna and Itay, and the journalist on the beach do not challenge but *partake* in "Western freedom." Like Tel Aviv, they wear a *kippa*—that is, they are identified and situated as Jews—while playing sports on the beach or drinking beer. Tel Avivian Judaism, understood here as a secular-liberal epistemological and political idea, thus enables a certain *normalization* of Judaism. It allows for intermingling under the umbrella of an urban, liberal lifestyle and Tel Aviv and Berlin's shared adherence to the constitutive ingredients of what Webb Keane calls the "moral narrative of modernity."[30] In Tel Aviv (or perhaps rather *as* Tel Aviv), the Jew is a person with whom one can plausibly share the same, decisively apolitical fun beach.

Tel Aviv can thus be made into a Mediterranean reflection of an imagined Berlin, and an "improved" one at that. In a German context, the sight of Jews is bound to the memory of the Nazi genocide and the German is, accordingly, a perpetrator, inevitably bound both to his or her historical skin and the context of the collective majority in which he or she is situated. This constellation does not allow for easygoing intermingling. Though strived for, it remains a yearning, as the memory of the Holocaust inevitably sets Jews at a distance, or even heightens a feeling of distance by situating Jews in (potentially) the same space as Muslims, as "religious minorities." In Tel Aviv, neither of these disturbances is likely to occur. For one thing, the separation of Jews from Muslims is ingrained in the city's ideological and architectural emergence (or is part of the narrative that preceded its emergence).[31] In Tel Aviv, the German tourist meets Jews as a hegemonic national collective, estranged from traces of Palestinian displacement, dispossession, and expulsion, and separated—in contrast to cities such as Jerusalem—from the very presence of Palestinians. However, possibly more importantly even, in being absorbed by a city "without history," the German tourist also loses his or her history: In Tel Aviv, the German tourist is not part of the majority national collective, but an individual in a kind of "Berlin of the Near East," where he or she can indulge and partake in Jewish *vitality*. Israel is, as the travelogue reminds its readers, a country "full of hope, full of possibilities, full of passion, full of joy of living, and full of extremes," and the Israelis of Tel Aviv emerge, accordingly, as sensual, erotic, lively, young, procreating people. These are not only markers of mobility, agency, and modernity, but also work as images that counterbalance (if not circumvent) another set of images, namely that of the annihilation of European and East European Jewry. In (or as) Tel Aviv, it is not only Judaism that is secularized and normalized, but also the past, which is neutralized. Tel Aviv provides a foil upon which a merging of persons and nations becomes possible, plausible, and banally easy.

NOTES

Initial versions of this text were first presented at ID Festival 2015 in Berlin and at the Annual Meeting of Israel Studies in Berkeley 2018.

1. Andrea Kiewel, "Denn wie immer flog ich nach Tel Aviv," *Wizoberlin* (2014): 73. All translations from German are my own.

2. For further examples see Claudia Schwartz, *Meschugge sind wir beide: Unsere deutsch-israelische Liebesgeschichte* (Berlin: Eden Books, 2017); Orit Arfa, *Underskin: A German-Israeli Love Story* (Berlin: Route 60 Press, 2017).

3. Christiane Wienand "From Atonement to Peace? Aktion Sühnezeichen, German-Israeli Relations and the Role of Youth in Reconciliation Discourse" (2012), in *Reconciliation, Civil Society, and the Politics of Memory: Transnational Initiatives in the 20th and 21st Century*, ed. Birgit Schwelling (Bielefeld: Transcript-Verlag, 2017).

4. Cf. https://www.kino.de/film/hannas-reise-2013/, retrieved July 11, 2018.

5. In colloquial German, "very cold" can be referred to as literally "pig-cold" (*schweinekalt*) and thus makes a pun with "pig meat."

6. Margarita Fortus, "Schlomi und Tina. Neun Deutschlerngeschichten für Israelis, easy-german," https://www.easygerman.co.il/single-post/SchlomiundTina1 (2017; retrieved July 20, 2018).

7. Ibid. Another movie that entails an Israeli-German love story is *Der Tel-Aviv-Krimi* (The Tel-Aviv Crime Story—incorrect hyphen in the original), a crime movie consisting of four episodes, which Germany's public television network ARD broadcasted between 2016 and 2017. The plot revolves around a German-Jewish criminal inspector, Sara Stein. Stein is portrayed as a young, energetic, and secular woman living in Berlin. She has an Israeli boyfriend (a musician), and eventually moves to Tel Aviv. In *The Tel-Aviv Crime Story* Sara Stein embodies a German gaze at Israel and specifically at religious Jews, in the words of the movie's webpage: "Upon solving her first case in her new place of living in Tel Aviv, secular Sara is confronted with a kind of religiosity entirely alien to her. She has to recognize the extent to which deeply religious people feel bound by their laws and conventions and can trigger human tragedies" (https://www.daserste.de/unterhaltung/film/der-tel-aviv-krimi/sendung/der-tel-aviv-krimi-shiva-104.html).

8. In total, approximately 150,000 migrants from the former Soviet Union had migrated as Jewish "quota refugees" and membership numbers of Jewish communities in Germany have risen from 29,089 in 1990 to 102,472 in 2003 as a result of migration. See Jonathan Laurence, "(Re)constructing Community in Berlin: Turks, Jews, and German Responsibility," *German Politics & Society* 19, no. 2 (2001): 22. Detailed statistics of community memberships are retrievable from the homepage of the Central Welfare Council of Jews in Germany—Zentrale Wohlfahrtsstelle der Juden in Deutschland e.V., http://www.zwst.org/medialibrary/pdf/Mitgliederstatistik-1990-2000-Ausz%C3%BCge.pdf.

9. See German Parliament, October 25, 1990, plenary protocol 11/231, 18359–18364. "Aktuelle Stunde," referred to in the following as Aktuelle Stunde.

10. See, for example, MP Gerster (Christian Democrats), German Parliament, October 25, 1990, plenary protocol 11/231, 18359–18364 (Aktuelle Stunde), MP Wetzel (Green Party), ibid., 18360, and MP Hoyer (Christian Democrats), German Parliament, June 26, 1996, plenary protocol 13/115, 10315.

11. Michael Demel, *Gebrochene Normalität* (Tübingen; Mohr Siebeck, 2011), 183.

12. Ibid., 185.

13. Cf. MP Bittner (Party of Democratic Socialism): "One will measure unified Germany by our behavior toward Jews," Aktuelle Stunde, 18363. See also MP Wetzel (Green Party), Aktuelle Stunde, 18360, and MP Bosbach (Christian Democrats), plenary protocol, June 6, 2003, 4119. Fittingly, the parliamentary debate opens with the exclamation "Germany is back again" (MP Wetzel, Green Party, Aktuelle Stunde, 18359). See also MP Glotz (Social Democrats), Aktuelle Stunde, 18360.

14. The works of sociologist Michal Bodemann about the transformation, that is, the institutionalization and "Germanization" of Holocaust memory, are instructive in this regard. See, for instance, Michael Bodemann, "Reconstructions of History: From Jewish Memory to Nationalized Commemoration of Kristallnacht in Germany," in idem., *Jews, Germans, Memory. Reconstructions of Jewish Life in Germany* (Ann Arbor: University of Michigan Press, 1996).

15. Laurence, "Re-constructing Community," 25.

16. Ibid., 32; and interview with author on February 26, 1999.

17. The position of the commissioner for Questions of Foreigners (*Beauftragter für Ausländerfragen*) is now named differently, namely "commissioner of Migration, Refugees and Integration." I could not find information as to when this renaming occurred. The quote is from Laurence, "Re-constructing Community," 44, interview with Hans-Burkhard Richter, Berlin Interior Ministry, Commissioner for Questions of Foreigners, February 16, 2000.

18. Malte Krause, Berlin Interior Ministry, head of section "Policies of Domestic Politics and Planning" (Grundsatzangelegenheiten der Innenpolitik und Planung), interview with Laurence on January 27, 1999, quoted in Laurence, "Re-constructing Community," 43–44. Laurence notes that "administration of subventions for Turkish associations occurs uniquely within the Senate's Commission for Foreigner Affairs, whereas matters of state subventions for Jewish groups is a matter of the culture senator, as the Commission for Foreigner Affairs 'does not deal with German organizations.'"

19. Ferruh Yilmaz, *How the Workers Became Muslims: Immigration, Culture, and Hegemonic Transformation in Europe* (Ann Arbor: University of Michigan Press, 2016).

20. Sultan Doughan and Hannah Tzuberi, "Säkularismus als Praxis und Herrschaft. Juden und Muslime im Kontext säkularer Wissensproduktion," in *Der inspizierte Muslim. Zur Politisierung der Islamforschung in Europa*, ed. Schirin Amir-Moazami (Bielefeld: transcript, 2018), 269–308.

21. Doughan and Tzuberi, "Säkularismus als Praxis und Herrschaft." See also Cynthia M. Baker, *Jew, Key Words for Jewish Studies* (New Brunswick, NJ: Rutgers University Press, 2016), 110ff.

22. For an elaboration of this argument see Hannah Tzuberi, "Plausible Conversions," in *Protocols* 3 (2018): http://prtcls.com/article/plausible-conversions, retrieved August 20, 2018.

23. One could argue, I think, that a dependence on memory's political effectiveness leaves Jews in Germany in a fundamentally unstable position. For if an acknowledgment of a minority's vulnerability follows exclusively from the memory of past atrocities, then what if memory withers, eventually *failing* to infuse conscience into the political, juridical, and media class?

24. Plenary protocol, June 6, 2003, MP Edathy (Social Democrats), 4123, and plenary protocol October 16, 2008, 19562, MP Reichen (Social Democrats). Mirroring this, also "the establishment of flourishing Jewish life" becomes "of importance for our country as a whole, for the entire society," MP Wolfgang Bosbach, Christian Democrats, plenary protocol June 6, 2003, 4120.

25. A brief glance at the recent emergence of the German "*kippa*-demonstration" may suffice to illustrate this: In the early summer of 2018, a Syrian refugee attacked an Arab-Muslim Israeli citizen who was wearing a *kippa*—exact reasons for this are hitherto unknown—with a belt. Following this attack, which occurred in an affluent, heavily gentrified neighborhood of Berlin, the city's Jewish Community (JGzB) initiated a "solidarity-demonstration," calling upon the demonstration's participants to wear a *kippa*. In media reports that covered the attack and advertised the demonstration, the attack's more intricate details (for example, that it involved an Arab Israeli and a Syrian and formerly Palestinian refugee) elided into the more easily discernible faultline "Jew versus Arab," and eventually "us versus antisemites." The act of wearing a *kippa* was extracted from the context of religious practice and became reframed as a practice, or posture, of the anti-antisemitic citizen.

26. https://www.bz-berlin.de/artikel-archiv/was-wenn-berlin-israel-waere, retrieved July 19, 2018.

27. https://www.bild.de/politik/ausland/israel/israels-krieg-gegen-den-hamas-terror -die-gesichter-der-gefallenen-37188346.bild.html, retrieved July 19, 2018.

28. Janosch, *Oh, wie schön ist Panama. Die Geschichte, wie der kleine Tiger und der kleine Bär nach Panama reisen* (Weinheim: Beltz & Gelberg Verlag, 2005 [1978]).

29. Architect Sharon Rotbard traces the emergence of Tel Aviv's modernist architecture in its architects' rejection of anything Eastern European or Middle Eastern in favor of a more European, Ashkenazi look. The marketing of Tel Aviv as "the White City" has its roots for Rotbard in the 1980s and was a reaction against a turn in Israeli politics that favored a traditionalist (and Likud-voting) identity whose emblematic city was Jerusalem, rather than a central European, modernist (and Labor-voting) identity centered in Tel Aviv. Sharon Rotbard, *White City, Black City: Architecture and War in Tel Aviv and Jaffa* (London: Pluto Press, 2015 [2005]). The travelogue affirms this Tel Avivian self-narrative.

30. Webb Keane, *Christian Moderns: Freedom and Fetish in the Mission Encounter* (Los Angeles: University of California Press, 2007).

31. Tel Aviv was planned by the Scottish urban planner, biologist, and botanist Patrick
    Geddes in 1927–1929 to circumvent and cut off Jaffa, then the largest city in Palestine.
    Jaffa was designated a Palestinian enclave in the partition plan of 1947, and after 1948,
    annexed to Tel Aviv. Jaffa's center was demolished and then reconstructed in the early
    1960s as a heritage district with residence restricted to artists. Sharon Rotbard, research-
    ing the construction of the "White City" narrative in the late 1980s, describes Tel Aviv
    as a city with a "forced geography," a place where "narrative precedes construction and
    accolades of progressive innocence—White City, creative city, gay-friendly city, capi-
    tal of the Start-Up Nation, etc.—proffer ideological cover for the literal and symbolic
    destruction of its neighbors." Rotbard, *White City, Black City*, quoted in Jonathan
    Moses, "Whiter Than White" (review article), *City* 20, no. 4 (2016): 650–653.

DOES THE GERMAN-JEWISH PAST HAVE A FUTURE IN ISRAEL?

MOSHE ZIMMERMANN

L ET'S START WITH three "establishing shots":

1. The roots of the Israeli historical profession are German. Like so many academics belonging to the first generation of the first Zionist university, the Hebrew University in Jerusalem (founded in 1925), most of the founding fathers of Israel's historical profession were either Germans or intellectual "products" of German universities. Both the departments of Jewish history and of so-called general history were headed in the early days of the Hebrew University by historians who were brought up in Germany. Itzhak Fritz Baer and Richard Michael Koebner, both experts on medieval history, were already faculty members of German academic institutions before emigrating to Palestine. Baer, who had been teaching in the *Hochschule für die Wissenschaft des Judentums* in Berlin, moved to Jerusalem in 1928 and Richard Koebner, who had been an associate (*ausserordentlicher*) professor at the University of Breslau from 1924, accepted the invitation to Jerusalem after he was thrown out of his university by the Nazis in 1933. The third most prominent historian of the first generation, Benzion Dinur (Dinaburg), though born in czarist Russia, studied at Berlin University before emigrating in the year 1921. Many of their colleagues and students felt at home working in the German language.[1]

2. Between Hitler's rise to power in 1933 and the founding of the Zionist state in 1948 around 80,000 Central European Jews, nicknamed "*Yekkes*," were able to make *Aliyah* (emigration) to Palestine. Central European Jews at this time made

up around a fifth of the Jewish-Palestinian population and played a decisive role not only in academic life, but also in Palestine's economic and cultural life. They introduced their imported heritage to the Eastern European Jewish community in Palestine, leaving deep imprints on theater, literature, music, sport, and so on.[2]

3. When the State of Israel was founded, the declaration of independence named the Shoah to be the single greatest catastrophe in Jewish history, and this was among the strongest arguments in support of the creation of a Jewish state in Palestine. The German-Jewish and the German past thus became an important element of Israel's raison d'être.[3]

Thanks to the so-called fifth *Aliyah,* German history and German culture were decisive to a great extent not only in the historical profession in Israel, but also in shaping Israeli society and its self-perception pre-1948. This was destined to gradually change because of the changing demographic structure of Israeli society. At the beginning, the effect of the German tradition on Israeli historiography and especially on historical education in Israel remained strong despite the demographic changes, but very soon it lost its quasi-monopolist status.

A glimpse into the future of the German-Jewish past raises a twofold question— one concerning historiography and the other concerning Israeli society in general. The two questions are closely intertwined: professional history puts the results of its newest research at the disposal of society and in turn society is expected to use these results in its process of socialization. Indeed, the intensive exchange of knowledge between Israeli and German historians has enabled a continuous presence of this tradition and of the German-Jewish past in both countries' curricula.[4] But this is not the decisive element in the equation. The future of the German-Jewish past in Israel is not going to be decided by professional historians but by the "consumers" of historical knowledge, by the agencies of socialization, and by politics.

We are talking about a society socialized by a leadership interested in a history that may serve its hegemonic political and ideological aims—aims deriving from postmodern Zionism. For official Israel history is an applied science and the past Israel is interested in is the past that could be used for very specific politics—both internal and external. Politics and ideology guide the educational system, and the system, including higher education, adapts and attempts to function in a "politically correct" manner. The search for a usable past is particularly conspicuous when we look at the place of the "German-Jewish past" in present-day Israel, casting a gloomy shadow over the prospects of this history's independent survival.

From the point of view of historical research, practiced by "the guild" (*Zunft*), the future we are discussing concerns the fourth generation of historians of German-Jewish history in Israel and the generations to come. The first generation, to which we referred earlier in this article, mainly imported German methodology—not so much German history as its field of research. Itzhak Baer was an expert on the history of the Jews in medieval Spain before and after he made *Aliyah* and Richard Koebner, upon arriving in Palestine, shifted his primary focus from medieval German to modern British history.

Among the second generation of historians with a German background (and with German as their mother tongue), some very important figures found their way back to German and German-Jewish history as their main area of research and teaching. Examples are Jacob Katz, Jacob Toury, Uriel Tal, Shaul Esh, Avraham Margaliot, Avraham Barkai, Dov Kulka, Shlomo Neeman, and Walter Grab. We may say that a critical mass of historians studying German history has been reached in this period. Saul Friedlander, a younger representative of this generation, became one of the most influential contributors to the German-Israeli historical dialogue.

Born in the 1940s, the "German-ness" of the third generation of historians specializing in German history was very different from that of previous generations. Either born in Israel or as very young immigrants, this generation grew up as "post-Holocaust Israelis" in an academic atmosphere that encouraged research and teaching of German and German-Jewish history that was hitherto avoided or marginalized before the late 1970s. This generation also enjoyed the privilege of having intensive contacts with the German historical community (the "*Historikerzunft*"). This contact helped institutionalize German history in Israel by establishing specialized centers for German and German-Jewish studies. There is truth in the argument that financial support provided by the Federal Republic of Germany for Israeli universities from the 1970s boosted German history in Israel. However, this argument is somewhat misleading as German investment in Israeli universities (via DFG, the Max Planck Society, etc.) was, and still is, predominantly in the natural sciences.

This third generation, to which Shulamit Volkov, Steven Aschheim, Michael Toch, Dan Diner, Henry Wassermann, and I belong, has been given the opportunity to take a lively role in public discourse in Israel, beyond the ivory towers of academe. This group of historians has made German and German-Jewish history accessible to broader audiences. Moreover, these historians, because of their expertise, have become an integral part of the liberal/left-wing part of the political scene. Israeli society has been aware that the messages these historians were sending concerned not only the German past but the Israeli present and future too. This also applies to Moshe Zuckermann and Jose Brunner (Tel Aviv University), who are examples of younger members of this generation. As the number of Israeli students of this generation who have written their dissertations outside Israel has risen, it is not surprising that some of them who have specialized in German and German-Jewish history have become professors at prominent American universities (e.g., Omer Bartov, Alon Confino) while remaining in close contact with the Israeli academic scene.

The fourth generation consists of historians such as Yfaat Weiss, Shmuel Feiner, Guy Miron, and others who concentrate on Jewish history alongside historians of "general" German history, such as Boaz Neumann, Gilead Margalit, Ofer Ashkenazi, Sagi Schaefer, and Oded Heilbronner. This is the first generation to "export" historians of German and German-Jewish history following studying for their PhD dissertations in Israeli universities (Adi Gordon, Gideon Reuveni, Udi Greenberg, and others).

The point of departure for this fourth generation could have been optimal in most respects if not for the ever-growing tendency in Israeli society toward a more nationalist, less universalist self-understanding. Not only are the faculties of humanities on the retreat; history as a discipline is expected to function on all levels primarily as an auxiliary for a one-dimensional state ideology, not as an instrument of analytical approach to humankind and its development over the centuries. Based on a rather reactionary understanding of Judaism and Jewishness, Jewish history has become the focal point of studying and learning of history, while at the same time so-called "general history," that is, history beyond the Jews, is being marginalized. The German-Jewish past is a typical chapter of Jewish history used (or misused) in order to achieve the aims set out by the Israeli establishment. The needs and wishes of the Ministry of Education, Ministry of Culture, and Ministry of Science also guide and influence *nolens-volens*, in the long run, the universities. In short: Given the situation at present, the future of the German and German-Jewish past appears to be rather bleak.

According to the hegemonic approach to Jewish history in Israel,[5] the German past serves the purpose of learning and internalizing the following "lessons":

1. The Shoah is the most important event in Jewish history and the ultimate justification not only for the existence of a Jewish state but also for its policies. According to Israeli-Zionist historical interpretation, life in the diaspora leads to antisemitism and catastrophe, whereas life in the Jewish nation-state guarantees security for its Jewish inhabitants.

2. For the so-called *Jewish problem* two main solutions were offered in the past: emancipation and integration for Jews in their place of residence in the diaspora; or a demographic concentration in a Jewish national home in which Jewish sovereignty is guaranteed. Until 1933, Germany provides an example of the first solution, a solution that totally failed. Israel, on the other hand, provides the only successful solution.[6]

3. Since 1948, the hegemonic narrative of Jewish history remained an Ashkenazi one for too long, even in Zionist historiography and despite the Oriental (*mizrachi*) influx into Israel and the ensuing change in Israel's demographic structure. Challenging this narrative is called for. The German Jews (*Yekkes*) are the most radical advocates of the old narrative and must therefore be marginalized.

4. The history of the Jews is unequivocally unique. Antisemitism cannot be perceived as part of the general phenomenon of racism and prejudice. Zionism is far from being just an example of modern nationalism, and the Shoah, even if understood as genocide, cannot be compared to other genocides. Jewish history as such is sui generis, that is, incomparable. The German-Jewish past serves as the ultimate proof for the exceptionality of the Jewish fate in history.[7]

Before moving on from this interpretation of the past to expectations for the future, I would like to add a few words about the implications of these "lessons" in the recent past. According to research that was conducted in schools and history departments since 1977, when a nationalist coalition took over Israel's government, there has been a change in historical perception and no alteration is to be expected in the near future. Israel's historiography and Jewish historiography outside Israel is drifting apart and the gap between them, as well as the gap between historical consciousness inside and outside Israel, is deepening.

An example of this is provided by the attitude toward the history of the Jewish religion. Since the end of the eighteenth century the historical debate about Jewish modernity focused primarily on the rise of the reform and liberal movement, which opened the gates for a new definition of Judaism. The German-Jewish past (i.e., between the middle of the eighteenth century and the year 1933) provided the framework for this historical breakthrough. As Reform Judaism became a successful export to the United States during the nineteenth century, the issue of Jewish religious reform attracted further historical attention. As paradoxical as it may seem, this focus on reform in Judaism also contributed to research about Jewish Orthodoxy, which was interpreted as a modern response to Reform Judaism—a response explained by the same sociopolitical circumstances in which both Reform and Orthodoxy evolved.

Theoretically *Aliyah* from both Germany and the United States should have created an optimal opportunity for taking up the discussion concerning modernization of the Jewish religion in Israel, if not for an inbuilt structural flaw that characterizes the Zionist movement. Secular Zionism positioned itself against the religious elements of Judaism, and especially against the section within Judaism that seemed unreachable—Reform Jews and liberal Jews. Indeed, Jewish Orthodoxy was as opposed to Zionism as the Jewish Reform movement in principle, but the religious segment that joined Zionism (for tactical reasons)—the *Mizrachi* (acronym for "Spiritual Center")—was Orthodox. This is how Zionism started its modus vivendi with Jewish Orthodoxy. Since 1967, this marginal segment of Israeli society has emerged as a surprisingly influential one.

This is the background for the suppression of the history of the Reform movement, which in the nineteenth century was a central component of the history of the German Jews, and also for the rise (since 1967) of a religious-Orthodox interpretation of the

history of Zionism. The process of *religionization*, which has characterized Israeli society since the 1980s, has not only led to rewriting the role of Orthodoxy in the history
of Zionism and to accentuating the negative effect of secularization on Jews in Central
Europe, but has also made the history of German-Jewish Neo-Orthodoxy (so different from Eastern European Orthodoxy) disappear.[8]

From the present (and perhaps also the future) Israeli perspective, not only liberal
Judaism and the secularization of Jewish life, but also the concept of Enlightenment
itself are perceived as negative messages deriving from the German-Jewish past:
Enlightenment (*Aufklärung*. Hebrew: *Neorut*)—a key concept in the history of Central
Europe and of the German Jews—became a dirty word in Israel. The tradition of
Enlightenment is therefore suppressed, together with two other closely related concepts
that played a decisive role in the history of the German Jews—assimilation and emancipation. The fact that Zionism considered itself a "self-emancipationist" movement
was forgotten and the efforts of German Jews at emancipation, assimilation, and inclusion became textbook examples for practicing the wrong "solution" for the "Jewish
question," in contrast to the exclusively nationalist, ethnocentric "solution" for which
Israel stands. In short: the stronger the nationalist interpretation of Jewish history in
Israel became, the less benevolent was the reference to the German-Jewish past.[9] This
specific past became the absolute opposite to what present and future Israel stands for.

This is not merely a theoretical matter; it explains why, in the year 2010, German
and Israeli members of the joint German-Israeli schoolbook commission (unlike the
situation with the previous commission during the 1980s) could not find common
ground for curricula and syllabi in which modern German-Jewish history could play a
positive educational role.[10] We are talking here about an ongoing process that deepens
the gap not only between professional historians in Israel and Germany, or between
the main concerns of Jewish historians inside and outside Israel, but also between the
relevant Israeli historians and the official educational system. Shulamit Volkov wrote
about the German-Jewish "Project of Modernity" and Shmuel Feiner about the Jewish
Enlightenment, but their important contributions to historical research have become
secondary to the Israeli public.[11] This includes the emphasis in schools. This important aspect of German-Jewish history is now irrelevant. It may even become a red rag
for postenlightened Israelis.

Israeli society, by and large, is convinced that living in the diaspora is itself the
real Jewish problem and that Zionism will remain forever the unassailable "solution."
Within this narrative, the demise of German-Jewish history under Nazi persecution
is also considered to be the ultimate argument for the validity of the official Israeli
line. Once you assume this perspective, the only merit or "value" of learning about
the history of the struggle for Jewish emancipation in Germany—a central topic in
historical research over a long period—is proving its utter futility. What is more, the

interrelation between emancipation on the one hand and inclusion or integration into German society on the other hand focuses in Zionist historiography, and particularly in the Israeli collective memory, on the phenomenon of assimilation. The very process of *religionization* of Israeli society turns assimilation into the number one enemy (becoming even more important than antisemitism) of collective Jewish endurance, and Jewish assimilation in Germany is reduced to nothing more than a logical precursor of the Holocaust. The German-Jewish past thus presents itself as the perfect opposite of the "correct solution" for the Jewish "problem." Against the background of an extremely aggressive campaign against assimilation that is currently taking place in Israel,[12] the German-Jewish past will either be misused for the purpose of this campaign or simply ignored.

There is no period in the German-Jewish past that demonstrates this attitude better than the history of the German Jews between the two world wars—or more precisely during the Weimar period. The Weimar era was perceived by those who lived through it, as well as by later historiography, as a kind of "golden age" that could be compared to the medieval golden age of the Jews in Spain. The role of the Jews in politics, in the sciences, in culture—including its modern facets like cinema and sports—the so-called Jewish renaissance,[13] all added up to a story of seemingly unprecedented success of Jewish emancipation and inclusion. The catastrophe that followed after the year 1933 made a benevolent appraisal of this period so problematic. But from the contemporary Israeli perspective it was not simply the allegedly predestined catastrophic end that cast its shadow over the history of Weimar Jews, but the very nature of its alleged success—its liberal, assimilationist, modern character.

It seems to me that if there is any future for the German-Jewish past in the context of the modern Israeli narrative, it will only survive as part of questionable arguments that Nazi anti-Jewish policies were a form of nemesis for radical Jewish attempts at assimilation and integration. The Israeli journalist and historian Amos Elon published a book that eventually became a best-seller, *The Pity of It All: A Portrait of Jews in Germany 1743–1933*, in Israel.[14] When it was published in 2002 (Hebrew title: *A German Requiem*) some readers were under the impression that the history of the German Jews, including the history of their contribution to the Weimar Republic, was redeemed. But Elon's success has much to do with the fact that he did not go beyond January 1933, that is, Hitler's rise to power, but practically disconnected the two chapters from each other and left his story as a "Requiem" for something that is dead and gone forever, leaving some room for nostalgia only for elderly *Yekkes*. This may explain why, despite the commercial success of the book, it did not change the attitudes of either the general public or the Israeli educational system toward the period. The Weimar years remain a discredited chapter of Jewish history. The blame for the catastrophe has shifted from the Nazis to the "assimilationist" Jews. Gershom Scholem, one of the founding fathers of the Hebrew University, was a *Yekke* who did not believe the so-called German-Jewish symbiosis ever took place. Perhaps he shoulders the responsibility for much of this negativity.[15]

The chapter about German Jews between 1933 and 1938 that was omitted by Elon has become, especially in Israel, a mere introduction to the history of the Shoah. The fate of German Jews from 1939 onward was practically left out of the history of the Shoah altogether.[16] This introduction explains the mechanisms of Nazi *Judenpolitik* during the Second World War rather than explaining the fate of the German Jews themselves. The spotlight is focused on the perpetrators during the pre-Second World War years rather than on the persecuted Jews. Since the general historical "framework" for attempting to comprehend Jewish behavior during the war is the Shoah, the main focus of the average Israeli is on the history of the Polish or Eastern European Jews. When it comes to the average Israeli pupil's learning, the history of the German Jews during the years of the Shoah remains at best marginal or, at worst, nonexistent.

There is an internal competitiveness between the different *Landsmannschaften* over their status as victims in the history and memory of the Shoah. If there is a chance of any community in modern Israeli society drawing attention away from the Shoah of the Polish Jews, it is not the German Jews but the Oriental Jews who wish to be "upgraded" in the hierarchy of Israel's society of victims. Thus, the attempt to be considered victims of the Shoah has caused representatives of Iraqi, Moroccan, and Libyan Jews to bring their cases before court. The history of the Polish Jews also "profits" from an inherent advantage, compared to that of German Jews, as it has become paradigmatic for multifaceted antisemitism. Israeli youth participate in the "March of the Living" trips to Poland—a centerpiece of the Israeli educational system, where they (the future citizens) learn not only about the antisemitism of the chief perpetrators, the Germans, but also about the behavior of the other victims, the non-Jewish Poles, who are usually presented as the henchmen of the Nazis.

The German-Jewish past is also less effective when it comes to proving the notion that "all the world is against us," especially since Israeli politicians attempt to put the blame for antisemitism on "the Arabs" or "the Palestinians," *en passant* shifting the blame for the idea of the Final Solution from Hitler to the Mufti of Jerusalem, as recently suggested by Israel's Prime Minister Netanyahu.[17] The German-Jewish chapter of Holocaust history poses yet a further challenge: Holocaust historians are looking for a generic category to which the Holocaust may belong. Historians such as Yehuda Bauer or Daniel Blatman refer the Holocaust to the category of genocide.[18] This has proved highly contentious: The critics insist that the Holocaust as *sui generis* even among genocides, not only posteriori but also a posteriori, must remain unquestioned. They fear competition and dilution when the word Holocaust is used to describe other catastrophes (the Armenian, the Polish, the Nanjing, but especially the Palestinian *Naqba*).[19]

A generic notion of genocide, or even of racism, when dealing with the Holocaust is regarded with suspicion. They fear that the use of the larger "frames," such as Nazi racism and genocidal policy, could theoretically undermine the idea of the uniqueness of the Jewish Holocaust.

The only generic framework for the Holocaust that does not meet real opposition in the public discourse in Israel (and in some cases also in academia) is antisemitism. The causal explanation for the most radical "solution" of the "Jewish problem" seems to be eternal and ubiquitous antisemitism, as mentioned previously, and not racism or prejudice in general. This is precisely why the German-Jewish past does not fit into the official narrative: Compared to antisemitism in other parts of the world, in Russia, France, or even the United States, German antisemitism was not especially virulent until the National Socialist government took over. On the contrary, as George Mosse wrote: if someone had pondered, back in 1913, about the question of whether the extermination of the Jews might happen in the years to come, the answer would have been: Yes, it might happen, because one never knows what the French are up to. The German-Jewish past is not a helpful example when it comes to supporting a mono-causal explanation of the Holocaust, unless of course one unreservedly accepts Daniel Goldhagen's far-fetched thesis concerning the eliminatory character of German antisemitism.[20] The overwhelming majority of historians don't. Here again, there is a rift between the mainstream of professional historians in Israel and the spirit of the official historical interpretation, which casts antisemitism in the leading role both in the past and in the future.

A fourth-generation representative, Guy Miron, dedicated a detailed article to the attitude of Israeli historiography to the history of the German Jews in the Third Reich.[21] He came to the conclusion that future generations of historians will continue to ponder the same old questions: Could the German Jews and their leaders have been more aware of the looming dangers? Did they miss chances to save more German Jews? And the crucial question: What could the Zionist movement and the *Yishuv* have done to prevent the catastrophe? With this last question, the cat is out of the bag. The real motive behind the preoccupation with this topic is the quarrel over a political issue: Who was more farsighted, who was right, and who was wrong in the 1930s—the socialist Zionists or the Revisionists? Again, this instrumentalization of the Nazi era focuses more on Eastern European Jews and offers little empathy for Central European Jews.

Premodern German-Jewish history, on the other hand, attracts much historiographic attention and is also utilized in the service of the hegemonic approach to Jewish history in Israel.[22] Medieval German history, that is, Ashkenazi history, highlights two allegedly typical characteristics of the Jewish past: a people of the Torah living in the shadow of eternal Jew-hatred. The *Shum* (Speyer, Worms, Mainz) communities and their halachic leaders (such as Rashi or *Rabenu* Gershom) are representative of the first characteristic, and the pogroms organized by the crusaders, the Black Pest, and so on, of the other. No doubt, the historical research undertaken by prominent Israeli historians of medieval German-Jewish history of the second and third generations—Avraham Grossmann, Michael Toch, Israel Yuval, and others—was not intended to support a one-dimensional Israeli approach to the German-Jewish past. But the results of that research will only harden attitudes to their subject matter in the future.

Last but not least: the history of German Zionism. Though a central chapter in the history of Zionism (Martin Buber, Max Nordau, David Wolffsohn, Otto Warburg, Arthur Ruppin, and Theodor Herzl are familiar names to the average Israeli), this history looks increasingly like a deviation from the "right" course. David Ben-Gurion was always dissatisfied with the political vision of the German-Jewish Zionists. The story of the Brit-Shalom group still serves as proof of the inability of the German Jews to cope with the challenge of Israel being "a villa in the jungle." Instead they were looking for dialogue with the Palestinians and the other Arabs in the region. A closer look at the Zionist aspect of the German-Jewish past does not seem to be helpful in strengthening a belligerent Israel, so this chapter, too, will either be forgotten or misused in the future. In the service of the hegemonic interpretation of history, it will be one case among many.

The future of the German-Jewish past in Israel? Not a rose garden.

NOTES

1. Robert Jütte, *Die Emigration der deutschsprachigen "Wissenschaft der Judentums": Die Auswanderung jüdischer Historiker nach Palaestina 1933–1945* (Stuttgart: Franz Steiner, 1991); Moshe Zimmermann, "Deutsche Geschichte in Israel," *Geschichte und Gesellschaft* 15, no. 3 (1989): 423–440.

2. For a comprehensive description: Yoav Gelber, *New Homeland: Immigration and Absorption of Central European Jews 1933–1948* [Hebrew] (Jerusalem: Yad Ben Zvi, 1990).

3. Tom Segev, *The Seventh Million: The Israelis and the Holocaust* (New York: Picador, 1993); Dalia Ofer, "The Past That Does Not Pass: Israelis and Holocaust Memory," *Israel Studies* 14, no. 1 (2009): 1–35.

4. Dan Diner and Moshe Zimmermann, eds., *Disseminating German Tradition* (Leipzig: Leipziger Universitätsverlag, 2009).

5. Arie Kizel, *Subservient History: A Critical Analysis of History Curricula and Textbooks in Israel, 1948–2006* [Hebrew] (Tel Aviv: Mofet, 2008); see also the chapter about Israeli education in Eliezer Schweid, *Zionism in a Postmodernist Era* [Hebrew] (Tel Aviv: Hakibbutz Hameuchad 1996), commenting on the development right after the assassination of Yitzhak Rabin.

6. In order to follow the arguments of nationalist interpretations of Jewish history one should get acquainted with the attack against the old school: Yoram Hazoni, Michael B. Oren, and Daniel Polisar, *The Quiet Revolution in the Teaching of Zionist History* (Jerusalem: Shalem Press, 2000).

7. A good example is provided by Yoav Gelber's comments in *History, Memory and Propaganda: The Historical Discipline at the Beginning of the 21st Century* [Hebrew] (Tel Aviv: Am Oved, 2007), 436–443.

8. A representative of the neo-orthodox German heritage was second-generation historian Mordechai Breuer, author of *Modernity within Tradition: The Social History of Orthodox Jewry in Imperial Germany* (New York: Columbia University Press, 1992).

9. Arie Kizel, "The Presentation of Germany in Israeli History Textbooks between 1948 and 2014," *Journal of Educational Media, Memory, and Society* 7, no. 1 (2015): 94–115, https://www.berghahnjournals.com/view/journals/jemms/7/1/jemms070105.xml.

10. Arie Kizel and Dirk Sadowski, eds., *Deutsch-israelische Schulbuchempfehlungen* (Göttingen: Vandenhoeck & Ruprecht, 2015).

11. Shmuel Feiner, *Cultural Revolution in Berlin: Jews in the Age of Enlightenment* (Oxford: Oxford University Press, 2011); Shulamit Volkov, *Das jüdische Projekt der Moderne* (Munich: Beck Verlag, 2001).

12. A group calling itself Lehava (Hebrew acronym: "Against Assimilation in the Holy Land") is responsible for physically attacking Arabs who had contacts with Jewish women and for setting a mixed Arab-Jewish school on fire.

13. Michael Brenner, *The Renaissance of Jewish Culture in Weimar Germany* (New Haven: Yale University Press, 1996).

14. Amos Elon, *The Pity of It All: A Portrait of Jews in Germany 1743–1933* (New York: Picador, 2003).

15. Gershom Scholem, "Reflections on the Wissenschaft des Judentums," *Haaretz Calendar* (1944) [Hebrew].

16. Moshe Zimmermann, *Deutsche gegen Deutsche: Das Schicksal der deutschen Juden, 1938–1945* (Berlin: Aufbau Verlag, 2008).

17. *Haaretz* (October 21, 2015).

18. Donald Bloxham, *The Final Solution: A Genocide* (Oxford: Oxford University Press, 2009); and its discussion in Israel is one example for the challenge posed by the concept of genocide to the Israeli community of Holocaust researchers.

19. Bashir Bashir and Amos Goldberg, eds., *The Holocaust and the Nakba: A New Grammar of Trauma and History* (New York: Columbia University Press, 2015).

20. Daniel Goldhagen, *Hitler's Willing Executioners: Ordinary Germans and the Holocaust* (New York: Alfred A. Knopf, 1996).

21. Guy Miron, "The German Jews during the Nazi Period and the Israeli Historiography" [Hebrew], *Yalkut Moreshet* 12, no. 95 (2014): 16–38.

22. Among the relatively small number of contributions about German-Jewish history published in recent years in the central Israeli historical journal *Zion* (founded by Baer and Dinur, 1936), the largest number deal with the Middle Ages and the early modern period.

New Perspectives for
German-Jewish Studies

THE PSYCHOLOGY OF
ANTISEMITISM REVISITED

ANTHONY D. KAUDERS

P SYCHOHISTORY HAS A bad name, and for good reason. Historians are loath to
psychoanalyze individuals, whether these be dead or alive, and they are equally
loath to pass judgment on personalities, whether these be ordinary or pathological. Students and laypeople, however, find the idea of combining history with psychology attractive, even commonsensical.[1] The appeal may be misguided and confirm the
reservations mentioned above. But I would like to suggest that the interplay between
psychology and history makes perfect sense, even though this interplay need not be
called psychohistory and even though the interplay I am concerned with highlights
the benefits for the historian rather than the advantages for the psychologist.

It makes perfect sense on several grounds: it is, for example, presumptuous to
suppose that hundreds of scholars working in either field are somehow deluded and
that their findings should therefore be discounted. The benefit of today's much-touted
interdisciplinarity is to recognize the possibility that experts dedicating their lives to
an area of study (related to one's own research) are doing so in good faith and not in
order to delegitimize other disciplines. While historians may question the search for
laws and behavioral patterns, they can profit from psychological theories. Not only are
these often derived from clinical observation or methodologically innovative experi-
mentation, they also proffer explanations that can refine the more mundane approaches
encountered in the historical literature. Finally, historians have regularly appropri-
ated ideas and models from sociology, economics, anthropology, literary theory, and
gender studies. To critically exploit the work of Weber, Marx, Foucault, or Butler,
but to refuse to consider the equally pathbreaking oeuvre of Freud, Lewin, Tajfel, or
Sherif is hard to justify.

The aim of this chapter is twofold: First, I would like to remind readers that psycho-logical theories have always informed the study of antisemitism. Historians have repeat-edly invoked psychological concepts, often assuming that these references sufficed as explanations. Historians have also resorted to psychoanalytic interpretations, often relying on sweeping judgments that are difficult to sustain. Second, I would like to suggest that past practice—believing that allusions to psychological terminology will do and relying unduly on Freudian theory—has led scholars to abandon the search for alternative (social) psychological models that might allow for a better under-standing of antisemitism. I hope to be able to show that revisiting the psychology of Jew-hatred is well worth the effort and that it may contribute to future research in German-Jewish history.

THE USES AND ABUSES OF PSYCHOLOGY IN ANTISEMITISM STUDIES

Hayden White's *Metahistory*, the most prominent attempt to disclose the narra-tive conventions underlying historical research, refers to archetypical emplotments (romantic, tragic, epic, pastoral, farcical, comic) that have determined the way in which historians write about the past.[2] Far from being neutral conveyors of meaning, narra-tive plots reveal political proclivities, moral attitudes, and religious sentiments. "As a symbolic structure," White writes, "the historical narrative does not *reproduce* the events it describes; it tells us in what direction to think about the events with different emotional valences."[3] Aside from contributing to debates about the epistemological status of history, White's perspective is helpful in uncovering narrative routines that, in the case of antisemitism studies, have shown little concern for the relevant theoret-ical underpinnings. Although the list of works that have used psychological terminol-ogy in this manner is extensive, I would like to illustrate my point by focusing on two classic studies in the field, Robert S. Wistrich's *Antisemitism: The Longest Hatred* and David Nirenberg's *Anti-Judaism*.

Wistrich is sensitive to the psychological dimensions of antisemitism. Although he concedes that, initially at least, antisemitism may have been a reaction to "Jewish exclusiveness" (which, clearly, also suggests a psychological explanation), he goes on to stress the ubiquity of Jew-hatred in places where the Jewish population had been expelled, such as medieval England or Spain after 1492. This kind of "free-floating anti-Semitism," Wistrich argues, thrived on "archetypal fears, anxieties and reflexes that seem to defy any rational analysis."[4] What is more, his accounts of both Christian and modern antisemitism rely on psychological explanations, including projection, repression, and feelings of guilt. According to the doyen of antisemitism studies,

Christianity's "morbid fear of all sexuality (. . .), the unrestrained invective against women and the downgrading of marriage to mere procreation were of a kind with the projection of all the repressed 'sinful' (i.e. sexual) impulses onto the 'carnal' Jew."[5] Repression was also at work in assaults on the Jews throughout the medieval period. Degrading their legal status and turning them into pariahs in European society, for instance, testified to the "latent doubts" Christians hoped to silence concerning the meaning of central tenets of their faith, most prominently transubstantiation.[6] These doubts persisted and contributed to the "well-poisoning hysteria" and subsequent conspiracy theories such as the Protocols of the Elders of Zion. In all these cases, the notion that Jews wished to take "revenge on their subjugators" suggested an underlying bad conscience about the way in which the Christian majority had treated the Jews in the past.[7] In short, Wistrich's plot relies on concepts culled from psychology, but he either dismisses these as beyond "rational analysis" or assumes that they are self-explanatory. References to the psychological literature are missing.

Nirenberg's aim is to establish how Judaism became a category with which non-Jews made sense of and criticized their world. Yet the absence or unimportance of anti-Judaism in certain cultures ("the vast seas of indifference") is left unexplained,[8] although the reasons for the difference between, say, Babylonia and Egypt would allow for an appreciation of why Babylonians did not require the "category" of Judaism to interpret their universe. But Nirenberg also wishes to downplay social or political explanations for the emergence of Egyptian anti-Judaism, including the argument that Egyptians resented the Jews as allies of the Persians, whom they regarded as oppressors.[9] Instead, he prefers to focus on "foundational" ideologies and "deep" antagonisms. The "infectious theory of knowledge" he associates with Mark, Matthew, and Luke, for example, suggests that several psychological processes were at work, including the fear that the emerging Christian order (or social dominance) was precarious and demanded ever stronger distinctions to uphold one's own self-categorization. It is only toward the end of the volume that Nirenberg draws attention to the underlying "goal" of his "project," namely to "encourage reflection about our 'projective behavior,' that is about ways in which our deployment of concepts into and onto the world might generate 'pathological' fantasies of Judaism."[10] Like Wistrich, Nirenberg is sensitive to the psychological dimensions of antisemitism, but his broad claims about "infection," "pathology," and "projection" imply that there is consensus on the meaning of these concepts and that the purported processes mentioned in this connection operate according to the same criteria, regardless of theoretical background, social category, and historical context.

Not all scholars of antisemitism have used psychological notions unselfconsciously or cursorily. In fact, there is a rich literature on the subject based in large part on Freudian theory. Much of this scholarship has alerted historians to the possibility that, in addition to cultural, economic, and political factors, psychology too can explain manifestations of Jew-hatred. Psychoanalytical readings of antisemitism range from the speculative and spectacular to more modest accounts of the phenomenon. Let me begin with a few of the former.

According to Bela Grunberger, monotheism installed an all-powerful father whose role it was to nip Oedipal desire in the bud. The Jews were identified with paternal authority, and antisemitism became the Gentile revolt against castration anxiety.[11] Rudolph Loewenstein similarly emphasized Oedipal dynamics to explain the persistence of antisemitism. The ancient conflict between Jews and Christians represented the struggle between an older and a younger faith—a religion standing for the fathers and a religion standing for the sons. The Jew, like the real father image of the antisemite, is hated, loved, and feared. The Holocaust, this reading suggests, was an attempt to destroy this personification of the superego.[12] Otto Fenichel maintained that antisemites responded to the uncanniness of the Jews. Jewish rituals, in particular, provoked feelings of apprehension. The practice of circumcision implied that Jews were a source of punishment and that this punishment took on sexual forms. Castration was written into the Jewish tradition, as it were. Like all human beings, Gentiles also repressed their sexual greed and murderous tendencies, projecting these cravings onto the Jews instead. As a result, the Jews were equated with the carnal, licentious, polluted, and deadly.[13]

It is easy to reject most of the arguments put forward by Grunberger, Loewenstein, and Fenichel. There is indeed little point in positing causal connections between antiquity and the twentieth century or in examining the way in which Jews have figured as the personification of the superego or in linking circumcision with castration anxiety and castration anxiety with Jew-hatred. Several counterarguments, ranging from the methodological (causality, representativeness, contingency) to the historical (antisemitism in non-Christian societies, circumcision in Islam, Jewish lack of power in the diaspora), rule out any meaningful consideration of these explanatory models. Some elements of the psychoanalytic approach, however, can be taken more seriously, not least "regression," "ambivalence," and "projection," all of which allow for slight modifications that can be assimilated to less totalizing accounts.[14]

A brief discussion of projection may illuminate the way in which an important Freudian term has been employed to great effect. *The Authoritarian Personality* remains the best-known attempt to analyse antisemitism with recourse to projection. For Theodor W. Adorno, Else Frenkel-Brunswik, R. Nevitt Sanford, and Daniel J. Levenson, Jew-hatred amounted to "a kind of compromise between underlying urges and hostile stereotypes on the one hand, and the demands of conscience and the weight of concrete experience on the other."[15] The absence of an inner superego required the individual to "seek some organizing and coordinating agency outside of himself."[16] The belief in and devotion to authority figures followed from such a search for an external superego. At the same time, unconscious impulses that could neither be integrated in the self nor expressed against the externalized authority were displaced or projected onto other groups. This process was not simply scapegoating, as the "authoritarian *must*, out of an inner necessity, turn his aggression against outgroups. He must do so because he is psychologically unable to attack ingroup authorities, rather than because of intellectual confusion regarding the source of his frustration."[17] Projection was therefore a device for "keeping id-drives ego-alien."[18]

This is a subtle analysis that tries to grasp projection not merely as the inability to confront one's own (carnal, sadistic, destructive) urges, but maintains that antisemitism exists because authoritarian personalities cannot vent their aggression against those whom they need as stand-ins for immature or unstable "superegos" (internalized social rules or consciences). A diverse group of historians has since then used projection to describe different forms of antisemitism: Jan Gross, for instance, has argued that Poles projected their own attitude of gratitude and relief toward the German occupiers in 1941 onto an "entrenched narrative" about how Jews allegedly behaved vis-à-vis the Soviets in 1939;[19] and Helmut Walser Smith has suggested that Germans in the Kaiserreich projected the unthinkable idea that the Eucharist resembled ritual cannibalism onto Jews whom they consequently blamed for ritually murdering Christian children.[20]

Mindful of specific contexts, such applications of "projection" (or "ambivalence" and "regression") can indeed provide insight into antisemitic behavior. Still, questions remain about the use of psychoanalytical models. Aside from the common critique that Freudian terminology connotes diseased minds (psychic weakness, psychopathology, mass delusion), there are several reasons for being prudent in this respect: first, scholars writing in the Freudian tradition do not distinguish between the personality psychology that this tradition rests on and the social psychology that they seek to invoke when analyzing antisemitism. From the perspective of personality psychology, differences in human beings are enduring dispositions that are reliably manifested in trait-relevant behavior. Social psychologists, by contrast, wish to fathom how persons are affected by or transformed into collectives. They accentuate the dynamic and situational elements of group behavior. Groups, they believe, arise in specific situations and do not depend on individual characteristics or specific social makeups. Given the performative nature of group behavior, social psychologists share a common belief in the volatility of behavior.

Second, because scholars beholden to Freudian discourse do not differentiate between personality and social psychology, they themselves tend to project notions traditionally associated with personality psychology (character/character structures, personality/personality structures) onto groups, peoples, and societies. In so doing, they tend to ignore the fact that personality psychology cannot tell us anything about the *truth* of certain assertions or about the *content* of certain cultures. From the point of view of such a personality psychology writ large, most societies in the past, with their torture chambers, auto-da-fés, witch hunts, infanticides, and crusades, must be diagnosed as psychologically disturbed, to say the least. Not only do historians reject such anachronistic approaches, personality psychologists themselves contend that the "big five" personality traits (extraversion, agreeableness, conscientiousness, neuroticism, and openness to experience) can be found in the same proportion of people across time, disputing the conclusion that some societies are more *prone* to psychopathological behavior than others.[21]

Third, psychoanalytical studies of antisemitism do not provide tenable narratives of historical change. Relying on the premise that certain forms of primary socialization produce deep character flaws, scholars working in this tradition must invariably presuppose rigid child-rearing practices to explain authoritarian conduct. They must also presuppose that these ingrained attitudes can only be changed through psychotherapy. Yet many cultures in the past (and present) have embraced such practices without distinguishing themselves as exceptionally prejudiced or antisemitic. In a similar vein, the relatively rapid decline of (overt forms of) antisemitism in West Germany since the Holocaust cannot be immediately linked to changes in child-rearing.[22] It would be impossible, finally, to postulate that the rise of Islamophobia and Judeophobia today, whether in Western Europe or the United States, was due to parenting styles that suddenly emerged one or two generations ago.

FUTURE AVENUES

Should historians of German Jewry dispense with psychology altogether, the occasional reference to projection (ambivalence, regression) notwithstanding? Although psychoanalysis has often proved fruitless in understanding the past, the case for integrating psychology into the study of antisemitism is difficult to dismiss. While attention to "discourse" enables us to imagine deep structures that transcend individual psyches, specific situations, or cultural boundaries, "discourse" fails to render intelligible how a particular semantic stock turns into praxis: the language of antisemitism, after all, does not do the maiming or killing on its own. Even Shulamit Volkov, a scholar recognized for formulating a particularly compelling semantic approach ("cultural code"), has made passing references to the "authoritarian personality" or the "therapeutic function" of Jew-hatred.[23] Indeed, she has also, in a later contribution, indicated that "cultural codes" prevail "in times of stability, or even growth and prosperity," not in "days of wrath."[24] The processes by which codes engender "days of wrath" or "days of wrath" transcend codes are left unexplored. Or, to put it in slightly different terms: just as it is impossible to predict behavior from emotions (fear, for example, elicits all sorts of responses), so it is impossible to predict behavior solely on the basis of the tenacity or popularity or ubiquity of a distinct discourse.[25]

Before I suggest how and where psychology can complement historical work, it is important to remind readers that a psychology that pertains exclusively to the field of Judeophobia, as if the minds of antisemites functioned differently from the minds of other racists or bigots, cannot exist. Psychological findings provide tools to comprehend Jew-baiters and Jew-hatred alike, but they do not provide definitions of *the* Jew-baiter or Jew-hatred *as such*. Applying psychology to the history of antisemitism must therefore be based on the much more modest hope of coming to grips with disparate forms of antisemitism rather than trying to identify one theory that can explain every antisemitic act, past and present. It also means that the psychology employed to this end can be used to address other forms of prejudice as well. Some scholars have criticized this caveat as foregoing any attempt at delimiting the specificity of antisemitism. But for historians who are convinced that behavior is always also context-dependent, psychology is meant to serve as a means to appreciate better how antisemitism came about rather than as a means to transform antisemitism studies into a sociology-inspired theory.

If one had to venture a guess as to which work on Jew-hatred that explicitly appropriates psychological findings has had the greatest impact, Christopher Browning's *Ordinary Men* immediately comes to mind.[26] Browning did not discount ideology as a motivating force, but sought to demonstrate that members of Police Battalion 101, most of whom belonged to Hamburg's working class, participated in the mass murder of Jews for several equally important reasons: careerism, the pressure for conformity, and the desensitization and brutalization that came with the killing routine. Browning engaged critically with the theories of well-known social psychologists, including Stanley Milgram and Philip Zimbardo. Later genocide scholars followed suit, bringing further concepts (deindividuation, diffusion of responsibility) and further social psychologists (Leon Festinger, Henri Tajfel) into play.

Browning has been criticized for failing to assess the relative significance of the various contributing factors mentioned in connection with the Holocaust.[27] The response to this legitimate objection, however, cannot be yet another overarching system of thought. Rather, it would behoove historians to try even harder to grasp the "pathways leading to certain outcomes." To achieve this goal, that is, to differentiate between "essential variables and contextual conditions,"[28] psychological theory may figure as an additional means, building on Browning's pathbreaking study. This interdisciplinary path, needless to say, should not be confined to genocide studies.

In the following section, I would like to discuss briefly several exemplary social psychological theories (social identity, cognitive redefinition, cognitive dissonance, escalating commitments) that, alongside other similarly powerful methods, could prove promising in future work on antisemitism. I will concentrate on social psychology for the simple reason that personality psychology is usually too static for the historian, positing as it does dispositional differences that would make it difficult to detect change over time. If there are approximately the same number of extroverts and introverts or neurotic and emotionally stable personalities in a given population, this information will hardly allow us to discern antisemitic prejudice, unless we state the obvious, namely that the extroverts can be found among the rabble rousers and the neurotics among the particularly sadistic perpetrators. The relatively stable (and low) number of "psychopaths" in a given society cannot account for recurrent mass violence, massacres, and wars in human history. In fact, people with so-called "antisocial personality disorders" would have hardly succeeded in the organizations (military, killing units, police battalions, SS, Reichssicherheitshauptamt) responsible for the Holocaust.[29] While the tendencies attributed to different personalities permit us to distinguish between *generalized* patterns of behavior (the quiet introvert, the conscientious academic, the agreeable cleric), they do not permit us to predict how people will act in specific situations, when otherwise consistent comportment is disrupted by unexpected circumstances. In short, antisemitism in large sections of the population cannot be put down to the traits of the individuals comprising these substantial groups of people.

How are the theories mentioned above relevant to antisemitism studies? According to *social identity theory*, individuals do not lose themselves (deindividuation) in groups or crowd-like situations, but shift their self-categorization from the individual to the group level. Social identity is therefore "understood as tied to action in the world."[30] This action regularly involves emotions toward other groups, the intensity of which waxes and wanes depending on the "salient levels of self-categorization."[31] When a group categorizes itself in a certain way (American or women), this can lead to higher levels of anti-Muslim sentiments, for instance. If the self-identification changes to other categories (such as students or citizens of the world), these feelings may diminish.[32]

Groups *recategorize* or *redefine* themselves regularly, depending on the situation they find themselves in. Individuals, too, engage in cognitive redefinition, often forming new groups in the process. Sometimes, neighbors and business associates become strangers, even enemies. Whether friends remain friends or business associates remain business associates depends on the power of rival modes of self-categorization (transforming the Jewish cattle dealer from a business associate to an enemy of the people, for example).[33] More dramatically, redefining one's own behavior allows perpetrators to fend off self-doubts or self-censure. Thieves, plunderers, rapists, and (mass) murderers thereby "preserve their view of themselves as moral agents even while they are inflicting extraordinary evil on others." Sometimes the victims are blamed for their victimhood in an effort to confirm processes of recategorization.[34]

Historians of both German antisemitism and the Holocaust have *alluded* to the psychology behind social identity theory. Alon Confino is perhaps the most vocal proponent of the view that Germans in the Third Reich ostracized, humiliated, and murdered the Jews in order "to strengthen the self and build an emotional community that defied this inner sense of transgression."[35] But he is not alone. Committing crimes against Jews and other groups, another prominent scholar writes, enabled Germans to unify the nation between 1933 and 1945, creating "a particular kind of belonging."[36] Various works have traced this development on the micro-level. During the April 1933 anti-Jewish boycott, for example, members of the police requested that the rights of Jewish citizens be curtailed so that the law enforcement officers would no longer have to be forced to protect the minority.[37] When the SS came together for "comradely" gatherings, moreover, they not only did so to enjoy each other's company or express their anger, but "also to consider themselves members of a community of fate."[38]

These forms of self- or recategorization can have a number of causes, including *cognitive dissonance*. When persons are confronted with an acute conflict between their ethically problematic beliefs or actions on the one hand and their own self-image (based on moral injunctions internalized over time) on the other, they must decide how to deal with the situation. Sometimes it may be possible to ignore the conflict or postpone its resolution, but more commonly a swift response is required. Restructuring one's self-image in such a manner as to conform to the morally problematic beliefs and actions is a typical strategy of dealing with cognitive dissonance.

Several historians have either touched on or directly addressed cognitive dissonance. Research on antisemitism in the German countryside, for example, has revealed the existence of a relatively mild form of cognitive dissonance, at least in light of the immediate consequences. Although Protestant peasants lit fires for the Jews on the Sabbath, accepted Jews into the local veterans' associations, and invited them to local festivities, the antisemitic movement in some villages gained between 74 and 84 percent of the vote in the late nineteenth century. This paradoxical behavior, it can be argued, was an attempt to accommodate both the relatively amicable relationship between Jews and Gentiles of the past and the more recent apprehension that the Jews were wielding too much power in the present. The "downfall" of the antisemitic parties in the years to come can be read as a sign that many peasants wished to rid themselves of this emotional quandary.[39] Cognitive dissonance has also been used as an explanatory model for the enactment of genocide. In the words of Aristotle Kallis, by "relativizing the problematic nature of the action" or "endorsing new definitions of what is acceptable," perpetrators rendered the "option of elimination more desirable or accessible."[40]

The conflict that is cognitive dissonance may stem from beliefs or actions. Some beliefs that collide with moral injunctions are due to comparisons between our experiences and our expectations. *Relative deprivation* rests on perceptions of injustice, usually distributive injustice—feeling that one's group has less than it deserves relative to other groups. Individuals tend to reflect on their own group's experience of social, cultural, or material capital and expect the future to be similar. The perceived status of other groups "generates expectations for how well we think our own group should be doing. In turn, we feel respectively deprived or gratified."[41] Prejudice against groups who appear to be thriving compared to one's own group may result from this interplay between experiences and expectations.

Relative deprivation can serve as a useful rejoinder to the strong reservations voiced by some researchers about the so-called correspondence (or "realist") theory of antisemitism. These experts have denied that Judeophobia proceeds from a real conflict between Jews and Gentiles, going so far as to declare that "antisemitism has nothing to do with real Jews."[42] This misgiving is understandable in view of the concern that Jews might appear responsible for the enmity that led to their persecution and mass murder.[43] But although there are plenty of instances where real conflict did exist and where real conflict was used as a pretext to conjure up antisemitic stereotypes, relative deprivation allows us to reframe the issue from one about conflicts over resources or theological truths to one about perceptions of social or cultural capital. Accordingly, we can acknowledge the psychological mechanisms at work without at the same time ignoring the transformation of German Jewry after emancipation. We can also avoid psychologizing about "the lack of self-confidence" among Germans, as if feelings of relative deprivation are confined to weak-willed and fainthearted people.[44]

Actions that challenge moral norms and occasion cognitive dissonance usually take the form of "a sequence of seemingly small, innocuous steps—a series of *escalating commitments.*"[45] Social psychologists have dubbed this the "foot-in-the-door-phenomenon," pointing to the common occurrence that people who commit themselves to small requests subsequently comply more easily with larger requests. The literature on escalating commitments suggests that initial, relatively inconsequential immoral acts can make subsequent evildoing less troublesome. Even so, once the evildoing is apparent, cognitive dissonance demands a redefinition of the act. Self-categorization—"I belong to a group that is threatened by another group and therefore needs to protect itself"—is a likely reaction to the dilemma. As in much of the foregoing discussion, it is genocide scholars who have recognized the advantage of social psychological theorizing, in this case with regard to escalating commitments. Some have described the matter in terms of a continuum, at the beginning of which stands something seemingly harmless that eventually culminates in extermination. Others have used the image of a "chain reaction" that, once set in motion, "*may* catalyse the transition from desire to concentrate intention to the enactment of genocide."[46] Common to this analysis is the notion of "small incremental steps" that help facilitate the illusion of "minimal change."[47]

THESE ARE SOME of the ways in which historians of antisemitism, in their quest to ascertain the interconnection between discourse and action, can borrow from psychology. A handful of Holocaust historians have already ventured along this path, most notably Christopher Browning. Yet colleagues in related fields, this essay proposes, might follow in his footsteps, all the more so because much academic work on the subject remains wedded to antisemitism as semantics, rhetoric, and ideology. The germination, proliferation, and dissemination of this hostility, as well as its metamorphosis from "linguistic violence" to arson, looting, boycott, assault, and murder, are bound to be understood with greater sophistication if we take notice of the way in which psychologists have endeavored to explain how collective behavior produces groups in the first place, why groups try to distinguish themselves from other groups, how group identity is strengthened through criminal acts, why criminal acts lead to further criminal acts, and how crime is viewed as indispensable in the struggle for group survival. This appeal to psychology does not mean that we should discount other methods, whether culled from sociology, anthropology, or political science. And it does not mean that we should discard more familiar psychological interpretations, especially "projection" and "regression." It simply means that we should embrace ideas and tools from all disciplines insofar as they make antisemitism more intelligible.

NOTES

1. Paul H. Elovitz, "The Successes and Obstacles to the Interdisciplinary Marriage of Psychology and History," in *Psychology and History: Interdisciplinary Explorations*, ed. Christian Tileaga and Jovan Byford (Cambridge: Cambridge University Press, 2014), 83–108, here 84.

2. Hayden White, *Metahistory: The Historical Imagination in Nineteenth-Century Europe* (Baltimore: Johns Hopkins University Press, 1973).

3. Hayden White, *Tropics of Discourse: Essays in Cultural Criticism* (Baltimore: Johns Hopkins University Press, 1978), 91.

4. Robert S. Wistrich, *Antisemitism: The Longest Hatred* (New York: Pantheon Books, 1991), xxv.

5. Ibid., 18.

6. Ibid., 25.

7. Ibid., 33.

8. David Nirenberg, *Anti-Judaism: The Western Tradition* (New York and London: W. W. Norton, 2013), 14–15.

9. Nirenberg, *Anti-Judaism*, 40.

10. Ibid., 468.

11. Bela Grunberger, "Der Antisemit und Ödipuskomplex," *Psyche* 16 (1962): 255–272.

12. Rudolph M. Loewenstein, *Christians and Jews: A Psychoanalytic Study* (New York: International Universities Press, 1951).

13. Otto Fenichel, "Elemente einer psychoanaytischen Theorie des Antisemitismus," in *Antisemitismus*, ed. Ernst Simmel (Frankfurt am Main: Fischer Taschenbuch, 1993), 35–57.

14. See, for example, Nathan W. Ackerman and Marie Jahoda, *Anti-Semitism and Emotional Disorder: A Psychoanalytic Interpretation* (New York: Harper and Collins, 1950), 35, 55–56; Mortimer Ostow, *Myth and Madness: The Psychodynamics of Antisemitism* (New Brunswick and London: Transaction Publishers, 1996); Jack Jacobs, *The Frankfurt School, Jewish Lives, and Antisemitism* (Cambridge: Cambridge University Press, 2015), 72–73.

15. T. W. Adorno, "Prejudice in the Interview Material," in *The Authoritarian Personality*, ed. T. W. Adorno, Else Frenkel-Brunswik, Daniel J. Levenson, and R. Nevitt Sanford (New York: Norton Library, 1969), 605–653, here 617, 627.

16. T. W. Adorno, Else Frenkel-Brunswik, Daniel J. Levenson, and R. Nevitt Sanford, "The Measurement of Implicit Antidemocratic Trends," in idem., *Authoritarian Personality*, 222–279, here 234.

17. Ibid., 233.

18. Ibid., 240.

19. Jan T. Gross, *Neighbours: The Destruction of the Jewish Community in Jewabne, Poland, 1941* (London: Arrow Books, 2003), 155.

20. Helmut Walser Smith, *Die Geschichte des Schlachters. Mord und Antisemitismus in einer deutschen Kleinstadt* (Frankfurt am Main: Fischer Taschenbuch, 2002), 108.

21. Karen Stemmer, *The Authoritarian Dynamic* (Cambridge: Cambridge University Press, 2005), 1, 150, 271.

22. Miriam Gebhardt, *Die Angst vor dem kindlichen Tyrannen. Eine Geschichte der Erziehung im 20. Jahrhundert* (Munich: Deutsche Verlags-Anstalt, 2009).

23. Shulamit Volkov, "Antisemitism as a Cultural Code: Reflections on the History and Historiography of Antisemitism in Imperial Germany," *Leo Baeck Institute Year Book* 23 (1978): 25–46, here 31, 35, 37, 44.

24. Shulamit Volkov, "Readjusting Cultural Codes: Reflections on Anti-Semitism and Anti-Zionism," *Journal of Israeli History* 25 (2006): 51–62, here 59.

25. Uffa Jensen and Stefanie Schüler-Springorum, "Einführung: Gefühle gegen Juden. Die Emotionsgeschichte des modernen Antisemitismus," *Geschichte und Gesellschaft* 39 (2013): 414–442, here 421–422.

26. Christopher R. Browning, *Ordinary Men: Reserve Police Battalion 101 and the Final Solution in Poland* (London: Penguin, 2001), 73–74.

27. Stefan Kühl, *Ganz normale Organisationen. Zur Soziologie des Holocaust* (Berlin: Suhrkamp, 2014), 14.

28. Henri Zukier, "Diversity and Design: The 'Twisted Road' and the Regional Turn in Holocaust History," *Holocaust and Genocide Studies* 27 (2013): 387–410, here 401.

29. James Waller, *Becoming Evil: How Ordinary People Commit Genocide and Mass Killing* (Oxford and New York: Oxford University Press, 2002), 19, 70–71.

30. John Drury and Steve Reicher, "Collective Action and Psychological Change: The Emergence of New Social Identities," *British Journal of Social Psychology* 39 (2000): 579–604, here 581–582.

31. Angela T. Maitner, Eliot R. Smith, and Diane M. Mackie, "Intergroup Emotions Theory: Prejudice and Differentiated Reactions toward Outgroups," in *The Cambridge Handbook of the Psychology of Prejudice*, ed. Chris G. Sibley and Kate Barlow (Cambridge: Cambridge University Press, 2017), 111–130, here 118.

32. Ibid.

33. Stefanie Fischer, *Ökonomisches Vertrauen und antisemitische Gewalt. Jüdische Viehhändler in Mittelfranken 1919–1939* (Göttingen: Wallstein, 2014), 171.

34. Waller, *Becoming Evil*, 187–188, 251.

35. Alon Confino, *A World without the Jews: The Nazi Imagination from Persecution to Genocide* (New Haven and London: Yale University Press, 2014), 80.

36. Thomas Kühne, *Belonging and Genocide: Hitler's Community, 1918–1945* (New Haven and London: Yale University Press, 2010), 91.

37. Michael Wildt, *Volksgemeinschaft als Selbstermächtigung. Gewalt gegen Juden in der deutschen Provinz 1919–1939* (Hamburg: Hamburger Edition, 2007), 173.

38. Jürgen Matthäus, "Controlled Escalation: Himmler's Men in the Summer of 1941 and the Holocaust in the Occupied Soviet Territories," *Holocaust and Genocide Studies* 21 (2007): 218–242, here 232. For a similar argument suggesting that, see David Bloxham, "Europe, the Final Solution and the Dynamics of Intent," *Patterns of Prejudice* 44 (2010): 317–335.

39. Richard S. Levy, *The Downfall of the Anti-Semitic Political Parties in Imperial Germany* (New Haven and London: Yale University Press, 1975).

40. Aristotle Kallis, *Genocide and Fascism: The Eliminationist Drive in Fascist Europe* (Routledge: New York and Oxford, 2009), 114.

41. Rupert Brown, *Prejudice: Its Social Psychology* (Oxford: Wiley-Blackwell, 2010), 168.

42. Ulrich Wyrwa, *Gesellschaftliche Konfliktfelder und die Entstehung des Antisemitismus. Das Deutsche Kaiserreich und das Liberale Italien im Vergleich* (Berlin: Metropol, 2015), 13–14.

43. Steven Beller, *Antisemitism: A Very Short Introduction* (New York: Oxford University Press, 2015), 3–4.

44. Götz Aly, *Warum die Deutschen? Warum die Juden? Gleichheit, Neid und Rassenhass* (Frankfurt am Main: S. Fischer, 2011), 80.

45. Waller, *Becoming Evil*, 205.

46. Kallis, *Genocide*, 114.

47. Henri Zucker, "The Twisted Road to Genocide: On the Psychological Development of Evil during the Holocaust," *Social Research* 61 (1994): 448.

JEWISH AND GERMAN
The Leo Baeck Institute Archives and Library

FRANK MECKLENBURG

AFTER WORKING FOR almost thirty-five years as an archivist at the Leo Baeck Institute (LBI), I have been wondering increasingly what this archive at the LBI actually is. What does it mean? What is the meaning of the 4 million–plus pages of documents and what does the archive as a "memory with legitimacy" mean? The archive and the library hold a managed collection of 80,000 titles and 10,000 mostly personal collections of documents from individuals, families, and businesses, plus some 5,000 artworks, all pertaining to a rather small group of people when looked at on the national scale—never more than 1 percent of the population in Germany, with a higher concentration of 4 percent in prewar Berlin. However, half a million people is still a very sizeable group with a high degree of diversity, and to look at the German Jews as a closed entity misses the aspects of participation and impact in a much larger society and its context. The Leo Baeck Institute probably holds the largest archival documentation of that group.

Michael Meyer wrote in his introduction to the fiftieth anniversary volume of the Leo Baeck Institute: "On May 25, 1955, sixteen men . . . came together in Jerusalem. Using German as their common language, they addressed the task of setting forth a program for a newly envisaged Leo Baeck Institute. . . . According to Buber, now that German Jewry had reached the end of its historical journey, the survivors possessed an obligation to determine how the German-Jewish 'symbiosis' came into being, how it functioned, and what remained of it after crisis and catastrophe."[1] Michael Meyer wrote this at a moment shortly after two major changes had taken place. The LBI in New York had moved into new quarters at the Center for Jewish History and the archives were associated with a new major German institution—the Jewish Museum

Berlin. He also wrote this shortly before the archives began to put the entire content on the World Wide Web. The German-Jewish legacy had begun its transformation process from a survivor-based *"landsmanschaft"* organization to a research institute that is now a solid part of a consortium of Jewish libraries at the Center for Jewish History in New York with a strong Internet presence, which so far has increased the archival usership tenfold. The German-Jewish legacy became part of the canon of American-Jewish history, an integral part of Jewish history at large, and also achieved recognition as part of the history of German-speaking lands. German-Jewish as we knew it as a distinct history has recently become more Jewish and more German, and also American-Jewish and part of American history.

The beginning of a new millennium brought two significant changes that took the Leo Baeck Institute, New York, into new contexts and directions. It joined with the two other major Jewish research libraries in the United States, American Jewish Historical Society (AJHS) and YIVO, to form the Center for Jewish History, which in the meantime has acquired more library and museum components; and it also banded together with the newly established Jewish Museum Berlin—which is a German institution, not the museum of the Jewish community—to create a joint archive facility; this decision put the LBI into previously unfamiliar cooperative settings. It created mutual recognition between significant but rather unequal partners, and it granted the LBI the stamp of acknowledgment of its importance in a global historical context. The New York joint venture of the Center for Jewish History admitted the LBI into the canon of American-Jewish history. The German tradition became an integral part of Jewish group identity in the United States. By way of a joint cataloguing facility with the Center for Jewish History, partner library overlaps between the different histories became visible, demonstrating how traditions moved across the continents and underpinning the transitions and demographic shifts of the global dynamic of the diaspora. The initial creation of the LBI in Jerusalem signaled a new relationship between the center and the periphery, with the immediate postwar triangularity between the main places of refuge, Israel, the United Kingdom, and the United States. This has subsequently shifted by adding another pillar of Jewish life, again in continental Europe and, of all places, in Germany. The move of all its archival collections in the form of microfilms and then digital images to Berlin signaled the acceptance of German-Jewish history as an integral part of German history (Austria is still procrastinating).

So, where are we now? It is fascinating to see that with the eightieth commemoration of the Anschluss and Kristallnacht, national identities are still standing in the way of a more common understanding of the many shared aspects of society, politics, and culture. Until the end of the twentieth century, and the symbolically charged end of a millennium, in the initial decades after the creation of the LBI, the institute was part of a network of intimately connected refugee organizations: the newspaper *Aufbau*,

Congregation Habonim, the social services organization Self-help, and so on, providing cohesion for its members and a platform for ideas and discussion. The audience was comprised entirely of *Yekkes* (Jews of German-speaking origin) and the staff came from the same pool of people. This has radically changed. Very few *Yekkes* are left to attend the lectures and events, and a younger crowd is gradually coming to listen—people who do not share the same ethnic background and cohesion but who are interested in what is now called the relevance of the German-Jewish experience. The LBI has become a research institute and it is the foremost place for the study of German-Jewish history.

Some of the central questions of modernity affecting Jews in German-speaking lands are: Who is a German Jew and who is to tell? Are people religious or not? How long have people lived in Germany or other German-speaking lands? The power of these concepts and definitions has started to shift and erode in an era of increasing inter-marriage between Jews and non-Jews, when turning away from religion became more common. After the end of the Weimar Republic, these issues took a sharp turn. Ismar Elbogen's notion of the position of Jews in German lands and of the ups and downs of the history of Jews in Germany, illustrated in his *Geschichte der Juden in Deutschland*, was to characterize the relationship over a thousand-year period.[2] In an article responding to the April boycott, published on the front page of the *CV Zeitung* of April 6, 1933, entitled "*Haltung!*" (which may be best translated as "Stance!"), Elbogen wrote: "Ten thousand have been pushed out of their jobs, many independent businesses have been uprooted. It makes no sense to ask what the reasons are, it makes no sense to accuse ourselves or others, this hour only knows one command: work and help! We can be condemned to suffer hunger, but not to starve to death!"[3] Elbogen drew a line extending the historical developments of centuries and understanding the severity of the situation. Two years later, he wrote in the introduction to his 300-page history account: "Since their settlement during the Roman times Jews have always lived in Germany, they went through evil and good days, . . ." ("*Seit ihrer Niederlassung in der Römerzeit haben immer Juden in Deutschland gewohnt, sie haben böse und gute Tage durchgemacht, . . .*"). He finished the manuscript in 1934 and the book was published in 1935.[4] After reporting on the history of settlement and pogroms, periods of stability and unrest, acceptance and rejection throughout the centuries, he concluded in view of the Nazi threat: "Once again, German Jews are confronted with the question of testing our resilience, to prove ourselves worthy."[5] Elbogen emphasized the permanence of Jewish life in Central Europe, and expressed his skeptical hope that history would continue. However, during the same year as the publication of Elbogen's book, the question of belonging was addressed from the Nazi perspective with the radical and cynical power of the racist state. The racial laws of 1935—the Nuremberg Laws—gave definition to a number of those questions, with dire consequences for those being subject to those verdicts. As we came to understand in the aftermath, the Nuremberg Laws were a turning point into the unimaginable, starving the Jews to death and worse. The archives of the LBI hold a rich collection of documents that are evidence of those questions and responses, and these documents can be examined in order to analyze those historical developments to attempt to put faces and names to individuals from this period of history.

The archive of the LBI represents a spectrum between urban and rural, "*Stadt und Land*," between Jews in Berlin and Frankfurt and the Jews in the countryside, thousands of small towns and villages, where Jews had lived for hundreds of years. There are those German Jews who increasingly moved from the rural areas to the cities and people who came from further east—Polish Jews and also from the eastern provinces of Germany. The religious spectrum developed from traditional to modern during the late eighteenth and nineteenth centuries, with the twentieth century adding a new form of belonging, being secular with ever dwindling religious connections.

And how German is it? And what does being German imply? It is not Germany (only since 1871) as a political entity within its borders, but rather German language and culture in all its diversity between the Baltic Sea and the Black Sea, from western Poland to eastern France, from the northern Adriatic to southern Denmark. There is no Germany without Jews, and in turn German is one of the more important Jewish languages.

That said, accepting the widely held notion that Jews were an integral part of German culture, what does that mean for the archives and library of the Leo Baeck Institute? There are, of course, larger archival holdings that contain the documents of the German-Jewish experience—the archives of the Centrum Judaicum in Berlin with the collections of the community archives of the Gesamtarchiv der deutschen Juden; there is the Heidelberg archive of the postwar communities; and there are the many local and regional archives mainly documenting the position of Jewish communities within the larger context. On the other hand, state and federal archives in Germany do not cover much of the Jewish experience. The effort to show what holdings exist in the archives of the five new postunification states has not rendered very much; it has rather confirmed how much of a recognition gap there is. But it is the archive of the diaspora that holds the most comprehensive documentation about the daily lives of Jews in German-speaking lands in the Leo Baeck Institute. Major holdings are found in Israel, in the National Library, in the Central Archives of the Jewish People, the Central Zionist Archives, and in Yad Vashem.[6]

On the other hand, having become part of the Center for Jewish History in New York, the LBI has entered the canon of the universalist Jewish identity and understanding of American Jewry, with the German-speaking Jews as major contributors to a broad demographic entity that is characterized by aspects of hybridity resembling the fabric of U.S. society in general. The question of belonging in the United States is being answered in ways reminiscent of Germany before the Nazi period—full civil rights and recognition, part of a broad demographic patchwork.

The surprise is to realize that in terms of German-Jewish history after the Holocaust, there were a quarter of a million Jews in immediate postwar Germany, mostly Polish refugees who had survived the war in the Central Asian provinces and in Siberia in the Soviet Union, and who after repatriation to Poland had subsequently fled to the American Zone of Occupation in Southern Germany. This fact has only surfaced in recent years.[7] By the mid 1950s less than 10 percent remained in Germany to become the "new Jews" and in subsequent years these Jews came to be regarded as the postwar German Jews. Since the 1990s they were the German Jews whose children and grandchildren were born in Germany, and who were then confronted with a new wave of immigration from the Soviet Union and postcommunist Russia and Ukraine, whose children and grandchildren in turn are born in Germany. However, we also recognize that this pattern was already valid, though to a lesser degree, before the First World War and certainly after 1918.[8]

Going back to prewar history, to what degree does the LBI archive represent "the German Jews"? Again, the mix of those born in Germany for generations and those one generation away from Eastern Europe comprise the Jews who fled Nazi Germany. They are the German Jews represented in the LBI archives. German-Jewish history functions also as a paradigm of demographic and social hybridity, and the German-Jewish archives are a reflection of this paradigm.

What we find in the archives are the utterances of individuals that go from the trivial to the profound. The collections display and reflect a spectrum of experience and expression that is much more colorful than the printed words vetted by publishers and editors. Daily life is encapsulated in these archives. German-Jewish history is also "general" German history—an integral part of that history. This said, the LBI then gains enormously in importance. There is no other archive documenting the lives and achievements of the German Jews in such detail. That the Jewish Museum Berlin holds a copy of the LBI's archives, which are now almost all online, speaks to the recognition of the LBI within the framework of German governmental policies by way of acceptance from official German museum institutions. But it is also the admission of German-Jewish history as part of German history.

To illustrate the work of the LBI, the latest example is the 1938 Project—a direct application of the original documents to a contemporary purpose.[9] What does the memory and experience of that year represent for us today? Whether the associations we make are political, social, personal, psychological, or philosophical is a matter of personal opinion. But the knowledge of the march of time on a level of great personal and geographic detail provides a more concrete look into what history means on the ground. Looking at the events at the time combined with the connecting tissue of the daily lives of ordinary people provides a different dimension of history. It offers a sense of our own daily life intertwined with various aspects of our own social existence. The history and stories of the luminaries don't tell us much about "the people." It is rather

the ordinary citizens who with their individuality display a range of behavior and experiences that enable us to learn about people in a general sense. We need to compare in
order to gain perspective. Compare the lives of Jews and non-Jews and recognize the
sense of a spectrum, not just polarity.[10]

With approximately 10,000 archival collections, donated by individuals and families, the archives represent over 50,000 names and stories, which is approximately
7–10 percent of the pre-1933 Jewish population of Central Europe. This is meant more
symbolically rather than as an accurate figure. But nevertheless, these were real people,
individuals, not abstract entities, not statistics or numbers. And fifty thousand is more
than any individual researcher could handle. Some current research employing the
methods of digital humanities seems to approach serious networking analyses, cluster
research and literary corpus analysis. The documents and written remnants of everyday life, used, for instance, in the aforementioned 1938 Project—the school report
cards, the *Schulzeugnisse* of the Central European education systems, highly valued in
Germany and even more among Jews, but completely useless in America; the endless
photo albums of the summer and winter vacation trips to the mountains or to the
sea—clearly signs and testimony of accomplishment and pride; and the letters in the
late 1930s and early 1940s between parents and children from the *Kindertransport*—
all of these archival items find increasing recognition and provide insight into people's
lives, giving color to the statistics.

What remains of the German-Jewish past? The children of the refugees are becoming more active, whether in retrieving the documents of their parents and taking an
interest in preserving the legacy, or by getting their children and grandchildren interested or writing memoirs and family histories, making reunions with former teachers, making contact with groups online and offline, and recently, by claiming German
citizenship in the form of a passport to which the descendants are legally entitled.
German-Jewish studies has found its way into German studies as well as Jewish studies
when looking at the annual meetings of the German Studies Association (GSA) and
American Jewish Studies (AJS). And Germany has become the third strong pillar of
scholarship, to quote Ismar Schorsch, in addition to Israel and the United States: *Wer
hätte das gedacht?* Who would have possibly thought that at the time of the establishment of the Leo Baeck Institute?

WHAT IS MISSING?

According to its mission, the LBI is not dealing with postwar history, at least not in
Germany. Postwar German-Jewish history is to be gathered, kept, and dealt with in
Germany and not by a foreign entity with a foreign view on that matter, this being

eagerly guarded by archives in Germany which have taken on that task. And in a way it is true. The LBI is an institution of the diaspora and is one of the few institutions that deals exclusively with the German-Jewish diaspora/refugee population and its history. However, the story is more interwoven in complex ways between the pre-Holocaust history, the diaspora, and the global community as signified, for instance, by the periodical *Aufbau*, which has recently become recognized for its important role.

What is still missing is an investigation of the connection between classical, traditional German-Jewish history and postwar history. Is postwar Jewish life in Germany another chapter in German-Jewish history? We need to take a serious look at the period between the end of the Second World War and Reunification, the GDR (the German Democratic Republic of [East] Germany) and the BRD (Federal Republic of [West] Germany) as two chapters in parallel, actually 1945 till 1949 as the first postwar chapter, and postunification the last chapter. Who knows what is to follow? Maybe Diana Pinto's vision of European Jewry will become a reality, although her concept has been somewhat reduced since the end of the Cold War.[11]

The silence about the GDR chapter goes hand-in-hand with the combination of anticommunism and antisemitism, including the question "Who is a Jew?" denouncing Jewish communists as not being "really Jewish," which on the other hand has to confront the fact that German Jews returning to postwar Germany often went to the GDR in the hope of building a new, antifascist Germany. In lining up all these chapters of modern German-Jewish history, from the time of Moses Mendelssohn to the present day, we can see the ups and downs, triumphs and defeats, rapid growth and total destruction. The reemergence of Jewish life in Germany after the Holocaust demonstrates the resilience and capacity of rebound, or as the old saying goes, that the end is also a new beginning.

NOTES

1. Michael Meyer, "Preserving the Legacy of German Jewry," in *A History of the Leo Baeck Institute, 1955–2005*, ed. Christhard Hoffmann (Tübingen: Mohr Siebeck, 2005), V.

2. Ismar Elbogen, *Geschichte der Juden in Deutschland* (Berlin: Erich Lichtenstein, 1935).

3. Ismar Elbogen, "Haltung!," *CV Zeitung* 14 (6.4.1933), 117.

4. Elbogen, *Geschichte der Juden*, 9.

5. Ibid., 314.

6. To this list one could also add the Wiener library archive in London, as well as the German-Jewish family archives at Sussex University.

7. Atina Grossmann, *Jews, Germans and Allies: Close Encounters in Occupied Germany* (Princeton: Princeton University Press, 2007).

8. What I described here is the story of the Bundesrepublik (West Germany); the history of Jews in the German Democratic Republic (East Germany) remains to be addressed and written, and it seems that that history is quite different. But that is another matter.

9. For more information see the project webpage: www.1938projekt.org.

10. A similar and yet very different approach to the 1938 Project is the Russian history website concerning the year 1917, https://project1917.com.

11. Diana Pinto, *European Jews in the 21st Century* (London: Weidenfeld & Nicolson, 2010).

TOWARD A TRANSNATIONAL JEWISH HISTORIOGRAPHY

Reflections on a Possible Future Path for the German-Jewish Past

GUY MIRON

I N 1983 THE historian Jacob Katz organized a conference on the impact of German Jewry. Participants were invited to reflect on the ways in which German-Jewish movements and processes such as Jewish enlightenment, social integration, German acculturation, and the transformation of religious life in Germany influenced other European Jewish communities.[1] The departure point for this discussion was the assumption that German Jews were the forerunners of Jewish modernity and a major source of influence and inspiration to other Jews. However, not all the historians who took part in the conference, some of whom were Katz's own students, shared this view. Thus, for example, Todd M. Endelman, a historian of the Jews in England, called for a differentiation between English Jewry and the German-Jewish model in his article entitled "The Englishness of Jewish Modernity in England," suggesting that there are different types of Jewish modernity, not only the one that was shaped by the German model.[2] Endelman's approach came to dominate the reading of modern Jewish history.

During recent decades social historians have been predominantly preoccupied with the peculiarities of the Jewish communities in various nation states—arguing for a separate English-, French-, Hungarian-, and Russian-Jewish path to modernity. This tendency is also dominant among historians of German Jewry. One might say that German-Jewish history has developed during recent decades into a subdiscipline of German studies and that the vast majority of those dealing with it were trained as German historians and not as historians of Jewish history. This is the situation not only in Germany, Europe, and the United States but also in Israel, where the field of Jewish history is institutionalized as a separate and independent department of so-called "general" (i.e., non-Jewish) history. As an Israeli historian who was trained in the 1990s in a department for Jewish history and turned to the field of German-Jewish history, I gradually came to realize that almost all the senior scholars as well as my colleagues working in the field came from departments for "general" history and were trained in German history rather than in Jewish history. This fact has implications for their research questions, the historiographical context of their scholarship, and also ultimately for the fruits of their work. Most of them did not interpret German-Jewish history in the nineteenth and twentieth centuries as part of wider pan-European Jewish developments, or were even aware of this historiography mainly of Eastern European history. Instead they focused their gaze on interpreting German-Jewish history in the wider context of German and European, non-Jewish, history.

In this short essay I will offer some thoughts on the future of the German-Jewish past. I will discuss the different implications of this conceptualization of German-Jewish history as a subdiscipline of German history and will offer some possible options for framing the German-Jewish past in the coming decades. These reflections will be presented through the prism of my own attempts to deal with German-Jewish history from a context of Jewish history.

THE SPATIAL TURN

The great wealth of scholarship that has been accumulated in the field of German-Jewish history in recent decades evokes questions about where it is heading. Scholars in the field sometimes get the impression that dealing with the German-Jewish past is close to exhaustion—we have now a rich and nuanced historical picture of the political, social, cultural, and religious phenomena that characterized German-speaking Jews from the late eighteenth century until the Holocaust. An international research network is spreading in North America, Israel, Europe, and especially in Germany, where Jewish studies are still generously funded by the state and produce a large number of publications on diverse German-Jewish topics.[3] This ever-growing research corpus, which includes an ever-growing number of case studies and regional projects, is so rich that it is becoming almost impossible to fully grasp and characterize it in its entirety. Undoubtedly, for younger scholars interested in doing research on the German-Jewish past, the challenge of finding a "research gap," or uncharted territory in German-Jewish historiography, is becoming ever more difficult. But every generation has its own need to reinterpret the past according to changing circumstances and new perspectives—and this is also valid for the German-Jewish past.

I believe that the variety of "turns" discussed during the recent decades in humanities and social sciences may inspire a regeneration of German-Jewish historiography.[4] The enormous corpus of sources and research projects that is available for German-Jewish historians can be used to ask new questions about language (the linguistic turn), culture (the cultural turn), body (the corporal turn), the economy (the economic turn), and so on. For the sake of the discussion here I will explore how the so-called "spatial turn" can inspire new questions and thus enrich our understanding of the German-Jewish past.

The spatial turn is based on the view that space is not simply a given but rather a product of social and mental construction. Its forerunner, Henri Lefebvre, rebuked the view of space as a neutral and empty container. In his seminal book entitled *The Production of Space*, published in 1974, he maintained that the transparency of space is just an illusion that should be replaced by a more subtle approach to space; an approach that will acknowledge "social space" and "mental space" as products of social construction.[5] Since the publication of Lefebvre's pioneering study, the use of concepts such as "space," "place," and "mapping," which in the past were primarily associated with geography and urban planning, have become dynamic and dominant components in the analysis of social and cultural developments.

The growing influence of the spatial turn can be associated with the accelerating process of globalization. Even if the decline of the nation-state as a worldwide phenomenon is still highly disputed, one cannot deny the fact that since the late twentieth and early twenty-first centuries, technological, political, and communication transformations have put an end to the era in which the nation-state was the undisputed dominant social, linguistic, and cultural unit. Moving beyond traditional social and historical fixation on the nation-state, scholars have become ever more aware of a variety of social and cultural phenomena that they regard as "transnational." These new impulses of the conceptualization of space are also referred to as "the transnational turn."[6]

JEWISH PLACE AND EUROPEAN SPACE

Jewish history offers a great and, at times, a unique setting for reevaluating a variety of topics in modern European history using the insights of the spatial turn. Based on the theories of Henri Lefebvre, Edward W. Soja, David Harvey, Karl Schlögel, and others, the meaning of "place," and "space" in Jewish history should be reexamined. For example, the complex relations between notions such as "homeland," "exile," and "diaspora" can be used for analyzing the "mental maps" through which Jews navigated the challenges of integration, inclusion, and exclusion in European societies during the age of emancipation.

In recent years a number of publications have benefited from this new research orientation. The volume *Jewish Topographies*, which was published in 2008, was devoted, according to its editors, to following Lefebvre and Soja in developing spatialization of the Jewish historical experience and mapping Jewish daily life.[7] Living in the margins as a minority without a sovereign territorial base throughout, Jews developed a variety of minority spatialization strategies.[8] Two more recent volumes offer a great variety of case studies, exemplifying the potential of the spatial perspectives for modern German-Jewish history.[9] Still, it seems that with the impact of the spatial turn a new transnational Jewish historiography is only now beginning to materialize.

What can be the influence of this new spatial orientation on the transnational thought in Jewish history and how can it inspire the future of German-Jewish historiography? The dominant attitude of European-Jewish historiography, as presented by Jonathan Frankel in the early 1990s, was based on a clear spatial view.[10] Seeking to break free from the bipolar and dichotomous distinction between assimilation (associated with modern Western and Central European Jewries) and Jewish nationalism (associated with modern East European Jewries), Jewish historiography tended to focus on European nation states, concentrating on the topics of civil emancipation, social integration, and acculturation. As a result, Jewish historiography produced a conspicuously large number of monographs and articles on the history of European Jews as a component in their nation-state.[11]

In the mid-1990s Shulamit Volkov reproached the inclination to view the history of European Jews solely from the perspective of the history of the nation-state within which they resided. Volkov did not underestimate the importance of the nation-state— after all, this was also the main thrust of her own work on German Jewry. Still, she emphasized the need to redress this approach by studying the history of European Jewries beyond the ethnocentric boundaries of the nation-state.[12]

A more recent challenge to approaches to Jewish history through the lens of nation-states was raised in Moshe Rosman's article "Jewish History across Borders." Coming from a predominantly North American school of social historians, Rosman asserted that many Jewish historians produced a great variety of "narrowly focused monographs" based on an impressive command of European languages and local historiography. Still, their exclusive focus on the national political borders, he added, might blind scholars and prevent them from recognizing and analyzing wider phenomena.[13] Influenced by the theoretical framework of the spatial turn, Rosman asked historians to pose new questions that would go beyond the nation-states and develop a new transnational approach to Jewish history. He also pointed to a variety of topics such as Jewish enlightenment, history of the Hasidic movement, and international Jewish solidarity—which in his opinion require a new spatial conceptualization.

TOWARD A COMPARATIVE APPROACH
TO THE GERMAN-JEWISH PAST

Such calls for a paradigm change in Jewish history have already shown preliminary results, but it is too early to evaluate whether they will lead to a fundamental transformation in the spatial perspective of modern Jewish historiography. It is perhaps more important for us to explore how the spatial turn will affect German-Jewish historiography.

Jacob Katz's initial view concerning the domination of the German-Jewish model of modernization as the direct source of influence on other Jewish communities is not necessarily valid. Decades of research have shown how the unique circumstances of various Jewish communities were part of unique developments of Jewish history in each national context. However, this preoccupation with the nation-state led to a growing detachment between historians working on Jewish communities in different countries. In the German-Jewish context this meant that accounts of German Jews became part of German historiography—a development that denied the rich research fruits of German-Jewish historians to a wider community of students of the Jewish experience.

The rich corpus of research dealing with German Jews can, and should, in my view, serve as the basis for a comparative study of modernization processes of Jewish communities in Europe. In so doing German-Jewish historiography will present an important contribution to the development of a nuanced narrative of a more integrative Jewish history. I will demonstrate this by using two case studies: Hungary and Iraq.

The comparison between German Jewry and Hungarian Jewry is useful for various reasons. The significance of the German-Jewish experience to our understanding of the European discourse on Jewish emancipation and the question of assimilation is undeniable. As an integral part of the Habsburg Empire, models of modernization that took shape in Germany reached Hungary, mainly through Vienna and Prague. The German-Jewish press also played a key role in Hungarian-Jewish polemics.[14] For modern Hungarian Jews, German Jewry served as a "reference group" or even as a role model. On the other hand, for conservative Hungarian Jews, from whose midst modern Orthodoxy and Ultra Orthodoxy would later emerge, German Jewry served as a negative model, the source of all evil—Jewish assimilation.

In addition to these historical connections, it seems that the extensive amount of historiographical scholarly attention devoted to problems of Jewish modernization and integration into German society and its various implications during recent decades should be able to enrich research into the Hungarian case.[15] German-Jewish historiography has significantly contributed to the elucidation of basic concepts such as "assimilation," "acculturation," "dissimilation," and "cultural code" and has yielded plenty of empirical studies in social history and Gentile-Jewish relations as well as gender history. The insights gained by this research can and should be implemented in the Hungarian-Jewish case in spite of all the clear differences.[16]

An especially fruitful product of German-Jewish historiography that can contribute to an innovative interpretation of Hungarian-Jewish history is the concept of co-constitutionality. In his book entitled *Jews and Other Germans*, which dealt with nineteenth-century Breslau, Till van Rahden aspired to transcend the more traditional concepts of "national homogeneity," which were associated with the interpretation of German-Jewish history in majority-minority terms.[17] Instead of viewing the German nation and national identity of the nineteenth century as a "given," van Rahden saw it as an ongoing process of *becoming*, in which Jews, like Catholics and Protestants, played an active role. Following van Rahden's analysis, Steven E. Aschheim suggested the concept of co-constitutionality as a guiding concept for the understanding of the formation of the German national identity and for the interpretation of German-Jewish history.[18] In Hungary, much more than in Germany, Jews had a crucial role in the development of the local middle class and of Hungarian liberalism.[19] The Jewish presence in bourgeois Budapest was more prominent in relative terms than in Berlin or Breslau. Imported from German-Jewish historiography, "co-constitutionality" can therefore be used as a key concept for a critical analysis of the development of Hungarian liberal nationalism in the late nineteenth and early twentieth centuries.

Hungary might be a good case study into the potential use of insights and concepts from German-Jewish historiography, but I believe that such a potential exists also in additional areas of Europe. Jewish integration in imperial Russia was very different and one cannot speak about a process of "co-constitutionality" of Russian nationalism on a large scale. Still, following the research developments in Russian-Jewish history of the last two decades that reveal a variety of social, cultural, and even political fields of integration on smaller scales, I believe that German-Jewish historiography can be an important source of inspiration for Russian-Jewish historiography.[20]

The challenge of a comparative, transnational, and interrelated modern Jewish history is even more complicated if we wish to apply it also to Jews outside Europe. The question of if and how basic categories used for German and more generally European-Jewish history could apply for Jews living in the new worlds is a matter to be discussed elsewhere. Here I would like to refer briefly to Jews living in Islamic countries.

In 2006 I published an article entitled "Between Berlin and Baghdad," which called for a development of a new historiography of Iraqi modern Jewry based on methods and insights from European and predominantly German-Jewish history.[21] Reflecting on a variety of works on Iraqi Jewish history, I argued that students of Middle Eastern studies and Arabic literature dominate this research rather than scholars trained in Jewish history. Certain works in the field, predominantly Reuven Snir's 2005 comprehensive study on *Arabness, Jewishness, Zionism*, clearly point to the need to interpret Iraqi-Jewish history within the wider horizon of Jewish (and specifically German-Jewish) history.[22]

In his book, Snir gives a few interesting examples of early twentieth-century Jewish intellectuals from Baghdad whose attitude to the Arabic language and tradition call for comparison with the German-Jewish enlightenment thinkers. A number of these intellectuals took part in the formation (or "invention") of modern Iraqi national-ism, and their activity can be analyzed with concepts such as "assimilation," "accul-turation," and perhaps even co-constitutionality. Naturally one should be wary of making simplistic comparisons. But the need to illuminate such developments as a transnational phenomenon seems evident.[23] The literature on German-Jewish identity formation may be helpful to free the Iraqi Jewish historiography from the simplistic Arab-Jewish dichotomy and offer new conceptualizations. This might help to develop more subtle models to interpret the process of Jewish integration and acculturation in Islamic societies.[24]

CONCLUSION

German-Jewish historiography proffers great potential not only for those with a specific interest in the subject matter, but also for a wider range of scholars. The complex past of Jews in German-speaking lands, from the Enlightenment to the Holocaust and their rich cultural heritage, render the German-Jewish experience a fascinating and relevant case study for any student interested in topics such as identity formation, inclusion versus exclusion, religious transformation, and diversity, to name just a few. Furthermore, the very fact that this field has yielded an enormous body of research literature in recent decades, utilizing innovative approaches and research methods, makes German-Jewish historiography an ideal starting point for a wider discussion of the Jewish experience in modern times.

The influence of the spatial turn as well as the proclivity of scholars from different disciplines and countries to collaborate might enable historians to reevaluate Jewish history across and beyond political borders. German-Jewish historiography should, in my opinion, become more involved in this process and contribute to the develop-ment of a more comparative, transnational, and entwined Jewish historical narrative.

NOTES

1. The proceedings of this conference were published as Jacob Katz, ed., *Toward Modernity: The European Jewish Model* (New Brunswick: Transaction Publishers, 1987).

2. Todd M. Endelman, "The Englishness of Jewish Modernity in England," in ibid., 225–246.

3. For Germany see Till Van Rahden, "History in the House of the Hangman: How Postwar Germany Became a Key Site for the Study of Jewish History," in *The German-Jewish Experience Revisited*, ed. Steven E. Aschheim and Vivian Liska (Berlin: De Gruyter, 2015), 171–192.

4. Compare to my previous discussion about this concerning Jewish history at large: Guy Miron, "Language, Culture and Space: The Challenges of Jewish Historiography in the Age of the 'Turns,'" *Zion* 76 (2011): 63–93 [Hebrew].

5. Henri Lefebvre, *The Production of Space* (Oxford: Blackwell, 1991).

6. On the growing challenge of writing transnational historiography se: Gunilla Budde, Sebastian Conrad, and Oliver Janz, eds., *Transnationale Geschichte. Themen, Tendenzen und Theorien*, (Göttingen: Vandenhoeck & Ruprecht, 2010). For a discussion regarding the connection between the spatial turn and the process of globalization see Matthias Middell and Katja Naumann, "Global History and the Spatial Turn: From the Impact of Area Studies to the Study of Critical Junctures of Globalization," *Journal of Global History* 5 (2010): 149–170.

7. Anna Lipphardt, Julia Brauch, and Alexandra Nocke, "Exploring Jewish Space: An Approach," in *Jewish Topographies: Visions of Space, Traditions of Place*, ed. Julia Brauch, Anna Lipphardt, and Alexandra Nocke (Aldershot: Ashgate, 2008), 2.

8. Ibid., 6. See also in the introduction of a special Jewish Social Studies volume about space: Elisheva Fonrobert and Vered Shemtov, "Introduction: Jewish Conceptions and Practices of Space," *Jewish Social Studies* 11, no. 3 (2005): 3–4.

9. Alina Gromova, Felix Heinert, and Sebastian Voigt, eds., *Jewish and Non-Jewish Spaces in the Urban Context* (Berlin: Neofils Verlag, 2015); Simone Lässig and Miriam Rürup, eds., *Space and Spatiality in Modern German Jewish History* (New York: Berghahn Books, 2017).

10. Jonathan Frankel, "Introduction," in *Assimilation and Community: The Jews in Nineteenth-Century Europe*, ed. Jonathan Frankel and Steven J. Zipperstein (New York: Cambridge University Press, 1992), 1–37.

11. Two volumes of articles can be used as examples for this tendency: Frankel and Zipperstein, *Assimilation and Community*; Pierre Birnbaum and Ira Katznelson, eds., *Paths of Emancipation: Jews, States and Citizenship* (Princeton: Princeton University Press, 1995).

12. Shulamit Volkov, "Jews among the Nations: A Unique National Narrative or a Chapter in National Historiographies" [Hebrew], *Zion* 61 (1996): 91–111.

13. Moshe Rosman, "Jewish History across Borders," in *Rethinking European Jewish History*, ed. Jeremy Cohen and Moshe Rosman (Oxford: Littman Library of Jewish Civilization, 2009), 22–23.

14. Michael Silber, "The Historical Experience of German Jewry and Its Impact on Haskalah and Reform in Hungary," in *Toward Modernity: The European Jewish Model*,

ed. Jacob Katz (New Brunswick & Oxford: Transaction Books, 1987), 107–147, see especially 127–129, 143.

15. See my article, which is based on this view: Guy Miron, "Between 'Center' and 'East', the Special Way of Jewish Emancipation in Hungary," *Jewish Studies at the CEU* 4 (2004/2005): 111–138.

16. For assimilation and dissimilation see for example David Sorkin, "Emancipation and Assimilation: Two Concepts and Their Application to German-Jewish History," *Leo Baeck Institute Year Book* 35 (1990): 17–33; Shulamit Volkov, "The Dynamic of Dissimilation: Ostjuden and German Jews," in *The Jewish Response to German Culture*, ed. Jehuda Reinharz and Walter Schatzberg (Hanover: University Press of New England, 1985), 195–211. For the concept of cultural code as an interpretation of modern German antisemitism see Shulamit Volkov, "Antisemitism as a Cultural Code," *Leo Baeck Year Book* 23 (1978): 25–46. German Jewry was also the first European Jewish community to get an extensive social history research on the gender problem; see Marion A. Kaplan, *The Making of the Jewish Middle Class: Women, Family and Identity in Imperial Germany* (New York: Oxford University Press, 1991); Benjamin Maria Baader, *Gender, Judaism and Bourgeois Culture in Germany, 1800–1870* (Bloomington: Indiana University Press, 2006).

17. Till van Rahden, *Jews and Other Germans: Civil Society, Religious Diversity, and Urban Politics in Breslau, 1860–1925* (Madison: University of Wisconsin Press, 2008).

18. Steven E. Aschheim, "German History and German Jewry: Junctions, Boundaries, and Interdependencies," idem., *In Times of Crisis: Essays on European Culture, Germans, and Jews* (Madison: University of Wisconsin Press, 2001), 86–92.

19. See in this context Gábor Gyáni, "Embourgeoisement as Jewish Identity," *Budapest Review of Books* (1997): 107–113; Kati Vörös, "A Unique Contract: Interpretations of Modern Hungarian Jewish History," *Jewish Studies at the CEU* III (2002/2003): 229–255.

20. A seminal work in this context is Benjamin Nathans, *Beyond the Pale: The Jewish Encounter with Late Imperial Russia* (Berkeley: University of California Press, 2002). For a critical review of additional projects in this field see Kenneth B. Moss, "At Home in Late Imperial Russian Modernity—Except When They Weren't: New Histories of Russian and East European Jews, 1881–1914," *Journal of Modern History* 84 (June 2012): 401–452.

21. Guy Miron, "Between Berlin and Baghdad—Iraqi Jewish History and the Challenge of Integrated Jewish Historiography" [Hebrew], *Zion* 71 (2006): 73–98.

22. Reuven Snir, *Arabness, Jewishness, Zionism: A Clash of Identities in the Literature of Iraqi Jews* [Hebrew] (Jerusalem: Ben-Zvi Institute, 2005).

23. Snir refers to it in pp. 469–470.

24. An important contribution to a more balanced historiography of Iraqi Jewry is Orit Baskin's book *New Babylonians: A History of Jews in Modern Iraq* (Stanford: Stanford University Press, 2012).

DIGITAL GERMAN-JEWISH FUTURES

Experiential Learning, Activism, and Entertainment

KERRY WALLACH

THE FUTURE OF the German-Jewish past is, in a word, digital, and not only in the sense of digital humanities or digital history. Future generations of scholars, students, and the general public will engage with the past online in the same ways—and for many of the same reasons—that they engage with everything else. There needs to be something redeeming, enjoyable, or at least memorable about studying history for people to feel that it is worthwhile. For many, the act of learning about the past serves as a kind of virtual travel, even an escape, to another time and place. Learning about German-Jewish history becomes possible on a regular basis when it is easily accessible through the newest media on computers, cell phones, and other electronic devices. Perusing a digital history project about the 1930s or reading posts on Twitter and Instagram does not take as much time, nor require the same level of commitment, as sitting down to read a history book. Watching a hit television show about the 1920s feels just educational enough to mitigate the guilt of partaking in a "guilty pleasure," yet not so stiflingly academic as to prevent it from being fun. Twitter is the new *Times*. Netflix is the new newsreel—and noir. We must begin to harness the potential of these platforms to cultivate opportunities to teach and learn about the German-Jewish past. In this essay, I explore three ways of establishing a connection to the past in digital forms suited to the twenty-first century: experiential learning in a traditional college classroom setting, social media activism, and streaming television shows.

As we consider how to reach those who will study and otherwise engage with German-Jewish history in the future, we must acknowledge that most younger students are three or more generations removed from those who experienced the "golden age" of

Weimar Jewish culture, as well as the Second World War and the Holocaust. Yet even seventy-five years after 1945, the past is no less relevant. New generations coming of age in the twenty-first century still confront a wide range of social and political questions that are intertwined with the legacy of German Jewry. Some reasons for making connections to the German-Jewish past are predictable, but others cannot yet be anticipated. In *Holocaust Memory in the Digital Age*, Jeffrey Shandler reminds us that it is possible to use resources and archives "against the grain" to examine issues other than those that are central to an institution's mission.[1] As scholars, and as educators, it is our role to help future generations gain digital access to, become more knowledgeable about, and determine how they as individuals will make use of the German-Jewish past.

EXPERIENTIAL LEARNING: MAKING GERMAN-JEWISH HISTORY MEMORABLE FOR GENERATION Z

Students of German and Jewish studies are among those who will continue to engage with German-Jewish history in an intensive way in the coming years. To be sure, an immersion trip or an extended period of study in Central or Eastern Europe would provide the ideal mode of experiential learning, but this is not an option for everyone. For those who cannot travel to such places as Berlin, Hamburg, Frankfurt, Munich, Vienna, Prague, and Budapest, there must exist more easily accessible ways to become passionate about the histories of these cultures. Although students might begin to study German-Jewish topics while still in high school, college and university students delve most deeply into online resources and thus represent a primary audience for many digital materials. Many college students obtain the majority of sources for their papers, presentations, and other projects via online searches. It is no surprise that virtual archives serve as key sources of information: the Jewish Women's Archive, for example, has one million visitors annually, most of whom find the site using Google.[2] It is my observation that college students respond best to digital assignments and activities when their mode of engaging with a project is highly interactive, thus constituting a memorable experience in its own right. Multiple forms of media (text, image, audio, video) enable students to experience material in different ways, and students with proficiency in more than one language benefit further from accessing this material in two languages. The design of the online resources and the assignments themselves affect the degree to which student experiences are interactive and potentially impactful.

By 2024, college courses will serve mainly post-Millennial students who differ in a number of ways from previous generations of students. Undergraduate courses in the United States, where traditional students range in age from 18 to 22, currently contain the last groups of students that combine Millennials (sometimes also "Generation Y," born between 1981 and 1996, according to the Pew Research Center) and members of "Generation Z."[3] The generation born from 1997 onward is now commonly referred to as Generation Z, although some locate the beginning of this generation in the post-9/11 era.[4] By most definitions, the majority of college students who graduate in 2020 and later can be considered part of Generation Z. Cohorts beginning with the class of 2024 contain students born after 9/11. Whereas most Millennials can still remember a time before smartphone technology and the rise of social media, members of Generation Z cannot. Many members of Generation Z prefer to communicate via text messages rather than phone or email, and they favor such image-driven platforms as Instagram, Snapchat, TikTok, and YouTube over Facebook and Twitter. They are "digital natives"; the ways that Generation Z and future generations consume information will continue to drive the ways scholars, institutions, and cultural producers choose to present it.

In my courses at Gettysburg College, where I have taught since 2011, I have used several digital history projects that focus on German-Jewish life and culture, and I have begun to make use of the wide array of digitized resources that deal with the Holocaust. Gettysburg is an undergraduate liberal arts college with an emphasis on small class size; course enrollment usually ranges from six to eighteen students. By far the most successful of my assignments using digital resources was a four- to six-page paper in my spring 2018 course, "European Jews: History, Holocaust, Future," which required students to find, view or listen to, and critically analyze the video or audio testimony of a Holocaust survivor. Here the vast digitized resources of the United States Holocaust Memorial Museum and the USC Shoah Foundation's Visual History Archive were invaluable. Without exception, the students agreed that they benefited from the act of searching for and accessing survivor testimony. Nearly all chose to write about video testimony, though one student noted that she preferred the audio-only format. Several opted to work with video testimony for which there was also a transcript available. Having the freedom to write about any testimony meant that some students voluntarily watched portions of multiple interviews, or viewed several hours of testimony by one survivor, in order to locate a segment that interested them and would lend itself to this paper assignment. Of course, there is a clear difference in terms of scope, resources, and audience when it comes to learning about the German-Jewish past versus the Holocaust, and I focus hereafter on ways of engaging digitally with specifically German-Jewish topics.

Inviting students to choose and analyze one short text that interests them is standard practice when I ask students to work with digital history projects. For a short homework assignment in my course on "The German-Jewish Experience," I asked students to work with the Jewish Museum Berlin's project, "1933: The Beginning of the End of German Jewry" (https://www.jmberlin.de/1933/en). This smaller-scale project, rolled out in 2013 to mark the eightieth anniversary of 1933, draws primarily from the collection of the Jewish Museum Berlin and the Leo Baeck Institute New York/Berlin (LBI). It was created in conjunction with the Berlin citywide theme year "Zerstörte Vielfalt (Destroyed Diversity): 1933–1938–1945."5 The 1933 project includes a selection of original documents matched to corresponding dates throughout the year, with an average of ten documents per month. It also contains transcriptions of hand-written German documents and translations into English. In other words, there is too much material to assign in full if only a short unit of the course focuses on the 1930s.

In November 2016, I asked students to visit the 1933 project's site and choose one document on which to focus. They were instructed to read both the English and German texts if able. In a discussion forum on our online course management system, Moodle, students responded to two broad questions: "What can we learn from this document about how Jewish life in Germany changed in and after 1933? What do you find particularly interesting about the document?" Using an online forum facilitates a wider variety of posts since students can see each other's posts and are encouraged not to examine the same document. One student noted the contemporary resonance of the document posted for January 30, 1933: a letter written by Rosa Süss in Mannheim to her daughter and son-in-law on the day when Hitler became chancellor. Süss wrote: "Well, they [he] won't be any different from all the others. We'll have to wait and see what happens! People abroad will be surprised." The student observed that Süss's reaction "has both elements of hope and fear at the same time," not unlike what the student and many of his friends felt shortly after the U.S. presidential election earlier that month. Although I do not wish to draw categorical parallels between events of the 1930s and 2010s, I would suggest that comparing and contrasting these two eras of political change made the assignment more meaningful for this student. His ability to understand January 1933 was informed by his experience of November 2016, and vice versa.

In spring 2018, in "European Jews: History, Holocaust, Future," I introduced students to the 1938 Projekt of the Leo Baeck Institute New York/Berlin in order to make a lesson on Jews in Nazi Germany more interactive. The 1938 Projekt (http://www.lbi.org/1938projekt) commemorates each day in 1938 through one post published on every corresponding day of 2018, exactly eighty years later, in both English and German. Materials used in the daily posts originate from over ten partner institutions. The posts were publicized widely; the LBI made them available on its website and in daily posts on social media sites including Facebook, Twitter, and Instagram. This approach suggests that the project format was designed to maximize impact on users. William Weitzer, the executive director of the LBI, suggested that these social media platforms allow users to have a "transactional" experience by scrolling through and interacting with the posts in a way that is personally meaningful.6 In a podcast inter-view about the 1938 Projekt, Frank Mecklenburg, the director of research and chief archivist of the LBI and also a contributor to this volume, points to the significance of 1938 as a historical reference point with respect to twenty-first-century political issues: refugees, the rise of right-wing political groups, and the gradual and incremental normalization of everyday restrictions.[7] In Mecklenburg's view, the broader issues of the past are inseparable from issues in the present.

In my "European Jews" course, we worked with the 1938 Projekt during class time to facilitate a collective encounter with this digital project. In other words, we made the use of social media a social experience in real life, at least for a few minutes. Together, we studied the post from March 5, 2018: "Homosexual Relations with a Jew." This post highlights the fact that the blond, non-Jewish German tennis star Gottfried von Cramm, who was accused of homosexual conduct and arrested on March 5, 1938, was not immune to Nazi persecution. Students found this story compelling both because it deviated slightly from the traditional narrative of persecution and because it challenged them to think about other groups who fell victim to the Nazis. After looking at one post together, the students accessed the 1938 Projekt individually. Most of the fifteen students present that day used cell phones, although a few pulled out laptops or Surface devices. I asked the students to scroll through the project's feed and select one additional post. Students then prepared short responses to the prompt: "How does this project use sources from 1938 to make a critical point about Jewish history? What point does this post seem to be making?" We integrated their responses into a group discussion, which also included their feedback on learning about the past through digitized media.

These students of German-Jewish history responded enthusiastically to the act of engaging with historical sources in an online platform. This mix of (late) Millennial and Generation Z students offered overwhelmingly positive feedback on their experience using the 1938 Projekt. They appreciated the concise summaries of historical documents as well as the translations of short, one-sentence quotes from the original German document into English, for example in the post from February 25, 2018, about the separation of young lovers Julius Hirsch and Elisabeth Schiff. The discussion of this post provided a natural complement to our earlier discussion of the difficulties many Jews faced in obtaining visas as they sought to emigrate. One German studies major noted that the 1938 Projekt is "not intimidating" because of its "short little stories" and appealing presentation of "facts not everyone knows." Another student pointed out that each story takes only about five minutes to read in full. A third said that the concept reminded her of the Timehop app, which can be paired with social media (Instagram, Facebook) and other apps such as photo albums to remind users what happened in their lives one or more years ago on that same day. In deploying strategies popularized by social media apps, digital history projects gain access to the students whose worlds are built around these apps.

In addition to online resources and digital history projects, access to German-Jewish topics through other digital means such as Skype or Zoom provides a different type of experiential learning. On several occasions, I have devoted a whole class period to a video call with one or two people who could provide insight into German-Jewish topics. This low-budget approach to incorporating guest speakers into a course relies on a free app, as well as the camera and microphone found in most computers, though it is also helpful to conduct calls in classrooms equipped with special video conferencing technology. One of these calls was in fall 2016 with Gabrielle Rossmer Gropman and Sonya Gropman, mother and daughter co-authors of *The German-Jewish Cookbook* (Brandeis University Press, 2017). Talking with these authors provided students in "The German-Jewish Experience" a different way of considering the campus-wide "Year of Food." After reading an excerpt from the cookbook about Sabbath and holiday foods, students prepared advance questions about recipes and traditions relating to specific dishes. The class sampled several Jewish foods during the Skype call, thereby adding additional participatory elements to the lesson and reinforcing the conversation with something tangible.

Digitally savvy students enjoy using platforms that are already familiar to them as they learn about the past. The experience of interacting with German-Jewish topics through websites and apps becomes memorable precisely because it borrows from a nonacademic sphere of life. Some of the digital projects and media that work well for experiential learning also provide individuals and institutions with opportunities for social outreach beyond the classroom.

THE REACH OF SOCIAL MEDIA ACTIVISM

The ways in which many institutions have begun to promote the German-Jewish past on social media can be interpreted only as a form of activism. The goals of these social and political activist efforts are linked to the ongoing struggle against antisemitism, racism, homophobia, sexism, and other forms of oppression. Such forms of activism often rely on historical lessons by connecting the events of the past to the present moment, sometimes in the form of political commentary. By examining a few different uses of social media, we gain insight into why academic, educational, and other nonprofit institutions—as well as some individuals—rely on digital activism to achieve their desired impact. This type of activism ultimately serves as a vehicle for promoting the content generated by virtual archives and digital projects to much wider general audiences. When disturbing content is involved, its shock value can further contribute to the reach of digital activism.

The use of the German-Jewish past has attracted considerable media attention in recent years and is not uncontroversial. One of the most extreme cases is the social media presence of the nonprofit Anne Frank Center for Mutual Respect

(@AnneFrankCenter), which since 2017 has regularly cited Anne's diary on Twitter, Facebook, Instagram, and YouTube in its overt criticism of specific acts and policies of the Trump administration. According to Emma Green for the *Atlantic*, the Anne Frank Center's "more aggressive and hyperbolic" approach runs the risk of undermining Anne Frank's legacy by politicizing it. Green suggests that whether Anne Frank or her father Otto would have wanted her legacy politicized is of little consequence to the center, which does not necessarily deserve the authority it gains through the use of her name.[8] Yet it is undeniable that millions of people have seen and interacted with the center's social media posts relating to Anne Frank's history, and it is possible that the media attention Anne Frank's family regularly receives is partly a result of the center's work. As of 2020, the center has nearly 104,000 Twitter followers and over 115,000 Facebook followers, and its activism has been featured in dozens of news articles from publications across the political spectrum. Whether "authorized" or not, more people have begun to consider the German-Jewish past as they attempt to make sense of the tumultuous twenty-first century.

More established academic and educational institutions are able to make less controversial use of social media, as their work is widely received as scholarly even when it tends toward the political. However, even these institutions are not immune to criticism. The United States Holocaust Memorial Museum (@HolocaustMuseum; USHMM) leads the pack with 322,000 Twitter followers, 1,169,000 Facebook followers, and 105,000 Instagram followers. It regularly uses social media platforms to commemorate important dates and occasions (often with the hashtag #OTD, On This Day), protest immigration or refugee policies, or raise awareness about antisemitism, hatred, and genocide. Yet in summer 2019, the USHMM came under fire when it implicitly criticized U.S. Representative Alexandria Ocasio-Cortez's comparison of the U.S. government's immigrant detention centers to "concentration camps," which also used the phrase "Never Again." In response, the USHMM released a statement regarding its unequivocal rejection of Holocaust analogies; this prompted historians Andrea Orzoff and Anika Walke to pen an Open Letter asking the USHMM to retract its statement.[9] Within a few days, 580 scholars had signed the letter, which was circulated through Google Docs. Several weeks later, on July 18, the USHMM published a response that cautioned against "careless comparisons and simplistic equivalencies" but conceded that the Holocaust "can and should also be carefully analyzed for areas where there may exist some similarities with and differences from other events, both historical and contemporary, utilizing appropriate contextualization and avoiding simple answers to complex questions."[10] This debate took place almost entirely in publicly accessible online platforms. It demonstrates the enduring significance of German-Jewish history and the Holocaust for the future of American politics, particularly within a digital framework.

On a smaller scale, and often in German, the Jewish Museum Berlin (@jmberlin; 9,500 Twitter followers, 33,500 Facebook followers) uses social media for some similar purposes, including showcasing items in its collection that relate to current events. Its Twitter feed is notably more political than its Facebook page, and the use of Twitter has also led to recent controversies. For example, retweeted articles about the kippah that led to the antisemitic attack in Prenzlauer Berg in April 2018 contributed to the ongoing dialogue about whether it is safe for Jews to wear kippahs in public in Germany and elsewhere in Europe. But Twitter revealed its potential to bring about more severe consequences when Peter Schäfer, the director of the Jewish Museum Berlin, resigned after a tweet endorsing a petition against a motion defining anti-Israel boycotts as antisemitic. When institutions or their affiliates use social media for activist purposes, they risk negatively impacting how the public engages with representatives of the German-Jewish past. Some institutions therefore tend to be more cautious in digital spheres. The Leo Baeck Institute New York (@lbinyc), for example, tends to post articles about German-Jewish individuals, places, cultural texts, or traditions; most of the institute's regular social media posts are not as overtly political.

Not only institutions, but also individuals from celebrities to artists use websites and social media to inspire social change. One particularly noteworthy example is Israeli-German satirical artist Shahak Shapira's short-lived YOLOCAUST project (www.yolocaust.de; YOLO = You Only Live Once), which went viral and was viewed by over 2.5 million people within one week in January 2017. The project used Photoshop to superimpose twelve selfies and other photographs taken at the Berlin Memorial to the Murdered Jews of Europe onto graphic images of the victims of Nazi death camps. Its goal was to call attention to the inappropriate and disrespectful ways many visitors interact with this massive memorial, which since its inauguration in 2005 has become part of the topography of central Berlin. Shapira found the photos on public social media accounts (Facebook, Instagram, Tinder, Grindr) and gave the photos' subjects the opportunity to request the removal of their images; all twelve of them contacted him within a week to have their photos removed. This sharply critical project supposedly reached as many as 100 million people due to the extensive media coverage it received. Through a combination of shocking satire, creative image manipulation, and incisive social criticism, Shapira persuaded his viewers to reflect on appropriate ways to commemorate the Holocaust.

Digital media provided Shapira a platform for calling attention to the potential consequences for sharing images that disrespect the Jewish past. His work serves as a warning of the Internet's power to publicize seemingly private acts of disrespect—as well as acts of hate. To be sure, Shapira's own activism is at times also offensive and his techniques of exposing and shaming individuals and corporations are as rife with controversy as with good intentions. (In August 2017, he spray-painted hateful tweets on the pavement near Twitter's Hamburg headquarters for his #HeyTwitter campaign.) Still, with 187,000 Twitter followers and over 132,000 Facebook followers—and Internet-related projects that reportedly have managed to reach 250 million people all told—Shahak Shapira has found ways to win what he terms "The Race for Attention" on several occasions.[11]

Institutions and activists who seek to reach a broader audience have much to learn from Shapira's stunts, as well as from the social media practices of such institutions as the Anne Frank Center. Successful outreach campaigns do not shy away from controversy; in fact, they benefit from shock value. Yet some of these politically motivated initiatives go awry. The German-Jewish past contains no shortage of events and incidents that provoke reactions of disgust, horror, anger, and fear, and references to these events tend to elicit strong responses. In this digital age of oversaturation and clickbait, one way to draw the public's attention to the past is to amplify it online in controversial and innovative ways.

STREAMING HISTORY TO ENTERTAIN THE MASSES

Whereas one previously needed access to a television and certain cable networks to enjoy cutting-edge trends in home entertainment, popular new streaming services such as Netflix, Amazon, and Sky now bring representations of the past to everyone with Internet access. In fact, Millennials have notoriously "cut the cord" and cancelled their cable subscriptions in favor of streaming television—and many members of Generation Z rely largely on streaming services. Historical dramas are all the rage and in the past few years several German-language television series have joined the ranks of such period dramas as *Downton Abbey* and *The Crown*. Two seasons (16 episodes) of the German series *Babylon Berlin* reached international audiences in late 2017 and 2018, and a third season was released in early 2020 (12 episodes; the third season is not discussed here). American audiences, too, have become obsessed with this crime series, set in the final years of the Weimar Republic, which is the most expensive non-English-language television drama series ever made.[12] The series is based on Volker Kutscher's bestselling novels, including *Der nasse Fisch* (2008), and was created by Tom Tykwer, Achim von Borries, and Henk Handloegten. In May 2018, I had the privilege of discussing how *Babylon Berlin* connects to my book, *Passing Illusions: Jewish Visibility in Weimar Germany* (University of Michigan Press, 2017), in conversation with film scholar Noah Isenberg at the Leo Baeck Institute, New York. The LBI sold roughly 100 advance tickets for this event, due in part to the popularity of the suspenseful *Babylon Berlin*. The potential mass audience for streaming television dramas far exceeds the readership of most academic scholarship and presumably also surpasses the potential audience of bestselling books and hit films, at least in the immediate sense. When audience size is of the essence, the best way to maximize the reach of the lessons of the German-Jewish past is to teach them through the mass medium de rigueur, which in this case is streaming television.

Jews are not foregrounded in most episodes of the first two seasons of *Babylon Berlin*, but their limited presence plays a significant role nonetheless.[13] This mainstream drama neatly embeds German-Jewish topics in its story without overemphasizing them. The plotline of the first two seasons, set in 1929, makes it impossible to ignore the growing tensions between political factions, as well as the fact that Jews are located at the heart of several conflicts. Still, some scholars have pointed to the omission of (other) Jewish characters as troubling and historically inaccurate.[14] The central Jewish character is Councillor August Benda (played by Matthias Brandt; perhaps loosely based on Bernhard Weiss), a Social Democrat and the head of the Berlin Political Police.[15] His Jewishness is made explicit in the sixth episode of the first season; we learn that Benda comes from a Jewish family and refuses to be baptized. Additional references to Benda's Jewishness can be found throughout the first two seasons: a number of menorahs on display in the interior of the Benda home (episode 7 and others); his strong preference for (kosher) sausages from the Scheunenviertel, the largely East European Jewish district near Alexanderplatz (episode 8); his use of a Yiddish expression— "*A leyb hot nit moyre far keyn flig*" (A lion is not afraid of a fly)—while conversing with Foreign Minister Gustav Stresemann, who claims his wife often uses the same phrase (episode 11); and Benda's tragic death when he becomes the target of an antisemitic plot carried out by a group of Nazis who turn his own maid, Greta Overbeck (Leonie Benesch), against him (episode 15). Benda is a generally likeable central character with whom viewers might sympathize. It is telling that the only obviously Jewish main character dies because of an act of deception perpetrated by someone he trusts. If nothing else, the first two seasons of *Babylon Berlin* teach that, with the rise of the Nazi Party, even the most seemingly benevolent average citizen could easily be turned against his or her Jewish neighbors or employers.

Although August Benda is the only explicitly Jewish character of note, the first two seasons of *Babylon Berlin* incorporate a few other subtle allusions to Jewishness that provide insight into exactly how Jews and Jewishness might have been relevant for the average resident of Weimar Berlin on an everyday basis. Police inspector Gereon Rath (Volker Bruch) lives for a time in a boarding house alongside journalist Samuel Katelbach (Karl Markovics), who writes for the historically significant left-wing journal *Die Weltbühne* and is thus coded as Jewish on several levels (name, appearance, profession, left-wing political leanings). Katelbach serves as a constant reminder of the perceived influence of Jews via liberal journalistic outlets. Described by historian

Peter Pulzer as the profession most "completely dominated by Jews," journalism was a field in which many Jews built successful careers.[16] Due to the prominent role of many Jews in liberal and left-wing publishing, this sector was slanderously termed the "*Judenpresse*." Throughout the series, Katelbach's articles represent this sector and indeed attempt to check the power of the political right, including those with close ties to the German military.

Other references to Jews in *Babylon Berlin* offer nuanced historical lessons by calling attention to well-known antisemitic stereotypes. In a rant about Berlin's downsides, the pharmacist at Severin pharmacy, where Gereon Rath obtains his illicit preparations, rattles off a long list: "the construction sites, the millions of visitors, the Jews, the hacks, the prices, only ugly women" (episode 7). Jews are depicted here as an unavoidable part of the urban landscape, and one that many Berlin residents regarded as a disadvantage. The one brief visual allusion to East European Jews in the very first episode of *Babylon Berlin*—an image of several Hasidic Jews in fur-trimmed *shtreimel* hats strolling near Alexanderplatz—reminds viewers of the highly visible position of traditionally clad East European Jews, as well as the major roles Jews played in the garment and fur industries. Later, when aspiring inspector Charlotte Ritter's (Liv Lisa Fries) mother dies, Charlotte's sister Ilse finds a wedding dress that their mother claimed she had long since taken "to the Jew," and Ilse suggests that "the Jew" will still give them a good price for the valuable prewar material (episode 10). Jews were indeed responsible for a disproportionately large portion of the trade in secondhand clothes in interwar Berlin. This relatively benign association of Jews with clothing dealers emerges again in a different, defamatory context, with the representation of the historical "fur coat affair" of Mayor Gustav Böß, who was accused of embezzling funds to buy his (Jewish) wife a fur coat in conjunction with the Sklarek brothers scandal (episode 15). By crosscutting between scenes that emphasize stereotypes about Jewish women and opulence, to scenes in which Benda is killed by a bomb planted in his elegant home, the first two seasons leave no doubt that Jews were targeted for their wealth and positions of power in the late Weimar years.

If we take *Babylon Berlin* as a prime example of how streaming television can reach and educate mass audiences, we get a sense of what will be possible in the increasingly digital age to come. Those who could benefit from learning about the German-Jewish past—students, activists, social media users, television viewers—require two separate things to engage with it: (1) something that captures their initial interest, from an interesting-sounding course to a provocative news article, trailer, or review; and (2) simple and engaging means of accessing information, for example, an attractively constructed digital history project, a well-crafted social media post, or a highly addictive form of streaming media. It seems obvious that more scholars should use social media to share their research and also incorporate more media into their teaching, but perhaps scholars should go further and prioritize collaborating on digital projects, serving as consultants for television or film projects, or even writing their own screenplays. For the past to remain relevant, it must also go digital.

NOTES

1. Jeffrey Shandler, *Holocaust Memory in the Digital Age: Survivors' Stories and New Media Practices* (Stanford: Stanford University Press, 2017), 4.

2. Gail Twersky Reimer, "Remarks Delivered upon Receiving the Lee Max Friedman Award at the American Jewish Historical Society's 2014 Biennial Scholars Conference," *American Jewish History* 99, no. 1 (January 2015): 93–98, here 97.

3. Michael Dimock, "Defining Generations: Where Millennials End and Generation Z Begins," Pew Research Center Fact Tank, January 17, 2019. https://www.pewresearch.org/fact-tank/2019/01/17/where-millennials-end-and-generation-z-begins.

4. Notably, *Forbes* contributor Neil Howe has written about the "Homeland Generation," which in his view includes people born in 2005 or later. See Neil Howe, "Introducing the Homeland Generation (Part 1 of 2)," *Forbes*, October 27, 2014, https://www.forbes.com/sites/neilhowe/2014/10/27/introducing-the-homeland-generation-part-1-of-2/#6eb70bfa2bd6.

5. The citywide 2013 exhibition included museum exhibitions and an open-air exhibition of posters displayed prominently in such public spaces as subway stations and Potsdamer Platz. See Moritz van Dülmen, Wolf Kühnelt, Björn Weigel, and André Schmitz, *Zerstörte Vielfalt. Berlin 1933–1938–1945: Eine Stadt erinnert sich* (Berlin: Kulturprojekte Berlin, 2013).

6. Conversation with William Weitzer at the Leo Baeck Institute, New York on May 15, 2018.

7. Jason Lustig, "Why 1938 Matters Today with Frank Mecklenburg," *Jewish History Matters*, March 11, 2018, http://www.jewishhistory.fm/why-1938-matters-today-with-frank-mecklenburg.

8. Emma Green, "Who Does the Anne Frank Center Represent?," *The Atlantic*, April 24, 2017, http://www.theatlantic.com/politics/archive/2017/04/anne-frank-center/524055.

9. See the "Statement Regarding the Museum's Position on Holocaust Analogies," June 24, 2019, https://www.ushmm.org/information/press/press-releases/statement-regarding-the-museums-position-on-holocaust-analogies. The open letter was published online as well: Omer Bartov, Doris Bergen, Andrea Orzoff, Timothy Snyder, and Anika Walke, et al., "An Open Letter to the Director of the US Holocaust Memorial Museum," New York Review of Books Daily, July 1, 2019, https://www.nybooks.com/daily/2019/07/01/an-open-letter-to-the-director-of-the-holocaust-memorial-museum.

10. "The Role and Relevance of the United States Holocaust Memorial Museum," July 18, 2019, https://www.ushmm.org/information/press/press-releases/the-role-and -relevance-of-the-museum.

11. Shahak Shapira, "The Secret of Going Viral: TEDxVienna," TEDx Talks on YouTube, November 17, 2017, http://www.youtube.com/watch?v=6od-uoPYMiU.

12. Noah Isenberg, "Voluptuous Panic," *The New York Review of Books Daily*, April 28, 2018, http://www.nybooks.com/daily/2018/04/28/voluptuous-panic.

13. There are numerous references to Jews in the third season that are not discussed in this essay. It is possible that Jews will play an even more central role in later seasons of *Babylon Berlin*, particularly if a fourth season is based in part on the third book by Volker Kutscher, *Goldstein: Gereon Raths dritter Fall* (2010).

14. See especially historian Darcy Buerkle's comments in the forthcoming *Babylon Berlin* Forum in *Central European History*, edited by Veronika Fuechtner and Paul Lerner.

15. Bernhard Weiss, the Jewish vice president of the Berlin police, plays a more prominent role in later books by Volker Kutscher; in contrast, August Benda dies at the end of season two of the series.

16. Peter Pulzer, *The Rise of Political Anti-Semitism in Germany and Austria* (London: Peter Halban, 1988), 13.

CONTRIBUTORS

Sandra Anusiewicz-Baer holds BA and MA degrees in education, Jewish studies, and Islamic studies. Before embarking on her doctoral studies, she was head of the educational and cultural department of the Jewish community in Berlin. Her dissertation about the alumni of the Jewish High School in Berlin asked how the education of the school influences the students' self-perception and identity. This study was published as *The Jewish Gymnasium in Berlin—Identity and Jewish Schooling since 1993*, winning the prestigious Humboldt Prize in 2017. Currently Anusiewicz-Baer is chief operating officer of the Zacharias Frankel College, a rabbinical seminary to train Masorti/Conservative rabbis.

Mathias Berek is a research associate at the Center for Research on Antisemitism, Technische Universität Berlin. After studying cultural philosophy and history, communication, and media studies, he acquired his PhD at the University of Leipzig in 2008 with a theoretical work on collective memory and the social construction of reality (published 2009). Recently, he has led a DFG-funded project on German-Jewish philosopher Moritz Lazarus at the Institute for the Study of Culture at the University of Leipzig, and the Minerva Institute for German History, Tel Aviv University, resulting in a monograph with Wallstein (2020): *Moritz Lazarus. Deutsch-jüdischer Idealismus im 19. Jahrhundert.*

Michael Brenner is professor of Jewish history and culture at the University of Munich and Seymour and Lillian Abensohn Chair in Israel Studies at American University in Washington, D.C. He is the international president of the Leo Baeck Institute and an elected fellow of the Bavarian Academy of Sciences and the Accademia Nazionale Virgiliana in Mantua. Brenner has authored eight books on Jewish and Israeli history, translated into twelve languages. His most recent publication is *In Search of Israel* (2018).

Sheer Ganor is an assistant professor of history at the University of Minnesota, Twin Cities. She is currently working on a book manuscript titled *In Scattered Formation: Displacement, Alignment and the German-Jewish Diaspora*, which deals with everyday experiences of displacement and their significance in shaping and affirming cultural identities among refugees from Nazi Germany.

Diana Franklin is the manager of the Centre for German-Jewish Studies at the University of Sussex. Her work involves editing research papers and the center's biannual newsletter, and organizing the center's events (notably Holocaust Memorial Day). She worked closely with Professor Edward Timms to found the center in 1995. Diana's father and grandparents came to England from Furth in 1936, and she feels a strong connection with her European heritage.

Michal Friedlander is head of the Judaica department at the Jewish Museum Berlin. She is the author of numerous articles on different aspects of Jewish material culture and the co-editor of *10 + 5 = Gott – Die Macht der Zeichen* (2004), and *Kosher & Co.–Über Essen und Religion* (2010). In 2013, she co-curated "The Whole Truth—Everything You Always Wanted to Know about Jews," an exhibition that sparked international debate. Friedlander's current research focuses on the concept of the Jewish object.

Nicola Glucksmann is the younger daughter of German-Jewish child refugees. In 1939, at age thirteen, her mother's life was saved by a passage on one of the last Kindertransports. Nicola's parents met at Stoatley Rough, a boarding school for German-Jewish children, from where they went on to marry and raise a family in northwest London. Formerly a documentary filmmaker, Nicola is now a psychotherapist in private practice. Her own three children have, she would suggest, shown admirable fortitude and good humor in the face of inherited trauma and the invisible shadows of their grandparents' past. Her contribution is for them.

Klaus Hödl is a historian at the Center for Jewish Studies at the University of Graz. He has published on Jews in Eastern Europe and the "Jewish body," new approaches to Jewish historiography, and Jews in popular culture. His most recent book, *Entangled Entertainers*, was published by Berghahn in 2019.

Anthony D. Kauders is professor of modern history at Keele University, UK. He is the author and co-editor of several volumes that deal with German and German-Jewish history, as well as the history of psychology. His most recent book, *Der Freud-Komplex* (2014), examined the reception of psychoanalysis in Germany. He is currently researching the social psychology of antisemitism.

Dani Kranz is a DAAD exchange professor at Ben Gurion University, Israel, and director of Two Foxes Consulting, Germany and Israel. Her thematic expertise covers migration, integration, ethnicity, law, state/stateliness, political life, organizations, as well as memory politics. She has been conducting long-term fieldwork in Europe and the Middle East; she headed "The Migration of Israeli Jews to Germany since 1990"

(GIF Grant 1186) jointly with Uzi Rebhun (Hebrew University of Jerusalem) and Heinz Sünker (Bergische University Wuppertal). Her current academic project concerns the genesis of moral economies in Germany. In her applied line, she is a consultant to the high commissioner of the German government for Jewish life and in the fight against antisemitism, member of the council for migration (Rat für Migration), and a range of other foundations, museums, and NGOs.

Frank Mecklenburg received his PhD from the Technical University, Berlin. Before becoming a German-Jewish historian he studied mathematics, physics, and computer science. Since 1996 he has been the director of research and chief archivist of the Leo Baeck Institute, New York. He has published several books and many articles on diverse topics such as German prison reform in the nineteenth century, migration, German Jews in exile, as well as on topics relating to his work in the archive.

Guy Miron is the vice president for academic affairs at the Open University of Israel and teaches Jewish history. He is also the director of the Centre for Research on the Holocaust in Germany at Yad Vashem, Jerusalem. His research focuses on modern German and Hungarian-Jewish history, Holocaust studies, and Jewish historiography. His publications include the books *German Jews in Israel—Memories and Past Images*, (Hebrew, 2004); *The Waning of the Emancipation, Jewish History, Memory, and the Rise of Fascism in Germany, France, and Hungary* (English and Hebrew versions, 2011). His current research deals with time and space in the German-Jewish experience under the Nazi regime.

Alan Posener, the son of a Jewish émigré from Berlin, was born in 1949 and grew up in London, Kuala Lumpur, and West Berlin. Posener worked as a Communist organizer before becoming a teacher in 1977. Later, he worked as a writer, translator, journalist, and rock singer. In 2000, Posener joined the newspaper *Die Welt*, where he still works. Posener has written biographies of such diverse figures as Elvis Presley, William Shakespeare, and the Virgin Mary; a polemic against Pope Benedict XVI; and a defense of the European Union. Alan Posener is married with one daughter and two granddaughters.

Gideon Reuveni is the director of the Centre for German-Jewish Studies at the University of Sussex. He has published widely on diverse topics such as historiography, sport, reading culture, and Jewish economic history. His most recent book, *Consumer Culture and the Making of Jewish Identity* (2017), won the National Jewish Book Award in 2018. Currently he is working on a book-length project on the history of German reparations after the Holocaust.

Joachim Schlör is a cultural historian with research interests in urban history and the history of German-Jewish migration. He received his PhD from Tübingen University in 1990 and his Habilitation from Potsdam University in 2003. Since 2006 he has been professor for modern Jewish/non-Jewish relations at the University of Southampton. He is the editor of the journal *Jewish Culture and History* and co-editor, with Johanna Rolshoven, of the online journal *Mobile Culture Studies*. His latest book is *Escaping Nazi Germany: One Woman's Emigration from Heilbronn to England* (2020).

Galili Shahar is professor of comparative literature and German studies at Tel Aviv University. His work is dedicated to research and teaching of German, Jewish, and Hebrew literature. Since 2013 he has served as a director of the Minerva Institute for German History and as the head of the study program in Arab-Jewish literature and culture. His publications include articles on Goethe, Hölderlin, Kleist, Kafka, Franz Rosenzweig, and Walter Benjamin. His most recent book, *The Stone and the Word: On Paul Celan's Poetry*, was published in 2019.

Björn Siegel studied Jewish history and culture at the University of Munich and Tel Aviv University. His PhD thesis on the Viennese *Israelitische Allianz* was published in 2010. Following his PhD he joined the Franz Rosenzweig Minerva Research Center in Jerusalem and then worked as DAAD lecturer at the Centre for German-Jewish Studies at the University of Sussex. Currently he works as researcher at the Institute for the History of the Germany Jews (Hamburg), focusing on his new book projects: *The Ship as a Place in Jewish Migration: Between Europe and Palestine 1920–1938* and *Fritz Pinkuss: A Modernizer on Both Sides of the Atlantic*.

Lisa Silverman is associate professor of history and Jewish studies at the University of Wisconsin–Milwaukee. She serves as contributing editor for the *Leo Baeck Institute Year Book* for German-Jewish history. She is author of *Becoming Austrians: Jews and Culture between the World Wars* (2012) and co-author with Daniel H. Magilow of *Holocaust Representations in History: An Introduction* (2015). Her co-edited volumes include *Austrian Studies 24: Jews, Jewish Difference and Austrian Culture: Literary and Historical Perspectives* (2016); *Making Place: Space and Embodiment in the City* (2014); and *Interwar Vienna: Culture between Tradition and Modernity* (2009).

Hannah C. Tzuberi is research assistant at Freie Universität Berlin, Institute of Jewish Studies. She studied Jewish studies and Islamic studies in Berlin. For her PhD she focused on sections of the Talmudic tractate Sanhedrin. Apart from her interest in the rabbinic tradition, her research interests involve broader questions related to the critical study of secularism, specifically, academic knowledge production in the context of Jewish studies and German "Jewish politics." Her latest publication is "'Reforesting' Jews: The German State and the Construction of 'New German Judaism,'" *Jewish Studies Quarterly* 27, no. 3 (2020): 199–224. She is also a blogger: www.mandolinaforpresident.wordpress.com.

Kerry Wallach is associate professor of German studies and an affiliate of the Jewish Studies Program at Gettysburg College. She is the author of *Passing Illusions: Jewish Visibility in Weimar Germany* (University of Michigan Press, 2017), as well as a number of articles that deal with German-Jewish literature, history and culture, visual and consumer culture and film, and gender and sexuality.

Liliane Weissberg is the Christopher H. Browne Distinguished Professor in the School of Arts and Sciences and professor of German and comparative literature at the University of Pennsylvania. She has taught as a visiting professor at universities in the United States, Germany, Austria, and Switzerland. Among her recent publications are *Über Haschisch und Kabbalah. Gershom Scholem, Siegfried Unseld und das Werk von Walter Benjamin* (2012); (with Karen Beckman), *On Writing with Photography* (2013); *Juden. Geld. Eine Vorstellung* (2013); *Münzen, Hände, Noten, Finger: Berliner Hofjuden und die Erfindung einer deutschen Musikkultur* (2018); (with Andreas Kilcher), *Nachträglich, grundlegend? Der Kommentar als Denkform in der jüdischen Moderne von Hermann Cohen bis Jacques Derrida* (2018).

Moshe Zimmermann's academic research focuses on the history of German Jews, German-Jewish relations, and antisemitism. He is the author and editor of more than twenty-five books and over 100 articles in leading academic journals. In 2005, he was part of a group of historians commissioned to examine the history of the German Foreign Service during the Nazi period and how it came to terms with its past after 1945. Zimmerman is the recipient of many prestigious awards including the Humboldt Prize, the Jacob and Wilhelm Grimm Prize, the Dr. Leopold Lucas Prize, and the Theodor Lessing Prize for Criticism.

INDEX

Brazil: German-speaking Jews in, xix, 15;
Jews in, 103n16; Pinkuss in, 97–100

Brenner, Michael, xv, 63, 105n37

Breuer, Mordechai, 203n8

Britain. *See* England/Great Britain/United
Kingdom

Brod, Max, 25, 89

Broder, Henryk M., 9

Browning, Christopher, 101, 213, 217

Brunner, Jose, 195

Buber, Martin, 221

Bundesrepublik Deutschland (BRD). *See*
Germany

B.Z. (daily tabloid), 186

Cabinet of Curiosities *(Wunderkabinett)*, 38

capitalism, Lazarus on, 79–80

Celan, Paul, 89, 93–94

Center for Jewish Cultural History
(University of Salzburg), 121, 123

Center for Jewish History (New York City),
222, 224

Center for Jewish Studies (University of
Graz), 121, 123

Central Archives for the History of the
Jewish People (Jerusalem), 26

Central Council of Jews in Germany, 8, 45

Central European Jews, in Palestine, 194

Centre for German-Jewish Studies
(University of Sussex), xviii–xix, xxii, 26

Chabad, 70–71, 75n23

change, Pinkuss on, 100

children, legal immigration papers for, 21n4

Chinese Jewry, 68

CIP (Congregaçao Israelita Paulista, Sao
Paulo), xix, 97, 99–100

circumcision, 210

civilization, thin crust of, 77

Clausewitz, Carl von, 159n21

clothing dealers, in interwar Berlin, 249

co-constitutionality, 234

coffeehouses, 156

cognitive dissonance, 215–16

cognitive redefinition, 214–15

color-blind racism, 138

commemoration, Pinkuss on, 97

commentary, Jews as people of, 155

complete assimilation, 51, 53, 59–60

"Confessions of a Former Assimilationist"
(Leander), 20

Confino, Alon, 215

Congregaçao Israelita Paulista (CIP, Sao
Paulo), xix, 97, 99–100

Conservative movement, 70–71, 109, 117n2

conversions, differing attitudes toward, 114

corporal turn, of German-Jewish history, 231

correspondence (realist) theory of antisemitism, 216

Covid-19 pandemic, xvi

Cox, Nigel, 39

Cramm, Gottfried von, 243

culture: cultural codes, 20, 84, 137, 212–13;
cultural differences, importance of, 9;
cultural memories of the Holocaust,
169; cultural turn, of German-Jewish
history, 231; German-Jewish culture,
relationship of feuilleton to, 157;
Lazarus's understanding of, 78;
native culture, commitments to, 20;
non-Jewish culture, question of definition of, 133n35; as process and practice,
33; thin blanket of, xix; white European
supremacy and, 83

Cultures of the Jews (Biale), 68

Czollek, Max, 10, 171, 177n40

Danziger, Walter M., 29–30, 31

Darwish, Mahmoud, 94

de Beauvoir, Simone, 140–41

Declaration of Montreux (World Jewish
Congress), 110

Dekel, Irit, 167

Demel, Michael, 183

Denkbilder (thought images), 157

Denkmal der ermordeten Juden (Memorial
of the murdered Jews, Eisenman and
Serra), 167

Dershowitz, Alan, 67

Pinkuss's mission and, 100–101; Muslims
in, 183–84; nationalist movements on
creation of, 86n14; Nazi sympathizers
in, post-Holocaust, 166; newspapers and
mid-nineteenth century Jewish emancipation, 150; postwar German-Jewish
history, control of, 226–27; research
centers for Jewish studies, 27; structural
racism in, 48n5; Tarbut for Jews, 70
Germany, Jews in: creating post-Holocaust
Jewish life in, 111–12; German-Jewish
community in, lack of interest in history,
xvii; incorporation of Jews into, 182–86;
inferiority complex of Jews in, xvii–
xviii; integration of, 40; isolation of,
116; Israeli Jews in, xviii; Jewish communities in, 73; Leo Baeck Institute and,
225; postunification nation-building,
incorporation of Jews in, 182–86; postwar, being Jewish in, 109–19; postwar
Germany, Jews, antisemitism and Jewish
difference in, 135–45; reconstitution of
Jewish life in, xxi, 66; return of Jews to,
xvi; urban versus rural Jews in, 224. *See
also* Israeli Jewish migrants; *entries begin-
ning "German-Jewish"*
German Zionism, 202
Gershon David Hundert, 127
Geschichte der Juden in Deutschland
(Elbogen), 223
Gettysburg College, 241
Ghettorente (ghetto pension), 167
Gilman, Sander L., 137, 143n3
Giyur Lechumra (pro forma conversion),
114, 115
Glinka, Mikhail, 48n5
globalization, 231
Glucksmann, Nicola, xv, xviii, 51
Goitein, Shlomo Dov (Fritz), 28
Goldfinger, Arnon, 169
Goldhagen, Daniel, 201
Goll, Iwan, 88
Gorbey, Ken, 39
Gordis, Daniel, 114, 117

Gould, Stephen Jay, 124, 127
Grab, Walter, 26, 28
Great Britain. *See* England/Great Britain/
United Kingdom
Green, Emma, 245
Gringauz, Samuel, 65–66
Gronemann, Sammy, 25
Gropman, Gabrielle Rossmer, 244
Gropman, Sonya, 244
Gross, Jan, 211
Großes Verdienstkreuz, 100
Gruber, Ruth, 71–72
Grunberger, Bela, 210
Guttmann, Julius, 98

Halakhah (Jewish legal system), 44, 109
Halbwachs, Maurice, 165, 169
Halevi, Yehuda, 92–93
Halle, Germany, attack on synagogue in, xvi
"Haltung!" (Elbogen), 223
Hamburger, Hans and Charlotte, 99
Handloegten, Henk, 247
Hanna's Journey (Hannas Reise, movie),
180–81
Harré, Rom, 33
Haselberg, Lea Wohl von, 177n40
Hasenclever, Walter, 88
Hayek, Friedrich August von, 82
Hecht, Evelyn, 6
Heine, Heinrich, 150, 154
*Heinrich Loewe. Zionistische Netzwerke und
Räume* (Schlöffel), 28
Heller, Otto, 64
Hermann, Georg, 154, 159n19
Herrmann, Fred, 19
Herrmann, Lazar (Leo Lania), 19, 20
Herz, Henriette, 152
Heyne, Christian Gottlob, 148
Heyse, Paul, 80
Hildesheimer, Esriel, 115
Hineni (here I am), 95
historians: of German-Jewish history in
Israel, generations of, 194–96; in Israel,
193